Understanding Close Relationships

Susan S. Hendrick

Texas Tech University

PEARSON

Boston   New York   San Francisco
Mexico City   Montreal   Toronto   London   Madrid   Munich   Paris
Hong Kong   Singapore   Tokyo   Cape Town   Sydney

Executive Editor, Psychology: Carolyn Merrill
Marketing Manager: Wendy Gordon
Composition and Prepress Buyer: Linda Cox
Manufacturing Buyer: JoAnne Sweeney
Cover Administrator: Kristina Mose-Libon
Editorial–Production Service: Susan Freese, Communicáto, Ltd.
Text Design/Electronic Composition: Denise Hoffman

For related titles and support materials, visit our online catalog at www.ablongman.com.

Between the time Website information is gathered and then published, it is not unusual for some sites to have closed. Also, the transcription of URLs can result in unintended typographical errors. The publisher would appreciate notification where these errors occur so that they may be corrected in subsequent editions.

Library of Congress Cataloging-in-Publication Data

Hendrick, Susan
    Understanding close relationships / Susan S. Hendrick
      p. cm.
    Includes bibliographical references and index.
    ISBN 0-205-34985-4
    1. Interpersonal relations.   I. Title.

HM1106.H46 2003
158.2—dc21

                              2002038548

Printed in the United States of America

10 9 8 7 6 5 4 3 2 1   09 08 07 06 05 04 03

To my students
■ ■ ■

Contents

3 | Friendship and Social Support   45

4 Romantic Love 71

5 | *Relational Sexuality*   93

Preface

Close relationships come in all shapes, sizes, and colors. My years of teaching courses on close relationships to college students have convinced me of the amazing diversity in relationships. Teaching has also convinced me that students are vitally interested in their own personal relationships—with romantic partners, friends, family members, work colleagues, and others. They want to understand these relationships and to improve them wherever possible. *Understanding Close Relationships* is designed to help students in both of these areas.

The interdisciplinary field of close relationships has emerged over the last two decades, providing an overarching framework for relational theory and research in such disciplines as communications; human development and family studies; sociology; and clinical, counseling, developmental, and social psychology. This interdisciplinary area explores a variety of close, intimate relationships with friends, family members, and romantic partners. The literature that has developed from this field is broad and influential. Although geared largely to scholars of close relationships and their students, this literature is becoming increasingly relevant in applied settings that deal with relationship problems.

Understanding Close Relationships is designed to build on this existing literature in an innovative way by constructing chapters around stories that serve as case examples and then using theory and research to explicate and further enrich the examples. In turn, the stories illustrate and highlight some of the research and theories, making them more alive for student readers. Everyone loves stories!

Overview of the Volume

This book takes what might be loosely described as a *developmental approach*. It begins where nonfamily relationships typically begin: with interpersonal attraction. It then goes on to explore the characteristics of relationships as they continue to develop, and to ponder the issues that affect them as they begin to disintegrate and dissolve.

The goals in Chapter 1, The Importance of Relationships, are to set a conceptual framework—the fundamental need to belong—and then to describe some salient aspects of contemporary relationships and to survey a few of the myriad approaches to gathering information about persons in close relationships. Chapter 1 also introduces the use of scenarios to illustrate the many facets of close personal relationships. A series of short scenarios are scattered throughout the chapter. Each of the remaining chapters begins with one or more Relationship Stories, longer scenarios that are much like case examples. These stories are drawn from real situations, and they display many of the themes and topics that are detailed in their respective chapters. Each story is meant to interest the reader in the chapter that it introduces.

Chapter 2, Attraction and Relationship Development, presents the attitudinal approach to attraction, drawing extensively from the experimental tradition within which much of this research originated. The chapter presents several theories of attraction (e.g., balance and similarity) and discusses environmental and personal influences on attraction. Mate selection, particularly from the evolutionary perspective, is also discussed. Relationship development is introduced, with an emphasis on romantic relationships. Social penetration is presented as a way of viewing relationship development, and phenomena such as romantic beliefs and illusions are touched on as well. The chapter concludes with a brief section on courtship theories.

Chapter 3, Friendship and Social Support, focuses on a particular type of relationship: friendship. Theories of friendship formation are discussed at some length, with particular emphasis on the exchange and equity models. Factors that influence friendship formation and continuation are presented next. Friendships may begin at different times during the lifespan and may last for varying time periods; thus, childhood, adolescent, young adult, and older adult friendships are all portrayed. The similarities and differences in how women and men conduct friendships, as well as the complexities and rewards of cross-sex friendships, are also presented. Social support—a basic aspect of family, friend, and romantic relationships—is addressed next in Chapter 3. Defining and measuring social support, along with the importance of social support in close relationships, are discussed. Social support in couples is treated at some length, including how social support is both affected by and, in turn, affects other relational characteristics.

It has been said that "Love makes the world go 'round." Chapter 4, Romantic Love, analyzes love through current theoretical approaches and relationship research. The ability to love as an adult is influenced strongly by early love relationships/attachments with caregivers—typically, parents. Thus, the roots of love are planted in infancy, and they grow and begin to flower, as least in a romantic sense, in adolescence and young adulthood. The theoretical approaches presented include the prototype and evolutionary approaches, with considerable attention accorded the love styles perspective. Love is also discussed in the context of different ages and cultures. The chapter concludes with an extended discussion of intimacy in relationships.

Sex is not present in all romantic relationships, but it is certainly an integral part of many such relationships. Chapter 5, Relational Sexuality, begins with a discussion of current sexual attitudes and behaviors, including sexual satisfaction and sexual desire. Sexual behavior typically occurs within a relational context, so the links between sexuality and love are explored next. And because sexual involvement is not confined to young, European American, heterosexual couples, it is also discussed briefly in the contexts of gay and lesbian couples, multicultural/multiracial couples, people who are aging, and people who have various disabilities and illnesses. Finally, the risky aspects of sexuality are addressed.

Beginning a relationship is only the first step in the process; even more critical is taking care of and nurturing the relationship. Chapter 6, Communication and Relational Maintenance, deals with how to take care of a relationship once it has begun. Various definitions of *relational maintenance* are offered, and maintenance strategies are discussed. Communication, in all its forms, is centrally important in relational maintenance and thus considered at length. Self-disclosure, or the intimate sharing of oneself with another, is explored in some detail. Nonverbal communication is discussed next, and the importance of day-to-day, garden-variety communication is noted. The chapter concludes with a brief discussion of relationship satisfaction, one vehicle for assessing the success of a relationship.

Chapter 7, Conflict and Abuse, addresses these two topics, which are different yet linked. Both the definitions and structure of *conflict* are presented initially, and then the processes of conflict, including attributional and exchange explanations, are discussed. Conflict will inevitably occur in most close relationships at some time, so the pluses and minuses of conflict are explored. Conflict between parents and children and conflict within friendships are discussed, and considerable attention is paid to conflict in romantic and married relationships. Methods of dealing constructively with conflict are also presented.

The second topic of Chapter 7, *abuse,* typically involves conflict, although most conflict certainly does not involve abuse. Abuse occurs more often in partnered relationships than most people realize, and some of the identified causes of abuse, as well as other characteristics related to abuse, are discussed. The consequences of abuse can be devastating for the people involved, particularly the victims of abuse, so this topic is explored at some length. Finally, sexual aggression, which is one particular manifestation of abuse, is discussed.

As relationships begin, the partners are typically excited and hopeful about the possibilities for their future in a friendship or romantic relationship. The other side of this hopefulness and positive emotion, however, is the sadness and even anger that can overwhelm people as a relationship disintegrates. Chapter 8, Breakup, Divorce, and Bereavement, deals with the inevitable losses of relationships that occur at some time in everyone's life. Jealousy and infidelity are two possible causes of relationship breakup, and they are discussed initially. Breakup itself is then described, followed by a detailed exploration of divorce. Some of the major theoretical perspectives on the divorce process are presented, and various aspects or kinds of divorce (e.g., emotional, financial, social network) are described as well. The consequences of divorce are many, so the effects of divorce on both adults and children are discussed. Breakup and divorce are not the only sources of loss; bereavement also occurs for everyone. Thus, bereavement, especially of a romantic partner, is addressed briefly.

As noted earlier, close relationships come in all shapes, sizes, and colors. Chapter 9, Diverse Relationships, employs a wide lens to examine some of the relationship forms that broaden traditional notions of relationship and family yet also reflect the realities of relationships today. The end of one relationship often means the beginning of another because so many people divorce one marital partner and then acquire a new one. The incidence of remarriage has increased substantially, which means belonging to a remarried family is part of many people's experience. Remarital courtship and quality, along with the issues concerning children in remarried families, are discussed.

Another family form has been created by gay and lesbian couples, who typically cannot marry legally but nevertheless create households and families. Chapter 9 also considers lesbian and gay relationships at some length in terms of courtship and maintenance, breakup, and family formation. The children of gay and lesbian parents are similar in most respects to the children of heterosexual parents, but they are also different in some ways (e.g., the children of gay and lesbian parents may have a more inclusive view of sexuality). The research on these differences is discussed briefly.

We may be of "one world," but different races and varied cultures are contained in that world. The section in Chapter 9 on multicultural/multiracial relationships begins with a brief discussion of families of color, since the individual's basis for understanding how to conduct close relationships is, to a large extent, learned within his or her family and surrounding culture. Research comparing relationships of different cultural and ethnic compositions is presented, noting briefly both the differences (e.g., interethnic and interracial couples may face more discrimination) and the similarities (e.g., same-race and different-race couples both report secure attachment styles).

Chapter 9 concludes by examining cohabitation and the pluses and minuses of romantic couples living together before or instead of marrying. Reasons for cohabitation and types of cohabiting couples (e.g., college-student dating couples, adults with children) are discussed.

Chapter 10, Gender, explores the complex issues surrounding sex and gender in contemporary Western society. The evolutionary and social structural perspectives on gender are presented, along with the concept of *benevolent sexism*. The relatively recent discussion of women's sexual plasticity is presented in some detail, along with gender in the context of partnered relationships (e.g., relationship beliefs and culture). Power and control, inextricably interwoven with gender issues, are presented next and related to the concept of *entitlement*. Gender and family work are discussed at considerable length, including such issues as maternal employment, occupational stress, multiple roles, housework and parenting, and so on. Perspectives on the future of gender and work conclude the chapter.

Finally, the Epilogue explores a couple of different topics. First, it shows how some of the Relationship Stories that introduce Chapters 2 through 10 might continue and asks readers questions about the relationships and the people involved in them. The Epilogue goes on to contrast life with and without relationships and to consider the choice points that couples inevitably encounter during their relational lives.

In sum, the chapters of this book cover most of the major topics in the area of close relationships. Given the breadth of the field, however, some topics are covered only briefly and other topics are not included. In contrast, topics such as gender and diversity are given more attention than they often receive in books that focus on relationships research. In this respect and perhaps in others, the text reflects my own background as a counseling psychologist and a marriage and family therapist. This is the lens through which I invariably view relationships theory and research, asking the questions "What does this mean?" and "How can this help clients, especially couples?" The material in this book offers answers to these and many more questions and can be very helpful to readers, including couples.

A variety of study aids will benefit readers as well:

- Each chapter opens with an outline that provides an at-a-glance overview of its content. And as noted earlier, Chapters 2 through 10 begin with Relationship Stories, followed by a series of probing questions, that will pique readers' interest and prompt them to think about the topic at hand.

- Within each chapter, boxes labeled Up Close present a variety of brief surveys and sets of guidelines that will engage readers in thinking about their own personal relationships.

- Each chapter ends with a summary of its content along with a list of key vocabulary terms and several recommendations for additional reading.

- The key terms, which are bolded within the text, are collected and defined in a Glossary at the end of the book.

- A comprehensive References section, also at the end of the book, provides complete bibliographic information for the more than 600 sources cited in the text.

Acknowledgments

Writing this book has been a major challenge and, for the most part, a joy. Much of the pleasure has been due to the excellent people with whom I have worked. First, I want to thank Carolyn Merrill, Executive Editor at Allyn & Bacon, for her enthusiastic support and excellent ideas. I also want to thank her editorial assistants and all those at Allyn & Bacon who helped produce the book, including Donna Simons, Senior Production Administrator. I also thank freelancers Denise Hoffman and Susan Freese for their creative work.

I am grateful to the excellent reviewers, whose insights, without question, have made this a better book: Julie M. Albright, California State University, Los Angeles; Duane A. Dowd, Louisiana Tech University; William Dragon, Cornell College; Renate Klein, University of Maine; Benjamin Le, Haverford College; and especially Maurice J. Levesque, Elon University.

Finally, I wish to thank a few very special people. I thank Robert Hogan for giving me my first break in publishing. I also thank John Harvey, who has been a generous and supportive academic mentor for over two decades. I thank Steve Duck, too, for his formative mentoring over many years. I also thank Ellen Berscheid for modeling such exquisite academic writing—writing that has always been an aspirational, if not an attainable, goal for me. And Clyde—thank you for everything.

The Importance of Relationships

Raquel and Elisia have been best friends since junior high. They have very different personalities and interaction styles, but they have always been able to talk to each other about everything. They have been roommates during their first year of college, but they've found that living together is different from just being close friends. In fact, they've been getting on each other's nerves and are wondering whether their friendship can survive another year of being roommates.

■ ■ ■

Brief scenarios, like this one, are interspersed throughout Chapter 1 to illustrate some of the relationship situations and dilemmas addressed in this book. For example, can long-time friends be roommates and also maintain their friendship? When is the right time in a romantic relationship for partners to begin having sex? How do married couples maintain their relationship after children are born? These questions and others are considered briefly in this chapter and at greater length in the case studies—called *Relationship Stories*—that open the following chapters.

What Do We Know about the Importance of Relationships?

It sometimes seems that relationships bring us our greatest joys—and our greatest heartaches. People are intensely interested in *close relationships,* which are those consisting of personal involvement, emotional connection, and ongoing interaction. Each of us has grown up within a set of family relationships—sometimes satisfying, sometimes not. As adults, we typically also have close relationships with friends and perhaps with a romantic partner.

What this means is that to some degree, every student of close relationships is a relationship expert. When taking a course in close relationships, we each have a level of knowledge and experience that would not necessarily be present in a literature course or a science course. But this knowledge can sometimes blind us to what we do *not* know. In fact, many people are rather inexpert experts about their own relationships. And much of what people actually do in relationships is governed by unconscious mental processes, rather than by what are perceived to be conscious choices (e.g., Bargh & Chartrand, 1999). So although we may believe that we know a great deal about relationships, we always have more to learn.

Relationships with family, friends, and romantic partners are all significant for our lives. The extensive literatures on all of these types of relationships could not be condensed successfully into a single volume. This book will focus primarily on romantic, partnered relationships, with some emphasis on friendships. Nevertheless, all these types of relationships contribute in one way or another to each person's life story.

As you read this book, it is intended that you will realize all the knowledge you already have about how relationships work; that you will learn new information that fills in the gaps in your knowledge; and that you will understand how to

Amy and Chin have been dating for several months. They have both dated several other people during their time in college, but they are tired of the dating scene. Now, they are nearing graduation and beginning to think more seriously about graduate school and their futures. They like each other a lot, and they are taking things very slowly in their relationship. They are not sure when or even whether to become sexually intimate. They think this relationship might actually be the right one, and they don't want to mess things up.

▪ ▪ ▪

engage in your own close relationships with greater satisfaction. There are many initial questions about the role of relationships in our lives: Why are relationships so central, so important to us? Why can relationships be so rewarding yet sometimes so painful? And why are they sometimes so complicated? One important perspective on these questions is discussed in the following section.

The Need to Belong

In a major theoretical article, Baumeister and Leary (1995) suggest what they call the *belongingness hypothesis.* Specifically, they propose that "human beings have a pervasive drive to form and maintain at least a minimum quantity of lasting, positive, and significant interpersonal relationships" (p. 497). They go on to elaborate their argument and support it with a vast array of psychological research.

Although this is not a new idea, as Baumeister and Leary acknowledge, the systematic nature of their argument and the precision with which they support it gives scientific credibility to what has been an intuitive truth. *People need other people.* This premise provides an overarching framework for the current volume.

There are several key elements to Baumeister and Leary's argument. They propose that the need to belong consists of two aspects, including (1) frequent and emotionally pleasant interactions with at least a few other people and (2) stability of these affectional relationships over time. They also propose that belongingness is a *need,* rather than a *want,* and thus an innate, fundamental part of human evolutionary makeup. Belonging is not optional, they argue; it is essential. Belonging to a family unit and a larger social group would have conferred survival and reproductive value on humans through improved food procurement, more effective defense against hostile forces, and so on. Thus, the need to belong could have been selected over long time spans.

If belongingness is a fundamental need, then it should be woven into human life in some specific ways. Humans should be motivated to form social bonds and not to break those bonds. Both cognitive and emotional processes should coalesce around such bonding, so that positive bonds are related to positive outcomes and the loss of such bonds is associated with negative outcomes. In addition, neither close bonds without ongoing interaction nor ongoing interaction without close bonds should be as satisfying as having both together. Finally, the need to establish social relationships should diminish after one's belongingness needs have been met, and the loss of one relationship should motivate the replacement of that relationship by another one.

Because key aspects of Baumeister and Leary's (1995) hypothesis center on the need to form social bonds and the consequences of both forming and breaking those bonds, special attention will be paid to these specific topics. One particularly influential approach to how young humans first form social bonds, which then becomes a guide or blueprint for later social relationships, is the *attachment perspective.*

LaDonna and Emmett got married five years ago, just after completing college. They had their first child about a year ago. LaDonna is totally infatuated with the baby, and between motherhood and her teaching job, she has very little time for Emmett. He loves the baby, too, but wonders if his marriage will ever be as good as it used to be. He feels like he has lost his wife!

▪ ▪ ▪

Attachment

The formation of social bonds, or **attachment** in its broadest sense, refers to a general affectional linkage between persons. Attachment involves physical contact, stability of relationship, and consistency in interaction. More specifically, the term has been used to describe how parents and infants maintain physical closeness (Bowlby, 1958) and how adults experience their connection to romantic partners (Hazan & Shaver, 1987).

Observational studies of humans and other primates indicate that infants and mothers interact with each other from the point of birth and that fathers are an integral part of this interactional system, as well. In fact, research indicates that father love is fully as important as mother love in the development and functioning of infants and children (e.g., Rohner & Veneziano, 2001). Whether the infant turns her head at the sound of her mother's voice or begins to smile at her father when he picks her up, the interactional system is being strengthened. Indeed, interaction is part of belonging, as defined by Baumeister and Leary (1995). Hrdy (1999) proposes that infant smiles and general adorableness are designed for survival value, in that an infant who interacts with and is strongly bonded to his parents is more likely to be taken care of and to survive infancy.

Physical contact is particularly important in this bonding process; that is one reason it drew so much attention from Bowlby (1958). Much of the knowledge about attachment has been drawn from studies of primates (Harlow, 1974; Harlow & Harlow, 1966, 1970). Infant monkeys seek physical proximity to and comforting from their mothers, and Harlow (1974) coined the concept *organic affection* to describe how the infant monkey clings to its mother long before it can actually recognize her. When deprived of such comfort in infancy, the monkeys' later development was arrested in various ways, particularly in terms of mating and rearing offspring. Human infants also seek physical closeness with caregivers. An infant who is dry and well fed may still cry, and that crying will typically cease when the infant is held close and soothed, sometimes by rocking. As Baumeister and Leary (1995) point out, an essential part of a close relationship is physical proximity.

Relationship stability is another aspect of full belongingness, and consistency is another aspect of the attachment process. It is through the consistency of caregiver attention that an infant learns to feel safe and secure. During the first year of life, infants who are well cared for are fed when hungry, changed when wet, held and fondled extensively, and talked to almost unceasingly. With affectionate and responsive caregiving, an infant learns that her world is consistent and predictable. Moreover, this process is reciprocal (Schaffer, 1971), with the caregiver and infant vocalizing, gazing, and imitating each other's movements.

Throughout the first year of life, an infant becomes increasingly attached to responsive caregivers, typically both mother and father, and also develops resistance to being physically separated from the caregiver. By one year of age, a toddler becomes possessive of the caregiver and becomes threatened and jealous if the caregiver pays attention to another child (Hart, 2001). Such possessiveness is very adaptive, since it is not in an infant's best interest for the caregiver's nurturing to be diverted elsewhere. Evolution mandates that a "me first" or even a "me only" attitude provides the greatest promise for infant survival (Hrdy, 1999).

The concept that humans are physically and emotionally linked to each other is an old one, but the beginning of what might be called *attachment research* occurred after World War II, when British psychiatrist John Bowlby was asked to study children who had been orphaned or otherwise separated from their parents and families. Bowlby systematically observed children over long periods of time and developed a general theory of attachment (Bowlby, 1969, 1973, 1980). Bowlby proposed that infants develop an attachment to their primary caregivers and that from this attachment, they develop an **internal working model,** or cognitive and emotional blueprint, of how relationships are likely to unfold in the future. What makes this concept so important is that it proposes that early relational bonds strongly influence the development of later emotional bonds.

Bowlby's work was followed by that of Ainsworth (e.g., Ainsworth, Blehar, Waters, & Wall, 1978), who developed an experimental approach called the *strange situation*. Briefly, this situation involves the separation of child from caregiver in an otherwise pleasant setting (e.g., a playroom in which another adult is present to attend to the child's needs). Observations of the child's behavior are conducted when the caregiver leaves, in the caregiver's absence, and when the caregiver returns. Based on how the child responds to all phases of this experience, he or she can be classified as demonstrating **secure, avoidant,** or **anxious** attachment.

A securely attached child gets upset when the caregiver leaves, then calms down and begin to play, and then is happy to see the caregiver when they are reunited. The caregiver functions as a *secure base* from which the child can go forth and explore the world (or the playroom). An anxiously attached child shows the same upset initially but never really calm downs. When reunited with his or her caregiver, the child is both clingy and resistant, exhibiting ambivalence. He or she is also reluctant to freely explore his or her environment. An avoidantly attached child does not necessarily get upset during separation and does not acknowledge the caregiver upon reunion. He or she seems, to some degree, insulated from the attachment experience. Based on numerous research studies, nearly two-thirds (65%) of middle-class U.S. children can be classified as secure, with the remainder being either anxious (23%) or avoidant (12%) (Erber & Erber, 2001).

It is wise to remember that the specific categories of attachment are only approximations of the research findings of Ainsworth and others, and there is some controversy about whether there are three or four (or perhaps more) attachment styles (see Chapter 4). Although attachment research is profoundly important and has proliferated in recent decades, attachment as a universal concept is much larger than attachment as a theory of the child/caregiver relationship or, as will be explored in Chapter 4, a theory of the adult romantic relationship. The distribution of attachment styles may show cultural variation, so that although actual infant/mother bonding, for example, is virtually universal, the exact expression of that bonding depends on the culture and the historical time period in which it is expressed as well as the options for caregivers that infants have available. Attachment styles may also change over time and with new and different relational experiences (Feeney, Noller, & Roberts, 2000). In addition, the belongingness hypothesis is broader than the concept of attachment theory; it goes beyond the infant/caregiver relationship and the adult romantic relationship to focus on an overarching and universal need to belong (Baumeister & Leary, 1995).

If the need to form social bonds is powerful, then the loss of those bonds is equally powerful.

The Loss of Attachments

Among the several concepts encompassed by Baumeister and Leary's (1995) belongingness proposition is the idea that it is as important to understand the results of *not* belonging as it is to understand the results of belonging. Cognitive factors are important, and emotional factors may be even more so. Baumeister and Leary make a strong case that "the main emotional implication of the belongingness hypothesis is that real, potential, or imagined changes in one's belongingness status will produce emotional responses, with positive affect linked to increases in belongingness and negative affect linked to decreases in it" (p. 505).

Research on happiness is consistent with this hypothesis. In writing about happiness, Myers (2000) cites the overwhelming research evidence that "most people are happier when attached than when unattached" (p. 62). This attachment may come in the form of family bonds, friendship bonds, or romantic bonds. Married people report greater happiness than either never-married or divorced people, as long as those married people are also in happy marriages. People in unhappy marriages report the least happiness of all groups sampled. The majority of people in marriages also have close friendships, since three out of four married Americans describe their mate as their best friend (Myers, 2000). And the connection between happiness and being married extends across cultures and countries (Stack & Eshleman, 1998). Positive attachment is also related to personality features such as hardiness and mental health (Neria, Guttmann-Steinmetz, Koenen, Levinovsky, Zakin, & Dekel, 2001).

Shannon grew up in a family in which there was no open conflict. It appeared to her that her parents never disagreed with each other, and she and her brother were not allowed to argue. Now, she is in college and away from home. She bottles up her emotions, afraid that if she exhibits any negative emotion at all, she'll alienate her friends. She has had one serious romantic relationship, but that boyfriend broke up with her. She is still hurt and angry about the breakup, but she hasn't talked to anyone about it. She feels very lonely and depressed.

■ ■ ■

Even as belonging is related to greater happiness and, potentially, to greater health, the loss of social bonds is related to decrements in both emotional and physical health. Whether social ties are broken because a friendship is disrupted, a loved one dies, or a partner is lost to divorce, anxiety is likely to rise and physical health is likely to fall (Baumeister & Leary, 1995; Myers, 2000). As Myers states, "When our social ties are threatened or broken, negative emotions may overwhelm us. Exile, imprisonment, and solitary confinement are progressively more severe forms of punishment" (p. 62). For example, one of the greatest concerns for many prison inmates is the loss of close relationships, and in fact, the loss of a relationship though divorce or death is a major risk factor for suicide (Correia, 2000).

One does not need to go to a prison to experience the threat of relational/belongingness loss. Any child who has experienced a "time out" for unacceptable behavior, any adolescent who has been "grounded" and unable to go out with friends, or any adult who has had a relational partner walk out on him or her knows the painfulness of being separated from a loved one. Thus, it would seem that the joy of belonging along with the sadness of isolation both highlight the profound importance of human connection.

In supporting their belongingness hypothesis, Baumeister and Leary (1995) also propose that because both positive relating and consistent interaction are important, relationships that have either quality individually are not as complete as relationships that have both qualities. People who have relatedness without interaction include those in prison, separated from loved ones; noncustodial divorced parents and their children, who may have greatly reduced contact; military families, who may be separated for up to a year at a time; and partners in long-distance relationships, including commuter marriages. Some of these relationships may be just as satisfying as more proximal relationships; however, the decreased opportunities for interaction are likely to serve as a source of stress (Baumeister & Leary, 1995).

The mirror images of these relationships are those that include ongoing interaction but fail to contain positive relating. Those in conflictual family settings or in unhappy marriages offer examples of interaction without the requisite positive emotional attachment. Having a loving relationship with a person one sees often will obviously be much more satisfying than having a loving relationship with a person who lives across the country or frequent interaction with a person one is no longer close to.

Two other aspects of Baumeister and Leary's (1995) argument should also be highlighted. First, even though relationships are a good thing, there can be enough of a good thing. Thus, when people's belongingness needs are satisfied by some number of good relationships, they are likely to be less motivated to form additional relationships. And second, when people lose a close relationship for one reason or another, sometimes that relationship can be replaced with a similar relationship. The need to belong is a strong motivator. Ultimately, as Baumeister and Leary conclude, "The desire for interpersonal attachment may well be one of the most far-reaching and integrative constructs currently available to understand human nature" (p. 522). Use the questions in the Up Close box on page 8 to help you examine your own experiences of belonging.

Considering Your Relationships

Answer the questions below as completely as you can.

- Do you feel a sense of belonging in your family? What is that like?
- Do you ever feel distance between you and either your parents or your siblings? What is that like?
- What is your earliest memory of belonging to a group other than your family? How did you feel as part of that group?
- Who was your very first best friend? How did you feel about that person?
- Have you ever been rejected by a friend or a relationship partner? How did you feel?
- Have you ever been excluded from a group that you wanted to be part of? How did you feel?
- Have you ever rejected someone else? How did you feel? How did the rejected person seem to feel?
- What person in your life is closest to you right now? Use three words to describe your relationship with that person.

Using the scale below, circle the number that best represents how connected you feel overall to the people in your close relationship network.

1	2	3	4	5	6	7
Very Disconnected	*Moderately*	*Slightly*	*Neutral* (neither disconnected nor connected)	*Slightly*	*Moderately*	*Very Connected*

Loneliness

One aspect of belonging involves the *feeling* of belonging, and that is something that may be absent when a person feels lonely. Loneliness can involve either an actual or a perceived deficiency in interpersonal relationships, and it is not necessarily related to the number of social ties that someone has. It may or may not relate directly to whether one is in a close romantic relationship or has lost such a relationship. One person may have

few relationships yet be emotionally satisfied, while another may have multiple relationships but still experience loneliness.

Mikulincer and Segal (1990) propose
four different subtypes of loneliness feelings:
(a) *depressive loneliness* (which can involve
longing for a loved one), (b) *emotional isolation* (feeling rejected), (c) *esteem loneliness*
(which has "fear, shame, and alienation" [p.
224] at its core), and (d) *social estrangement*
(no social ties). Based on this classification,
it is easy to see that different events could
produce different types of loneliness. For instance, losing a partner could result in depressive loneliness, while losing a job could
result in esteem loneliness. Moving to a new
location might precipitate social estrangement. For some people, loneliness is situa-

> *Natalie and her husband, Jack,
> have been married for about
> a year. Natalie loves Jack, but
> whenever they disagree about
> something, he begins yelling at
> her and calling her names. She
> knew before they got married
> that he had a bad temper, but she
> thought that after they were mar-
> ried, he would feel more secure
> emotionally and that his temper
> would improve. She was wrong!
> She loves him, but she's growing
> increasingly unhappy.*
>
> ■ ■ ■

tional and experienced periodically throughout the lifespan, depending on the circumstances. Interestingly, loneliness is experienced more commonly by adolescents and
young adults than by older adults (Rubenstein & Shaver, 1982).

For some people, however, loneliness is chronic, no matter what the circumstances. People who are chronically lonely may experience a number of depressive and
related features (Myers, 2002) and may be more negative in judging others as well as
more negatively judged by others (Jones, Sansone, & Helm, 1983). Therapeutic strategies such as increasing one's social contacts (through volunteer work, for example) and
learning better interaction skills (such as more effective listening) may help people to alleviate chronic loneliness (Jones, Hansson, & Cutrona, 1984). It is important to remember, however, that whereas *loneliness* may be loosely related to belongingness, the *need
to belong* is a much broader concept. If people did not have a fundamental need to belong, loneliness, as we know it, would not exist.

Contemporary Relationships

Although the foundational premise of this book is that people have a fundamental need to
connect with each other and that these connections (called *relationships*) are important
for researchers to study, a few additional ideas should be considered when looking at relationships today. The first thing to consider is the *context:* both the immediate context and
the larger societal context. Many of us live in a rushed and complicated world, so the context of our lives is complex. For those of us in technologically developed countries, modern conveniences and labor-saving devices do not seem to have freed us up to have more

Graciela and Luis are trying to finish college and are living together with their 2-year-old daughter, Lourdes. They got married when they were very young, and they love each other (and Lourdes) very much. But life is not easy. Trying to take care of Lourdes, go to college, and work to support themselves leaves them almost no time for each other. They aren't fighting, but they also aren't talking. Sometimes, they feel like nothing more than roommates.

■ ■ ■

time for ourselves, much less for each other. E-mail, answering machines, faxes, cell phones, and surfing the Internet may actually make us less free, rather than more free. We may sometimes wish for the simplicity of the "good old days," thinking that we could have the same kind of uncomplicated relationships that appear to have existed then. It seemed that people simply met, fell in love, and lived happily ever after. But the simplicity of the past is a myth (Coontz, 1992). Life has *never* been that simple. In fact, our modern world offers a complex context of positives and negatives that include medical advances and educational opportunities along with what are often inconvenient conveniences and labor-saving devices that cost us time! Today's context for relationships thus may be simpler in some ways and more complicated in other ways, as compared to past relational contexts.

A second aspect of contemporary relationships is their variety, or *diversity*. Relationships come in different colors and sizes, just like people, a fact that is essential to remember. In one recent undergraduate relationships class, students spoke about what kinds of families they had grown up in, and the descriptions varied widely. Of course, some students were raised in two-parent homes where the mom stayed at home and the dad worked outside the home, but the following were also represented: a family where the kids were raised by the mother after the parents divorced and the father went on to have multiple remarriages; a family where the dad worked outside the home, the mom stayed home and raised the kids, but the housework was done by a housekeeper; a family in which the kids did all the housework, since both parents worked outside the home; a family where the parents had a home-based business and worked at home, sharing parenting, housework, and business duties; and yet another family where the grandparents served as the parents. All sorts of shapes and sizes of families were represented in that single classroom; one size clearly did not fit all.

Relationships also exhibit racial, ethnic, sexual orientation, age, and religious diversity. It can be said that at some level, every relationship is cross-cultural because no two people grow up with exactly the same set of experiences and expectations. As an example, take a couple who are white, heterosexual, middle-class college students and come from families that have the same number of kids, live in the same part of the country, and have the same religion. These relational partners will still have differences that at times seem to represent contrasting cultures. He comes from a family that goes to church on Sundays, always eats dinner together, and expresses little negative emotion. She comes from a family that goes to church only occasionally, seldom eats together, and is very expressive of all emotions, whether positive or negative. Can this be a cultural clash? Yes! So even though much of the relationship literature discussed in this book has been based on European American, heterosexual college students, many of the dynamics that will be discussed are at least loosely generalizable to other groups of people. If relationships are indeed part of our evolutionary heritage, then we should expect there to be relationship characteristics and processes that are virtually universal across cultural and racial groups.

A final aspect of relationships is the level of *knowledge* that we have about them. We live in a time in which people are fascinated by relationships and acknowledge their importance. Books, movies, TV talk shows, and magazines all testify to the importance that people place on their intimate relationships: the ones they want, the ones they have, and the ones they have lost. In the past, most people did not so closely examine their relationships, yet today, we are sometimes obsessed with relationships. It is not clear whether all our knowledge about relationships has made us wise about them; nevertheless, knowledge is one key to improving relationships.

Relationship knowledge is communicated through the media, but it is also communicated through a variety of books, including handbooks, that attempt to cover specific fields or topic areas very broadly (e.g., Andersen & Guerrero, 1998; Duck, 1997; C. Hendrick & S. S. Hendrick, 2000). The underlying basis for relationship knowledge, however, is actual research about relationships. Specific research approaches are discussed in the next section.

Methods of Research

If the extent of contemporary knowledge about relationships is greater than ever, how was this knowledge acquired? And as we try to learn more about relationships, how do we go about it? First, it is important to consider the questions that we are asking because that will influence the methods we employ (Duck & Montgomery, 1991). We may have a conjecture or hypothesis about the relationships between two or more concepts or behaviors (often called *variables*). For example, we may believe that intimacy affects satisfaction, that satisfaction affects intimacy, or as occurs most often in everyday life, that both satisfaction and intimacy affect each other. Or we might be curious about relationships that have been studied relatively less often, such as sibling relationships. We may simply want to ask questions about these relationships, with no preconceived ideas about what we might find.

Terrance and his girlfriend, Latrice, live together and are planning to get married when they graduate from college. Terrance works almost full time to support himself, and Brandi, one of the girls at work, has sought him out as a friend and counselor. Terrance doesn't mind being supportive, and he kind of likes the counselor role. But Latrice is starting to get jealous of his relationship with Brandi.

■ ■ ■

Although a detailed consideration of the research methods used in close relationships and in social science more generally is beyond the scope of this volume, we will consider very briefly a few of the more common techniques for acquiring new relationships knowledge. More thorough explanations of such methods are contained in some of the Suggested Reading at the end of this chapter (Allen & Walker, 2000; Harvey, Hendrick, & Tucker, 1988).

Self-Report Approaches

The most common method of acquiring knowledge about relationships is through **self-report** (Harvey et al., 1988), which requires asking people to provide information about themselves and their relationships. Self-report methods include questionnaires, interviews, behavioral records, and personal accounts.

Questionnaires are most popular in relationship research because they are inexpensive and easy to administer and can vary in length. Moreover, questionnaires can elicit a range of information, so one lengthy questionnaire can ask about the participant's family background, current romantic relationship (e.g., love, self-disclosure, satisfaction, sexual attitudes), and personality characteristics (e.g., anxiety, depression, extraversion, perfectionism). A potential wealth of information can be secured from a number of people with relative ease and efficiency. Many of the measures presented in the Up Close boxes throughout this book have been designed specifically for use in research on close relationships.

A time-honored approach to obtaining information is through conducting *interviews*. Well-constructed interviews given by effective interviewers may elicit particularly accurate responses from participants. Although conducting interviews is time consuming and costly, doing so may yield rich, highly descriptive information. Interviews may be highly structured, with all the questions detailed in advance, or less structured, with some basic questions and a great deal of leeway for respondents to elaborate. An interesting interview format used typically with married couples is one in which the respondents identify key events or turning points in the relationship that positively or negatively affected their movement toward marriage. These events are then marked on a timeline and plotted on a graph, such that the development of the relationship can actually be visualized (Fitzgerald & Surra, 1981; Surra & Hughes, 1997).

Rani is devastated. His girlfriend of over a year just broke up with him. She said that she had met someone else and didn't love Rani anymore. He has talked to a few of his friends, and they told him to forget her and find someone else. But Rani can't stop thinking about her. He has even driven over to her apartment building and parked across the street, hoping to catch sight of her. He has lost weight and is having trouble sleeping.

▪ ▪ ▪

Other self-report approaches are gaining popularity in relationship research. *Behavioral records* involve having participants record their experiences in a type of journal: for instance, at specific times of the day (e.g., morning and evening), when particular events occur (e.g., a couple has an argument), or when contacted by the experimenter (e.g., via beeper, pager, or phone). One approach, the Rochester Interaction Record, has people record social interaction of a particular type for one or two weeks (Nezlek, Wheeler, & Reis, 1983).

Finally, there is a wealth of information contained in people's *personal accounts* or narratives of relationship events and processes (Harvey, Weber, & Orbuch, 1990). Conclusions may be drawn from individuals' personal stories, or relationship partners or family members may provide accounts from which particular themes can be derived. Narrative approaches allow the researcher and the participant to co-create the work, and the account-making process may even be therapeutic for the participant involved (Harvey et al., 1990; Pennebaker, 1990).

Sophia and Marco have been in a romantic relationship for nearly two years, but Sophia is wondering if they should call it quits. Marco is intensely jealous, even though she has assured him that she loves him and would never betray him in any way. He keeps track of everyone she sees and everything she does, and it's getting worse, not better. He has never hurt her physically, but nevertheless, she is sometimes afraid of him.

■ ■ ■

There are disadvantages to questionnaires and other self-report approaches, however. It is difficult, if not impossible, to know if participants have understood all the questions, if they have interpreted the questions in similar ways, or even if they have answered the questions honestly and carefully. Other problems concern people being less accurate than they believe they are, being influenced by how the questions are asked (e.g., phrased positively or negatively), and perhaps becoming bored while answering a questionnaire (Erber & Erber, 2001).

Observational Approaches

Observation can include field observation, in which researchers simply observe a couple or a group in a natural setting, but most relationship observation is conducted systematically in the laboratory. One approach involves having relationship partners sit at either end of a table and take turns speaking, typically about a relationship problem (Bradbury & Fincham, 1989). Partners rate the intent of their own communications as well as the impact of one another's communications, and they are also rated by observers. Self-reports and other behavioral ratings may also be used along with the talk-table approach.

Some researchers observe participants from behind one-way mirrors, but much observation is done via videotape. For example, a couple might be videotaped during the discussion of a potential conflict, and the tape would later be coded for specific communication and other relational behaviors. If the research also had a therapy component, the couple might be shown the videotape so that they could actually see how they handle conflict. A picture can indeed be worth a thousand words.

Kevin recently graduated from high school and started college. He has a few friends, but somehow, he just doesn't feel that he fits in. There is an active gay/lesbian/bisexual/transgendered (GLBT) student group on his campus, and he is thinking about attending a meeting. He has wondered for a long time if he is gay, and he thinks maybe it's time to answer that question.

■ ■ ■

Ickes and his colleagues (e.g., Ickes & Barnes, 1978; Ickes, Bissonnette, Garcia, & Stinson, 1990) have used a dyadic interaction paradigm, in which video equipment and specialized software programs are used to tape pairs of persons in brief, unstructured interactions outside the lab, while they are supposedly waiting for a research study to begin. Then the participants (who might be friends, romantic partners, or even strangers) are asked to review the videotape and record the feelings and thoughts they remember having at particular points during their interaction with the other person. This approach thus combines observation with self-analysis and self-report.

Another approach that can be considered observational is the research that assesses physiological arousal and other physical phenomena, such as immune system response. Such research involves considerable equipment and has frequently been employed to increase understanding of men's and women's responses to relationship conflict (e.g., Gottman & Levenson, 1988; Kiecolt-Glaser, Newton, Cacioppo, MacCallum, Glaser, & Malarkey, 1996).

Observational approaches have the advantage of achieving considerable accuracy, but they have the disadvantage of being very labor intensive. In addition, it is not always clear how well behavior (or coding) that occurs in the laboratory will generalize to daily life.

Archival Approaches

Archival approaches use information that already exists in order to answer particular research questions. Census data, hospital records, and large-scale data sets from the National Health and Social Life Survey (NHSLS) are examples of quantitative archival information. Personal letters and journals represent other, more narrative sources of information for the archival researcher. Such information is analyzed in various ways. An obvious advantage to archival research is that the participants do not have to be recruited. A disadvantage is that the researcher has no control over the quality of the information that has been obtained.

Experimental Approaches

Experimental approaches typically take place in a structured setting and involve giving a task or experience (a *treatment*) to some participants but not to others. For example, a researcher might have two groups of participants, all of whom are in current romantic relationships. One group might be asked to write essays about recent relationship conflicts they have had, while the other group would be asked to write about what they did on their last vacation. Then the groups would complete surveys assessing conflict and other characteristics (e.g., love) in their relationships. The question of interest would be whether having people think carefully and write about specific conflict incidents influences their more general attitudes toward conflict and other relationship qualities. If participants were assigned randomly to the two groups and if the groups were treated in exactly the same way, except for the topic assigned for their written essays, then any differences between the groups on the other measures might be presumed to be due to the essay-writing exercise.

Experimentation is used widely in the social sciences, since it allows considerable control over the research process as well as sophisticated analysis of the information (Kashy & Levesque, 2000). One difficulty with experiments, however, is that there are many real-world questions that cannot be explored in the lab.

Additional Issues

As noted at the beginning of this section, the choice of research method is influenced by the type of question being asked. It is also influenced by the *researcher.* Some researchers prefer a more controlled and predictable research situation; they might lean toward experimentation. Other researchers might view research as a cooperative venture between the researcher and the participant (Allen & Walker, 2000). They might lean toward qualitative methods that include unstructured interviews, written accounts, and so on.

No matter what approach they take, relationship researchers must be particularly sensitive to the ethical issues involved in working with people in close relationships. Rubin and Mitchell (1976) note that researchers may affect people and their relationships by the questions asked, the issues raised, and the methods employed.

For example, if a dating couple participates in a research study in which they fill out questionnaires asking about love, communication, commitment, and so on, the partners might well begin to think more deeply about these issues and even talk with each other about them. Such a process could result in a relational turning point (Surra & Hughes, 1997), moving the couple toward or away from marriage. As another example, suppose a married couple participates in research on couple conflict. Could the various research tasks (e.g., being interviewed about how they handle conflict, engaging in a discussion of a conflictual topic) increase or decrease the couple's actual conflict outside the laboratory?

Julia is in her mid-60s and lost her husband to cancer about a year ago. Some friends recently fixed her up with Hal, a divorced man about her own age. They hit it off immediately and have been dating regularly since they met. Now, they are talking about getting married. Their grown children are concerned and have urged them to wait, but Julia and Hal don't think they want to listen to their kids.

■ ■ ■

Thus, researchers need to fully inform potential research participants about the procedures to be followed and at least some of the potential effects of participation. Researchers also need to be interpersonally skillful in working with participants. "Whenever research touches on important areas of the participants' lives, the processes of research and counseling are likely to merge" (Rubin & Mitchell, 1976, p. 25).

Summary and Conclusions

Relationships may bring people some of their greatest pleasure but also their greatest pain. It has been proposed that humans have a *need to belong,* or a need to be attached or bonded to others in close personal relationships. To be fully satisfying, such relationships should involve frequent and emotionally pleasant interactions and be relatively stable over time. One aspect of the belongingness need is the motivation to form social bonds. Infants form such bonds with caregivers from birth onward, and indeed, interaction with caregivers fosters infant development and even survival. Physical contact is an important aspect of bondedness, also called *attachment.* Attachment research has resulted in the identification of three different styles with which infants and young children interact with those closest to them: secure, anxious, and avoidant. Humans may internalize early close relationships in the form of internal working models, which provide a blueprint for future relationships. Attachment styles and what they actually signify may vary depending on culture and the availability of caregivers. Research on attachment has been very influential.

Social bonds are impactful both by their presence and their absence. People who have satisfying relationships report greater happiness, greater health, and so on. People who are separated from loved ones or who have lost relationships are at greater risk for such conditions as depression. It is likely that relationships that have both positive relating and ongoing interaction will be more satisfying than relationships that contain only one of these two elements. When people have enough social bonds, they may have a reduced need to develop additional bonds, and when a relationship ceases, people are typically motivated to replace it with another relationship.

In studying current relationships, it is important to remember that such relationships are conducted in a very complex world, that there is great diversity in current relationships, and that even though there is perhaps more knowledge today about relationships than ever before, more knowledge is still needed. And *knowledge* is not the same as *wisdom.*

Knowledge about relationships is gained through research, which can be conducted in several ways. Self-report approaches involve asking participants about themselves, using questionnaires, interviews, personal narratives, and the like. Observational approaches involve researchers watching or observing participants, either in person or on videotape, and then documenting and analyzing those observations. Archival approaches use information that already exists, such as census data and other large-scale data sets along with personal letters and journals. These sources of information are analyzed in various ways. Experimental approaches involve systematic comparisons, typically of two or more groups, under controlled conditions. Decisions about which methods to use are typically based on the types of questions being asked. It is important that relationship researchers be particularly sensitive to the impact that their research may have on the participants involved.

Key Terms

Anxious (p. 5)

Archival (p. 14)

Attachment (p. 4)

Avoidant (p. 5)

Experimental (p. 14)

Internal working model (p. 5)

Observation (p. 13)

Secure (p. 5)

Self-report (p. 12)

Suggested Reading

Allen, K. R., & Walker, A. J. (2000). Qualitative research. In C. Hendrick & S. S. Hendrick (Eds.), *Close relationships: A sourcebook* (pp. 19–30). Thousand Oaks, CA: Sage.

Baumeister, R. F., & Leary, M. R. (1995). The need to belong: Desire for interpersonal attachments as a fundamental human motivation. *Psychological Bulletin, 117,* 497–529.

Feeney, J. A., Noller, P., & Roberts, N. (2000). Attachment and close relationships. In C. Hendrick & S. S. Hendrick (Eds.), *Close relationships: A sourcebook* (pp. 185–201). Thousand Oaks, CA: Sage.

Harvey, J. H., Hendrick, S. S., & Tucker, K. L. (1988). Self-report methods in studying close relationships. In S. Duck (Ed.), *Handbook of personal relationships* (pp. 99–113). New York: Wiley.

Myers, D. G. (2000). The funds, friends, and faith of happy people. *American Psychologist, 55,* 56–67.

2

Attraction and Relationship Development

Relationship Stories

First Date Scenario 1

Nora thought it was unfair and stupid! At the restaurant where she was on the waitstaff, management had said that only the male waitstaff had to carry out trash as part of cleanup before closing. How sexist was that? Nora typically ignored the rule and carried out trash along with all the guys. If that was part of the job for them, then it was part of the job for her!

Nora was used to working hard. She was the oldest of four kids, and her parents had taught them all the value of hard work—the "gift of work," they called it. Nora was responsible for most of her college expenses, so she was a full-time student and sometimes almost a full-time waitperson. She liked this restaurant and was good at her job; the clientele was nice, the management was young and pretty relaxed most of the time, and the other waitstaff were college students like she was.

This particular Friday night, they had been extremely busy and no one had a chance to breathe all night. They were closing later than usual, and Nora was hauling out yet one more bag of trash when someone walked up behind her and said, "Let me get that." She looked up and saw Tomas, one of the other waitstaff. Tomas was fairly new, and she had seen him quite a few times but hadn't really talked to him. "I'm doing fine," she said. But then, not to seem rude, she said, "Thanks anyway." Tomas walked along with her out to the dumpster and started talking. He was a transfer student and new to the university and the town, not just to the restaurant.

After "they" dumped her trash, they walked back into the restaurant and started wiping off tables and straightening up, all the while talking and getting to know one another. It turned out that Tomas was from a large family like hers, and both of them were oldest kids. Both of them were living in apartments with roommates, in the same part of town. They even shared the same minor (English), although he was a political science major and she was majoring in psychology. Nora thought Tomas seemed very nice, and as they were closing, he asked her if she would go out with him after work the next night. Nora said yes, although she wasn't absolutely sure she wanted to. After all, she really didn't know him very well.

As Nora walked out to her car with her friend Jennifer, one of the other waitstaff, she told Jennifer that Tomas had asked her out, and she was surprised when Jennifer said, "It's about time." Jennifer went on to say that she had seen Tomas watching Nora and knew that he was attracted to her. Somehow hearing this made Nora feel better about going out with Tomas.

When she was getting ready for work on Saturday, Nora made a point of spending extra time on her hair and makeup, trying to dress up her T-shirt-and-jeans uniform a little bit. She got a ride to work from Jennifer so that she wouldn't be stuck there with her car. Tomas and Nora were both supposed to get off at 9:30 that night, but business was brisk, so they worked until 10:00. Then Tomas suggested they go out for something to eat! They both laughed, given that all they had been doing for several hours was serve food to other people, but in fact, they were starving. So they went over to another, quieter place and were shown to a booth.

After ordering, they started to talk at the same time. They were both a little nervous—that "first date" nervousness. But as they talked about school, their families, and some of their high school experiences, they both started to relax. Nora found that Tomas was someone she could really talk to. He seemed genuinely interested in what she said and asked lots of questions about her background and her interests. He was a very good listener. And he didn't just listen; he talked a lot, too. She learned about his younger brothers, his parents, his previous junior college (where he had played basketball), and about his hopes to go to law school.

They finished eating and kept talking, and before they knew it, the restaurant was closing. As Tomas drove Nora to her apartment, they talked about work—what they liked and what they didn't like. When they got there, he walked her to her door. There was one awkward moment, and then he said, "I really had fun tonight. You're so easy to talk to. I'd like to go out again. Can I call you tomorrow?" Nora assured Tomas that she would like to go out with him, and as he left, she thought that her job had given her a bonus she hadn't planned on! Tomas was *very* special.

■ ■ ■

First Date Scenario 2

James was laughing at something his friend Jamal said, and as he turned his head to say something smart to Jamal, he saw a girl he hadn't seen before, walking through the food line. The dormitory dining hall was not the place where he usually looked at girls, but this woman was an exception. She was tall, with short curly hair, and something about the way she carried herself really struck him. She looked proud. That was it; she looked proud! And proud was a good thing.

"What are you looking at?" Jamal asked.

"See that tall girl over by the salad bar? She is what I am looking at!" Jamal looked, even stared, and then told James that he was not all that impressed. She just looked like one more college girl to him. But not to James.

James was almost finished eating, and he watched to see where the girl sat. She was at a table with three other girls, in the back corner of the dining room. He hung out with Jamal for awhile, glancing over at the girl every now and then. Finally, he saw her get up and walk toward the dessert table. "I think I want some dessert," he told Jamal, and he walked toward the table—and the girl.

Keisha was her name. After he said "Hi" and introduced himself, they stood around the chocolate cake for a couple of minutes, making small talk. He found out she had just moved from another dorm to this one, and she was majoring in art. He told her a little about himself and then asked if she wanted to go to a free concert on campus the following night. She looked a little surprised, but she said, "Okay."

They met in the dorm lobby the following evening. James was impressed with the way Keisha looked, even in boots, jeans, and a sweatshirt. They walked over to the student center, where the concert was being held, mostly talking about school and work. Keisha worked in the university library, and James worked for a computer store in town. (He was a math major.) They realized that the auditorium in the student center was crowded, but Keisha and James found seats near the back. James glanced at Keisha now and then, thinking how much he already liked her. She was one fine-looking woman.

For her part, Keisha wasn't sure how interested she was in James. He was a nice enough guy, but she had recently broken up with her boyfriend of several years, her high school sweetheart, and she wanted to date different people for awhile. She didn't want to get into a serious relationship again any time soon. She was fairly sure that James was interested in her—he kept looking at her. And she was really enjoying the concert. Maybe they could date each other without getting too involved.

When the concert ended, James and Keisha went over to a pizza place near the campus and sat down at a small table in the corner. They talked in a casual manner about their backgrounds, their families, their interests, but no particular topic of conversation went very far. They ate their pizza and then walked back to the dorm. When they got in the lobby, Keisha thanked James for asking her to the concert, and he told her how much he had enjoyed their date. But they both knew that there probably wouldn't be any more dates. That was that.

■ ■ ■

First Date Scenario 3

Alicia was almost ready to leave the apartment she shared with her sister and slam the door behind her. They were having a conversation that Alicia did not like, and she was ready to split. You see, her sister, Amy, wanted to fix Alicia up with a good friend of Amy's boyfriend, Todd, and Alicia wasn't having any of it. She could get her own dates, thank you very much! And besides, she was too busy this semester to worry about going out with anyone except her girlfriends. She was taking 19 hours and also working, and she hardly had time to sleep, much less date!

"Wait—wait, don't leave!" shouted Amy. "I promise you that Todd says his friend from work, Dan, is a great guy, and he thinks you two would really hit it off. Todd has *never* wanted to fix anybody up before, so he must think this is going to work. If you will just agree to go out with Dan once, I will let you borrow my red leather jacket for all of next semester. And I'll never try to fix you up with anyone again. Please say you'll go out to the basketball game on Friday."

Alicia felt herself relenting. She and Amy were very close and usually got along. And she was pretty well caught up on schoolwork for now. And she had Friday night off from work. And she really liked that red leather jacket of Amy's!

So they made a date for the next men's basketball game at the university. Amy and Todd would double-date with Alicia and Dan. They would go to the game and then out to eat. Alicia tried to forget about the whole thing during the week, but all too suddenly, it was Friday evening. As she and Amy got dressed for the date, Alicia was sorry she had ever agreed to this, red jacket or no red jacket. Finally, they heard a knock at the door of their apartment, and Amy opened it. Standing there were Todd and a tall, dark-haired, and rather nice-looking guy. Amy told them to come in, and as Alicia and Todd were introduced, each was checking the other out. Alicia was pleasantly surprised by Dan, and he thought she was cute, with her short dark hair and big blue eyes.

The basketball game was great. Both teams played hard, and everyone was cheering and yelling. Dan tried to explain some of the fouls to Alicia, but she stopped him cold. "My Dad loves basketball, and Amy and I are his only kids. So we know as much about basketball as he does. And by the way, that last foul shouldn't have been called, because . . ." And she went on to explain the fine points of the referee's mistake! Dan seemed impressed with her basketball knowledge, and they enjoyed the rest of the game.

Later, the four of them went out for burgers, and they all had a good time replaying the game and also talking about school and other things. Dan had a wicked sense of humor, so Alicia found herself laughing more than she had in a long time. Todd and Dan knew each other from work, so they told some work stories, and both Amy and Alicia laughed some more. Finally, it was time to go home. The girls invited the guys in to listen to some music, and they listened and talked. As he and Todd were getting ready to leave, Dan pulled Alicia aside and asked if he could call her. She smiled at him and said, "Absolutely."

They left, and after Amy closed and locked the door, she turned to Alicia and asked, "Well, what do you think? Do you like him? Are you going to see him again?"

Alicia waited before she said anything—she didn't want to make this too easy for Amy. Finally, she said, "Yes, I like him. And yes, he's going to call me. But I still don't like blind dates. And I still want your red leather jacket for all of next semester!"

■ ■ ■

Questions to Consider in Reading This Chapter

- In reading about the three couples described in the Relationship Stories, which one did you identify with most?
- What in your dating history is like their story?
- Based on their first date, which couple do you believe has the best chance of developing a long-term relationship? What are your clues?
- Which of these couples do you think you would most like as friends? Why?

What Do We Know about Attraction and Relationship Development?

As discussed in Chapter 1, people need to connect with other people. There are many ways to bond with others, and one of the most profound ways is through a partnered romantic relationship. Marriage is one such prototypic relationship. Not everyone desires this type of relationship, of course, and in fact, many never-married and divorced men and women have no particular desire to enter into marriage (e.g., Frazier, Arikian, Benson,

Losoff, & Maurer, 1996). Yet marriage as a form of long-term, stable attachment has been linked with greater perceived general well-being, happiness, and other positive psychological and physical characteristics (e.g., Diener, 2000; Myers, 2000). Most people want to be connected to others, and marriage is one form of very deep connection.

Marriage and other long-term relationships do not just happen. They occur as the result of a complex set of emotions and behaviors that typically stems from initial attraction.

Theories of Attraction

There are many theories of attraction. The focus in this book is on the approaches most relevant to the development of romantic relationships.

Attraction as an Attitude

An *attitude* can be thought of as an orientation toward or away from a particular object that involves an emotion, some sort of belief or knowledge, and a tendency to behave in a certain way. Viewing *attraction* as an attitude, it can be defined as "an orientation toward or away from a person that . . . consists of a *cognitive* structure of beliefs and knowledge about the person, *affect* felt and expressed toward him or her, and *behavioral tendencies* to approach or avoid that person" (S. S. Hendrick & C. Hendrick, 1992a; italics in original). Viewing attraction as a composite of thought, **affect** (or emotion), and behavior means that theories attempting to understand and explain attraction may take some or all of the three components into account.

Balance Theories

Balance theories are concerned with harmony and are built on the original theory developed by Heider (1958). For example, Newcomb's (1961) *A-B-X model* is a balance model particularly relevant to attraction. The basic idea is that people like to have harmony in the people, things, and relationships around them. For example, if you are person A and you like persons B and C, you would likely prefer that persons B and C also like each other. If they do not, then you will have to manage your friendships with B and C separately, making sure that you see them at different times, avoid planning occasions where they will run into each other, and so on. A less problematic but still annoying example might be a situation where you, an avid movie-goer, are in a relationship with a romantic partner who hates going to the movies. This isn't a major conflict, perhaps, but it does mean that you will have to go to the movies without your partner, plan to see fewer movies than you would like, or handle the dilemma in some other way.

Essentially, balance theories say that life is simpler and attraction is greater when people and things are in harmony. Balance theory may have been at work for Amy's boyfriend, Todd, who liked both Dan and Alicia and hoped they would like each other. Research has supported the basic principles of balance theory (e.g., Davis & Rusbult,

2001) in a relational process called *attitude alignment*—namely, "individuals experience discomfort when they discover that their attitudes are inconsistent with those of a close partner and are motivated to change their attitudes to achieve congruence with the attitudes of the partner" (p. 65).

Reinforcement/Reward Theories

Some theories of attraction are built on basic learning processes: *classical conditioning* (a stimulus is followed by a response) and *operant conditioning* (a response/behavior is followed by a reinforcement). As an example of classical conditioning, if Kristen is in a class that she likes and Sam is in the same class, Kristen may begin associating Sam with the positive experience of being in the class, especially if they walk out of class together, study for exams together, and so on. Sam becomes liked because he is associated with a reward (the class), although he could also be liked under other conditions, such as being disassociated from a punishment (Martin & Seta, 1983). It is also possible that the class has become liked because it is associated with Sam! If Ann is in the same class and nearly always agrees with the comments that Kristen makes, then Kristen may begin to like Ann, also; this would illustrate operant conditioning.

It is hard to describe precise examples of situations in which pure conditioning operates, but Byrne (1969) has developed the learning-based model of reinforcement and attraction most effectively. He states that "attraction toward X is a function of the relative number of rewards and punishments associated with X" (p. 67). Assuming that X is a person, then attraction to that person is based on the rewards (positives) and punishments (negatives) associated with that person.

The general reinforcement approach provides much of the basis for *exchange theory,* which will be discussed in more detail in Chapter 3. Exchange theory is a theory of the marketplace that has been adapted for the study of social relationships (e.g., Blau, 1964). It emphasizes the rewarding and punishing aspects of people's interactions and has led to considerable research about close relationships, particularly why people do or do not continue them. In the case of initial attraction, the rewards available with a particular partner may be more obvious than the costs, particularly if the partner is on his or her best behavior at the start of the relationship. One specific application of reinforcement theory is the construct of similarity.

Similarity

The idea that "Birds of a feather flock together"—or that the more similar two people are in a variety of ways, the more attracted they will be to each other—has prompted a volume of research, a great deal of it conducted by Byrne (1971). Much of the research has taken place in laboratory experiments, in which participants completed attitude questionnaires and then rated their degree of liking for a stranger who had supposedly also filled out the questionnaire. Attraction increased in direct proportion to increases in **similarity** between the participant and bogus stimulus stranger (Byrne & Nelson, 1965). These findings have been supported by considerable additional research (e.g., Gonzales, Davis, Loney, Lukens, & Junghans, 1983).

The relationship between attraction and similarity has been shown for a variety of factors, including economics, personality attributes, self-esteem, and so on, but it is not an invariant relationship. For example, Neimeyer and Mitchell (1988) studied friendship formation outside the laboratory. They found that similarity predicted early attraction between friends, but for the longer term, aspects of friends' personalities and thoughts were better predictors of attraction. Similarity is only part of a broad perspective on how humans relate to one another (Byrne, 1997).

Although similarity is thought to influence attraction, it is likely that attraction also influences similarity. People who are attracted to each other may grow more similar over time and may also perceive themselves to be more similar than they really are. (See the section Positive Illusions on pp. 38–39.) Similarity is also central to balance theories, in that our desire for harmony and balance requires similarities between partners in terms of attitudes and behaviors, as is true for attitude alignment, discussed earlier (Davis & Rusbult, 2001).

Thus, similarity is important but not exclusively so. The perspective that "Opposites attract" has also been given some research attention (e.g., Winch, 1958), but it is much less powerful than the notion of similarity. Similarity was important for Nora and Tomas on their first date, as they learned about each other.

Arousal Theories

No, this is not the chapter on sexuality! *Arousal* here refers to physiological arousal and the part it plays in emotional states. According to Schachter (1964; Schachter & Singer, 1962), the presence of physiological arousal plus situational cues that seem relevant and comprehensible constitutes *emotional experience.*

Classic research on arousal and attraction (Dutton & Aron, 1974) involved having male research participants walk individually across one of two bridges: one, suspended and swaying over a deep canyon; the other, stable and closer to the ground. Each participant was then met by a research assistant, either female or male, who asked the participant to view a picture, answer some questions, and write a brief story about the picture. The participant was also told that if he had any further questions, he could call the research assistant at home. Participants who had been on the suspension bridge and had been met by a female assistant wrote stories that were later rated as having the highest sexual imagery, and they also were more likely to call the assistant. The conclusion was drawn that the physical arousal of walking across the seemingly dangerous bridge appeared to prompt greater attraction.

Thus, if you are on a first date with someone and you come across a car accident, in which you both help the people at the scene, the physiological arousal of the situation plus your helpfulness and teamwork in the accident situation are likely to accelerate your attraction for each other. This type of situation has also been called *misattribution of arousal* (Erber & Erber, 2001).

"Fatal Attractions"

If similarity increases attraction, then what about *dissimilarity?* In fact, research on dissimilarity indicates that when romantic partners are too different, the relationship is often less likely to succeed. Felmlee (1995) has studied what she calls *"fatal attractions,"* or "qualities once seen as alluring and fascinating in a romantic partner [that] are often the same or very similar to those considered flaws and weaknesses after a breakup" (Felmlee, 1998, p. 235). Felmlee conjectured that people will experience these fatal attractions under particular conditions, specifically conditions of (1) a partner being dissimilar to oneself, (2) a partner being unique or different from the average, and (3) a partner being different from normative gender role expectations (i.e., what is expected of a woman or man).

After systematically coding and analyzing quantitative and qualitative information from over 300 people describing terminated relationships, Felmlee (1998) found her conjectures to be largely correct. First, dissimilarity between partners did lead to more breakups, particularly when the qualities that were dissimilar were ones that had caused one partner to become attracted to the other person in the first place. For example, if a rather shy person becomes attracted to an extremely outgoing person, then the outgoingness or extraversion could become a "fatal attraction." If, however, two people simply discover dissimilarities between themselves in the course of developing their relationship, that seems to be less problematic and, in fact, is just a normal aspect of being in a close relationship. Felmlee also found that the more unique or extreme a partner's qualities, the more one might become disillusioned with them. Finally, it appeared that behaving in ways not typical for one's gender role was not related to relationship breakup.

If you are currently in a relationship with someone whose behavior is driving you crazy—or is at least annoying you—think about whether that behavior is new or whether it was obvious when you first met your relationship partner. In fact, could that behavior even be one of the things that attracted you to your partner? If so, then you understand well Felmlee's concept of "fatal attractions."

This brief discussion of theoretical approaches to attraction offers some of the broad perspectives on how people become interested in one another. Particular environmental and personal factors also influence attraction. These factors will be considered in the next two sections.

Environmental Influences on Attraction

Proximity

Homans (1961) noted that if people interact positively, then the more they interact, the more they will like or be attracted to each other. In order to interact often, they must be near each other, or in spatial **proximity.** The idea is that people who are in the same space—be it the workplace, the college classroom, or an apartment complex or housing development—will interact more frequently and become more attracted to each other.

Remember that Nora and Tomas met at work, and Keisha and James met in the dorm dining room.

Of course, if people interact negatively, proximity can also increase disliking. Ebbesen, Kjos, and Konecni (1976) surveyed occupants of a condominium complex about people in the complex whom they either liked or disliked. In each case, the people selected for liking or disliking lived in the same part of the complex as the respondents.

One key aspect of proximity is the *frequency of exposure* that people have to one another—in other words, how often they see each other. Zajonc (1968) proposed a general hypothesis that "mere repeated exposure of the individual to a stimulus is a sufficient condition for the enhancement of his attitude toward it" (p. 1). That is, just seeing something or someone over and over again can increase our liking for it. Empirical support for the "mere exposure" effect has come from a variety of research studies, including exposure to slides of specific objects, exposure to other people while drinking pleasant and unpleasant liquids, and exposure to pictures of relationship partners.

Body Language

Attraction can also be affected by nonverbal presentation, or *body language,* a term popularized by Fast (1970). Body language refers to facial expressions; body moves such as posture, lean, and so on; and even physical adornments such as clothing, jewelry, and makeup. As noted in the next section, physical attractiveness plays a powerful role in attraction, and many aspects of body language are closely tied to attractiveness. An individual may not be attractive in a classic sense, but if he or she carries himself or herself well, with erect posture and head held high, then he or she can seem attractive. Remember how James noticed Keisha's "proud" body language?

Facial expressions have been studied particularly intently because the face can express a wide range of emotions. These expressions can portray both what a person is feeling at a particular time and the level or intensity of that feeling (Ekman, Friesen, & Ancoli, 1980). Visual interaction, consisting of eye gaze and eye contact, is important because it can be used to signify either intimacy or aggression. People gaze more at those whom they are close to, and more eye contact is typically considered better than less eye contact (Kleinke, 1986). Eye contact may increase as partners become more attracted to and more intimate with each other.

More generally, nonverbal behavior is an important aspect of the attraction process, whether it is attraction to a romantic partner or simply affection for a family member or friend. For example, Friedman, Riggio, and Casella (1988) were interested in observers' evaluations of both physical attractiveness and emotional expressiveness of research participants. Physically attractive and emotionally expressive participants were evaluated more positively, but even when physical attractiveness was not considered (the effects were removed statistically), the people who were more emotionally expressive were better liked. Like other aspects of body language, emotional expressiveness may be part of a person's presentational composite, which is much more than mere attractiveness.

People differ in their nonverbal expressions or body language, and they also differ in how they express this body language to different people. Foot, Smith, and Chapman (1979) observed 9-year-old children in dyadic interactions with both friends and strangers and found that children in the friendship dyads were more nonverbally alike than were children who were paired with strangers. And more recently, Guerrero (1997) conducted a study in which she analyzed how men and women communicated verbally and nonverbally when observed within three different types of relationships: opposite-sex romantic relationships, opposite-sex friendships, and same-sex friendships. Guerrero was particularly interested in how communication might change when people interacted with these different types of relationship partners. She found substantial consistency in people's behaviors with their three different partners, but she also found inconsistencies.

When interacting with a romantic partner, people gazed more, touched more, had more physical closeness, and displayed greater general interest. In this same situation, however, they exhibited less fluency, less nodding, and less vocal interest but the most silence and the longest response time. Thus, on some dimensions, romantic partners appeared more intimate than friendship pairs, yet on other dimensions, they appeared less intimate. Frequent nodding and indications of vocal interest were greater for friendship relationships than romantic ones, and same-sex friends had more congruent body posture than did opposite-sex friends. Finally, women and men differed slightly, with men doing more forward leaning and showing posture similar to that of their partner and women showing more direct gaze and body orientation. As Guerrero noted, "These findings paint an intriguing behavioral profile of romantic partners as more immediate but less fluent than friends" (1997, p. 51).

Body language is powerful and informative in the process of becoming attracted to and developing a relationship with someone. Although body language is considered here as an environmental influence on attraction, it could arguably be considered among the personal influences, such as physical attractiveness and desirable characteristics, considered in the following section.

Personal Influences on Attraction

Physical Attractiveness

One of the most powerful factors in whether one person becomes attracted to another is outward appearance, or *physical attractiveness*. Physical attractiveness is important in contemporary culture (Hatfield & Sprecher, 1986b). Although it might seem to be a shallow criterion for evaluating another person, outward appearance is often the first thing we notice when meeting someone new. Facial features, hairstyle, body build, posture—all are evident characteristics that can influence our first impressions of someone. For example, Tomas noticed Nora's physical appearance, and James noticed Keisha's physical appearance.

There is some cultural similarity in defining beauty, as Cunningham and his colleagues (Cunningham, Roberts, Barbee, Druen, & Wu, 1995) found when assessing people's judgments about Asian, Latino, and white women's facial attractiveness. Asian, Latino, and white raters all favored pictures of women with small noses, small chins, and large eyes, no matter what culture the rater or the person being rated represented. The facial qualities that were preferred emphasized youth as opposed to age (baby-faced as opposed to mature-faced), a preference that evolutionary psychologists (e.g., Buss, 1999) suggest supports the evolutionary approach to attraction and mate selection (discussed later in this chapter). Physical form is also important to overall attractiveness, and waist-to-hip ratio is one such aspect of form. Men tend to prefer women with a waist-to-hip ration of 0.7 (Singh, 1993), which signifies a smaller waist relative to hips and thus a curvy appearance. On the other hand, women appear to prefer men with a 0.9 waist-to-hip ratio (Singh, 1995), signifying a waist and hips that are similar and thus a more straight-up-and-down appearance.

Yet there are also cultural differences in attractiveness ratings. Ford and Beach (1951) examined primitive cultures' values for body build (plumpness versus thinness) and found that they had different standards for what was considered attractive. Thus, characteristics that are portrayed currently by Western media as critical for a woman's attractiveness, such as body build and weight, are not necessarily considered important everywhere.

Of course, the media influences notions of attractiveness, but more than the media is at work here. Evolutionary psychology offers one perspective for why attractiveness matters, and this approach will be discussed later in the chapter. But what do other social scientists say about how physical attractiveness influences the choice of a romantic partner?

The Matching Hypothesis

One view holds that no matter what we look like, we will seek a romantic partner who is at our same level of attractiveness or social desirability. If we believe we are a 10 on a 1 to 10 scale, then we'll look for another 10. If we believe we're a 6, then we'll be looking for 6s. This perspective is called the **matching hypothesis.**

Although some research has not found support for the matching hypothesis (Walster, Aronson, Abrahams, & Rottman, 1966), other research has found that matching does occur. For example, Berscheid, Dion, Walster, and Walster (1971) designed two experiments to test whether the possibility of rejection would influence people's dating choices. In the first experiment, participants signed up for what they thought was a computer date. Half the participants thought they would briefly meet a potential partner and that the partner would have the option of turning them down as a date. The other participants believed they would simply go to the dance with the partner assigned to them. Participants then rated the characteristics they desired in a date. The possibility of rejection did not influence participants' ratings, and in fact, a matching effect was indicated. Namely, the more attractive the participant was, the more attractiveness that person desired in a potential partner. In the second experiment, participants viewed six photographs of prospective dates and selected the one they preferred; once again, the group was divided into those who believed they could possibly be rejected and those for whom rejection was not a possibility. As before, participants chose a prospective partner who matched them in attractiveness level and were not influenced by the possibility of rejection. In other words, the 6s sought 6s, and the 10s sought 10s!

Matching effects have been found for middle-class, middle-aged married couples (Murstein & Christy, 1976) as well as for same-sex friends (Cash & Derlega, 1978). In a meta-analysis of 18 studies concerned with physical attractiveness in friendship pairs and romantic pairs, Feingold (1988) found some support for matching in romantic partners, with correlations between partners' attractiveness ranging from 0.40 to 0.50.

In addition to a tendency for matching to occur, there is also a tendency to generalize a partner's personal qualities based on physical attractiveness.

The "Beauty Equals Goodness" Hypothesis

There is a stereotype about physical attractiveness that says "What is beautiful is good." Dion, Berscheid, and Walster (1972) had both male and female participants rate photographs of females and males who differed in attractiveness. Some participants rated same-sex photographs, whereas others rated opposite-sex photographs. Results indicated that people who were rated as more physically attractive were also rated as having more socially desirable personalities, greater occupational success, and greater marital, professional, and general happiness than were less attractive persons. Other research suggests that people who are perceived as attractive may also have better interactions than those perceived as less attractive (Snyder, Tanke, & Berscheid, 1977), and indeed, some research has found a small but significant and positive relationship between physical attractivenss and psychological adjustment (O'Grady, 1989).

It appears that people will even lie about personal characteristics such as appearance, personality, and income in order to appeal to attractive prospective dates (Rowatt, Cunningham, & Druen, 1999). And this preference for attractiveness begins early in life; even small children have shown a preference for attractive as opposed to unattractive faces (Dion, 1977).

In fact, attractiveness is just one facet of the whole attraction/beauty issue. The corollary of "What is beautiful is good" is "What is ugly is bad." Just as people generalize additional positive qualities based on someone's outward attractiveness, so also do people sometimes generalize additional negative qualities based on someone's unattractiveness (see Erber & Erber, 2001). It undoubtedly would be wise for all of us to remember that "Beauty is only skin deep" and to limit our assumptions about what people's physical attractiveness or unattractiveness might mean in terms of their personality or character.

Another old saying is that "Beauty is in the eye of the beholder," and to some degree, that is true. But while beauty or attractiveness may be one of the first characteristics noticed about someone, it may diminish in importance as a relationship progresses.

Murstein (1976) proposed a *stimulus-value-role (SVR) theory* of relationship development, suggesting that stimulus characteristics (e.g., physical attractiveness) are important early in a relationship, but in later stages, values (e.g., attitudes, beliefs) and role compatibility assume greater significance.

Other Desirable Characteristics

Physical attractiveness is only one of a number of desirable characteristics that influence attraction. Research has shown that individuals who disclose about themselves appropriately and who reveal attitudes and values similar to those of an evaluator are considered more appealing (Daher & Banikiotes, 1976), and people who are cheerful are liked better than those who are not (Folkes & Sears, 1977). In other research, extraverts were evaluated better overall than were introverts (Hendrick & Brown, 1971), and people who were moderately selective about potential dating partners were viewed more positively than those who were either extremely selective or nonselective (Wright & Contrada, 1986). Still other research (Aronson, Willerman, & Floyd, 1966) showed that people like others with high ability (in this case, high intelligence) who also have some human flaws (clumsiness, in the case of the Aronson et al. study). That is, we like people who are superior but not perfect.

Aron, Dutton, Aron, and Iverson (1989) found that desirable characteristics were among the most important factors in respondents reporting falling in love with someone or developing a strong friendship with someone. Also important were similarity and how well the potential partner liked the respondent. Remember that Nora felt better about going out with Tomas when Jennifer told her that Tomas had been attracted to Nora for awhile. *Reciprocity*—or feeling that emotions and behaviors are given and received fairly equally in a relationship—also appears important for attraction as well as for relationship continuation (e.g., Gouldner, 1960). Indeed, reciprocity of social attraction in relationships increases people's positive emotions (Vittengl & Holt, 2000).

Numerous environmental and personal factors influence attraction, and a number of theories purport to explain them. One of the most comprehensive explanatory systems for attraction is the evolutionary psychology approach to mate selection. The questions in the Up Close box that follows will help you consider just how important attraction has been in your own relationships.

Mate Selection and Evolutionary Psychology

The evolutionary perspective has been applied increasingly to areas of psychology, including the area of close relationships (Simpson & Gangestad, 2001). This approach considers attraction as important to the human condition largely because of the role it plays in mate selection, which is central to reproduction and survival of the human species. Although some species reproduce asexually and thus have only one sex, many more species, among them humans, require two mating parents. Sexual reproduction

Up Close

The Nature of Attraction

Think about the best romantic relationship you have ever had. If you are in a relationship currently, it might be that relationship—or it might not. If you are not in a relationship at the present time, think about a past relationship.

Consider these questions:

- How did the two of you meet? Did you meet in school, at work, or in some other place? Were you fixed up by friends, or did one of you ask the other one out on a date? Did you meet because you were part of the same group? Did you start your relationship by being just friends? Or were you romantic from the beginning?
- What did you do on your first date?
- What qualities in the *other* person appealed to you the most? In other words, what attracted you to him or her?
- What qualities in *you* did your partner find appealing? What attracted her or him to you?
- How early in the relationship did you know that this other person was someone special?
- If your relationship is still continuing, what keeps the two of you together? If you have broken up, why did you break up?
- Finally, what have you learned from this relationship?

promotes offspring that are genetically diverse, that can occupy a variety of ecological niches, that can keep parasites at bay by continuously changing the host environment (the human body), and so on (Buss, 1999).

Given that humans reproduce sexually, what are the driving forces behind selecting an appropriate mate? A key explanation of mate selection based on evolutionary psychology is Trivers's (1972) theory of *parental investment,* which proposes that men and women have different reproductive strategies. Women, who typically invest more in each single offspring, will be more selective about mating, will be more discriminating in both long-term and short-term sexual relationships, and will seek men who have the skills to be both capable and responsible providers for potential offspring. Men, on the other hand, will be less discriminating about sexual relationships, particularly short-term ones, and will look for women who have the attributes to conceive, bear, and raise healthy offspring (Buss, 1999).

Considerable research within the evolutionary psychology perspective has focused on attraction and mate choice. Buss and Barnes (1986) found in two studies that women and men desired many of the same qualities in a partner. For example, both genders desired a partner who was kind, understanding, and intelligent and who possessed an exciting personality. Thus, it seems people seek qualities that may contribute to a long-term, committed connection and satisfy a fundamental need to belong (Baumeister & Leary, 1995).

The genders differed on some qualities, however, with women more than men seeking a partner with good earning capacity and who was a college graduate and men more than women seeking a physically attractive partner. Consistent with evolutionary theorizing, men also tend to prefer a partner who is both attractive and younger, whereas women tend to prefer a partner who is both successful and older (Kenrick & Trost, 1989). Such findings also occur across cultures. In addition, men are also more likely to compromise their preferences than women are in the context of a casual or short-term sexual relationship (Buss & Schmitt, 1993). *Sexual strategies theory* (Buss & Schmitt, 1993; Schmitt, Shackelford, Duntley, Tooke, & Buss, 2001), in fact, proposes that since women and men have evolved different short-term and long-term strategies for mate selection, these differences may be expressed in a number of ways. For example, one large difference is men's greater desire for sexual variety, particularly in short-term relationships (Schmitt et al., 2001).

Because of the consistency and robustness of many of these findings—for example, that men seek attractiveness and that women seek resources—it is easy to circumscribe issues of partner choice into a relatively narrow "pretty versus big bank account" model. But mate choice is not unidimensional. Feingold (1992) analyzed the results of over 30 studies of mate selection and found that women consistently valued partner resource potential more than men did and that men consistently valued partner physical attractiveness more than women did. But he noted that evolutionary explanations are compatible with cultural ones. In other words, men's greater power and economic resources in virtually all cultures means that women must exploit personal resources such as beauty in order to achieve their goals. Eagly and Wood (1999) found in their analyses of 37 countries, using data provided by United Nations researchers, that as gender equality increased, mate preferences changed. Specifically, as gender equality increased, women's preferences for men who were older and who had greater earning potential decreased, as did men's preferences for women who were younger and who had domestic skills. Preferences for physically attractive women as mates did not correlate with gender equality.

Other research found that gender differences in mate preferences varied slightly based on sociodemographic characteristics such as age and race (Sprecher, Sullivan, & Hatfield, 1994). Still other research (Stewart, Stinnett, & Rosenfeld, 2000) revealed that women's and men's preferences for short-term and long-term relationship partners were consistent with "a qualified differential parental investment perspective" (p. 843). The genders showed several similarities, with "trustworthy/honest," "kind/understanding," and "dependable" among the top characteristics sought in a long-term partner by *both* women and men. Indeed, even for physical attractiveness, women rated it a 7.6 for a long-term partner (on a 1 [unimportant] to 10 [important] scale), and men rated it a 7.7. Both women and men also had higher standards or requirements for long-term relationship partners than for short-term ones.

Thus, women and men have similar preferences for most of the qualities they seek in relational partners, particularly long-term ones. And mates are chosen on the basis of much more than just having a pretty face or a fat bank account. If evolutionary pressures caused women to seek a mate who was a good provisioner, then it also influenced them to seek a dependable, nonharmful, faithful mate who would provide for them and their offspring. And in their turn, men needed more than an attractive, apparently healthy mate. A woman who could reproduce successfully was also one who could forage productively and defend her offspring effectively (Hrdy, 1999). Nature is indeed complex.

Flirting

Part of the attraction process for many people is *flirting,* which typically involves smiling and talking with someone in order to indicate romantic interest. Flirting may also involve nonverbal behaviors, such as increasing eye contact or touching someone on the arm, and the message offered may indicate anything from "I'm interested in you" to "I want to have sex with you." Flirting may range from friendly to seductive and may differ somewhat for women and men (Koeppel, Montagne-Miller, O'Hair, & Cody, 1993). Although flirting in the work setting may have negative effects for women (Satterfield & Muehlenhard, 1997), for many people, flirting in social settings is a routine part of getting to know potential romantic partners. A very modern form of flirting occurs on the Internet, as discussed briefly in the following section.

Attraction Online

A number of people form friendships and romantic relationships through the Internet (Knox, Daniels, Sturdivant, & Zusman, 2001). Internet relationships have several unique qualities. For instance, they allow greater intimacy in terms of such things as self-disclosure (Cooper & Sportolari, 1997), perhaps because face-to-face contact does not occur initially. Physical attributes are typically less important in computer-mediated relationships, and people may actually get to know each other better without the distraction of physical attraction (Cooper & Sportolari, 1997). But deception is widespread in Internet relationships (Knox et al., 2001) and can lead to major disappointments. Turning an Internet relationship into a face-to-face one within a month or so of meeting online can help keep the relationship on a realistic footing (Levine, 2000). Since it is expected that the level of online relating will increase, methods for relating online safely, ethically, and successfully will need to be developed further.

Attraction to and selection of romantic partners are significant parts of beginning to form a close relationship. There are also several perspectives on the ongoing process of relationship development.

Relationship Development and Processes

How do relationships progress and grow? What does relationship development look like? Theories of relationship development and courtship are useful in answering these questions.

Social Penetration Theory

Social penetration theory (Altman & Taylor, 1973) is a comprehensive theory of relationship development as well as a theory of self-disclosure processes in relationships. **Social penetration** really means just what it says: that social masks and outward appearances must be penetrated so as to get to the inner core of someone. Altman and Taylor (1973) describe relationships as progressing in intimacy systematically over time and including all communication and related behaviors. "Social penetration refers to (1) overt interpersonal behaviors which take place in social interaction, and (2) internal subjective processes which precede, accompany, and follow overt exchange. The term includes verbal, nonverbal, and environmentally oriented behaviors, all of which also have substantive affective/emotional components" (p. 5). One tenet of this theory is that the social penetration process of really getting to know another person is orderly and progresses through stages over time. A second tenet is that social penetration involves an assessment of rewards and costs throughout the process of development. Presumably, if rewards predominate, the relationship will continue, but if costs predominate, the relationship will terminate.

One important aspect of social penetration is *self-disclosure,* or the process of revealing one's feelings and thoughts to another. Altman and Taylor (1973) view disclosure as varying in both *breadth* (variety of topics) and *depth* (intimacy of topics), with both qualities increasing as the relationship continues.

This theory and others, as well as extensive research findings, support the importance of self-disclosure to both the initiation and maintenance of relationships (Derlega, Metts, Petronio, & Margulis, 1993). Research has also shown that self-disclosure and social attraction are related both to each other and to positive emotions, even in a laboratory setting in which people are first getting acquainted (Vittengl & Holt, 2000). "Self-disclosure within get-acquainted conversation is accompanied by liking or feelings of social attraction to conversation partners and by an increase in positive emotions" (p. 62). Self-disclosure was important for Tomas and Nora on their first date and to a lesser extent for Alicia and Dan.

Although the social penetration/acquaintance process is an important aspect of relationship life, Altman (1975) recognized early on that *privacy* is a concept that contrasts with the closeness aspects of social penetration and that offers balance to people in relationships. Altman, Vinsel, and Brown (1981) propose that partners alternate between intimate and superficial communication and interactions throughout the duration of their relationship.

The concept of *dialectics*—or polar opposites that need to be integrated in order to function optimally—is an important one and is discussed more fully in Chapter 6. The social penetration/privacy dialectic is an example of the larger closeness/distance issue that was explored by Feeney (1999). Feeney conducted a qualitative study in which she asked partners in 72 dating couples to complete questionnaires on attachment and relationship satisfaction and then to spend about five minutes describing their relationships and how they and their partners got along. The five-minute descriptions were tape recorded, transcribed, and then content coded for themes, particularly themes of closeness and distance. Closeness/distance themes were important, particularly for those who were insecurely (as opposed to securely) attached to their partners. "Of the 72 couples, 37 included at least one partner who explicitly mentioned overall differences in the partners' needs for closeness-distance" (p. 579). Differences in such needs were also related to satisfaction for men (greater difference correlated with lesser satisfaction). A particularly important finding was that closeness/distance issues could be transformed over time due to changes in the partners, the relationship, or their external circumstances, but for many couples, the issues were not solved but rather ongoing.

The importance of the closeness/distance dialectic was also confirmed by Baxter and Erbert (1999), who examined the basic importance to relational partners of six different contradictions, or dialectics, in relational events seen as turning points. Across a number of different relational turning points, the contradictions that were considered most important were the autonomy/connection (similar to distance/closeness) and the openness/closedness contradictions.

Although having contradictions and being able to resolve at least some of them is a significant part of the relationship development process, many other factors are also important.

Additional Factors Affecting Development

Romantic Beliefs Romantic beliefs—for instance, that love overcomes obstacles and that there is only one true love for everyone—have been *associated with* relationship quality (Sprecher & Metts, 1989) but do not actually *predict* relationship quality or stability (Sprecher & Metts, 1999). Researchers assessed couples periodically for four years and found that romantic beliefs did not contribute in a substantial way to love or satisfaction over time and did not predict which partners would stay together and which would break up. Romanticism or endorsement of romantic beliefs at an earlier time did predict greater commitment at a later time for men only, and the reverse was true for women (commitment predicted romanticism) (Sprecher & Metts, 1999). Therefore, romanticism may be linked to cognitive aspects of relationships, since commitment has been viewed as a decision and thus as a cognitive factor.

Flora and Segrin (2000) assessed relationship and other qualities in 200 people: 100 who were in romantic relationships and 100 who had recently broken off relationships. Results indicated that getting to know each other more quickly and more deeply (perhaps representing more effective social penetration), conceptualizing the relationship in terms of "we" rather than "you" and "me," glorifying the relationship's survival of hard times, and experiencing minimal disappointment in the relationship were all associated positively with relationship satisfaction. In addition, all these factors were related negatively to personal loneliness. It thus appears that framing our relationships (including their struggles) positively and thinking of ourselves as parts of relational teams is important to the processes of relationship development and satisfaction.

Positive Illusions What we believe about a relational partner is extremely important, and research indicates that our thoughts and beliefs about the partner and about what the partner may think or believe are extremely important (Sanderson & Cantor, 2001). Murray and Holmes (1997) conducted extensive research on the occurrence of **positive illusions** in romantic relationships, or the idealized beliefs that relationship partners may have about each other (see also Murray, Holmes, & Griffin, 1996a, 1996b). What they discovered is that reality is fine up to a point, but relationships can have too much reality! In other words, it is useful to hold some illusions about one's partner—his or her attitudes, beliefs, and behaviors—so as to allow him or her at least to be seen through rose-colored glasses occasionally. Murray and Holmes (1997) discovered "that relationship illusions predicted greater satisfaction, love, and trust, and less conflict and ambivalence in both dating and marital relationships" (p. 586). Believing that one's partner is similar to oneself supports a feeling of being "kindred spirits" (Murray, Holmes, Bellavia, Griffin, & Dolderman, 2002).

Relationship illusions also predicted relationship continuation for the dating couples as well as increased satisfaction at a later time. Interestingly, illusions are typically grounded partly in reality, but if they were fully realistic, they would probably be *knowledge,* rather than *illusions.* Illusions are also more than subjective feelings of satisfaction with the relationship. Rather, they encompass a positive and optimistic outlook that appears to cause relational partners to behave better and ultimately to improve their relationships. Thus, positive illusions appear to facilitate a positive reality.

Additional research on romantic illusions and ideals (Knee, Nanayakkara, Victor, Neighbors, & Patrick, 2001) indicated that illusions are not uniformly helpful—or at least, the lack of them is not necessarily hurtful. It may depend on one's general philosophy about relationships, as articulated by Knee (1998). If someone believes that *destiny* governs relationships and that two people either are or are not meant for each other, then having a partner who falls short of one's ideal may reduce satisfaction greatly. If, on the other hand, someone believes that the way to develop a relationship is to overcome obstacles and grow closer in the process, which is a *growth* perspective, then faltering illusions may not be such a problem. In fact, Knee et al. (2001), in studying both individuals in dating relationships and couples in dating relationships, found that positive illusions may be less powerful and less necessary for people who believe that relationships are places for change and growth rather than destined or made to order. For some people, it is less important what the relationship is *today* than what it can become in the *future*. Indeed, Karney and Frye (2002) found that marital partners cared more about how their relationship had recently improved than about their relationship quality at a single point in time.

Trust   A discussion of relationship development would not be complete without examining the issue of partner *trust*. According to Boon (1994), interpersonal trust is the "expectation that a partner is intrinsically motivated to take one's own best interests into account" (p. 88), even when the partner's best interests might point in a different direction. Because relationship development involves increasing intimacy, greater interdependence, and a heightened sense of vulnerability, both hope and fear increase commensurately. Thus, trust is necessary for the partners and their relationship to move forward (Holmes & Rempel, 1989).

Trust is an *intrapersonal* phenomenon, in that people may have a general disposition to be trusting or mistrusting, yet it is also *interpersonal,* in that one will either trust or mistrust a specific other person. Holmes and Rempel (1989) evaluated low- and high-trust partners in how they assessed their respective partners' motives during a conflictual discussion. Both before and after the conflict discussion, high-trust couples were more optimistic, were more willing to attribute positive motives to the partner, and had fewer negative and more positive reactions overall. In addition, trust is not static in a relationship but rather changes and deepens with the relationship. Boon (1994) noted that the qualities necessary for trust include dependability, faith, responsiveness, and the capability of resolving conflict. Trust is not "blind faith" because it involves an acceptance of the partner's imperfections, yet it grants an overall positive assessment of the partner and his or her motives. The resulting tendency is then to emphasize positives and relatively de-emphasize negatives in the relationship (Holmes & Rempel, 1989). Ultimately, "A sense of confidence pervades the relationships of those who have successfully achieved a comparatively full capacity to trust each other" (Boon, 1994, p. 102).

What happens when trust is broken? Broken trust erodes confidence in the partner and the relationship and can fuel self-doubt, partner-doubt, and pessimism about both immediate interactions and long-term outcomes. Trust is difficult to achieve and perhaps even harder to re-establish, once it has been broken. One way that trust can be broken is through relational infidelity (discussed in more detail in Chapter 8), and another can be through deception. Partners in intimate relationships endorse a standard of honesty for the relationship (Boon & McLeod, 2001), and indeed, honesty is a highly valued quality when people rate what they want to find in a potential partner (Stewart et al., 2000). Yet people also endorse deception and dishonesty as acceptable behaviors/strategies to achieve certain relational goals, whether to protect one's partner from some upsetting information (Boon & McLeod, 2001) or to gain a more attractive date (Rowatt et al., 1999). In a particular situation, deception may seem a better alternative than honesty, but it is a risky choice.

Commitment   As a relationship progresses, it typically develops along the *commitment* dimension. **Commitment** has been defined in various ways, such as a person's declared intention to stay in a relationship (Rosenblatt, 1977), and it has been measured in several ways, too (e.g., Lund, 1985). Most descriptions of commitment refer to a general, overall attitude and intention, or *personal commitment,* but Johnson, Caughlin, and Huston (1999) make the point that *moral commitment* (feeling morally obligated to remain in the relationship) and *structural commitment* (having barriers to ending the relationship) are important aspects of commitment, as well.

Frank and Brandstätter (2002) have shown that *approach commitment,* which is similar to personal commitment, represents positive reasons for maintaining a relationship (e.g., affection) and is related positively to various aspects of relationship quality (e.g., well-being). On the other hand, *avoidance commitment,* which is similar to a combination of moral and structural commitment, represents negative reasons for maintaining a relationship (e.g., fearing the pain of breakup) and is related negatively to various aspects of relationship quality.

Rusbult (1983) has been persistent in focusing on commitment as a central characteristic of close relationships. Working within the *investment model* framework, which posits that how much one invests in a relationship is indicative of commitment as well as other relational qualities, Rusbult found that greater investment, greater reward, and poorer prospects for an alternative partner all increased commitment for 34 persons in romantic relationships. And over time, commitment increased as investment and satisfaction increased and alternatives decreased. Rusbult's work on commitment has also been interwoven with her extension of interdependence theory (Rusbult, Wieselquist, Foster, & Witcher, 1999).

Interdependence theory (Drigotas, Rusbult, & Verette, 1999) emphasizes the degree to which relational partners are reciprocally involved in the relationship and involves two key constructs: (1) *level of dependence* refers to how much someone depends on the relationship for meeting his or her needs, and (2) *mutuality of dependence* refers to how similar the partners are in their dependence/involvement in the relationship. Dependence is greater when investment and satisfaction are high and alternatives are low. *Interdependence* can be conceptualized as a factor influencing commitment, and Drigotas et al. (1999) explored issues of interdependence, commitment, trust, and other variables in two studies, one with dating couples and one with married couples. Consistent with what the researchers had predicted, "both level of commitment and perceived mutuality of commitment . . . [were] associated with healthy functioning in relationships" (p. 404). Thus, not only the sheer amount of commitment but also the *mutuality* of commitment were important. Finally, the association between commitment and couple well-being was largely mediated by trust. Besides affirming the importance of both commitment and

The Nature of Commitment

Think about a romantic relationship, either one you are in currently or one you were in recently. Which of the following types and aspects of commitment are most characteristic of that relationship? Which types and aspects of commitment promote the strongest and most stable relationships, in your opinion?

- *Personal commitment:* an attitude or intention to stay in a relationship
- *Moral commitment:* feeling morally obligated to stay in a relationship
- *Structural commitment:* having barriers to ending a relationship
- *Approach commitment:* positive reasons for maintaining a relationship
- *Avoidance commitment:* negative reasons for maintaining a relationship
- *Mutuality of commitment:* how similar partners are in their commitment
- *Relationship-driven commitment:* smooth progress that takes time
- *Event-driven commitment:* more rapid progress, with more ups and downs

mutuality in relationships, these findings reaffirm the central role that trust plays in close relationships (Drigotas et al., 1999; Holmes & Rempel, 1989).

Surra and her colleagues (Surra & Gray, 2000; Surra & Hughes, 1997) have identified two general types of commitment processes that characterize couples as they move toward marriage. The first, *relationship-driven commitment*, has relatively smooth progress and involves positive feelings about the partner and the relationship, assessment of partners' compatibility, and willingness to take time for the relationship to develop. *Event-driven commitment* involves more rapid and more extreme changes in commitment, issues of trust and ambivalence (especially for men), and uncertainty about the relationship. A slower progression of commitment also seemed to indicate a smoother progression (Surra & Gray, 2000). Cate, Levin, and Richmond (2002) view commitment as a central aspect of premarital relationship stability. Read the Up Close box above to help you clarify some of your own experiences of and attitudes toward commitment.

As a relationship continues to develop, at some point, it evolves into actual courtship, which has been described in a number of ways (Cate & Lloyd, 1992; Surra, 1990).

Courtship Theories

Although courtship is, in a sense, just one type of relationship development, it is a very important one. *Compatibility models* of courtship are concerned with how well partners get along with each other, or with their similarities and differences. Earlier in this chapter, we discussed the importance of similarity as a basis for a relationship. As noted there, complementarity is a less effective basis.

One way to consider compatibility is as something that is achieved in different ways at different relationship stages. Kerckhoff and Davis (1962) proposed a *sequential filtering model,* wherein the similarity of certain personal and contextual variables is important early in the relationship, agreement on personal and family values becomes important at a later stage, and complementary needs become important farther on. Murstein's (1976) SVR (stimulus-value-role) theory, discussed earlier, is similar to the sequential filtering theory. In the stimulus stage, variables such as physical attractiveness are important. In the value stage, variables such as religious and moral values gain prominence. Finally, compatibility of roles becomes most important.

Interpersonal process models of courtship are less concerned with relationship *stages* and more with the relationship *process,* or how partner characteristics and environmental forces interact and change over time (Cate & Lloyd, 1988). One approach to interpersonal process models has focused on couples' trajectories, or paths toward marriage (e.g., Cate, Huston, & Nesselroade, 1986; Lloyd & Cate, 1985). This research approach involves interviewing couples and asking the relational partners to identify significant events and turning points in their relationships (see also Surra & Gray, 2000; Surra & Hughes, 1997). Such events may propel a couple toward marriage or deter them from it. These events are also placed in a timeframe, so that their timing, intensity, and degree of positivity or negativity are all taken into account.

Cate et al. (1986) identified three different types of relationship development in courtship. One type was *prolonged courtship,* characterized by slow and difficult progress, and another was *accelerated courtship,* which was rapid and seemingly almost problem free. The third type, *intermediate courtship,* had characteristics that fell between the other two types and had the smoothest progression toward marriage. Moderation has long been thought to be the best approach in many situations, and that appears to hold true for courtship progress, as well.

Summary and Conclusions

Attraction can be considered as a type of attitude, which has a cognitive component, an affective component, and a behavioral component. Theories of attraction include balance theories (humans value harmony in their close relationships); reinforcement theories (good relationships have more rewards/positives than costs/negatives); similarity theories (the more similar people are, the more attracted to each other they will be); and arousal theories (physiological arousal plus appropriate interpersonal cues can produce attraction). When someone is attracted to a person who is very dissimilar to himself or herself, this dissimilarity may ultimately hurt the relationship and has been referred to as a "fatal attraction."

Attraction is influenced by environmental factors, such as proximity and body language (e.g., facial expressions, eye contact, body lean). Physical attractiveness is a powerful force in initial attraction, and there are both cultural similarities and differences in what is seen as attractive. It is thought that people seek a romantic partner who matches them in attractiveness, although people often just seek the best-looking partner they can find. Beauty is sometimes equated with other positive qualities, such as good personality, greater happiness, and so on. A tendency also exists to generalize negative qualities to unattractive people. Desirable characteristics (in addition to beauty) also increase attractiveness.

An important theory of mate selection comes from evolutionary psychology, which proposes that women will mate more selectively than men and invest more in each offspring. This theory also proposes that men will seek to mate with women who are physically attractive, and women will seek to mate with men who have resources. There is some indication that gender differences in mate preferences vary somewhat based on sociodemographic characteristics and on the degree of gender equality in a given culture. Flirting may occur as relationships are forming. Some people develop romantic relationships online.

Relationships may develop due to social penetration, or the process of getting to know one another more intimately. Self-disclosure is part of this process and is thought to be broader at the beginning of a relationship and to grow deeper as the relationship continues. Privacy is an important counterpart to disclosure, and indeed, the balance between closeness and distance is an important one for close relationships.

A number of factors impact relationship development, including partners' romantic beliefs, ability to see a relationship in terms of "we" rather than "you" and "me," and positive illusions about one another (as long as the illusions have some grounding in reality). Trust is also extremely important, and broken trust can seriously damage a relationship. Commitment involves a number of factors and is important to relationship development and continuation.

Models of courtship include compatibility models, which emphasize how well partners get along or how similar they are to each other. Interpersonal process models emphasize courtship processes, or how slowly or quickly partners develop their relationship. In general, having a courtship that is neither too short nor too long might offer the best option for relationship success.

Key Terms

Affect (p. 24)
Commitment (p. 40)
Matching hypothesis (p. 30)
Positive illusions (p. 38)

Proximity (p. 27)
Similarity (p. 25)
Social penetration (p. 36)

Suggested Reading

Boon, S. D., & McLeod, B. A. (2001). Deception in romantic relationships: Subjective estimates of success at deceiving and attitudes toward deception. *Journal of Social and Personal Relationships, 18,* 463–476.

Drigotas, S. M., Rusbult, C. E., & Verette, J. (1999). Level of commitment, mutuality of commitment, and couple well-being. *Personal Relationships, 6,* 389–409.

Felmlee, D. H. (1998). "Be careful what you wish for . . ." A quantitative and qualitative investigation of "fatal attractions." *Personal Relationships, 5,* 235–253.

Flora, J., & Segrin, C. (2000). Relationship development in dating couples: Implications for relational satisfaction and loneliness. *Journal of Social and Personal Relationships, 17,* 811–825.

Murray, S. L., & Holmes, J. G. (1997). A leap of faith? Positive illusions in romantic relationships. *Personality and Social Psychology Bulletin, 23,* 586–604.

Myers, D. G. (2000). The funds, friends, and faith of happy people. *American Psychologist, 55,* 56–67.

Stewart, S., Stinnett, H., & Rosenfeld, L. B. (2000). Sex differences in desired characteristics of short-term and long-term relationship partners. *Journal of Social and Personal Relationships, 17,* 843–853.

3

Friendship and Social Support

Relationship Stories

Friends Forever

"No, he's not my boyfriend. No, I'm not jealous that he's going out with Jenny." Erin was trying to explain her relationship with Mike to one of her college friends, and she realized that she was starting to get annoyed. She got so tired of explaining; she felt like she had been explaining herself and Mike all her life.

Erin remembered the first time she met Mike. Her parents had just moved to the small midwestern city where she was to eventually grow up and where her parents still lived. The white frame, two-story house had looked very large to 5-year-old Erin as her family drove up and parked in the driveway. The moving truck was on its way and would arrive any minute. As Erin and her parents got out of their car on that hot summer morning, she noticed a little boy playing in the frontyard of the house next door. The two children looked curiously at each other from a distance, but then the moving truck arrived and things were hectic for the next several hours. Late in the afternoon, there

45

was a knock on the screen door, and when Erin's mother answered it, she found a dark-haired woman about her own age standing on the doorstep with a plate of brownies.

"Hi. I'm Alice Jones, and I live next door. I just wanted to welcome you to the neighborhood. I hope you like brownies. This is my son, Mike." And from behind her emerged the little boy whom Erin had noticed that morning.

"Come in for a minute," said Erin's mother. As the two women talked for a few minutes, Erin and Mike stood by their mothers, not knowing what to do. It turned out that the children were the same age and would be starting school together in a couple of months. The next day, Mike's mother offered to take care of Erin so that Erin's mother could unpack. And once the children started playing—especially running through the sprinkler in their bare feet—they became fast friends. And that was how it stayed.

In elementary school, most of their playing was done on weekends or in the summer. At school, they had separate friends; Erin had girl friends, and Mike had boy friends. But they still were each other's best friend. When Mike got chicken pox, Erin drew pictures for him and made "Get Well" cards, which she delivered to his front door. When Erin went away to visit her grandparents for a week each summer, Mike got lonesome.

As they grew older and went to junior high school, their friendship changed. They didn't exactly drift apart, but their interests diverged. Mike was into sports and Erin was into music, so they didn't have a lot of time for each other. But every once in awhile, they would talk on the phone or sit out at the picnic table in Erin's backyard and just catch up on things. They didn't see each other a lot, but neither one could imagine being without the other.

High school was a different story. It seemed like everyone started dating, and that included Erin and Mike. Erin's first real romance happened when she was a sophomore and started dating a senior. When things ended after a couple of months, Erin thought her heart was broken! And the first person she turned to was Mike. He let her cry on his shoulder—literally and figuratively—and gave her advice on guys and how they thought. Mike dated a lot, too, and he was always bringing questions for Erin to answer: Why do girls want to talk so much about the relationship? Why do girls want a commitment? Why are girls always trying to change guys? Mike thought of girls as a puzzle that could never quite be solved, but if anyone could help him, it would be Erin. Sometimes Mike thought that Erin was the only girl he knew who had any common sense, and sometimes Erin thought that Mike was the only guy in the world she could really trust.

When Mike started playing varsity basketball in their senior year, Erin made it a point never to miss a game. And when Erin was picked to sing a solo at the school's Christmas concert, Mike and his whole family sat right in the front row of the school auditorium to show their support for Erin. You see, they were not just close to each other, they were also close to each other's parents and even brothers and sisters.

Once in awhile, their friends would ask one of them why they didn't date each other, but the answer was unequivocal: "We're friends!" At their high school graduation, Erin and Mike felt like things would never be quite the same again. Their lives were filled with endings and beginnings, and they didn't know exactly how they were going to keep each other in their lives; they just knew that somehow they would. Mike had planned to go to a small college in the East, but toward the end of the summer, he suddenly changed his mind and decided to go to the state university only a couple of hundred miles away. Since that was where Erin planned to attend college, they both were glad that they would already have a good friend when they went off to school.

Both Erin and Mike made friends fairly easily at college, but they were still happy to have each other. They lived in different dorms but close enough to walk over if they wanted to. They developed new interests and new friendships. But they still talked to each other on the phone nearly every day, and if neither of them had a date on a Saturday evening, they would catch a movie or go to some campus event together.

They didn't often think about the future of their friendship. They both planned on having careers and someday getting married and probably having kids. Neither one knew exactly what he or she was going to be doing—or where. Sometimes, though, they talked about their individual hopes and dreams for the future. Whatever pictures they painted of the future, always, always they saw each other in the picture. As they had said since they were children, "Friends forever."

■ ■ ■

Going Off Road

Tamika picked up the package and headed toward the dorm elevator. Normally, she used the stairs, but this package was just too heavy to carry up seven flights. It was a package for her roommate, Jonelle, from Jonelle's mother. It was the most recent TLC package that had arrived since Jonelle's biking accident, and both Jonelle and Tamika were enjoying the benefits of homemade cookies, new music CDs, and assorted other goodies.

Although it had been a month since the bike accident, both Tamika and Jonelle were still adjusting to a new routine. Tamika was glad that if the accident had to happen, it happened in the second semester of their freshman year instead of the first semester. They had spent the first semester getting used to college, to living in a dorm, and to being roommates. The first time they met was the weekend before Fall semester started, when they were both moving their stuff into the dorm. They hit it off right away, although Jonelle's outgoing personality and wacky sense of humor sometimes made Tamika feel like she was living in the middle of a tornado! Tamika was more quiet and reserved by nature, but it was hard to be reserved around Jonelle. Jonelle didn't "do" quiet!

It was that outgoing energy of Jonelle's that led her to take her mountain bike off road on that Saturday afternoon, when the weather softened and warmed for a couple of hours and you could almost smell spring in the air. Jonelle was mountain biking with some friends, not too far from campus, when she said, "Let's go down this unmarked trail" and then took off. Her friends followed, more slowly, and so they didn't really see what happened when

Jonelle hit the bump and flipped over her handlebars, landing awkwardly in the brush with her arm twisted under her. All they knew was that one minute she was far ahead of them on the trail, and the next minute she was crying and holding her arm, saying, "It's broken. I know it's broken."

Tamika had gone to a baseball game with some friends, so she didn't hear about any of this until later, when Jonelle called her from the hospital emergency room. "Tamika, it's Jonelle. I'm at the hospital. I just broke my arm, but they won't put a cast on it until I get insurance information from my parents. Can you try to track them down for me and get them to call the emergency room?"

Tamika did just that. In fact, she took care of everything at the beginning. She and her younger sister had grown up with just their mom (their dad died when they were small), so Tamika learned very early how to be responsible and steady, especially in a crisis. She called Jonelle's parents and helped Jonelle get home from the emergency room to the dorm. She took care of her until Jonelle's mother came to stay in town for a few days to help Jonelle out. Tamika helped Jonelle's mom arrange for Jonelle to make up class work, to get to and from doctors' appointments, and to manage all the small things that suddenly seem large when someone gets sick or breaks a bone. Jonelle's mom could see how capable Tamika was, and when she left town, she gave Jonelle and Tamika each a big hug and told Jonelle that she was being left in good hands.

They got into a routine, Tamika and Jonelle, with Jonelle trying to do as much for herself as possible. She could feed herself and shower, go to class and take notes, get her mail, and even dress herself (mostly). But Tamika filled in on so many small things, like carrying Jonelle's tray in the cafeteria, cleaning up their dorm room, and picking up packages and carrying them upstairs, like today.

Jonelle looked up from her history book as Tamika walked into the room carrying the package. "What's up?"

"Your Mom sent another TLC package to you—oops, this one is actually addressed to both of us. I wonder what's in it. Those chocolate chip cookies she sent last week were fantastic!"

"If she sent more of those, girl, consider them yours," said Jonelle. Delicious cookies were small thanks for all Tamika was doing. What a great roommate, and more than just a roommate, what a great friend. Of all the people she could have been paired off with as a roommate, how did she ever get so lucky as to draw Tamika?

They had been friends almost since the first day they moved into the dorm, on that hot and sticky August weekend. They didn't do everything together because they each had their own friends, but they often ate dinner together, studied together, and just hung out. Tamika was in the nursing program, and she suffered through an anatomy course during the Fall with some help from Jonelle, who quizzed her before each exam to make sure she knew all the terms and definitions. For her part, Tamika provided a great audience as Jonelle practiced for her speech class. They figured they had done a pretty good job of helping each other study, since they each got a B average for the semester.

They supported each other in additional ways, also. Jonelle served as the pair's "recreation director," making sure that Tamika didn't study all the time and got out on the weekends to movies or parties. And when the Jonelle "tornado" revved up a little too much, Tamika put the brakes on and got her settled down. In other words, they provided good balance for each other.

Tamika and Jonelle sometimes felt like sisters, and just like sisters, they got on each other's nerves from time to time. They argued about small things, like how late to leave the lights on, who was spending too much time on the phone and interfering with the other's studying, and who borrowed whose sweater and spilled Coke all over it. But most of the time, they were there for each other. Tamika didn't mind that she needed to be an extra pair of hands for Jonelle right now; she knew Jonelle would do the same for her. That's what friends were for.

■ ■ ■

Questions to Consider in Reading This Chapter

- Do you have any friends whom you have known since childhood?
- What kinds of personal qualities do you look for in a good friend?
- Do you have any close opposite-sex friends?
- How are those friendships similar to and different from your same-sex friendships?
- Who are the people you can really count on for social support?
- Are they also the people who can count on you for support?
- Has someone close to you ever failed you when you needed his or her support?
- Have you ever failed to support someone who needed you?

What Do We Know about Friendship and Social Support?

As described in the previous chapter, attraction is a powerful process, drawing people together in romantic relationships. Yet attraction is also a central factor in **friendship,** which can be a relationship as close as any romance or family/kinship tie. If the need to belong is indeed part of our human evolutionary heritage, then friendship is central to that need.

One quality that sets friendship apart from other close relationships is its voluntary nature. Unlike the people in our families, our friends are chosen. Of course, romantic partners are chosen also, but if these partnerships result in legalized marriage, then some of the voluntary quality is reduced. With friends, the voluntary aspect remains. Unlike kin relationships, there are no blood ties between friends. And friendship typically does not contain the possessive and sexual aspects common to romantic love relationships (Rawlins, 1992). Friendship also lacks the prescribed contractual elements that are part of work relationships. Rawlins (1992) argues that the "marginal position" of friendship both strengthens and weakens it, and he emphasizes the dialectical nature of friendship. The four major dialectics Rawlins proposes are independence/dependence, affection/instrumentality, judgment/acceptance, and expressiveness/protectiveness (similar to closedness or privacy).

A number of theories have been proposed to explain how and why friendship works as it does.

Theories of Friendship

Fehr (1996) provides a clear and succinct description of several classes of theories relevant to friendship. She notes that *cognitive consistency theories* (or what were referred to in Chapter 2 as *balance theories*) propose that humans strive for balance or consistency in many aspects of their lives, including relationships. We want people whom we like to like each other, too, and we want our relationship partners (whether romantic or friendship) to like and dislike the same things we like and dislike.

Developmental theories are theories of relational chronology, or how relationships change over time. Altman and Taylor's (1973) social penetration theory, described in the preceding chapter, is developmental in nature. As both a theory of self-disclosure and a more general theory of relationship development, it describes the increases in breadth and depth of disclosure that occur as a relationship progresses. Levinger and Snoek (1972) have proposed a theory of relationship development in which partners vary along a continuum of relatedness. At point 1, there is zero contact—two people are unaware of each other. At point 2, there is unilateral awareness, where one person is aware of the other but there has been no interaction. At point 3, surface contact, people have had limited interaction. At point 4, mutuality, the partners are at least moderately interdependent. Movement on the continuum from point 1 to point 4 occurs over time. Levinger (1980, 1983) has extended this model to include relationship breakup, and the resulting ABCDE model goes from A/Acquaintance to B/Buildup to C/Continuation to D/Deterioration to E/Ending.

Fehr (1996) also discusses *reinforcement theories,* which are built on behaviorist traditions and emphasize the importance of rewards (and costs) in maintaining relationships. Theories built on reinforcement principles but that deserve particular consideration here are *exchange* and *equity theories.*

Exchange Theory

Exchange theory is a theory of the marketplace, adapted for relationships by Blau (1964) and others. It emphasizes both giving *and* receiving in relationships and has concepts of rewards, costs, outcomes, and comparisons levels. It can be applied to both friendships and romantic relationships.

A *reward* is a reinforcement, something that gratifies an individual. A *cost* is a punishment, but it can also refer to rewards that are foregone or missed out on. An *outcome* refers to a reward minus the cost, or what is left over after a particular interaction or in a particular situation. Finally, the *comparison level* refers to what a person expects to get out of a particular interaction or situation, based on what he or she estimates would be ideal and/or probable outcomes.

Thibaut and Kelley (1959) particularly emphasize comparison level and also point out the importance of the comparison level for alternatives, or what a person thinks his or her options might be outside the current relationship in a relationship with someone else. Thibaut and Kelley also emphasize the importance of the rising and falling of comparison levels during the life of a relationship. To understand comparison levels and alternatives in relational terms, consider the following:

Comparison level	I am entitled to and expect certain behaviors from my friend.
Comparison levels go up	The nicer my friend gets over time, the nicer I expect him or her to become.
Comparison levels go down	The less my friend gives, the less I come to expect from him or her.
Comparison level for alternatives	Would someone else be a better friend?

A great deal of research and theorizing characterizes exchange theory. Kelley (1979) has proposed that intimate relationships should be evaluated in terms of partners' *shared* rewards and costs, as well as their rewards and costs as individuals, and that the outcomes could be calculated mathematically. Foa and Foa (e.g., Foa, Converse, Törnblom, & Foa, 1993) have developed the *resource theory* of exchange, stating that relationship partners exchange a variety of resources, including goods, love, information, money, services, and status. Rusbult's work on the investment model and *interdependence theory* (e.g., Rusbult et al., 1999) is another example of an exchange-based theory.

Equity Theory

An extension of exchange theory, **equity** theory (Walster, Berscheid, & Walster, 1973), is concerned with issues of fairness in relationships, based on propositions about people's desires to maximize their personal outcomes, be rewarded equitably for what they do, and minimize incidences of inequitable treatment (being either overbenefited or underbenefited). Research by Utne and colleagues (Utne, Hatfield, Traupman, & Greenberger, 1984) showed that women and men who believed they were treated equitably by their marital partner were more content and perceived their relationship to be more stable than did those who felt either underbenefited or overbenefited. Sprecher (2001a, 2001b) found that romantic partners were in relative agreement about equity issues in the relationship and that underbenefiting equity but not overbenefiting equity was linked with lower satisfaction, greater distress, and greater likelihood of breakup.

Exchange versus Communal Relationships

Although exchange theories emphasize balances of rewards and costs as well as equity between relationship partners, Clark and Mills (1979) distinguish between exchange and *communal relationships.* In the former, someone gives a benefit with the expectation that a similar benefit will be returned. In the latter relationship, however, someone gives a benefit based on the other person's need, rather than with an expectation of return. In a **communal** relationship—which can be a friendship, family, or romantic relationship—the purpose of giving is to give what is needed, without expectation or obligation.

Numerous experiments have supported the distinction between communal and exchange relationships. In one case, Clark, Mills, and Powell (1986) assessed research participants, some of whom desired an exchange relationship with another person and some of whom desired a communal relationship with another person. When the other person was in a position to reciprocate benefits, those desiring an exchange relationship kept better track of the partner's needs. When the other person was not in a position to reciprocate benefits, however, those desiring a communal relationship kept better track of the partner's needs. Whether an exchange or a communal orientation exists may depend on the particular relationship in question or how an individual tends to approach his or her relationships more generally (Erber & Erber, 2001).

Erber and Erber (2001) note that there has been some criticism of the communal/exchange distinction: first, because it is based almost solely on laboratory research, and second, because there is a question "whether communal relationships are really exchange relationships with a fairly long time perspective" (p. 106). Weiss (1998) also speculates that elements of exchange exist even in very communal relationships. What seems likely is that some relationships are primarily exchange while others are primarily communal, but most relationships, including friendships, have both communal and exchange features. In other words, we give to our friends on the basis of their needs, but we expect that when we have needs at some time in the future, our friends will reciprocate. Reciprocity is not measured in an exact fashion, but its presence is expected and its absence is noted.

Additional Models of Friendship

It is appropriate to view friendship as developing along a number of dimensions, and indeed, Blieszner and Adams (1992) proposed a multidimensional model of older adults' friendships that incorporated both psychological and sociological perspectives. The authors noted that individual characteristics such as age, gender, and personality style affect friendship patterns, and friendship formation takes place within varying cultural, structural, and historical contexts. Adams and Blieszner (1994) refined this model, which attempted to identify virtually all the ingredients of friendship, and proposed that individual characteristics affect friendship patterns via what is called a *behavioral motif*, or a style of life and of "doing" friendship.

As difficult as it may be to conceptualize the complexities of friendship, it is even more daunting to try to measure those complexities. Dugan and Kivett (1998) operationalized part of Adams and Blieszner's (1994) model by surveying nearly 300 older adults who had relocated in retirement and found that certain individual characteristics influenced friendship patterns. For example, women respondents characterized themselves as closer to their best friend than men did, and perhaps more interestingly, proximity was not a positive influence on the most important friendships, since "the warmest thoughts and feelings were reserved for friends who lived farther away" (Dugan & Kivett, p. 620). Overall, this complex model did not map onto these authors' friendship findings very well, but the model is still promising in clarifying certain aspects of older adults' friendships.

Although scholars have developed a wide variety of models of friendship formation and maintenance, Cole and Bradac (1996) were interested in how ordinary people who were actually participating in friendships felt about friendship. Based on previous research, the authors had identified qualities thought to characterize best friendships, including acceptance, trust, social support, and so on. But the authors were particularly interested not in friendship generally but specifically in satisfaction with a friend or a friendship. Their initial question was "What do people think leads to satisfaction with a best friend?" (p. 61).

In a series of studies, Cole and Bradac (1996) sought to answer that question. In their first study, the authors had 221 people list the qualities and characteristics that they would want in a best friend in order to have a satisfying friendship. Many different items were generated, and they were streamlined to a list of 43 characteristics desired in a best friend. Interestingly, when these characteristics were ranked for their importance, women and men did not differ markedly in their rankings, so the characteristics appeared to be generally important to friendship, unrelated to gender specifics. Additional complex analyses identified three underlying dimensions for the 43 characteristics: an activity dimension, a closeness dimension, and a partner demeanor or style dimension.

In their final study, Cole and Bradac (1996) tried to identify how people thought these characteristics might be causally related. They also used this process to identify which qualities in a best friend would be seen as more important or more central. Using a reduced set of qualities for rating and analysis, the authors found that only a few of the 14 characteristics used were immediate or close causes of satisfaction in a friendship: namely, "approachable," "admits mistakes," and "not abusive." These qualities were, in turn, influenced by other qualities, so that if a friend had one of the immediate qualities, he or she was also assumed to have the influencing qualities. For example, someone who admitted his or her mistakes would be thought to be open minded, emotionally balanced, and possessing good communication skills. This is much like the "beauty equals goodness" issue discussed in Chapter 2, in which one quality generalizes to many other qualities.

Ultimately, Cole and Bradac (1996) found that the most central qualities viewed as important in an ideal best friend were "approachable," "emotionally balanced," "good communication skills," "inspires and enriches my life," "open minded," and "socially popular." One useful contribution of this series of studies is the affirmation "that people have specific, intricately structured beliefs about the causes of satisfaction among best friends" (p. 79).

Theories about satisfaction in friendship and friendship in general are rightfully important, but they are only part of the friendship puzzle. Also important are the actual qualities and processes that form and maintain friendships.

Forming and Maintaining Friendships

Friendships may seem relatively simple to deal with, as compared to either romantic relationships or family relationships, but because of their voluntary nature and their importance to human connection, they are, in reality, quite complex. Fehr (1996, 2000) has written at length about friendship and identified four levels of factors that must converge in order for a friendship to form: environmental, individual, dyadic, and situational.

Environmental Factors

Two people must meet in order for a friendship to develop (an exception is an Internet acquaintance), and many friendships begin at school, in housing complexes or confined residential areas (planned communities, retirement communities, military bases), and in the workplace. Friends are also made through voluntary organizations such as churches and through family and current friends. The environment is actually quite significant in this process, since two people may have great potential for friendship, but if they never meet, they will not realize this potential. Proximity was an important factor in both of the Relationship Stories for this chapter.

Individual Factors

Many of the qualities relevant to romantic attraction, discussed in the preceding chapter, are also relevant to friendship, including physical attractiveness, social skills, and responsiveness (Fehr, 2000). And as noted earlier, Cole and Bradac (1996) found that people identified qualities such as approachability and good communication skills as important, also.

Dyadic Factors

It is sometimes hard to know where individual factors end and dyadic factors begin. For example, physical attractiveness is strictly individual, but self-disclosure is both individual (given by one person) and dyadic (given in a relational context). Hays (1984) tracked friendship formation in college students and found that the behavioral elements of affection, companionship, consideration, and communication/self-disclosure all occurred with greater frequency and intensity in friendships that were progressing successfully than in those that were less successful. Thus, friendship doesn't just happen; it requires effort.

Similarity, a force in romantic attraction, is also important in friendships. Although friends do not necessarily have to share similar personalities, they do best when they enjoy many of the same activities and when they view the world in a similar fashion (Fehr, 1996). Tamika and Jonelle became friends even though their personality styles were quite different. In addition, friends are more similar in both communication styles and social skills than are nonfriends (Fehr, 2000).

Closeness and intimacy are also important concepts in friendship. Parks and Floyd (1996) expanded on previous research in order to clarify how women and men perceive closeness and intimacy in their good same-sex and cross-sex friendships. Participants generated 13 different meanings for *closeness,* with "self-disclosure" being by far the most frequently expressed meaning. Rounding out the top five meanings were "help and support," "shared interests and activities," "relational expression," and "comfort and ease." Meanings for *closeness* were similar for both women and men and for both same-sex and cross-sex friendships.

Participants were also asked whether they would apply the word *intimate* to their close friendships, and although about half said they would, about half said they would not. The primary reasons for not equating *closeness* and *intimacy* in these relationships were the belief that *intimacy* had romantic or sexual connotations and should not be applied to a friendship and the belief that the friends didn't engage in enough deep, personal self-disclosure for the friendship to be truly intimate. In this particular study, then, closeness was considered to be a consistent part of good friendships, whereas intimacy was more variable.

Situational Factors

A number of factors in the friendship situation are influential, such as how often friends see each other (affected by many things, including how close they live to each other) and how likely they are to continue interacting. Also important is the friends' availability to sustain their friendship. For example, many people have experienced the loss of a friend due to a geographic move, but losing a friend through marriage also occurs. Marriage changes individuals' lives and priorities, such that the friends who were once centrally important become more peripheral to a newly married couple's lifestyle. Fehr (2000) refers to a "friendship budget," which may accommodate a certain number of friends and no more. If we are extremely busy with work, school, a romantic partner, family obligations, and ongoing friendships, we may not have room in our lives for a new friend, no matter how interesting or attractive that person might be.

One social/environmental factor that can both facilitate and inhibit friendships is the **social network,** or "an individual's array of close associates including friends and kin relations" (Milardo & Helms-Erikson, 2002, p. 33). It is this network that often provides a backdrop to a developing romantic relationship or friendship. A social network of two friends can be described in terms of (1) *network overlap,* or the proportion of network members shared by the two friends; (2) *boundary density*, or the cross-links between members of both friends' social networks; and (3) *cross-network contact*, or the communication between each friend and the other friend's social network (Milardo & Helms-Erikson, 2002). If two friends have dense, overlapping networks, this can simplify their social interactions and reduce the competition of other network members for the friends' time and attention. But overlapping networks also have costs. As an example, friends who have highly overlapping social networks and who have a disagreement may find that if they tell one or two others in the network about the disagreement, virtually everyone they know will have seemed to hear about it. "You can run but you can't hide" if your social networks overlap too much.

Fehr (1996, 2000) made a good case for the convergence of environmental, individual, dyadic, and situational factors being important in successful friendship formation. Consider the Relationship Stories for this chapter. For Erin and Mike, living next door to each other, having compatible personalities, and even knowing each other's families all served to strengthen their friendship. For Tamika and Jonelle, having complementary personality styles and being roommates contributed to their friendship, but the situational event of Jonelle's bike accident really propelled their friendship forward. See the Up Close box that follows to help you consider the major influences on your closest friendships.

Just as these different types and levels of factors are important, so is the developmental period in which these factors occur. In Blieszner and Adams's (1992) multidimensional model of friendship, individual characteristics affect friendship patterns within cultural, structural, and historical contexts. It is the characteristics of age and developmental periods to which the discussion will turn next.

Friendship across the Life Course

Friendship is important across the lifespan, and although there are many commonalities among friendships at various ages and life stages, there are also some differences.

Childhood Friendships

Selman (1981) has proposed a model for children's friendships, which encompasses the years of preschool through midadolescence. The stages move from being short-term playmates, through superficial play and temporary cooperation, to autonomous interdependent friendships, or friendships that involve a healthy balance of dependence and interdependence. Schofield and Kafer (1985) agree that children develop interpersonal understanding and friendship skills gradually, perhaps through broad stages, but these scholars do not view the stages as having rigid boundaries. Individual children develop differently, girls and boys develop somewhat differently, and development is an irregular, even cyclical process.

Rose and Asher (2000) discuss the benefits that friendship may provide to children in terms of alleviating loneliness, buffering victimization and bullying, and aiding in various aspects of school adjustment. They have also identified six particular benefits that friendship provides to children: (1) validation and ego support, (2) emotional security, (3) self-disclosure, (4) help and guidance, (5) reliable allies, and (6) companionship and stimulation. As Rose and Asher note, even though children's friendships may become

Influences on Close Friendships

Think about one of your close friendships. It might be your best friend or simply another friend who is very important to you. Consider these questions:

- How did you two meet? Were you in the same class at school, or did you meet in a social organization, on a sports team, at a camp, or in the neighborhood?
- Did you know right away that you were going to be good friends, or did your friendship take awhile to develop?

Now think about some of the factors discussed in this chapter: environmental factors, individual factors, dyadic or relationship factors, and situational factors.

- Which of these factors was most important in the development of the friendship you are thinking of? Did your individual qualities make the biggest difference? Or was it the environment you were in? Did any event or situation occur that made your friendship better—or that perhaps almost destroyed your friendship?
- What qualities make your friendship strong at the present time?

increasingly complex and stable as children get older, "even young children's friendships have significance and can be quite enduring" (p. 47). Certainly, this was the case for Mike and Erin, as relayed in their Relationship Story.

When considering the friendships of young children (and even older adults), it is easy to overlook those within the family, but many friendships can be found there. As Hart (2001) points out, "The enchanting friendship and companionship that young siblings provide for each other is within the grasp of most families. Once established, these bonds last a lifetime. In fact, the sibling relationship outlasts every other relationship we have in our entire lives" (p. xiii).

Adolescent Friendships

Friendship is one of the primary tasks of adolescence, a developmental period that has forming same-sex friendships as a central task. Collins and Laursen (2000) have outlined a process in which adolescent friendships in essence evolve out of family relationships. Of course, childhood friendships may endure into adolescence, but the primary point is that children learn much about how to conduct friendships by how relationships are handled in the family. Family relationships and peer relationships (friendships) become increasingly differentiated in adolescence, but then in early adulthood, the two types of relationships become part of an integrated and "unified social structure" (p. 60).

During adolescence, social networks expand and friendships become more sophisticated and more central. Friendships are, in some ways, a training ground for later romantic relationships, in that adolescents learn social skills and communication processes. "Friendships are perceived as the most important source of support during adolescence, and intimacy, mutuality, and self-disclosure with friends peak during the period" (Collins & Laursen, 2000, p. 67). Although friendship is exceedingly important both to girls and boys, adolescent boys may have broader, more extensive friendship networks, whereas adolescent girls may have deeper, more intensive networks (Fehr, 1996; S. S. Hendrick & C. Hendrick, 1992a). It is also important to realize that adolescents may experience different types of friendships that are all equally successful (Way, Cowal, Gingold, Pahl, & Bissessar, 2001).

Young Adult Friendships

As older adolescents move into young adulthood, they presumably integrate their friendship, family, and romantic relationships. Friends are confidants, providers of social support, and companions with whom one can enjoy fun and relaxation (Fehr, 2000). Indeed, much of the theory and research on friendship provided earlier in this chapter has been based on friendship in young adulthood.

Young adults value their friends and employ both explicit and implicit strategies to maintain their friendships. Three of these strategies are especially important: supportiveness, self-disclosure, and spending time together (Fehr, 2000). The significance of simply spending time together—doing nothing in particular other than just being together—turns out to be an important binding force, not only for friendships but also for romantic relationships.

Yet as important as friendships become in young adulthood, if young adults marry or otherwise become permanent partners, friendships may recede in importance. If children are born, that also affects friendships—sometimes deepening them, sometimes lessening them. More social needs may be met within the family or extended family, and indeed, family commitments may mean that there is less time available for friendships (Dickens & Perlman, 1981). As people age and family obligations change, however, friendships may again increase in importance.

Older Adult Friendships

There is no age limit on friendship formation. Shea, Thompson, and Blieszner (1988) interviewed older adults who had recently relocated to a retirement community and who had made new friends as well as retained some old friends. "Affection," "communication," and "respect" were qualities of the new friendships as well as the older ones, and "liking" was equally high in both kinds of friendships. But old friends were "loved more dearly" (p. 88).

As Blieszner (2000) points out, both friendships and family relationships are important to older adults and they provide different resources and supports. Family members may provide more help with chores and ongoing tasks, whereas friends are sources of emotional support and companionship. Yet this task differentiation is far from strict, since friends also provide instrumental support and family members can offer emotional and psychological support.

As people age, they may divest themselves of some of the peripheral relationships in their lives, but "they increase the emotional closeness to those deemed most significant" (Blieszner, 2000, p. 92). And there are ways to increase friendship success for older adults. "Educational programs, self-help groups, and informal support groups can supplement naturally occurring friend networks by both helping with relationship or other problems and by providing opportunities to develop new friendships" (Blieszner & Adams, 1992, p. 114). In addition, housing, recreation centers, and larger communities can be planned in ways that will facilitate friendships and other social relationships.

Friendship is important across the lifespan, beginning with the play relationships of children and culminating in the rich, age-worn friendships of older years. Yet friendship can also have negative aspects.

Friendship Deterioration and Restoration

The factors that Fehr (2000) proposed as fostering friendship can also dissolve friendship. Environmental factors, such as infrequent contact, can impair friendship, as can individual qualities such as moodiness and boredom. Dyadic factors, such as increasing dissimilarity and, more seriously, betrayals of the friendship, are definite negatives. If situational factors, such as one friend's availability for friendship, shift, the friendship can shift, as well.

Unfortunately, when conflict arises between friends, it is often ignored rather than resolved. Both men and women tend to avoid dealing with conflict, and women are particularly reticent in confronting problems directly (Fehr, 1996). This failure to deal with conflict adequately can contribute to a friendship's demise. Although there are specific strategies for restoring a faded friendship (such as two friends having a heart-to-heart talk), most deteriorating friendships involve a sort of drifting apart, rather than an active severing of the relationship. Ironically, this somewhat passive approach to conflict deterioration can be positive, in that it allows for the possibility of restoring the friendship (Fehr, 2000). If the door has been left open after a traumatic event, rather than being slammed shut, the relationship can be more easily restored.

Gender and Friendship

Although friendships appear to be equally important to women and men, there are some differences in how men and women conduct their friendships. In addition, friendships between men and women, or *cross-sex friendships,* have a number of special characteristics.

Women's and Men's Friendships

There are both differences and similarities in men's and women's same-sex friendships. Although the overall amount of time spent with friends is similar for men and women, women spend more of their friendship time simply talking, whereas men spend more of their time doing activities (Fehr, 1996). For women, this dialogue in friendship cultivates intimacy, serves therapeutic functions, and provides a forum for both coping with and sometimes resisting other relationship problems and social pressures (Johnson, 1996).

Men also have close friendships, although the ways in which they enact closeness may differ from women's ways (Inman, 1996). Again, men are more likely to engage each other in activities than in conversation, but as Inman and others point out, to define *friendship* primarily as "verbal interaction" is to impose feminine standards on a masculine activity. If we were to put a masculine stamp on friendship and assume that going to sports events together is a demonstration of closeness, then women's friendships would often likely be found deficient.

The differing gender styles of doing friendship start relatively early (Rose & Asher, 2000). Young boys engage in more rough-and-tumble play with friends and spend more time in larger peer groups, whereas girls spend more conversation time one to one. Girls' friendships also involve more validation, and boys' friendships, more competition.

In adult friendships, women have more conversation about both intimate and nonintimate topics, although both men and women conceptualize *self-disclosure* as synonymous with *intimacy* in same-sex friendship (Monsour, 1992). Women and men both discuss personal topics with friends; women simply do this more frequently (Aries, 1996). Based on extensive research, it appears that men do not "lack the capacity for intimacy, but rather that they prefer not to exercise it in their interactions with other men" (Fehr, 1996, p. 140).

Tannen (1994) has proposed that because women and men have somewhat different stylistic approaches to communicating, women may sometimes feel that men are not listening to them. But that is because listening is evaluated in feminine terms. Taking a broader view of friendship, it is important to remember that authentic friendship is more than just words. Male friends may not talk explicitly about their closeness, but such closeness exists, nevertheless (Inman, 1996). In fact, gender disparities in communication and other behaviors are often exaggerated. Aries (1996) points out that gender ultimately does not account for a great deal of people's behavior in social situations, and this likely includes friendships.

If women and men both value friendship yet tend to enact friendship in different ways, what are the resulting implications for friendships *between* men and women?

Cross-Sex Friendships

Cross-sex friendships are not uncommon, even though some people assert that "Men and women can't just be friends." Although the stylistics of friendship may be different, with women more conversational and men more activity oriented, stylistics are not a great barrier to cross-sex friendships. In fact, men report that their cross-sex friendships are closer than their same-sex friendships (although women report the opposite) (Fehr, 1996). Women and men seem to blend their friendship styles when interacting in a cross-sex friendship (West, Anderson, & Duck, 1996).

As Werking (1997) has stated, society focuses on heterosexual romantic relationships as the most important relationships, so heterosexual friendships seldom if ever take center stage. In fact, she reported a study in which research participants said that they put priority on their romantic relationships over their friendships, even though they described "their cross-sex friendships as more stable and beneficial" (p. 406). Cross-sex friendships have been described as similar to same-sex friendships in such aspects as acceptance, enjoyment, respect, spontaneity, and trust but less intimate, stable, satisfying, supportive, self-disclosing, and so on.

Cross-sex friendships offer a particular challenge to friendship partners because society may tend to sexualize the relationship. There are fewer opportunities for cross-sex as opposed to same-sex friendships, both because they may be more difficult to initiate and because maintaining them may involve explaining the relationship to others (Fehr, 1996). Recall that this was the case with Erin and Mike.

There is also the possibility that the partners themselves may have difficulty keeping romance out of the friendship. Men, more than women, may view cross-sex friendships in a sexual light (Fehr, 1996; West et al., 1996). In one study, 48% of cross-sex friendships ended because the partners had tried a romantic relationship with each other that didn't work, because one partner wanted to turn the friendship in a romantic direction and the other partner did not, or because one person became involved romantically with someone else (Werking, 1997).

Nonetheless, the issues in cross-sex friendships are not as simple as "Will we have sex or not?" Reeder (2000) found that participants reported four primary types of attraction toward opposite-sex friendship. *Objective physical/sexual attraction* occurred when one's friend was viewed as physically attractive or sexy. *Subjective physical/sexual attraction* involved feeling sexually attracted to the friend. *Romantic attraction* referred to one partner wanting to turn the friendship into a romantic relationship, and this was reported rarely. Finally, *friendship attraction* involved growing to like and even love each other *as friends.* Most of the participants acknowledged this type of attraction.

Even when friends engage in sexual activity, it does not necessarily transform the relationship into a romantic one. Afifi and Faulkner (2000) found that about half of a sample of college students had engaged in sex within a cross-sex, otherwise platonic friendship, and many of these friendships continued on as they had been before the sexual encounter. As the authors noted, "Many of those individuals who engage in sexual contact in a cross-sex friendship seem to experience it as relationship-enhancing, but also recognize the activity as part of the friendship, rather than as a behavior that accompanies a change in relational definition (i.e., from friend to romantic partner)" (p. 218). This has sometimes been referred to as "friends with benefits." Many cross-sex friends work hard to maintain their relationships as platonic, largely because they don't want to risk a valued friendship for the possibility of a less satisfactory romantic/sexual encounter (Messman, Canary, & Hause, 2000). Cross-sex friendships provide many positives, one of which is to better understand romantic partners. For example, Bleske and

Buss (2000) report that in their research, both women and men said they had received information about how to attract romantic partners from their cross-sex friends. Mike and Erin clearly helped each other out in this way.

Cross-sex friendships may be highly valued and very satisfying, but they must be managed even more carefully than same-sex friendships. Given women's and men's somewhat different styles of doing friendship, cross-sex friends must learn new behaviors. Moreover, given the possibilities for sexual involvement and the resulting complications, cross-sex friends must be very clear about what they want (and do not want) from their friendship. Afifi and Faulkner (2000) found that sexual involvement could sometimes deepen a cross-sex friendship. However, in a study that compared participants' ratings of two types of friendship—a current cross-sex friend who was once a romantic partner and a cross-sex friend who had always been a platonic friend—Schneider and Kenny (2000) found that people felt differently about the two types of friends. More positive features were associated with the platonic friend, whereas more negative features and romantic desires were associated with the friend who had once been a romantic partner. Thus, letting romance enter a cross-sex friendship can be risky. (For a very detailed discussion of cross-sex friendship, see Monsour [2002].)

Friendship, whether cross sex or same sex, is complex, multifaceted, and centrally important among the close relationships that humans have. One aspect of friendship and other close relationships that will now be considered is social support.

Social Support

Social support has been defined in both general and specific ways. More generally, it is thought of as responsiveness to and fulfillment of another person's needs, involving such things as affection, validation, trust, and emotional or material resources. Considered more specifically, social support emphasizes responsiveness to and fulfillment of needs that occur particularly because of stressful life events or other negative circumstances (Cutrona, 1996). Cunningham and Barbee (2000) suggest that a person's social support network includes all the people from whom that person might expect to receive support when needed. In addition, these authors propose that humans have evolved both to seek and to provide social support.

This chapter takes the broad or general view of support. Although support may be particularly dramatic during an obviously stressful time (e.g., an accident, illness, or divorce), it would be a mistake to overlook the everyday kind of social support that involves someone listening when we need to talk, cheering us up when we're feeling down, or doing all the home chores when we need to study for an exam. This kind of social support is part of the fabric of daily existence, and ultimately, it is daily existence, rather than dramatic events, that defines life for most of us.

Social support may be emotional, cognitive, or behavioral. Wortman and Dunkel-Schetter (1987) propose the following as supportive behaviors: (1) expressing positive emotion, (2) supporting feelings or beliefs, (3) encouraging expression of emotions, (4) offering information or advice, (5) giving material aid, (6) helping with a particular task, and (7) letting someone know he or she is part of a supportive group. Burleson and Goldsmith (1998) emphasize the importance of providing comforting messages, which can also be central to social support.

Researchers have measured social support in a variety of ways, using brief questionnaire measures (e.g., Sarason, Sarason, Shearin, & Pierce, 1987) as well as interviews and observational techniques (Cutrona & Suhr, 1992). And as Brock, Sarason, Sarason, and Pierce (1996) have noted, it is important to differentiate between measures of global support and measures of support from specific relationships. Barbee and Cunningham (1995) have developed a *sensitive interaction system theory (SIST),* which takes into account the individual characteristics of the support seeker and support provider, the relationship between the two people, and the nature of a given situation or problem when assessing short-term and long-term outcomes. This perspective is similar to Fehr's (1996) model of friendship development as consisting of individual, dyadic, and situational factors.

Although support can be measured by asking support givers what support they have provided to someone, it is preferable to ask people who have supposedly been provided with support whether they, in fact, *feel* supported. This is known as **perceived support.** As Cunningham and Barbee (2000) note, "An individual's subjective belief that support is available generally is a better predictor of major outcomes, such as health, than are objective assessments of the person's social support network" (p. 277). So within this perspective, if one person feels supported by another person, then support exists, no matter what the perceived support provider has or has not done. But if a person does not feel supported, then effective support has not been provided.

How does support actually occur in friend and family relationships and in romantic relationships?

Social Support from Family and Friends

In some sense, social support from family begins when a baby is born. "The prototype for a supportive relationship is the nurturant behavior of a loving parent to a child" (Cunningham & Barbee, 2000, p. 274). And for many, if not most, people, family members remain a component of their support system throughout life. Family and friends each contribute uniquely to a person's social support (Brock et al., 1996).

Friendships are an important source of social support for adolescents (Collins & Laursen, 2000) and young adults, and indeed, young adults have more friends and fewer family members in their social support networks than do older adults (Walen & Lachman, 2000). If young adults marry or have children, the family members in their support group may regain importance, as noted earlier. Yet friends will also remain significant resources. DeGarmo and Forgatch (1997) found that for divorced mothers with children, the quality of supportive behaviors offered to the mother by a close confidant (friend, family member, or intimate partner) was related to the mother's ability to parent, regardless of who gave the support. In other words, no matter who the support provider was, receiving positive support contributed to more successful parenting.

As adults grow older, their social network grows smaller, but family and friends both remain important. Older adults may prefer the help of family members for such things as personal care, daily chores, and so on (Blieszner, 2000), but friends may be preferred as confidants and companions. Friends may be perceived to provide support through choice, whereas family support may seem more obligatory (Walen & Lachman, 2000).

Social support is important, irrespective of gender and ethnic background, yet it cannot be assumed that supportiveness occurs with the same behaviors or even the same meanings for all groups. For example, Samter, Whaley, Mortenson, and Burleson (1997) compared African Americans, Asian Americans, and European Americans in their assessment of the importance of verbal comforting behavior, particularly emotional comforting in friendships. The results showed both similarities and differences among the groups. All the groups (various combinations of gender and ethnicity) believed that it was better to be emotion focused than problem focused in supporting a friend in a difficult situation and that comforting strategies that validated the friend's feelings were most sensitive and effective. Nevertheless, differences were found most consistently between African American and European American women, with the former placing significantly less emphasis on the emotional aspects of support. The other groups did not differ as greatly. Samter et al. (1997) concluded that since the study's focus was *verbal* support, African American women may show support to friends though nonverbal behaviors in preference to verbal means. They may "walk the walk" more than they "talk the talk." This was clearly the case in the Relationship Story of Tamika and Jonelle. Tamika did not give Jonelle a great deal of verbal consolation when Jonelle broke her arm, yet Tamika offered countless acts of support.

Social support provided by family and friend networks is not without its downside, however, particularly for women. Research indicates that women have wider social networks and support resources and thus receive more social support than men do (Cunningham & Barbee, 2000; Cutrona, 1996). Yet women are also more affected by strain in their support network than are men and can be impacted negatively, both emotionally and physically, by disruptions among family and friends (Whalen & Lachman, 2000). Being involved actively in reciprocal social support is thus both a gift and a burden.

Ultimately, the knowledge that we can count on a friend, a family member, or a partner for emotional and physical support offers a psychological "safety net" that few of us would wish to be without. In addition to the sustaining safety net that may be provided by a friend, the social support provided by a partner or spouse is also very important.

Social Support in Couples

Situations inevitably occur in which one partner in a relationship requires some type of social support. The first step toward securing support is to tell one's partner about the problem or at least one's feelings about it. Women more than men may employ indirect strategies for getting support, such as complaining or behaving emotionally (e.g., crying). Such strategies are more difficult for the partner to interpret and may backfire, as when a man asks his girlfriend, "Why don't you just tell me what you want instead of beating around the bush?"

Because men in many cultures have been explicitly or implicitly taught not to reveal their feelings but instead to present a facade of complete mastery and control, men may be reluctant to ask for social support when they need it. If they ask anyone for help, it is likely to be their intimate partner. Thus, in general, women, who are more willing to display feelings and ask for support, have more resources from which to draw, as noted earlier (Cutrona, 1996). Even so, gender is clearly not the most important factor influencing support in couples.

Gurung, Sarason, and Sarason (1997) examined supportive interactions by relationship partners. They found that *personal characteristics* of the relationship partners (e.g., depression, loneliness), *relationship factors* (e.g., closeness, commitment), and *aspects of the situation* (e.g., discussion of a conflict, a novel stressful situation) all influenced partners' perceptions of supportive behaviors. Persons who were depressed, anxious, and had lower self-esteem were less supportive of their partner, reflecting personal characteristics. Previous experience in the relationship and expectations of the partner influenced whether behaviors were viewed as supportive or nonsupportive, reflecting relationship factors. But this reliance on relationship factors occurred more strongly in a conflict discussion over relatively familiar material. In novel situations, partners relied more on one another's personal characteristics. Thus, personal factors, relationship characteristics, and the particular situation all influenced the support interaction.

It is also essential to remember that the relational context influences not only what supportive behaviors might be enacted but also whether supported behaviors will even be interpreted positively. Sometimes, well-intentioned behaviors are misunderstood, if they are delivered in an atmosphere of conflict and attendant mistrust.

Cutrona, Hessling, and Suhr (1997) were also concerned with personal or individual characteristics and situational variables in their study of nearly 100 married couples, who completed questionnaires and were observed in two discussion interactions concerning stressful (but not conflictual) events. Although the personal quality of extraversion (outgoingness) was expected to contribute to supportiveness in multiple ways, it predicted only greater provision (but not receipt) of support behaviors in the first interaction. In other words, extraverts gave but did not get more support. In analyses of the second discussion interaction, what predicted the number of support behaviors a person received was the number of support behaviors that person had previously given his or her partner. People who gave a lot of support in the first interaction received a lot of support in the second interaction. Thus, what goes around comes around. But personality characteristics such as extraversion and emotional negativity emerged as important in other analyses.

Individual characteristics were also significant in Ognibene and Collins's (1998) exploration of adult attachment styles, social support, and coping strategies. Social support behaviors differed on the basis of attachment style, with people evaluated as having secure attachment perceiving that they both gave and received more social support than did insecurely attached participants.

Negativity was a central focus for Pasch, Bradbury, and Davila (1997), who assessed 60 newly married couples engaging in two 10-minute discussions. In the first discussion, one of the spouses was instructed to talk about something he or she wished to change about himself or herself. The other partner was simply to respond as he or she wished. In the second discussion, the roles were reversed. When these interactions were analyzed, some of the findings were surprising. First, women overall were not more effective support providers than men were. There were few gender differences, and those differences that did appear occurred largely when the person being helped was negative. Specifically, women were more emotionally negative when they talked about something they wanted to change, and in these cases, husbands exerted *less* supportive behavior. When husbands were negative, however, wives tended to be *more* supportive helpers. The authors noted that husbands and wives do not differ generally in social support behaviors, but they differ in specific situations, depending on the emotional tone of the person receiving the support.

Negative emotionality is often a part of couple conflict and ensuing couple dissatisfaction, which are implicated in both the enactment and effectiveness of social support behaviors. For example, Saitzyk, Floyd, and Kroll (1997) observed social support interactions in both satisfied and dissatisfied couples. They were particularly interested in how the couples appeared to balance issues of autonomy and interdependence. In fact, these issues were handled better by satisfied couples. Yet these couples had their own flaws in communication under some circumstances. Two skills seemed especially problematic for dissatisfied couples: the ability to provide support to the partner in a positive way and the ability to encourage a partner to take initiatives and independent actions. Thus, satisfied couples are not necessarily flawless in their communication, and dissatisfied couples are not always flawed.

Interestingly, in comparing violent and nonviolent couples, Holtzworth-Munroe and her colleagues (Holtzworth-Munroe, Stuart, Sandin, Smutzler, & McLaughlin, 1997) found few group differences in social support behaviors. The wives in these couples were very similar. The nonviolent husbands, however, offered more support to their wives than did the violent husbands, who appeared to be more generally negative, no matter how the wife was behaving or what kind of interaction was occurring.

It is clear from all the findings just discussed that negativity in individuals and couples has some problematic implications for couples' social support. However, Cutrona (1996) chose to turn things around conceptually and focus on how social support itself can impact positively on couples' negativity and conflict. Social support can (1) prevent relationship deterioration from stress, (2) alleviate depression, (3) reduce conflict intensity, and (4) promote intimacy, trust, and positive construals of the partner. "Support within the marital relationship can promote a positive emotional tone and . . . can foster intimacy and closeness that hold couples together through difficult times" (p. 59). Strategies to foster social support, some of which were adapted from Cutrona (1996), can be found in the next Up Close box.

Social Support Strategies and Suggestions for Relationships with Friends and Partners

Social Support Is Essential

- No one can go it alone. Everyone needs help and support at some time.
- Be ready to support friends and partners on small issues as well as large ones, and expect them to do the same for you.

Communicate Clearly

- Whether you are a support seeker or a support provider, try to figure out what you want or need or what you can provide. Then be straightforward in communicating this to others.
- Don't expect someone else to read your mind, and don't try to read his or hers. If you have a question or concern, always ask. Check things out.

People Are Different

- People have different styles of helping: some are serious, some use humor, some jump right in, some hold back awhile. Appreciate all of the help you get.
- Some people provide support emotionally, some through help with problem solving, and others through helpful actions.

Preventive Medicine

- When things are going well, make sure you continue both to seek and to provide support.
- Realize that just as you take care of yourself physically, so as to prevent illness or at least make it less debilitating, you also need to take care of your relationship, so as to prevent some problems and to make other life stresses and crises less severe.

Teamwork

- Use tough times to unite you and your relationship partner. Deal with problems as a team, where you combine resources to deal with a common issue.
- Remember that teamwork involves communication, strategizing, and having everyone doing the job that he or she does best. Use this approach in handling problems.

Ask Others for Support

- No one person can provide all the support required in coping with most large problems. Your friend or partner may be your primary source of support, but that does not mean he or she should be your only source.
- Remember that if you allow others to support you, then you will be giving them the gift of your trust. So understand that by asking, you are also giving.

Source: Some strategies adapted from Cutrona (1996).

Indeed, in a study by Sokolski and Hendrick (1999), perceived social support by one's spouse was found to be highly related to relationship satisfaction, for both husbands and wives. And according to Cutrona (1996), the most effective support is that which is provided voluntarily and caringly, rather than grudgingly or only after a specific request, as well as that which is matched to what is needed and desired. In the second Relationship Story, Tamika helped her roommate, Jonelle, in multiple ways over several weeks. Jonelle didn't have to ask—Tamika was just there when needed. She was willing, not reluctant, and she didn't either hold back on what was needed or try to do more than what was required. She matched the support to the stressor.

Ultimately, social support is an important construct because it transcends all types of relationships, from family ties, to friendships, to romantic liaisons. It is at the root of the ties that link people, and it is intertwined with the sense of belongingness that is so important. If we have a need to belong, then one way of demonstrating our belonging is through both providing and receiving social support. Social support is one ingredient in the affectional "glue" that binds us to our loved ones.

Summary and Conclusions

Friendships are important, voluntary personal relationships that add meaningful connections to our lives. Theories of relationship development and, more specifically, friendship development include cognitive consistency, developmental, and reinforcement theories. An important reinforcement-based theory is exchange theory, which emphasizes both giving and receiving. Rewards, costs, outcomes, and comparison levels are all part of exchange theory. Equity theory is an extension of exchange theory and is concerned largely with issues of fairness in what people both give to and get from a relationship. Although exchange relationships emphasize both giving and receiving, communal relationships are concerned primarily with giving what someone needs, without expecting something in return. Family and close friend relationships are thought to be communal, whereas work and other business relationships are thought to be exchange. But it has been argued that there are elements of exchange (i.e., reciprocity) in even the most communal relationships.

Friendships may seem to develop in a simple fashion, but the process is really rather complex, involving individual, dyadic, situational, and environmental factors. Friendships also develop within cultural, structural, and historical contexts. Although proximity is important to friendship, one's closest friends psychologically may be the farthest away geographically. Good communication seems to be an important factor in most friendships. A person's social network encompasses both friends and family, and there are both costs and benefits when relationship partners have highly linked and overlapping social networks.

Friendship is important throughout the lifespan. Children's friendships can be important buffers against loneliness and stress, and although most of these relationships change as children get older, some can endure. Sibling relationships can be the most enduring of all. Friendship formation is a central developmental task in adolescence, so friends become more important and families typically less so. Adolescent friendships may be a training ground for later romantic relationships. In young adulthood, ideally, friendship and family relationships are both incorporated into ongoing life in a satisfying way. If people marry and have children, family may become relatively more important and friends less so. In older adulthood, friends may resume substantial importance, although family relationships remain significant, also. The number of friends someone has may depend on his or her "friendship budget," or the time he or she has available for friends. Friendships can deteriorate for a number of reasons, but if there has not been a catastrophic event, a friendship can often be restored.

Friends are important both to women and men but different in nature; women's friendships are characterized more by communication and men's by activities. Cross-sex friendships can be difficult to maintain, both for personal reasons (one friend might become romantically interested in the other friend) and social pressure (society doesn't know how to handle cross-sex friendships). Yet cross-sex friendships can be deeply rewarding, offering qualities that are not available in same-sex friendships.

Social support consists of responsiveness to and fulfillment of another person's needs. Everyone requires support at one time or another, and most people are also called on to give support. Support may be emotional, cognitive, or behavioral. The most useful way to define *social support* is as perceived support, or whether someone believes that he or she has been supported. Social support is important at all ages and stages of life and has been related to greater relationship satisfaction, better parenting, and so on. There are some cultural and gender differences in support provision, with women typically providing more support within the social network and also being more negatively impacted by stresses within the network.

Romantic partners look to each other for support; men, in particular, rely on their partner as the primary support provider. Support provision may vary depending on the personal characteristics of the people involved and the situation. For example, extraversion may lead to greater support provision, whereas negativity may lead to less. Wives and husbands do not so much differ in the amount of support as in the style in which support is given. Social support both affects and is affected by other relationship characteristics. Support can lessen many relationship negatives and can provide a strengthening effect for both friendships and couple relationships. Both friendship and social support are central aspects of human social ties.

Key Terms

Communal (p. 52)
Equity (p. 51)
Exchange (p. 50)
Friendship (p. 49)

Perceived support (p. 63)
Social network (p. 55)
Social support (p. 62)

Suggested Reading

Blieszner, R. (2000). Close relationships in old age. In C. Hendrick & S. S. Hendrick (Eds.), *Close relationships: A sourcebook* (pp. 85–95). Thousand Oaks, CA: Sage.

Cunningham, M. R., & Barbee, A. P. (2000). Social support. In C. Hendrick & S. S. Hendrick (Eds.), *Close relationships: A sourcebook* (pp. 273–285). Thousand Oaks, CA: Sage.

Cutrona, C. E. (1996). *Social support in couples.* Thousand Oaks, CA: Sage.

Fehr, B. (1996). *Friendship processes.* Thousand Oaks, CA: Sage.

Hart, S. (2001). *Preventing sibling rivalry.* New York: Free Press.

Inman, C. (1996). Friendships among men: Closeness in the doing. In J. T. Wood (Ed.), *Gendered relationships* (pp. 95–110). Mountain View, CA: Mayfield.

Monsour, M. (2002). *Women and men as friends: Relationships across the life span in the 21st century.* Mahwah, NJ: Lawrence Erlbaum.

4 Romantic Love

Relationship Story

Swimming in the Ocean

No one thought of Sandy and Joe as extra-ordinary people. Joe was a high school history teacher of 40. Tall and lanky, with thinning brown hair and just the hint of a paunch, he wasn't someone you'd pick out of a crowd. He was a conscientious teacher who wanted his students to learn history without it being too boring, but he wasn't "Teacher of the Year" material at the urban high school where he taught. Students liked him well enough.

The other teachers liked him, too, al-though he wasn't a leader and avoided active participation in the teachers union. What Joe *could* be counted on for were simple things. If someone's car wouldn't start on a winter after-noon, Joe was the guy with the jumper cables who would help start the car and wait until it was running smoothly before leaving. In early September, when the school year stretched ahead unendingly, it was Joe who brought tomatoes from his garden for anyone who wanted them. And Joe was the one who always, always knew the latest basketball scores. He loved basketball!

Sandy was a little on the quiet side, someone people invariably referred to as "nice." She was of average height and somewhat plump (although not so plump these days) and her short, reddish-brown hair had just started to gray. Now in her late 30s, she was a substitute teacher who alternated her busy days in unfamiliar elementary school classrooms with busy days as the mother of two children and occasional quiet time spent with good friends. Sandy was not what you would call outgoing, but she had a lot of good friends—some of them, the same girlfriends that she'd had since grade school. She loved them dearly, as they did her. When someone needed a person to talk to or a shoulder to cry on, he or she called Sandy. And she always listened and tried to help, in her own quiet way.

Joe and Sandy had been married about 10 years; they were "late bloomers" in the relationship department. They had met at a workshop for teachers one spring, sitting in the same small-group discussion. They went out to dinner the first night they met and then started seeing each other more and more frequently, until they were seldom apart. That was the way it had been ever since; they were only apart when they had to be. They got engaged and married pretty quickly. It had taken them a long time to find each other, and they didn't want to waste any time.

Sandy and Joe had two children: a son, John, who was 6, and a daughter, Sarah, who was almost 2. The children were extremely important to Joe and Sandy. During those long years of being single, neither Sandy nor Joe had been sure that they would ever find someone to love and marry, much less have children with, so by the time Sarah was born, they sometimes felt that they were living a miracle. After awhile, Sandy went back to teaching part time, and when she was at work, the children were with one or another set of grandparents. Money was tight—teachers don't get rich—and Joe had some minor health problems, but all in all, everything seemed almost too good to be true.

Then Sandy found the lump. One day, when Sarah was nearly 2 years old, Sandy was taking a shower. As she moved the soapy washcloth over her body, she felt—something. It was in her left breast, just below and to the outside of the nipple. It felt hard, like a little pebble. Sandy never forgot the wave of panic that washed over her in that moment, how her stomach lurched and her heart began to race, how she couldn't believe that this was happening to her. The next few days were a blur. There was a telephone call to her family physician and an office appointment where the physician said, "It's probably nothing, Sandy, especially at your relatively young age, but let's just check it out to be sure." Then came the mammogram (labeled "suspicious" by the radiologist), a consultation with a surgeon, and a biopsy. And always, there was the waiting—the endless, interminable waiting. Finally came her doctor's call and the words *breast cancer.*

Sandy was stunned—and so was everyone else. Joe had just started his second year as assistant basketball coach at the high school, something he had always wanted to do. It was taking up all of his after-school hours and many of his evenings, but he loved every minute. John had just started first grade, a big adventure for the shy 6-year-old. He was excited about going to school all day, but it took him awhile to adjust to changes. John seemed to have been born wanting things to be predictable! And then there was Sarah, who was just getting ready to turn 2. "This can't be happening" was the reaction of basically all of Joe and Sandy's family and friends. Joe was very supportive and went with Sandy to talk with the surgeon and later with the oncologist, who would be her physician for the foreseeable future. And Joe supported her also when she decided to have a mastectomy, rather than a lumpectomy with radiation. She didn't want to lose her breast, and the lumpectomy would have conserved much of the breast, but she would have had to have six weeks of five-days-a-week radiation treatments. And as the mother of two small children, she felt that she just didn't have time for 30 radiation treatments.

That was how it happened that one week before Sarah's second birthday, Sandy went into the hospital for a mastectomy. She was so depressed and so scared; she cried and cried. The thing that haunted her most was the image of Sarah and John growing up without a mother. They might not even remember her when they got older. She felt she couldn't bear it.

But she did bear it. They made it through the surgery, the recovery, and being told that "There are no guarantees with cancer, of course, but your lymph nodes were clear, so the prognosis is good." Sandy knew there were no guarantees, and so did Joe. Then came the chemotherapy. If you have ever been wading in the ocean, knocked down by a wave, and then struggled to your feet only to be knocked down again, you have a hint of how Joe and Sandy (especially Sandy) felt during that first year after Sandy's diagnosis. Get swept over. Get up. Get swept over. Get up. Surgery. Recovery. Chemotherapy. Recovery. "A day at a time" was what they lived by. Their parents put in long hours of child care; Sandy's friends brought in meals; Joe's colleagues pitched in and his head coach got someone to fill in when Joe couldn't get to practice. Even the guys on the basketball team tried to help. They would somewhat awkwardly ask, "How's it going, Coach?" hoping that he'd say, "Fine," and leave it at that but also wanting him to know that they were aware of his family situation and that they cared.

Little Sarah didn't seem to understand much of what was going on; a loving family member was always there to take care of her. Outgoing and ready to engage the world at a moment's notice, Sarah seemed relatively untouched by the distress around her. John, on the other hand, got clingy and fearful on occasion and sometimes did not even want to go to school, even though he loved first grade. He required elaborate assurances that his mother would be there when he got home from school. If she was out somewhere, he wanted to know exactly when she would be home. All John wanted was for his world to be predictable again.

And finally, slowly, after the end of that first year, life did become more predictable. Sandy was starting to feel almost like herself again, minus a breast, of course. Joe didn't seem to mind her scarred chest; their lovemaking was much the same as it had always been. Joe had always had a way of making Sandy feel special. Right from that first day that they met in the teachers workshop, he always told her she looked nice, that her hair was pretty—

basically, that he loved her just as she was. She remembered going out to dinner a week before John was born, Sandy feeling very pregnant, but Joe telling her that she was the most beautiful pregnant woman he had ever seen. And to him, she was.

So, life was getting almost back to normal. Sandy's girlfriends stopped calling her to see how she was feeling but called instead to see if she wanted to get together for lunch. The grandparents stopped worrying all the time. Joe's basketball team had had an almost-winning season the previous year and was looking forward to an even better year ahead. John was excited about being on his first T-ball team. The family was drifting through the summer, breathing a little easier.

Then Sandy got a cold and cough that she just couldn't shake off. She went to see her physician, who took a chest x-ray just to be sure there was no pneumonia. While the x-ray didn't show any pneumonia, it showed a spot on the breast bone—a spot that turned out to be cancer. This was deja vu all over again, the rerun of a nightmare, but a nightmare from which Sandy couldn't wake up. Yet there, in the midst of everything, was Joe, filling in everywhere and anywhere, and consistently telling Sandy, "You'll make it. We'll all make it."

Even so, those words were hard for Sandy to hear as she endured six weeks of radiation—the radiation she didn't have time for only a year before. She pushed Joe away, saying, "It's my cancer, not yours. And there's nothing you or anybody can do." After radiation ceased, the chemotherapy started again. She'd have chemo, be sick for a week, feel increasingly better over the next two weeks, and then start all over again. And one of the worst parts was the chemotherapy "brain fog" that kept her fuzzy most of the time. The ocean waves kept knocking her down, and Sandy was afraid that this time, she might not be able to get back up; she might drown. But just when she felt herself going under, Joe was there with a life preserver—himself. He held her head when she threw up and took care of her when she couldn't take care of herself. He hated to do it, but he gave up his coaching job. History teachers have predictable hours and time for their families; coaches have long hours and a lot of away games. Basketball and breast cancer just didn't compute. Joe loved basketball, but between his family and the game, there was just no contest.

Love is a two-way street, and so is strength. Sandy fought to stay above water, coping with all chemo's side effects to go on with her life, one day at a time. Whenever she was tired and thought about letting go, she looked at Joe and the children standing on the shore, and she started swimming again. She swam for her life.

It *may* be true that it takes a village to raise a child, but it is *definitely* true that it takes a village to cope with cancer. And Sandy's village was as busy as it needed to be. Her mother took care of Sarah, and her father drove John to T-ball. Her mother-in-law helped Sandy buy a wig when her hair fell out, and her father-in-law fixed the broken screen door and weeded the garden. Her brother mowed their lawn, and her friends cooked again. And they got by.

Amazingly, as ill as Sandy felt, she responded well to her treatment, just as she had before. Eventually, chemo was over, the spot on her breast bone disappeared, and she was deemed "in remission." In some ways, it was scarier to be off chemo than on it. On it, she felt she was doing something; off it, she wasn't sure what she was doing. Slowly, so slowly,

Sandy and Joe eased back into some of their life as it had been before the breast cancer. Some of it, but not all of it. The "good prognosis" that Sandy had received after her first bout with breast cancer had turned out to be an illusion, so Sandy and Joe had no illusions this time. They had faith—strong faith—but no illusions. Sandy started to think about going back to substitute teaching, partly to help pay the medical bills not covered by insurance but mostly because she missed the classroom. Sarah and John seemed to be doing fine. Joe even started thinking about coaching basketball again—not now, but sometime. Sandy and Joe held hands tightly, and ever so slowly, they began to take tentative steps into their future, one step at a time.

■ ■ ■

Questions to Consider in Reading This Chapter

- How did Sandy and Joe express their love for each other before Sandy's diagnosis of breast cancer?
- How did their expressions of love change after the diagnosis?
- Do you think *companionate love* or *passionate love* is a better basis for a relationship? Why?
- What love theories discussed in this chapter are most applicable to your own personal experience?
- Does intimacy precede love, does love precede intimacy, or do both occur at the same time?

What Do We Know about Romantic Love?

The story of Sandy and Joe may seem to provide an unusual introduction to this chapter. So often, we think of stories of **love** as two movie stars who have a glamorous wedding and jet off to the French Riviera or the South Pacific for their honeymoon. Or we think of the young, beautiful people who look longingly at one another in television and magazine advertisements. But much more often, love is about the people in our neighborhoods, our families, ourselves. Love is both very idealized and very much a part of our daily lives.

   Love is a word that we all believe we understand. Dictionaries refer to *love* as "liking with great emotional intensity" and may mention qualities such as desiring and providing for the loved one's welfare and happiness. Romantic love can be envisioned on a continuum, with *attraction, falling in love, being in love,* and *loving* all occupying points along it. Falling in love occurs when people who are attracted strongly to each other deepen their feelings and begin to think that they want the relationship to continue. Falling in love typically involves heightened physical arousal, increased emotionality, and frequent thoughts of the loved one. Of course, the whole concept of *falling* in love only makes sense to certain kinds of people, as will be discussed later in this chapter. Other types of people *grow* into love over time.

The actual state of being in love appears to be somewhat different from love more generally. Meyers and Berscheid (1997) found that being in love was typically associated with a sexual attraction/desire component, whereas more general loving did not involve a sexual component and could refer to romantic partners, family members, or friends.

There are many different types of love, aspects to love, and influences on love, which explains, in part, why the theory and measurement of love have endured some controversy. Although love is applicable to a variety of relationships—parent/child, brother/sister, friend/friend—the focus here is on adult romantic love. This chapter will discuss theory and research exploring romantic love in some detail, beginning with romantic attachment.

Attachment

Humans have a need for connection, as discussed in Chapter 1 (Baumeister & Leary, 1995). One form of connection involves a great deal of infant/caregiver (often mother) interaction. Part of this interaction is physical closeness, which implies emotional affection, and this has been referred to as *attachment*, also discussed earlier.

Bowlby (1973) focused on attachment behavior in the context of an infant or toddler seeking proximity or closeness to the caregiver, and he viewed such behavior as evolutionarily adaptive, conferring a safety advantage on infants who seek such closeness. Other scholars (e.g., Ainsworth, Blehar, Waters, & Wall, 1978) built on Bowlby's work, developing an approach to assess infants' attachment styles. The three traditional attachment styles are *secure, avoidant,* and *anxious* or *anxious/ambivalent.* Attachment relationships begin in infancy but are important throughout the lifespan and can include relationships with parents, siblings, and close friends as well as with romantic partners (Feeney, Noller, & Roberts, 2000).

Romantic Attachment

Hazan and Shaver (1987) were groundbreaking in applying attachment theory to adult romantic relationships, in large measure, initiating the study of **romantic attachment.** In their early research with community respondents and college students, they found that 54% of respondents could be categorized as *secure,* 25% as *avoidant,* and 19% as *anxious/ambivalent.* Subsequent researchers (e.g., Bartholomew, 1990) refined and expanded both the theory and measurement of attachment to encompass four, rather than three, styles: *secure, preoccupied* (similar to *anxious/ambivalent*), *dismissing avoidant,* and *fearful avoidant.* Many researchers now acknowledge four styles of adult attachment, and considerable research has been generated to explore the stability of attachment as well as the implications of attachment style for other relational factors (Feeney & Noller, 1996).

As outlined in detail by Feeney et al. (2000), there is ongoing debate about the stability of attachment styles. Attachment styles change over time for many people, and some researchers say this is due to measurement factors (e.g., questionnaire or interview techniques that do not produce reliable results from one administration to the next). But changes in attachment styles are substantial enough to be more than just measurement error. They could be due to changes in the fundamental ways one experiences relationships (e.g., having a happy and stable marriage), or they could reflect more short-term, situational changes (e.g., a relatively stable period during which one experiences satisfying friendship and romantic relationships). Stability could also be affected by individual characteristics such as temperament (Feeney et al., 2000).

What is perhaps most likely is that our early experiences and our unique, individual makeup predispose us toward a certain attachment style in our close relationships. (For most of us, fortunately, that appears to be the *secure* style.) Yet we are constantly exposed to new relationships and life experiences, in which our secure attachment may be shaken by a partner's betrayal or our preoccupied attachment stabilized by a consistently and predictably loving romantic partner. So, as with many other aspects of who we are, the questions "Are we born with it?" and "Did we learn it?" can both be answered with a qualified yes.

Outcomes of Attachment Styles

Attachment has been related to many aspects of romantic relationships, including communication, conflict, emotional regulation, relational quality, and relationship stability over time (described more fully in Feeney & Noller, 1996; Feeney et al., 2000). People with different attachment styles may seek different things from their romantic relationships and their relationship partners. For example, secure persons may welcome intimacy, whereas avoidant persons may fear it. Anxious persons may be afraid of abandonment. People may seek certain attachment qualities in a partner, or being with a certain partner may change a person's attachment style. As an example, secure persons may seek other secure persons as romantic partners, or a long-term relationship with a secure partner might allow an anxious or avoidant person to become more secure (Feeney et al., 2000).

People may also behave consistently with their attachment styles in such ways as to elicit particular behaviors from others. In a study of 125 persons who kept structured diaries of their social interactions for one week (Tidwell, Reis, & Shaver, 1996), results showed that people with different attachment styles actually recorded different patterns of social interaction. Secure persons reported the greatest enjoyment, intimacy, and positive emotions. Anxious/ambivalent persons were similar to secure persons but were more changeable emotionally. Avoidant persons reported lower levels of the positive emotions and also appeared to "structure social activities in ways that minimize closeness" (p. 729).

It seems predictable that securely attached persons tend to be more successful in most relational arenas, but some outcomes are complex. Secure attachment involves not only higher disclosure but more flexible communication, as well as a greater reliance on positive problem solving during conflict. Persons with insecure attachment styles (particularly persons who are anxious/ambivalent or preoccupied) are less effective in handling both conflict (tending to alienate partners) and communication (avoidant persons, less disclosing; anxious/ambivalent persons, less flexible and appropriate) (Feeney et al., 2000). Less negative emotion and more positive emotion has characterized secure attachment (Simpson, 1990). Consistent with Hazan and Shaver's early work (1987), subsequent research has associated secure attachment with greater relational quality.

Interestingly, however, *secure* does not necessarily mean *stable*. Kirkpatrick and Hazan's (1994) four-year longitudinal study (i.e., a study tracking people over time) found that secure and insecure persons reported comparable overall degrees of stability, even though secure persons tended just to remain in their relationships whereas insecure persons were more likely to get in and out of the same relationship several times. So although secure attachment is related to greater relationship positivity in a number of areas, insecure attachment does not necessarily doom a relationship.

Diamond (2001) proposes that research on adult attachment should study the physiological effects of forming attachments. Attachment appears to be one form of expression of a fundamental need to belong (as discussed in Chapter 1), and it is therefore part of our evolutionary heritage. Because attachment is so important, according to Diamond, successful attachment should relate to positive physical outcomes (perhaps a more regular heart rate) and fewer negative physical outcomes (perhaps a reduction in stress-related hormones). Psychophysiological research (discussed in Chapter 10) has already shown relations between couples conflict and increased stress hormones, especially for women (Kiecolt-Glaser, Newton, Cacioppo, MacCallum, Glaser, & Malarkey, 1996). It thus seems logical that emotional positives, such as secure attachment, and emotional negatives, such as insecure attachment, should have measurable physical effects as well as psychological effects (Diamond, 2001).

In considering the Relationship Story (and remembering that over half of persons report secure attachment), Sandy and Joe appear to be securely attached to each other. They are not intense in their communication, but they are relatively successful in areas of disclosure and problem solving. Their attempts to maintain as normal a life as possible for their children, John and Sarah, as well as the helpful involvement by both Sandy's parents and Joe's parents, indicate that warmth and responsiveness (characteristics of the caregiver in secure attachment) are clearly present in this extended family.

Theories of Love

Attachment can be thought of as the foundation for successful loving, and just as research on attachment has exploded in recent decades, so has research on romantic love. Moreover, just as there are differing perspectives on aspects of attachment (e.g., its measurement, its stability), there are also several theories of love, a representation of which is provided here.

Three General Theories Applied to Love

Several general theories of human behavior have been applied specifically to love, and three of those theories will be considered briefly here.

Evolutionary psychology, an outgrowth of sociobiology and general evolutionary theory, has been proposed as an overarching theory for the social sciences (e.g., Buss, 1995). While much attention has been devoted to such phenomena as mate selection in the context of this theory, love has also been a focus. Mellen (1981) proposes that love is the modern version of more primitive emotional bonding that evolved to link adult parents who would then provision and protect their infants. Such bonding would thus facilitate infant survival and species survival. Buss (1988) defines more specific *love acts* that also lead to mating, relationship exclusivity, and so on and ultimately to species survival. These love acts tend to be differentiated in large measure on the basis of gender, according to evolutionary theory. Evolutionary theory and attachment theory have many commonalities, since attachment theory is really evolution based.

Social structural and social learning theories state that much of what we think of as natural behaviors, including behaviors in intimate relationships, are socially and culturally structured and learned rather than mandated as part of our evolutionary heritage (e.g., Eagly & Wood, 1999). Interpretations of these behaviors are also constructed, shaped, and reshaped by one's particular culture and historical period. For example, evolutionary psychologists might say that men fall in love with women who have big breasts and small waists because in humans' distant past, such women would more likely be fertile and produce healthy offspring. Social learning theorists, on the other hand, might say that men in the current historical period in Western society have simply been taught by the culture that big breasts and small waists are a sign of beauty and thus are attracted to women who have them (as opposed to historical periods where plump women were valued). In turn, women have learned that they may be valued based on breast and waist size and thus seek cosmetic or surgical ways to make their breasts larger and their waists smaller. (Evolutionary psychology and social learning theories are discussed in more detail in Chapter 10.)

A third meta-theory applied to relationships is Aron and Aron's (1996) *self-expansion theory,* in which it is proposed that humans seek to grow and to expand the self by incorporating people, experiences, and even possessions into one's conception of oneself. The ultimate goal of self-expansion is not to aggrandize the self but rather to unite the self with the universe—with all that there is. The love shared with another person can be a fundamental source of self-expansion, according to the Arons.

Although these three general theories are interesting, their focus is much broader than love. Thus, it would probably be difficult for Sandy and Joe to apply these theories to their own marriage. They might be most likely to identify with self-expansion, acknowledging that each of them has grown and prospered from their relationship, their partnership.

Passionate and Companionate Love

Passionate love consists of intense arousal and absorption with a partner; it is emotion laden. **Companionate love,** on the other hand, consists of a deep and abiding affection for a partner with whom one's life is linked. These conceptions of love were foundational in the study of love, as articulated by Berscheid and Walster (1978) as well as Walster and Walster (1978). Passionate love supposedly occurs early in a relationship, and if the relationship endures, passion evolves into companionate love. Such a view ascribes an almost statelike (i.e., temporary) quality to passionate love and a more traitlike (enduring) quality to companionate love. Hatfield and Sprecher (1986a) developed a measure of passionate love, the Passionate Love Scale, that is used widely, and companionate love has been measured in various ways, as well.

More recent research indicates that passion is not a quality that necessarily evolves into companionability but rather that the two types of love co-exist in intimate relationships. For example, S. S. Hendrick and C. Hendrick (1993) requested that participants write accounts (essentially mini-stories) about their romantic relationships. These accounts were analyzed for love themes, the most frequent of which was a friendship-type love theme. In another study that was part of this research, almost half of the college-student participants described their romantic relationship partner as their "best friend." Sprecher and Regan (1998) reported similar findings, with both passionate and companionate love related to commitment and relationship satisfaction. "Both passion and friendship appear to be necessary for the maintenance of enduring romantic relationships" (S. S. Hendrick & C. Hendrick, 2000, p. 205).

Fehr and Broughton (2001), however, studied personality and gender differences in love, finding that both men and women respondents viewed companionate love, rather than passionate love, as more generally representative of love for them. In addition, "people with nurturant personalities conceptualized love in companionate terms, whereas those with non-nurturant personalities conceptualized love in passionate terms" (p. 134).

Joe and Sandy's relationship has certainly been characterized by both passionate features and companionate features, although companionate love predominated during Sandy's cancer treatment. From their first meeting, they developed a strong attraction for and friendship with each other, and both aspects of their love have only deepened over time. They would hate to have to choose one aspect of love over another.

Prototype Approaches

A *prototype approach* defines a concept such as love not in terms of its *complete* set of characteristics (i.e., all of what it is and all of what it is not) but rather on the basis of its *best* or most representative set of features, referred to as the **prototype** of the concept. Fehr (1988, 1993) has explored the prototype approach to love, finding that companionate features were considered more important than were passionate features and that romantic love was considered less prototypical of love in general than were such types of love as parental love (Fehr & Russell, 1991). The prototypical features of love found across several studies were caring, friendship, honesty, trust, and respect (Fehr, 1993).

Although most prototype research has focused on the general concept of love, Regan, Kocan, and Whitlock (1998) analyzed only romantic love, finding passionate and sexual aspects to be much more important to romantic love than Fehr had found them to be for the more general concept of love. However, companionate characteristics such as honesty and trust were still more important than were sex and passion.

Sandy and Joe would agree with that. As noted earlier, passion and sex have certainly been a part of Sandy and Joe's relationship, especially at particular times in their relational development, but compassionate aspects are what have seen them through both the good times and the tough times. For example, each partner trusts the other in virtually all ways. They are also honest with each other. When they hear the word *love,* their immediate thoughts are of their deep affection for each other, their devotion to their children, and the circle of caring from family and friends that has enveloped them and sustained them.

Love Ways

Several scholars have emphasized the communicative aspects of love, noting that "communication is the fundamental action which both expresses and determines the subjective experience of romantic love" (Marston, Hecht, & Robers, 1987, p. 392). Marston et al. interviewed persons in romantic relationships and then used qualitative, or *content,* analyses of the interviews to derive categories of communicative behaviors, both from the self to the partner and from the partner to the self (e.g., saying "I love you," touching, and so on). These authors went on to develop a typology of the ways in which love is both experienced and expressed (*love ways*), with the typology including *active love, intuitive love, secure love,* and *traditional romantic love.* Each type of love was communicated in somewhat different ways (e.g., communicating love nonverbally in intuitive love; discussing emotions in active love).

Sandy and Joe communicate love in much of what they do with each other. Sandy is more likely to talk about her feelings than is Joe, whereas he is more inclined to show his love nonverbally, such as by quitting his coaching job in order to spend more time at home during Sandy's illness and recovery.

Triangular Theory

Sternberg (1986) proposed a *triangular theory of love,* in which love is comprised of three major components: *intimacy, passion,* and *commitment.* These three components can be combined in different proportions to create eight different types of love: nonlove (all three components absent); liking (primarily intimacy); infatuated love (primarily passion); empty love (primarily commitment); romantic love (intimacy and passion); companionate love (intimacy and commitment); fatuous love (passion and commitment); and consummate love (all three components present).

Measurement of the three components has been somewhat problematic because the components are highly related to each other (e.g., Acker & Davis, 1992). Nevertheless, they have been shown to be very important in romantic relationships. For example, Aron and Westbay (1996) factored 68 of the prototype features used by Fehr (1988, 1993) in her research and found an underlying three-factor structure, with the factors reflecting intimacy, passion, and commitment. And Marston, Hecht, Manke, McDaniel, and Reeder (1998) gathered a variety of data from approximately 80 romantic couples and found that intimacy, passion, and commitment were present. So, these three components do seem to be central themes of love.

If Sternberg's eight love types were applied to Joe and Sandy, it is likely that over-all, the couple would be characterized as having consummate love (all three components present), although they might appear to have more of a companionate love (intimacy and commitment), particularly at this time in their marriage. Passion can be hard to access for any couple on a day-to-day basis; it is even harder to find when a couple has two small children and can seem very elusive when dealing with a life-threatening illness. But the measure of passion is not how much sex a couple has had over the last week or month; rather, it is based on physical enjoyment and pleasure both in and with the other. And this broader definition of passion definitely applies to Sandy and Joe.

The Love Styles

People have personality styles, work styles, and even styles of dress. So why not love styles? A theoretical approach to love initiated by Lee (1973) and developed in a research program by C. Hendrick and S. S. Hendrick (e.g., 1986) proposes that just as people have individual interaction styles and personality styles, they also have **love styles.**

Six major love styles have been identified and researched: Eros (passionate, in-tense love); Ludus (game-playing love); Storge (love based in friendship); Pragma (prac-tical love); Mania (dependent, possessive love); and Agape (giving love). A central part of the love styles research has focused around precise measurement of the six styles. A measure was originally developed (Hatkoff & Lasswell, 1979; Lasswell & Lasswell, 1976) and then revised extensively and refined into the Love Attitudes Scale (C. Hen-drick & S. S. Hendrick, 1986). In addition to the general 42-item form, this scale now has a partner-specific form (C. Hendrick & S. S. Hendrick, 1990) and a 24-item short form (C. Hendrick, S. S. Hendrick, & Dicke, 1998). An 18-item version of the Love Attitudes Scale is shown in the following Up Close box. Answer the items and see what your pre-ferred love styles might be.

The goal of love styles research has been to identify, measure, and then relate the love styles to relationship-relevant constructs, such as gender, personality, ethnicity, self-disclosure, relationship satisfaction, and so on, but also to such things as personal con-struct systems (ways of viewing the world) and aspects of eating disorders. The research has been wide ranging (S. S. Hendrick & C. Hendrick, 1992).

Gender-based differences and similarities in love styles have been relatively con-sistent. Men typically describe themselves as more game playing, and women often describe themselves as more oriented to friendship, practicality, and dependence/possessiveness. But these differences (except for game playing) are modest. Research looking specifically at love and sex attitudes and other relational constructs (S. S. Hen-drick & C. Hendrick, 1995) found that, for the most part, women and men are more the same than different in how their attitudes toward love and sex are linked. For example, men may be somewhat more game playing than are women, but for *both* women and men, game playing is related negatively to relationship satisfaction.

Abbreviated Form of the Love Attitudes Scale

Using the scale below, rate each statement according to how well it describes your current romantic relationship. Then go back and add up your scores in each of the six parts so that you get a total score for each love style. Find your three highest scores to see what your preferred love styles might be. (Note that a total of 15 is the highest possible score in any area.)

1 = Strongly disagree   2 = Moderately disagree   3 = Neutral
4 = Moderately agree   5 = Strongly agree

Eros
1. _____ My partner and I have the right physical chemistry between us.
2. _____ I feel that my partner and I were meant for each other.
3. _____ My partner and I really understand each other.

_____ = Total

Ludus
4. _____ I believe that what my partner doesn't know about me won't hurt him/her.
5. _____ I have sometimes had to keep my partner from finding out about other partners.
6. _____ My partner would get upset if he/she knew of some of the things I've done with other people.

_____ = Total

Storge
7. _____ Our love is the best kind because it grew out of a long friendship.
8. _____ Our friendship merged gradually into love over time.
9. _____ Our love is really a deep friendship, not a mysterious, mystical emotion.

_____ = Total

Pragma
10. _____ A main consideration in choosing my partner was how he/she would reflect on my family.
11. _____ An important factor in choosing my partner was whether he/she would be a good parent.
12. _____ One consideration in choosing my partner was how he/she would reflect on my career.

_____ = Total

Mania
13. _____ When my partner doesn't pay attention to me, I feel sick all over.
14. _____ Since I've been in love with my partner, I've had trouble concentrating on anything else.
15. _____ I cannot relax if I suspect that my partner is with someone else.

_____ = Total

Agape
16. _____ I would rather suffer myself than let my partner suffer.
17. _____ I cannot be happy unless I place my partner's happiness before my own.
18. _____ I am usually willing to sacrifice my own wishes to let my partner achieve his/hers.

_____ = Total

Hahn and Blass (1997) found that Storge and Agape were the most appealing love styles (and Ludus, least appealing) when research participants were given descriptions of persons with different love styles and asked to rate them. People also tended to prefer others who were similar to themselves. (Recall the similarity/attraction link discussed in Chapter 2.) Love partners do indeed tend to be relatively similar in their love styles, including Eros, Storge, Agape, and Ludus (Davis & Latty-Mann, 1987) and Eros, Storge, Agape, and Mania (S. S. Hendrick, C. Hendrick, & Adler, 1988).

Love styles are related strongly to relationship quality (Morrow, Clark, & Brock, 1995) and satisfaction (S. S. Hendrick et al., 1988). More recently, Meeks, Hendrick, and Hendrick (1998) found that positive love (a combination of Eros, Storge, and Agape) and a person's perception that his or her relationship partner was a good perspective-taker were both predictors of greater relationship satisfaction. Game-playing love and negative conflict styles were predictive of lesser satisfaction.

The love styles seem to be easy for people to understand. Sandy and Joe could be described (and likely could describe themselves) pretty easily in terms of the love styles. Neither partner is at all game playing—not before, not now. They have a strong Storge component (they're good friends), less Eros (but still some) since Sandy's breast cancer, but much more Agape (giving love) in the relationship, especially on Joe's part. Practical love and possessive/dependent love don't seem too relevant to their relationship. Although some people might believe that romantic, partnered love is relevant primarily to young people, who are either seeking partners or who are newly partnered, Sandy and Joe would disagree with that.

Many theoretical perspectives on love have been presented in this chapter. The following Up Close box shows how these perspectives are similar and different.

Love across Ages and Cultures

Although young love has been the focus of many researchers, Grote and Frieze (1994, 1998) have conducted considerable research exploring love, relationship satisfaction, and related issues for middle-aged married couples, realizing that people like Sandy and Joe have a lot to tell us about love. In one study (1994), these authors examined love predictors of marital satisfaction for middle-aged, married couples, finding that friendship love and passionate love positively predicted marital satisfaction, whereas game-playing love negatively predicted satisfaction. In another study (1998), they found that passionate love was still somewhat strong and friendship love was quite strong for these older partners in long-term relationships. Another interesting finding was that husbands reported more altruistic love for wives than wives reported for husbands.

Montgomery and Sorell (1997) assessed relationship variables, including love styles, with four groups: (1) college-aged adults who had never been married, (2) married persons under 30 without children, (3) married persons (ages 24 to 50) with children in the home, and (4) married persons (ages 50 to 70) with no children in the home. The greatest number of differences between the groups were not due to either age or parent-

A Comparison of Some of the Major Approaches to Love

This chart shows how some of the major love approaches converge and diverge. It appears that passionate and companionate love are the most agreed-upon types of love.

Approach	Passionate Love	Companionate Love	Other
Berscheid & Walster (1978)	✗	✗	
Fehr (1988, 1993)		✗	
Hatfield & Rapson (1996)	✗		
C. Hendrick & S. S. Hendrick (1986)	✗ (erotic)	✗ (friendship)	✗ (game-playing, practical, possessive, altruistic)
Marston, Hecht, & Robers (1987)	✗ (romantic)	✗ (secure)	✗ (active, intuitive)
Sprecher & Regan (1998)	✗	✗	
Sternberg (1986)	✗	✗ (intimacy)	✗ (commitment)

hood but rather to marital status. The young, unmarried group reported greater game-playing and possessive/dependent love and less altruistic love than the other groups reported. Interestingly, neither passionate love nor friendship love differed across the groups. As these authors noted, "Individuals throughout the life-stages of marriage consistently endorse the love attitudes involving passion, romance, friendship, and self-giving love" (p. 61). In research with married couples, Tucker and Aron (1993) found that passionate love continued throughout the duration of marriage, although it lessened slightly with major transitions, such as the birth of children.

Just as love spans many ages, so, too, does it span many cultures. For example, Contreras and her colleagues (Contreras, Hendrick, & Hendrick, 1996) assessed love and sex attitudes and relationship satisfaction in a sample of married Mexican American and European American couples (ranging in age from 20 to 60 years). Passionate love was the strongest predictor of satisfaction for all groups, again reaffirming the importance of some amount of passion to couples, no matter what their age. In addition, there were only modest love and sex attitude differences between the ethnic groups (European American, bicultural, Hispanic American), with the groups similar in their endorsement of relationship satisfaction as well as passionate, friendship-based, and altruistic love.

Indeed, many scholars believe that the central qualities of love transcend cultures and historical periods. Hatfield and Rapson (1996) and Jankowiak and Fischer (1992) concluded that passionate love is nearly universal. Cho and Cross (1995) found that themes of passionate love, devoted love, obsessive love, and casual love were present in Chinese literature dating from 3,000 to 500 years ago, and they also found many similarities in love styles between Taiwanese students living in the United States and American samples of respondents. There have been similar findings in other cross-cultural samples, including Sprecher et al. (1994), who compared American, Japanese, and Russian love styles, attachment, and other relationship characteristics.

Given that human beings are a group species, oriented toward contact with one another, then similarities in basic inclinations toward love are not surprising. And the need for intimacy, which can be considered as both a precursor to love and an outgrowth of love, is not surprising either.

Intimacy in Relationships

Intimacy is defined here as "emotional closeness." As noted earlier, such closeness has been proposed as a fundamental need, characterizing relationships of many different types: parent/child relationships, other familial relationships (e.g., sibling/sibling), close friendships, romantic relationships that endure, and so on. These are clearly the same types of relationships that also experience love.

This chapter discusses intimacy in terms of the *degree* of closeness (very close versus less close), rather than whether the closeness is positive or negative. Baumeister and Leary (1995) describe a need for positive relationships, but in fact, relationships that are positive overall can include periods of negativity. And it is ironic that of the four major spatial zones of human interaction identified by Hall (1966), the *intimate zone*, extending from physical contact to about 18 inches, is the area in which both great positivity (e.g., a father rocking an infant; a couple making love) and great negativity (e.g., physical abuse) occur. So, intimacy allows the potential for both positive and negative interaction. The positive face of intimacy is emphasized in the current chapter, whereas the negative face of intimacy is dealt with in Chapter 7.

Conceptualizing Intimacy

Hatfield and Rapson (1994) view intimacy as a woven tapestry containing threads of love and affection, trust, self-disclosure, and positive forms of nonverbal communication. There are various theoretical approaches toward why and how people seek intimacy, and some research addresses factors related to intimacy. Prager (1995, 2000) has written widely about intimacy, noting that it has been difficult for scholars to agree on a basic way to define intimacy, much less how to measure it. Her approach has been to frame intimacy as a type of *interaction* rather than simply as a type of relationship.

Intimate interactions can occur in a variety of contexts, as noted earlier, but when they occur with some frequency and over time, they come to constitute intimate relationships. For example, partners in a romantic relationship exhibit intimacy-inducing behaviors, which in turn affect their own and their partner's intimacy experience in the relationship. Prager (2000) has proposed that intimate experience is composed of positive emotion, self-disclosure, and a feeling of being understood by one's partner. Over time and with sustained interaction, intimate experiencing will lead to a truly intimate relationship. Taking this systematic approach to intimacy, it becomes easier to understand why Sternberg (1986) would characterize love that is composed of passion and commitment but missing the essential quality of intimacy as "fatuous," or silly and mindless.

Sandy and Joe's relationship seems to exemplify the step-by-step or building-block approach articulated by Prager. The very first day they met, Joe impulsively invited Sandy out for dinner, and she accepted. Each person was genuinely interested in the other, and they really enjoyed themselves, just talking about their families, their growing up, how they became teachers, and so on. They got along so well that Sandy cautiously invited Joe to a reunion that her family was having the following weekend. Joe accepted the invitation eagerly and had a great time. At the end of the day, Joe suggested that he and Sandy go to a concert later in the week. As each of them enacted an *intimate behavior* that increased their knowledge of each other, the other partner reciprocated with another such behavior. The behaviors led, in turn, to Joe and Sandy feeling *intimate experience*. Eventually, they perceived themselves as having developed an *intimate relationship*.

Prager (2000) has written about specific aspects of interaction having more influence on intimate experiences than do partners' overall perceptions of their relationship. Such phenomena as "self-disclosure, listening, interaction pleasantness" (p. 232) are influential interaction characteristics. Both verbal (e.g., responsiveness, self-disclosure) and nonverbal (e.g., eye contact, leaning forward) behaviors are involved in intimate interaction.

Lippert and Prager (2001) were interested in people's "working definitions of intimacy" (p. 283), which reflect the characteristics and behaviors that persons in actual relationships believe are intimate. Detailed responses (e.g., questionnaires and diaries) from 113 cohabiting couples indicated that such things as disclosing emotions and personal information, expressing positive feelings, having pleasant interactions, and feeling understood by one's partner were examples of interaction characteristics deemed to be intimate.

Reflect on the intimacy of one of your own romantic relationships by considering the questions in the Up Close box on page 88.

Measuring Intimacy

The measurement of intimacy, just as the conceptualization of intimacy, can take different forms. One can measure relationship satisfaction or adjustment and say that they represent intimacy, or intimacy itself can be measured as a unidimensional or multidimensional construct.

A recently developed measure of intimacy, the Interaction Record Form for Intimacy (IRF-I), is a diary-type instrument that requires research participants in partnered relationships to rate their daily interactions with their partner on 17 different items (Prager & Buhrmester, 1998). These ratings are then dimensionalized or factored into

Up
Close

The Nature of Intimacy

Think about your current romantic relationship (or a recent romantic relationship). Consider how you and your partner get along.

- Do you have positive emotional feelings toward your partner? Do you believe that your partner has positive feelings toward you?
- What about your communication? Do you self-disclose to your partner? Does your partner self-disclose to you?
- Do you know each other's motivations, hopes, fears, and dreams? How well do you listen to and understand your partner?
- How well does your partner listen to and understand you?

If you and your partner have positive emotional feelings toward each other, self-disclose to each other, and understand each other, then according to Prager's (2000) definition of *intimacy,* you and your partner have *intimate experience.* If you do not have one or more of these components, you might want to think about what is missing.

- Do you want to bring these components into your relationship? Why or why not?
- Do you think your relationship is intimate? Why or why not?

three broader dimensions: an intimate *behavior* factor (factor A), largely comprised of self-disclosure/communication items, and two intimate *experience* factors. One of these experience factors (factor B) reflects positive affect and the absence of conflict, whereas the other (factor C) reflects a feeling of being listened to and understood (Prager, 2000).

Other measures could also be used to assess the three individual factors or components listed above. For example, the Self-Disclosure Index (Miller, Berg, & Archer, 1983) assesses the amount of self-disclosure (factor A) that one partner offers to the other, while a companion measure, the Opener Scale, documents one's perceived ability to evoke disclosure from others. A measure of closeness could begin to tap into the positive affect of factor B, whereas a measure of conflict could assess the presence or absence of that behavior (Canary, Cunningham, & Cody, 1988). Finally, one way of measuring the third component of the IRF-I (factor C, feeling listened to and understood) might be to examine perspective taking, or the ability to take the partner's point of view (Long, 1990). Perspective taking is an aspect of empathy, a quality very important to intimacy.

Using the example of Joe and Sandy's relationship, it is possible to understand how disclosure, positive affect and the absence of conflict, and perspective-taking ability all work together to increase intimacy. Disclosure was a part of the getting-acquainted process when Sandy and Joe first met. They also experienced a great amount of positive affect and virtually no conflict at that time in their relationship. As they courted, married, and had children, their relational intimacy grew, but it was Sandy's breast cancer that jump-started their perspective-taking abilities—abilities to see issues from the other partner's point of view.

The development of intimacy requires great vulnerability on the parts of both partners, who may differ in their needs for intimacy, their tolerance for intimacy, and the like. Thus, intimacy must be negotiated and, to some extent, regulated in ways that allow the partners' individual intimacy needs to be compatible (Prager, 2000).

The Context of Intimacy

The achievement of romantic intimacy is a dynamic process that occurs at multiple levels and in multiple contexts (Prager, 2000). First, there is an *individual context.* Individual partners in a couple must be considered—their temperaments, personality traits, earlier family experiences, previous romantic involvements, and so on. What each individual "brings to the table" is incredibly important and influences the direction that the relationship will take. Next, there is a *relational context,* which involves relational interaction, including intimacy compatibility, reciprocity of self-disclosure, emotional give-and-take, and so on. These issues are all essentially relational in nature because they don't depend on just one partner. Partners bring individual qualities to the relationship, but how these qualities are expressed *with a specific partner* yields the relational context.

A relationship also occurs in a larger *social network context.* For example, romantic partners in a relatively new relationship may need a lot of time by themselves, away from the crowd. If each partner has a large social network (or family network) that expects the couple to show up for various social events and then spend time with everyone in the group, the partners may not achieve the amount of get-acquainted time that they need. So, also, the larger *sociocultural context* affects relationship intimacy. A couple who crosses cultural, religious, or racial barriers, or a gay or lesbian couple, might face greater barriers and less support as their relationship intensifies. The sociocultural pressures may be divisive or they may cause the couple to bond even more strongly and become more deeply intimate as a reaction to the external forces trying to drive a wedge between them. Thus, it is unclear just how social network and sociocultural forces influence intimacy, but they certainly do.

Prager (2000) also talks about an *immediate context* for a relationship in which a given relationship is acted out in space and time. For example, if partners are separated for long periods while they are still developing intimacy and can only communicate by phone and e-mail—without the benefit of reading each other's nonverbal behaviors, touching each other, and so on—they may struggle with intimacy more than they would if they could be together throughout the intimacy-acquiring period. On the other hand, they may learn to be more intimate verbally since they cannot be as intimate nonverbally.

Although intimacy is related to love, the two are not interchangeable. Intimacy is one of the three components of Sternberg's (1986) triangular theory of love and is implied by some of the other theoretical approaches. Yet the love styles perspective (C. Hendrick & S. S. Hendrick, 1986) would include intimacy in the form of emotional closeness as a part of some love styles (such as Eros) but not others (such as Pragma). Some couples may be more emotionally expressive and others more reserved, but both types of couples can be loving. In the relationship example, Sandy and Joe experienced great love and support in their marriage, but sometimes they felt more intimate with each other and at other times, less intimate.

Unrequited Love

Although love and intimacy may be almost uniformly important, they are not uniformly positive. As noted earlier, both great love and great conflict may occur in an intimate context. Love experiences can also be *loss* experiences because of breakup, divorce, and bereavement (discussed in Chapter 8). Another painful aspect of love—and one that has been experienced by nearly everyone—is *unrequited love,* which occurs when one person gives love that is received by another person but is not returned. There is no reciprocal love—it only goes one way.

Baumeister, Wotman, and Stillwell (1993; see also Baumeister & Wotman, 1992) explored unrequited love through two studies, primarily using respondents' narrative accounts of their unrequited love experiences. The studies provided a number of interesting findings. Although people who offered love to someone and those who rejected love from someone had different experiences, they also had similar emotions of distress, lack of control over their feelings, uncertainty, erratic behavior, and more. The persons who offered love were preoccupied with their own needs and wishes, often ignoring the signals of rejection coming from the other person and interpreting any ambiguous response as positive. The love offerers also experienced a blow to self-esteem when their love was rejected. "To love is to put one's self-esteem at risk" (Baumeister et al., 1993, p. 392). The rejectors of love felt guilt at spurning the other person yet also felt hounded by the other's overtures. Rejectors, more than would-be lovers, were negative about the whole unrequited love experience, wishing it had never happened. Rejectors focused on morality issues, typically saying that they didn't want to hurt the other person but also didn't want to lead him or her on. Not surprisingly, rejectors and offerers differed in their assessment of whether anyone had indeed been led on.

Although the context differed, no one escaped pain in the unrequited love experience. To give love or receive love without reciprocity is profoundly upsetting. As Baumeister et al. (1993) concluded, "It is perhaps the mutuality of love, rather than either the giving or the receiving, that makes it a pleasant, desirable, fulfilling experience" (p. 393).

If love is either unrequited or lost because of breakup or divorce, how does someone survive the loss and move beyond it? The next section deals with strategies for surviving the loss of love.

Recovering from Love

Love is typically considered something to be savored, rather than survived, but many times, survival and recovery are what are needed the most. Although it is never easy to get over a lost love, a variety of strategies can facilitate the process (S. S. Hendrick & C. Hendrick, 1992a).

First and foremost, it takes time to recover from a lost love. If humans have a need to bond, then losing that bond is a powerfully negative experience. No one should expect immediate recovery. People should remember principles of self-care during this time. Eating and sleeping well, exercising, and staying focused on school or work can all aid in recovery. Relying on a support system is also important. Friends and family can often be very helpful, from providing a sympathetic ear to suggesting activities that can get the recovering person back into a social life.

There are also some specific behavioral strategies—dos and don'ts—that an individual can use to speed recovery. The *don'ts* are fairly clear: Don't keep reminders of the partner (e.g., pictures and mementos) around. Don't call the ex-partner or drive by his or her house or apartment. Don't ask mutual friends about the ex. If a recovering person starts thinking about the ex, he or she should visualize a stop sign as a way to end that train of thought. If certain music is a reminder of the ex, then that music shouldn't be listened to. Finally, it is not wise to pretend the relationship never happened. Acknowledge the pain and move on.

The *dos* include those mentioned earlier—taking care of one's physical self, relying on a support system, and so on. In addition, it is useful for the person in recovery to try to be as successful as possible in school, work, or both. This time can be used for self-improvement ventures (e.g., diet, exercise). Volunteer work helps; nothing takes people out of themselves like helping someone else. This is a good time to take up a sport or hobby. It is important to remember the old saying that "Success is the best revenge." Finally, the recovering person should remember that the need to belong (Baumeister & Leary, 1995), which causes pain when someone loses a love relationship, will very likely draw that person into a new and hopefully more successful love relationship.

To the extent that humans do have an intrinsic need to belong—a hard-wired propensity for bondedness—then the development of intimacy should be nearly universal. Thus, women and men, homosexual persons and heterosexual persons, and persons of varying ethnic and racial backgrounds should all yearn for intimacy. That yearning may be expressed somewhat differently due to socialization and context differences, however.

Summary and Conclusions

No one is intended to be an island, an entirely self-sufficient woman or man. We are meant to be connected to one another in loving and intimate ways. We begin our experiences of bonding or attachment in infancy, based in large measure on the interactions we have with our primary caregiver, often our mother. These experiences influence whether we are secure, preoccupied, fearful, or dismissing in our attachment style. Subsequent experiences and relationships influence our attachment style, just as early experiences and relationships do.

Love may be thought of as a product of evolution, as something created by cultures and other social structures, or as something that allows persons to grow and expand themselves. There are many ways to enact love, including romantic love. Passionate and companionate love are two types of love once thought to be sequential in romantic relationships (passionate first; then companionate). More recently, the two have been seen as co-existing in a romantic relationship. The prototype of romantic love, or its best representation, can be considered or love can be understood in terms of the ways in which people communicate and experience it (e.g., verbally, nonverbally). Intimacy, passion, and commitment are three components that are central to love. The love styles approach offers six different ways of experiencing love.

Although love may be expressed somewhat differently in various cultures and in different historical periods, elements of love (such as passionate love) have been expressed virtually universally, across both cultures and historical eras. It is also true that different experiences of and styles of love cross age ranges and lengths of relationships. For example, both dating couples and long-married couples experience passionate, intense love as well as companionate, friendship-oriented love.

Intimacy can be viewed as a precursor of love, as overlapping with love, or as growing out of love, and in a sense, all three perspectives are true. Intimacy involves an emotional closeness, but it is also more. Intimate behaviors lead to intimate interactions/ experiences, which in turn lead to intimate relationships. So, intimacy is less a condition to be achieved than it is a process to be cultivated. Intimacy can be conceptualized and measured, and it should always be considered within a context (ranging from an individual context to a sociocultural one).

Attachment, love, and intimacy are all separate yet related phenomena that impact romantic relationships, and they are all important. To say that one is more important than the other is as inappropriate as saying that oceans are more important than mountains or that prairies are more important than marshlands. All these and many more relational constructs are important to the ecology of a healthy relationship.

Key Terms

Companionate love (p. 79)
Intimacy (p. 86)
Love (p. 75)
Love styles (p. 82)

Passionate love (p. 79)
Prototype (p. 80)
Romantic attachment (p. 76)

Suggested Reading

Feeney, J. A., & Noller, P. (1996). *Adult attachment.* Thousand Oaks, CA: Sage.
Hendrick, S. S., & Hendrick, C. (1992). *Romantic love.* Newbury Park, CA: Sage.
Latham, A. (1997). *The ballad of Gussie & Clyde: A true story of true love.* New York: Villard.
Pickett, K. (1995). *Love in the 90s: B. B. and Jo: The story of a lifelong love.* New York: Warner Books.
Prager, K. (1995). *The psychology of intimacy.* New York: Guilford Press.
Sternberg, R. J. (1998). *Love as a story.* New York: Oxford University Press.

5 | *Relational Sexuality*

Relationship Story

The Red Nightgown

Noah kissed her, turned on his side facing away from her, and almost immediately fell asleep. His breathing slowed and became quieter. Katherine laid there in the dark, smiling, before getting out of bed. She reached for her nightgown, casually tossed over a chair, and pulled it over her head, feeling its silky folds drop down to her feet. It was a new nightgown, cut low in the front to reveal her breasts and deep crimson in color. The nightgown was Katherine's early birthday present to herself, and although it was rather more expensive than the nightwear she typically purchased, it was *well* worth the investment. Red was Noah's favorite color, so when Katherine walked into the bedroom just as Noah was settling down to watch some late-night television, she definitely caught his attention. His eyes widened as he looked at her, and he abruptly clicked off the TV and set the remote aside. His arms were already reaching for her as she slipped into bed beside him, and he covered her with kisses before gently removing her new nightgown.

If one were to consider the cost of the nightgown in relation to the length of time it was actually worn that evening, then it was prohibitively expensive: a $50 nightgown worn for approximately two minutes. Nevertheless, it accomplished its mission. It took Katherine awhile to fall asleep because she kept thinking about their lovemaking earlier and how sweet yet passionate it had been. Sex had always been an important part of their relationship, even before they actually had sex. They had dated for many months and learned a great deal about each other before they had sex for the first time.

In fact, Katherine remembered the very first time she saw Noah. They were both guests at the wedding of some mutual friends and had been in the buffet line next to each other at the reception. When their hands collided while they were both reaching for some of the chilled jumbo shrimp, both were apologetic and courteous, offering to let the other person go first. They began talking as they continued walking down the buffet line, learning that each was involved in the computer industry, that both had grown up in the Southwest, and that they both always headed for the shrimp bowl first when they went to a party. Noah asked Katherine if he could join her to eat as they headed toward a nearly empty round table near the edge of the dance floor. He retrieved glasses of champagne for both of them, while Katherine got two pieces of wedding cake. As they made small talk and tried to get to know one another, a band began playing and the bride and groom had the first slow dance. Soon the wedding couple was followed by other couples, and the dance floor was filled with couples of all ages—young friends of the bride and groom, older married couples, children playing at being grown up, and eventually Katherine and Noah. They eased out on to the dance floor, and as she felt his arm firmly on her back and placed her hand lightly on his shoulder, she gave a deep relaxed sigh. She felt so comfortable, almost as though she were coming home.

In spite of that feeling of comfort, Katherine was in no rush to begin a relationship with Noah. She had recently broken up with a boyfriend after two years of serious dating and even talk about marriage, so she wasn't interested in having her heart broken again. But Noah asked her out for a movie, and she agreed to go. At first, they continued to go out about once a week, and although they enjoyed each other's company, they continued casually dating other people now and then. The more time they spent together, however, the better they liked each other. Noah was funny, always seeing the humor in things, whereas Katherine's ironic humor was a little more subtle.

And then there was the physical attraction. Katherine and Noah had a sexual spark between them—they said it probably started when their hands collided over the shrimp bowl! When they walked down the street, he always put his arm around her or held her hand. When they kissed, it was long and deep and eager. They were hungry to touch each other, and they liked just being near one another. When Katherine walked into the room, Noah felt a slight rush; she always looked beautiful to him. And Katherine felt the same way about Noah. When they went somewhere together, she always told him he was the most attractive man in the room. So why, then, did Katherine and Noah date each other for several months before actually having sex—or as they preferred to call it, making love?

They talked about it, of course, and came close on several occasions, but they had agreed that their relationship was very special, and they didn't want to spoil things by "doing it." Both of them had been in relationships before and had found sex to be a complicating factor that sometimes actually got in the way of the development of the rest of the relationship. Sex was like a lens that could color the relationship positively or negatively, no matter what else was going on.

So they waited. And then, one autumn Saturday afternoon, several months after that June wedding reception where they had met in the buffet line, Noah and Katherine took a long walk in a local park, looking at the fall leaves of gold and red and orange. They could feel the slight nip of cold in the air, and they knew that winter would be on its way before too long. They went back to Katherine's apartment to warm up, and before long, their attraction for each other simply couldn't be restrained any longer. There, on Katherine's couch, they made love for the first time. It was exciting and awkward and intense and imperfect, but all in all, it was wonderful. They were *so* ready to be fully sexual with each other. But they were glad that they had waited to begin having intercourse because it made sex much more special to both of them. Besides, sex was a lot more than just intercourse to them. Those months of passionate kissing, hand holding, and eager fondling had reminded them both of how much they could enjoy each other sexually without just limiting it to intercourse.

Their first lovemaking experience on that autumn afternoon deepened but did not fundamentally change their relationship. For one thing, they didn't have sex all that often. Both Katherine and Noah had demanding jobs, their own apartments, and part-time school, so although they could and did show their affection for each other in many small ways every day—e-mails, phone calls, funny cards, quick but romantic lunches during the week at an out-of-the-way downtown café—intercourse itself probably didn't happen more than a couple of times a week. That didn't seem to be a problem for either of them, however. Noah and Katherine both understood that quality, rather than quantity, made their sexual relationship exciting and very, very special.

They talked about the future but didn't make specific plans until one evening when Noah looked at Katherine across the little table in his apartment. They had just finished eating a delicious dinner that both of them had worked together to prepare, as they so often did. Noah usually cooked the meat while Katherine put together a huge salad full of as many tasty and colorful vegetables as she could find. Typically, they would be squeezed together in Noah's tiny kitchen, but working literally side by side was part of the pleasure of cooking. Then they would pour two glasses of wine and sit down to enjoy the meal that they had prepared together. From the very beginning, they had done this kind of sharing in the work of "doing their relationship." Katherine sat back with a sigh of contentment and lifted her glass of wine to her lips. All of a sudden, Noah looked at Katherine and said, "I want to do this all the time. I want us to get married. Katherine, will you marry me?" "Yes, Noah," she said, blushing, crying, and laughing at the same time. "Yes, I will marry you."

And marry each other they did, in a church wedding witnessed by family and friends and co-workers, followed by a wedding reception that featured an elegant three-tiered wedding cake and a *huge* bowl of chilled shrimp!

Katherine and Noah moved into a new apartment and began to develop new friends as a couple, adding to the social network of friends and family that each had separately. Their sexual relationship got better and better, and since they were together more of the time, love-making also became more frequent. Although they learned more and more about pleasing each other sexually, specific sexual behaviors didn't seem as important as their increasing comfort and security with each other and their ability to communicate with each other—about sex as well as about other aspects of their relationship.

Heading into their second year of marriage, both Noah and Katherine started talking babies. They didn't tell anyone else that they were thinking of starting a family because they didn't want the pressure or the scrutiny of people wondering (or asking) if they "had any news yet." Before too long, they did have news. They were expecting a baby, and they were very excited. Katherine had some morning sickness, but for the most part, she felt well. She and Noah proceeded through the pregnancy together. Their sexual relationship didn't change, except perhaps to become a little more intense. They stopped having intercourse toward the end of Katherine's pregnancy, but they continued to kiss and touch as much as ever.

When baby Nicholas finally arrived, two tired but very happy parents greeted him, along with assorted grandparents, aunts and uncles, and friends. Having a new baby was exciting and exhausting from the get-go. Both Katherine and Noah used up all their parental leave trying to give Nicholas the best possible start in life. By the time they both finally had to go back to work, they had child care arrangements for Nicholas that made them feel very secure. The baby was happy and healthy, and they enjoyed him more and more each day. The only problem—and it wasn't a huge problem—was how much work it required to take care of a baby. Between their jobs during the day and caring for Nicholas in the evening and on weekends (not to mention the sleep deprivation that is inevitably part of the job description of new parents), both Noah and Katherine basically felt tired all of the time. They were happy, but they were tired.

And one of the major byproducts of this constant fatigue was a sharp reduction in (if not cessation of) their sex life. There was no question that they loved each other more than ever and that they were still extremely sexually attracted to each other. Their sexual desire was stronger than ever. However, desire wasn't enough when they collapsed into bed at night exhausted and fell asleep almost as soon as their heads hit the pillow. Sleep was their first priority, and sex—even great sex—came somewhat lower down on the list. Noah and Katherine didn't take the temporary decrease in their sex life too seriously, but both were aware of it and frequently commented to each other that they *wanted* to make love, they "just didn't have the energy tonight."

That was how it happened that one Saturday afternoon Katherine was shopping at the local mall, looking for a nightgown. Actually, she wasn't really looking for one. Noah thought she needed a little time for herself, so as an early birthday present, he said that he would take care of Nicholas for a few hours while Katherine went out shopping for something special for herself. When she drove into the mall, her intention was to buy a couple of little things for Nicholas and then go home. But without consciously intending to, she wandered into an upscale shop that featured women's lingerie. She looked casually at various displays, and then she saw several nightgowns hanging against a wall. And among those silky, lacy, pastel-colored garments, one nightgown immediately caught her eye. It was a deep crimson color, cut low in the front, and with lots of lace. It was elegant and feminine and oh, so sensual. She looked at the price on the gown and realized it wasn't exactly in her budget. But she finally decided to buy it. After all, it really wasn't so much an extravagance as it was an investment. That's what it was—an investment in her relationship with Noah.

So Katherine purchased the nightgown, but when she got home and showed Noah what she had bought, she only showed him the things she had gotten for Nicholas. She wanted the nightgown to be a surprise. Later that evening, after she and Noah had put Nicholas to bed and straightened things up a bit, they decided to go to bed a little early. That was when Noah first learned about the red nightgown. It was indeed a very beautiful nightgown. And it was indeed a very good investment!

■ ■ ■

Questions to Consider in Reading This Chapter

- Do you consider Katherine's red nightgown an extravagant purchase or an investment?
- What are some ways that Katherine and Noah could have revitalized/renewed/reenergized their sexual relationship?
- How do you feel about the idea of waiting awhile in a relationship before having sex?
- Should intercourse wait until marriage?
- What are some ways of being passionate and sexual with a partner that do not include intercourse?

What Do We Know about Relational Sexuality?

If human beings have a need to belong in a relationship (Baumeister & Leary, 1995), then one major way of both seeking and expressing such belongingness is through physical contact. Touching the people we care about and being touched by them are ways of connecting with them as well as means of showing affection. *Touching* may mean hugging and holding hands in a parent/child relationship, squeezing someone's shoulder or patting his or her back in a friendship, or kissing, intimate touching, and sexual intimacy (often leading to orgasm) in a partnered romantic relationship.

This chapter will consider the touching that occurs in a sexual context, most often in a partnered relationship. **Sex** is typically dyadic (exclusive of masturbation and group sex), and Laumann and his colleagues note that "sexual behavior is fundamentally structured by social factors" (Laumann, Gagnon, Michael, & Michaels, 1994, p. 78). When we think of sex in a romantic relationship, we frequently are referring to sexual intercourse in heterosexual couples. And much of this chapter will discuss research on the behaviors, attitudes, and so on that characterize heterosexual sexuality (often intercourse) and often in married couples. Thus, this chapter will consider the couple in the Relationship Story in light of a range of theory and research. We must always remind ourselves, however, that such a perspective is necessarily limited and touches on only part of the wider sexual experience that is an aspect of being human.

The chapter will begin by discussing briefly the topic of sexual behavior—what we actually do—and then explore some of the attitudes, values, and other motivating forces that appear to cause us to do what we do, including sexual attitudes and sexual attractiveness.

Sexual Behavior

One important area of sexual scholarship is *premarital sexuality,* or the issues involved with deciding whether or when to become sexual. Research indicates that some young adults remain virgins, although most eventually become sexually active (Christopher & Sprecher, 2000). These decisions are made based on values, attitudes, desires, and a host of influences, ranging from peers to parents. Indeed, "social forces are powerful and persistent in determining sexual behavior" (Michael, Gagnon, Laumann, & Kolata, 2001). Women, more than men, pair sex with emotional involvement and relational commitment (Christopher & Sprecher, 2000; Michael et al., 2001), so women and men may have very different agendas when engaging in premarital sex. Premarital sexuality is an extremely significant topic and is addressed more fully in many books and articles (e.g., Christopher, 2001; Christopher & Sprecher, 2000).

An important issue for people in close relationships, and for the researchers who work with them, is the frequency of certain sexual behaviors. A variety of studies have been conducted over the past six decades to determine the frequency with which couples in ongoing relationships have sex, including intercourse, oral sex, and anal sex. The most predominant of these behaviors is heterosexual intercourse (Laumann et al., 1994).

Interestingly, although **sexual frequency** increased somewhat (from about 2.5 times per week in the earliest research to a little over 3 times per week in later research) (Sprecher & McKinney, 1993), the phenomenal impact of this increase on the average couple is likely unremarkable. Sprecher and Regan (2000) found that "young married couples have sexual intercourse two or three times a week on average" (p. 221). More important, however, such couples can expect sexual frequency to decline during their relationship, due both to the ages of the partners and to the length of the relationship. This occurs more rapidly in the beginning and more slowly as time goes on, but over the course of the relationship, this is not a drastic change for most couples. Situational factors—such as pregnancy and resulting parenting, work demands, illness, and so on—can also cause a decline in *sexual frequency*. Call, Sprecher, and Schwartz (1995) found that the two factors impacting the sexual frequency of married couples most negatively were increasing age (and all that goes with it, such as illness) and marital dissatisfaction.

Great variability among couples in sexual frequency rates was reported by Greenblat (1983), who also noted that the rate of intercourse during the first year of marriage was the single best predictor of rates in later years. Cohabitation has been described as a "sexy living arrangement," since cohabiting couples have sex more frequently than married couples. Gay male couples have sex relatively more frequently, whereas lesbian couples may have more physical contact but less actual sex than some other couple types (Blumstein & Schwartz, 1983).

In fact, according to Laumann and his colleagues (1994), U.S. couples do *not* have sex a great deal more than they used to or as much as the media says they do (or should). "American adults fall roughly into three levels of activity in partnered sex. About 35% of the total have sex with a partner at least two or more times a week, and nearly 30% have partnered sex once or several times a month" (p. 89). Call et al. (1995) analyzed responses from an extremely large sample of single, cohabiting, and married adults that span a wide age range. Using just the data from married persons, they found that "the average number of times a married couple had sex was 11.7 times a month at ages 19 to 24, 8.5 times a month at ages 30 to 34, 5.5 times a month at ages 50 to 54, 2.4 times a month at ages 65 to 69, and 0.8 times a month at age 75 or older" (p. 646).

The majority of couples are heterosexual, and most sexual encounters for these couples involve vaginal intercourse. Oral sex has become more common, but vaginal intercourse is by far most common. Interestingly, masturbation remains the most widely practiced sexual activity that is still very stigmatized (Laumann et al., 1994).

Although the frequency of sexual interaction is what often makes the pages of popular magazines or the evening news, it may be less important to the people actually having those interactions than are the attitudes toward, feelings about, and satisfaction with those interactions. For both women and men, being in a relationship that is enduring and sexually exclusive is related to greater emotional satisfaction with sex in the relationship (Waite & Joyner, 2001). Men and women appear to experience sexuality somewhat differently, with women integrating their sexual selves in more complex ways than men (Christopher, 2001; Cyranowski & Anderson, 1998). Yet both women and men value sex in the context of connection.

Sexual Attitudes

The most potent sexual organ is reputed to be the brain because what we think and feel about sexuality—that is, our **sexual attitudes**—determines much of what sexuality will ultimately come to mean to our lives. Attitudes and values about sex can be examined in a number of different ways and with a number of different approaches. For example, attitudes toward sexual permissiveness have become more positive over time, whereas attitudes toward homosexuality and toward infidelity have changed less and remained more negative (T. W. Smith, 1994; Sprecher & McKinney, 1993).

Orientations to Sex

An approach toward understanding people's sexual frameworks or schemas or scripts that has been proposed (e.g., DeLamater, 1989) consists of three orientations to sex: procreational, recreational, and relational. The *procreational orientation* views the purpose of sex as reproduction. Not just a simple "continuation of the species" viewpoint, this perspective views having children and building a family unit as the outcomes for which sex is meant. Sex is a means to something else. The *recreational orientation,* in contrast, views sex as good fun, a pleasant experience, and altogether fine when it occurs between two consenting adults in a positive context. In this light, sex is an end in itself. The third perspective, the *relational orientation,* views sex as a meaningful experience for relationship partners, a way of expressing affection and experiencing closeness, and something that can bind partners more securely (and with greater fulfillment) in their life together. Sex is thus both a means and an end within the relational orientation. Noah and Katherine are prototypical of the relational perspective, since they are very passionate and sexual with each other, enjoying sexual relating for its own sake yet also viewing the creation of a family as a significant life value.

Michael et al. (2001) used similar categories when dividing research respondents into three broad groups based on their responses about a variety of attitudes and values. The categories—*traditional, relational,* and *recreational*—represent differing attitudes toward such issues as premarital sex, homosexuality, and the like. For example, people classified in the traditional group expressed the belief that based on their religious values, premarital sex is wrong.

Although it appears that young people today are having sex earlier and sometimes with more partners, their attitudinal orientation does not seem particularly recreational. Many teens still are searching for connection, and thus their attitude is relational. But the experience of early sex is often problematic. "Two thirds of teens are sexually active by the end of high school. More than one third say that they regret it" (Mulrine, 2002, pp. 48–49).

The procreational/traditional, recreational, and relational orientations are not necessarily good or bad; they are merely ways of framing people's attitudes and values about sex and the role of sex in human experience. A person's framework for sexuality has implications both for what he or she does sexually and how he or she thinks and feels about it. One's framework also has implications for whom he or she will seek as a sexual partner.

There has been considerable research on sexual attitudes, and a number of attitudes measures have been developed. One such measure, the Sexual Attitudes Scale (S. S. Hendrick & C. Hendrick, 1987), was developed based on existing theory and research and contains 43 items that encompass four subscales. The subscales, their content, and the number of items in each are as follow: Permissiveness (casual sexuality; 21 items), Sexual Practices (responsible, tolerant sexuality; 7 items), Communion (idealistic sexuality; 9 items), and Instrumentality (biological sexuality; 6 items). A modified form of this scale is shown in the Up Close box on page 102. Answer the questions in this scale and see how you believe your answers might fit into the relational, recreational, and procreational attitudinal orientations proposed by DeLamater (1989).

Influences on Sexual Attitudes and Behaviors

Although sexual attitudes are typically thought to influence sexual behaviors, the reverse is also true: Behaviors influence attitudes. And both behaviors and attitudes are influenced by many other factors, including personality characteristics of the people involved, aspects of their relationship, and social environmental influences (family, friends, other peers, etc.) (Christopher & Roosa, 1991). Broad sociocultural and religious values also affect sexual attitudes and behaviors, with religion, level of education, ethnic and racial background, and even location all exerting influences on people (Laumann et al., 1994). In other words, the development of sexual attitudes and a more general sexual orientation is a complex process.

Sexual Attraction

Sexual attraction and *sexual desirability* are very individual (i.e., "Different strokes for different folks"), but there are also some nearly universal features. For example, as discussed in Chapter 2, Buss and Barnes (1986) found that both women and men evaluated "kindness and understanding," "exciting personality," and "intelligence" as the top qualities in a potential marriage partner. These authors, as well as others, also found a partner's physical attractiveness to be more important to men than to women whereas a partner's economic prospects and earning potential were more important to women than to men.

These findings on physical attractiveness and earning potential have been awarded a great deal of attention. Yet the findings of gender *similarity* on the most important qualities (kindness, understanding, personality, intelligence) have often been overlooked or at least downplayed. Interestingly, Winstead and her colleagues (Winstead, Derlega, & Rose, 1997) surveyed an array of research and concluded that people's actual choices of romantic partners don't always coincide with the qualities people say are important

Another aspect of sexual attractiveness is an individual's sexual experience level. Previously, it was considered quite important for a woman to be a virgin when she married (even though this was more ideal than real for a substantial percentage of women). According to Sprecher and McKinney (1993), much research indicates that persons prefer a moderate amount of sexual experience in a relational partner, although men may

Abbreviated Form of the Sexual Attitudes Scale

Using the scale below, please rate each statement according to how well it describes your current romantic relationship. Then go back and add up your scores in each of the four parts so that you get a total score for each sexual attitude. Look at your scores to see which is highest and lowest. (Note that a score of 15 is the highest possible and a score of 3 is the lowest possible.) Do your scores reflect a procreational, relational, or recreational sexual orientation or some combination of orientations?

1 = Strongly disagree   2 = Moderately disagree   3 = Neutral
4 = Moderately agree   5 = Strongly agree

Permissiveness

1. _____ I do not need to be committed to a person to have sex with him/her.
2. _____ Casual sex is acceptable.
3. _____ One-night stands are sometimes very enjoyable.

_____ = Total

Sexual Practices

4. _____ Birth control is part of responsible sexuality.
5. _____ Sex education is important for young people.
6. _____ Masturbation is all right.

_____ = Total

Communion

7. _____ Sex gets better as a relationship progresses.
8. _____ Sex is the closest form of communication between two people.
9. _____ A sexual encounter between two people deeply in love is the ultimate human interaction.

_____ = Total

Instrumentality

10. _____ Sex is best when you let yourself go and focus on your own pleasure.
11. _____ Sex is primarily the taking of pleasure from another person.
12. _____ The main purpose of sex is to enjoy oneself.

_____ = Total

prefer more rather than less experience in a short-term partner as opposed to a longer-term partner. Moderation in sexual experience as well as indications of nonrecreational sexual attitudes and experience (e.g., Bettor, Hendrick, & Hendrick, 1995) may make a potential partner attractive to both men and women.

When a person finds someone attractive and the two begin a romantic relationship, decisions about whether or when to have sex become important. Some people appear just to have sex with no actual decision making involved, but sexual behavior reflects a decision, whether or not the decision is acknowledged as such. Behavior reflects decision.

Sexuality is less likely to occur in the beginning stages of relationship development than it is during the later stages of development. "Many couples wait for a particular stage of relationship development to begin to have sex" (Sprecher & Regan, 2000, p. 220). Interestingly, research does not show consistent links between the timing of the first sexual experience (early versus later in relationship development) and relationship outcomes such as continuation or termination of the relationship. Although waiting to have sex was an important part of relationship development for Noah and Katherine, it is not similarly important for all couples. Certainly, for some couples, sex waits until marriage.

The nature of partners' ongoing interactions is likely much more important than when the first sexual interaction occurred. Sexual satisfaction and sexual communication are central aspects of those ongoing interactions.

Sexual Satisfaction

According to Sprecher and Regan (2000), "Most couples report that they are satisfied with the sexual aspects of their relationships" (p. 221). Some number of specific sexual behaviors are related to greater satisfaction, including more frequent sex, consistency of orgasms, sexual sharing, and so on. Waite and Joyner (2001) found that for heterosexual couples, the more frequently the woman partner had orgasms during sex, the more emotionally satisfied both partners were. Relational factors such as communication and intimacy are also extremely important to sexual satisfaction and, in turn, to overall relationship satisfaction (Sprecher & Regan, 2000).

For example, Lawrance and Byers (1995) assessed persons' **sexual satisfaction** using a number of measures, including a checklist of 46 items that reflected a variety of sexual rewards and costs experienced in their sexual relationship with their partner (e.g., sexual spontaneity, affection expressed while being sexual). Respondents indicated for each item whether it was a reward, a cost, both a reward and a cost, or none of these. The results of this research were interesting on a number of dimensions. First, sexual satisfaction was related positively to rewards exceeding costs. In other words, to the degree that persons experienced more sexual positives than sexual negatives in their relationship, they were more satisfied sexually. Overall relationship satisfaction was also (not surprisingly) related to sexual satisfaction. Women and men reported similar *levels* of rewards and costs, even though the rewards and costs were somewhat different. And while both women and men rated feeling comfortable with one's partner at the top of the rewards list (number 1 for men and number 2 for women), by and large, "women were more likely than men to report rewards reflecting emotional, relational qualities of the sexual relationship" (p. 282). Clearly, sex is about much more than frequency and technique.

Consistent with this research, Byers and her colleagues (Byers, Demmons, & Lawrance, 1998) found that relationship satisfaction was an important predictor for dating couples' sexual satisfaction, even more important than for married couples in the earlier research study just discussed. The authors' conclusion was that a global appraisal of satisfaction was more important to sexual satisfaction in relatively new relationships, whereas specific aspects of the sexual relationship (e.g., differences between perceived benefits and costs of sexuality, perceived equality of costs for both partners in the relationship) were more important for married persons in longer-term relationships.

Sexual satisfaction is linked not only to relational satisfaction but also to actual relational outcome. For example, Sprecher (2000) found that greater sexual satisfaction led to a lower rate of breakup for couples (under some conditions), although she hypothesized that relational quality may have a stronger influence on sexual satisfaction than sexual satisfaction may have on relational quality.

Satisfaction with sexuality is sometimes thought to be a function of sexual excitement or novelty, and those aspects of sexuality can certainly be important. But sexual stability and predictability can also be related to satisfaction. For example, Lawrance and Byers (1995) found that having sex several times with the same partner was related to sexual satisfaction for women. And Laumann and his colleagues (Laumann et al., 1994) determined that those respondents who described themselves as the most physically and emotionally satisfied in their intimate relationship were also those persons who were in monogamous, partnered relationships. These people also reported themselves to be the happiest of all respondents. Married persons were the most satisfied physically and emotionally, followed by cohabitors and those in long-term relationships without cohabitation. The authors noted that "having one sex partner is more rewarding in terms of physical pleasure and emotional satisfaction than having more than one partner" (p. 364) and that "a widespread myth about sociosexual activity is that it becomes routinized, dull, and progressively less frequent in the context of marriage" (p. 92). (But see Liu [2000] for a different perspective.)

Sexual Communication

One possible reason that sex continues to be satisfying in ongoing relationships is that long-term partners feel secure with each other, both emotionally and physically, and learn to communicate about sexuality in their relationship. It is common knowledge that many people find sex quite difficult to talk about; nevertheless, partners learn to communicate about sex over time. For example, offering subtle nonverbal cues of kissing or hugging may not be as direct as walking naked into the room where one's partner is watching TV, but it may be just as effective in communicating one's interest in lovemaking and sex. Katherine's red nightgown proved to be a powerful communication to Noah!

In the same way that initiating sex is important, refusing sex is equally or more important. "A rejection (of a sexual interaction) in a well-established relationship is likely to be direct and accompanied by an account that reduces conflict and protects the partner's feelings" (Sprecher & Regan, 2000, p. 222). Because sexuality tends to be a sensitive area for most couples, tactfulness and sensitivity are important in both initiating and refusing sexual interaction. It was important for Katherine and Noah to reassure each other that they wanted to make love after the baby was born; they were simply too tired. They didn't so much refuse lovemaking as postpone it until the time was right.

General Communication

Good general communication in a relationship, as well as good sexual communication, contributes to relationship quality (Cupach & Comstock, 1990), and self-disclosure has been related to sexual satisfaction (Byers et al., 1998). Cupach and Metts (1995) explored the complex interrelationships between partners' similarities in sexual attitudes, sexual satisfaction, relational satisfaction, commitment, and satisfaction with sexual communication. These authors found that "sexual communication satisfaction appears to mediate the influence of (sexual) attitude similarity on sexual satisfaction for both partners and on relational satisfaction for men" (p. 298).

Thus, communication—both general and sexual—and partners' satisfaction with that communication are essential factors in sexual satisfaction and in overall relational satisfaction. So, communication influences satisfaction, which in turn influences communication. All these aspects of close relationships are intricately intertwined.

Chapter 4 considered love, and this chapter has thus far been concerned with sexuality. The convergence between love and sex is important, also.

Sexual Desire

One of the ties between sex and love is **sexual desire.** Recent writings about sexual desire (e.g., Regan & Berscheid, 1999) have highlighted its importance to our sexual choices. Desire occurs at many levels and is influenced by many factors—hormonal, emotional, relational—and it in turn influences how we behave. Sexual desire is a part of wanting, yearning for another. It is also clearly related to love.

Berscheid and Myers (1996) asked undergraduate women and men to list (by initials) three groups of people: those they loved, those they were in love with, and those they felt sexually attracted to/desirous of. Most of those listed in the "in love with" group (some 85%) were also listed in the "sexually desirous of" group. This was not the case for people listed only in the "love" group, which could include family and friends. Rather, being in love with someone was related to sexually desiring him or her. And Regan and Berscheid (1995) found that physical attractiveness was the most important quality in increasing sexual desire for a partner.

The kind of love most typically linked with sexual desire is passionate love, described in an earlier chapter. This type of love is intensely emotional, involves physiological arousal, and in many ways fits the popular stereotype of being in love. Hatfield and Rapson (1996) have commented on the sometimes "roller coaster" emotional quality of passionate love, which can cause a person to rise to ecstatic heights one day and sink to the depths of despair the next. A contrasting perspective on passionate love is offered by S. S. Hendrick and C. Hendrick (2000) in their description of Eros, one of the sub-scales of the Love Attitudes Scale. Eros is intense, to be sure, but it is uniformly positive, focusing on physical attractiveness, sexual attraction, being "in sync," and so on.

Other researchers (Regan, Kocan, & Whitlock, 1998) have also suggested "that passionate love is more strongly associated with positive emotions than with negative emotions" (Sprecher & Regan, 2000, p. 224). Couples can expect sexual desire to ebb and flow during the life of their relationship, much as other aspects of sexuality ebb and flow (Metts, Sprecher, & Regan, 1998; Sprecher & Regan, 2000). The links between sexual desire and passionate love are particularly noteworthy because sex, desire, passion, and love have seldom been considered together by scholars who study sex and love.

Linking Sex and Love

Philosophers and social scientists have questioned several aspects of love and sex, including whether they are related to each other and which of the two is most important. Some scholars propose that romantic love is really about sex, or at least sexual desire (e.g., Berscheid, 1988). Still others view love as predominant and sex as secondary. The philosopher Vannoy (1980) envisions love and sex as separate, with sex as certainly equal to and perhaps even superior to love. Yet he sees the two as somewhat unrelated. Hatfield and Rapson (1996), on the other hand, view sex and love as largely overlapping, at least insofar as sex is manifested in sexual desire and love is manifested in passionate love. Hatfield and Rapson's position would be the one that Katherine and Noah would be most comfortable with; they definitely don't see sex and love as separate events for themselves.

This puzzle about whether or how love and sex are linked prompted S. S. Hendrick and C. Hendrick (2002) to pursue research questions linking sex and love. First, they asked undergraduate college students (some of whom were older, nontraditional students) about how love and sex were linked in the respondents' romantic relationships. The authors defined *sex* broadly as "any type of physical affection." About 70 responses to this question were obtained and carefully read. What was very apparent was that these respondents had no doubts about whether love and sex were linked for them—they were! In fact, virtually no one viewed the two as unrelated; the question was simply *how* they were related. These responses were distilled into *themes,* which were then converted into item format.

These items comprised part of a much longer measure of relationship attributes, including love attitudes, sexual attitudes, relationship satisfaction, and a number of other measures. Hundreds of men and women (college students) answered this questionnaire, and after some complex analyses of the information, it seemed that 17 of the original items could be grouped into four *sets* of items, each capturing a different aspect of how people view love and sex in their own romantic relationship. These four groupings, or item sets, included the ideas that (a) love is the most important thing (e.g., more important than sex); (b) sex demonstrates (is a way of showing) love; (c) love comes before sex (e.g., people should have a love relationship before they have a sexual one); and (d) the idea that sex can decline in a relationship.

Extensive research with this measure linking sex and love seemed to show two overarching themes or messages. The first message was that love is more important than sex, although sexuality is itself extremely important. Sexuality is a significant part of the fabric of an ongoing, partnered relationship, but it is love that drives sexuality in people's perceptions, not the reverse. Noah and Katherine would agree wholeheartedly. Toward the end of Katherine's pregnancy and during the first weeks and months after Nicholas's birth, what anchored them and kept them tender with each other was *not* their sexual relationship. Actual intercourse was not even happening. So, love was the binding force that kept their marriage strong. Love, rather than sex, seems to be the dominant theme in relationships, and this emphasis on love is related to both satisfaction and commitment.

The second major theme that emerged from the research is in interesting counterpoint to the first one, however. Namely, the second theme says essentially that while love is the most important entity and that sex is a way of showing love, sex may become more important than love *if it is declining*. That concept of sex declining in a relationship is related to lower satisfaction, lower commitment, and a number of other relationship negatives.

Sex and Gender

Gender Differences in Sexuality

Although there are many similarities between women and men in the area of sexuality, there are also a number of differences. "Men are more inclined than women to interpret social behavior in a sexual way . . . (and) may wear sex-colored glasses" (Cupach & Metts, 1991, p. 99). Men are more likely to agree with an attitude of sexual permissiveness (S. S. Hendrick & C. Hendrick, 1987) and to sexualize a person or a situation (Cupach & Metts, 1991). "The available evidence strongly supports the proposition that males view females in more sexual terms than females view males" (Shotland, 1989, p. 253).

Evolutionary psychology theorists, such as Buss (1999), find such gender differences predictable based on the evolutionary perspective that men maximize their reproductive success by mating with more women and mating more frequently. Women, in contrast, maximize their reproductive success by being more discriminating in their sexual choices, since they must invest so much in any single offspring. Findings such as men's expressed desire for more sexual partners and greater willingness to have sex after knowing a partner only a short time (Buss & Schmitt, 1993) are consistent with evolutionary theorizing.

One area of concern that intersects with sex and gender is the issue of date rape, discussed briefly in the next section. Date rape is approached from the perspective of women as victims and men as perpetrators because that is the most common pattern.

Date Rape

Acquaintance rape involves sexual assault of a victim by someone she knows: a family member, friend, co-worker, or the like. *Date rape* is a subtype of acquaintance rape and involves assault by a romantic partner. As discussed in the previous section, men are more likely than women to see situations as sexual (Abbey, 1982). So, women may behave in ways that they do not consider extremely sexual but that may be perceived as sexual by their male partner or by others. For example, a woman may ask a man out or go to his apartment, and under such conditions, date rape would be judged by respondents as more justifiable than under other conditions (Muehlenhard, Friedman, & Thomas, 1985). In fact, women who initiate dating activities may actually be perceived as more willing to have sex (Muehlenhard, 1988). Thus, sexual miscommunication certainly occurs.

However, sexual communication is only one factor in a complex process involving the sexual violation of one person by another (Wiehe & Richards, 1995). There may be many reasons for date rape, but there are no excuses for it. Date rape has traumatic consequences for many of its victims and some of its perpetrators, and a preventive orientation toward date rape is important. One way to avoid being involved in date rape, as either a victim or a perpetrator, is to learn more about it, especially the myths surrounding it. Some of these myths are shown in the Up Close box that follows.

Sex for All Couples

It would be impossible to consider *all* sexual relational issues for *all* types of couples in this chapter. Even so, the point must be made that young, attractive, European American, heterosexual couples are not the *only* kind of couples or even the majority of the couples who are sexual. Sexuality, along with the relationships of which it is a part, is a cross-cultural imperative. Sexuality is also an important part of both the initial attraction process and the relationship maintenance process for lesbian and gay couples, just as it is for heterosexual couples.

Gay and Lesbian Couples

Sexuality is an important relationship element for most partners, and although heterosexual intercourse is what people typically think about when they hear the word *sex*, there is more to lovemaking than intercourse (e.g., Peplau & Spaulding, 2000).

Research has been mixed concerning sexual frequency for gay and lesbian couples. This may be due to a number of methodological issues, including the fact that the stereotype of sex as intercourse may influence gay and lesbian responses to questions about sexual frequency. But it is safe to say that there are not drastic differences in lovemaking frequency between different types of couples, based on sexual orientation. In addition, "preconceptions based on heterosexual models of sexuality might lead researchers to ignore important erotic components of same-sex relationships" (Peplau & Spaulding,

Up Close

Myths about Date Rape

- Date rape is the victim's fault.
- She asked for it.
- Women "want it."
- When women say "no," they really mean "yes."
- Women who dress in sexy clothes want sex.
- Women who tease deserve what they get.
- A woman can refuse sex if she really wants to.
- A real man is sexually forceful.
- A man needs to show who's in control in the bedroom.
- If a man gets sexually aroused, he needs to have sex.
- It's okay to force sex unless the woman is a virgin.
- A little rough play makes the sex more exciting.
- If a man spends a lot of money on a woman, he has a right to expect sex.
- It's not a big deal—it's only sex.

Source: Some of these myths have been adapted from Wiehe and Richards (1995).

2000, p. 118). In fact, sex in a relational context is similar across lesbian, gay, and heterosexual relationships, with sexual satisfaction similar for all the groups of couples (Christopher & Sprecher, 2000).

The one area in which couples may differ is in their acceptance of nonmonogamy. Gay male couples, more than lesbian and heterosexual couples, engage in nonmonogamous behaviors and report nonmonogamy to be unrelated both to relationship satisfaction and to commitment to the relationship (Christopher & Sprecher, 2000; Peplau & Spaulding, 2000).

Multicultural Couples

Multiracial and multicultural romantic relationships have all the complexities of other romantic relationships and more. Partners in multicultural relationships need to deal with social stereotypes that other people hold about their relationships as well as their own internalized stereotypes. Some of these stereotypes revolve around sexuality, often black/white sexuality, cast in the light of *miscegenation,* or racially mixed relationships. Mixed relationships consisting of Asian women and European American men receive kinder treatment from the media than do other racial pairings (Gaines & Liu, 2000).

In an extensive review, McLoyd and her colleagues (McLoyd, Cauce, Takeuchi, & Wilson, 2000) noted many similarities (e.g., in major predictors of marital quality and marital conflict) between couples from different ethnic and racial groups. Consistent with that perspective, Contreras et al. (1996) found only modest differences between European American and Mexican American married couples in sexual attitudes. The biggest differences were in attitudes toward birth control. Although both groups of couples were positive toward birth control, the European American couples were significantly more positive than were the Mexican American couples. Yet overall, the similarities were more prevalent than the differences between groups.

Couples as They Age

Sexuality is important for couples irrespective of sexual orientation and race/ethnicity. So, also, is the physical aspect of a relationship important for older couples. The end of reproduction doesn't mean the end of sexuality, and although sexuality in later life is not a new phenomenon, it is now more visible than it once was. Most older persons enjoy being sexual if they are at least reasonably healthy and if they have an appropriate partner with whom to share that sexuality (Levy, 1994).

As noted earlier in this chapter, sexual frequency declines across the length of a relationship, but the steepest decline occurs early in the relationship. A 1992 report by the University of Chicago's National Opinion Research Center examined survey data from over 5,000 respondents and found that among married couples age 60 and older, 37% had sex at least once a week (Mathias-Riegel, 1999, pp. 47–48). Other research has proposed that sexual activity among the elderly may be overestimated, however (Call et al., 1995). Nevertheless, it is important to widen our concept about sexuality beyond stereotypes to include those who are no longer young but who are actively (and sometimes joyously) sexual.

People with Disabilities and Illnesses

Another group who may not fit sexual stereotypes is comprised of those who are disabled or seriously ill. Yet again, one's sexuality does not disappear just because he or she deviates from the prevailing stereotype.

In fact, disease *can* interfere with sexuality. For instance, someone taking chemotherapy for cancer may have reduced sexual desire, and men who are diabetic may have erectile difficulties. Moreover, certain physical disabilities, such as spinal cord injuries, may require massive adjustments in sexual practices. Yet other ongoing disabilities, such as hearing difficulties and vision problems, may involve fewer adjustments in the sexual arena than in other life arenas.

Schiavi (1994) documented in detail the physical disorders (e.g., neurological, endocrine, metabolic, cardiovascular, anatomical) that may impair sexual functioning and also noted prescription and other drugs that are problematic (e.g., antihypertensives, antipsychotics, antidepressants, cancer chemotherapy agents, drugs of abuse, etc.). But

Schiavi also highlighted very clearly the lack of uniformity in sexual outcomes, even with accompanying physical and drug conditions that create barriers to maximum sexual functioning. "For example, unrealistic expectations about sexual functioning in older men or ignorance that satisfying sexual interactions and orgasmic release remain possible in impotent diabetics can result in undue distress" (p. 331).

In sum, medical conditions can result in lessened sexual satisfaction, but they do not have to. What appears to be most important is an *awareness* of one's own and one's partner's general physical and sexual capabilities as well as a knowledge of the medical, pharmacological, and psychological impacts on those capabilities. That awareness must be supported by communication between relational partners and communication with health care providers. In other words, what partners understand, acknowledge, and communicate about has the potential to be dealt with in the area of partnered sexuality. Thus, sexual sharing and satisfaction are possible for most, if not all, relational partners (Rossi, 1994).

Sex, Risk, and Trust

Throughout history, sex has often been viewed as occurring in the shadows due to such stigmas as moral judgment, ignorance, fear of discovery, and fear of pregnancy. Sex has also posed the potential danger of contracting sexually transmitted diseases, such as syphilis and gonorrhea. Contemporary society offers no exception. Indeed, "the consequences of sexual intimacy include the risk of sharing bacterial and viral infections, and the perpetuation and spread of several diseases are an important public repercussion of this very private behavior" (Laumann et al., 1994, p. 376). Only abstinence offers full safety, and even the technical abstinence practiced by some young people today does not provide complete protection (Mulrine, 2002).

For many *sexually transmitted infections (STIs)* and *sexually transmitted diseases (STDs)*, occurrence rates are highest among people in their late teens and twenties and then level off and eventually drop dramatically. A range of disorders put people at risk, from unpleasant problems such as herpes and genital warts to life-threatening diseases such as hepatitis and acquired immune deficiency syndrome (AIDS). And there "is compelling evidence that the number of sex partners is in fact an important risk factor when it comes to contracting these infections" (Laumann et al., 1994 p. 385). Thus, having multiple partners magnifies one's risk, and both familiarity and exclusivity with partners are important issues in determining such risk. The fewer partners one has, the lower his or her risk of contracting STIs and STDs, and the more familiar one is with sexual partners (and possibly their sexual histories), the greater his or her presumed ability to make safer sexual choices (Laumann et al., 1994).

Virtually everyone realizes that sex can be risky—even dangerous—and that issues of safety must be considered by anyone having a sexual relationship. What is most germane to this discussion of relational sexuality, however, is how sexual safety is negotiated (or not negotiated) in relationships.

As was discussed earlier, communicating about sex is not easy but is nonetheless important, both for reasons of pleasure and satisfaction and for safety reasons. Although the incidences of STIs and STDs are minimal to negligible for monogamous partners in long-term relationships, virtually everyone else runs at least some risk. In some ways, *risk* and *trust* become counterpoised in intimate relationships (Lear, 1997). "The over-arching struggle between risk and trust in relationships remains the difficulty of attaining a balance between protecting oneself by assuming one's partner poses some risk and be-lieving that the partner is trustworthy" (p. 101). Some partners deny the risks entirely, other partners acknowledge the risks but avoid using condoms, and still other partners accept using condoms as a way of minimizing the risks.

Condom use interacts with gender and power in relationships. At least in hetero-sexual relationships, the women may be most motivated for condom use, but the men must agree to use condoms. The partner with the greater power in the relationship is likely the one with final decision-making authority concerning condom use. In addition, women may still face greater negative sanctions for sexual initiatives, including pre-paredness (e.g., a conditional double-standard; Sprecher & McKinney, 1993). Women who are prepared for sex by possessing condoms may forfeit the claim to being "swept away and therefore not accountable" for engaging in sex (Lear, 1997, p. 109).

Discussing condoms with a new partner may be awkward, but raising the issue with an ongoing partner may be downright threatening to the relationship itself: "What do you mean you want me to use a condom. Don't you trust me?" So, risk versus trust may become a serious theme in a couple's negotiation of sexual behavior, in general, and sexual protection, in particular. Here, as in virtually all other areas of relational life, the ability to communicate openly and with some measure of skill is important.

Summary and Conclusions

One aspect of human bonding is manifested in sexuality between partners, particularly romantic partners. Sexuality is typically a behavior between two people, but it occurs within a social context (e.g., religious rules, societal norms). When researchers study sexuality, important topics include premarital sex and sexual frequency (often under-stood to be heterosexual intercourse). Although sexual frequency declines over the long term, particularly the long-term marriage, the steepest drop occurs over the first year. Frequency thereafter declines only very gradually for most couples. And even the most drastic declines may only be from four times a week to two times a week, for example.

Sexual attitudes seem to have a bidirectional influence on sexual behavior—each affects the other. Three sexual frameworks for envisioning the purpose and role of sexu-ality are the procreational (sex is to have children), recreational (sex is to have fun), and relational (sex is to strengthen the relationship). Many factors influence sexual attitudes and behaviors.

Sexual attraction is a first step in sexual interaction. Although physical attractive-ness is a significant attractor for both women and men, characterological qualities such as kindness and understanding are even more important in evaluating a potential partner, for both genders. A moderate amount of sexual experience is also viewed as attractive in a potential partner, although when such experience begins in the life of a particular couple is not very important. More important is sexual satisfaction, which is linked to both relational satisfaction and stability. Feeling comfortable with one's partner is extremely significant to both men and women, and both women and men report experiencing similar levels of rewards and costs in their intimate relationships. Although sexual novelty may contribute to satisfaction, sexual security and stability contribute, also. A major survey of U.S. sexual practices found that the persons most physically *and* emotionally satisfied in their intimate relationships were those who had one partner, with whom they were monogamous.

One aspect of partnered sexuality that can improve over time is sexual communication. The ability to communicate skillfully one's sexual interest (or lack of interest) at a particular time is a significant asset in relational life. Satisfaction with both the sexual communication and the general communication in one's relationship is important.

Sexual desire is something that can tie sex and love, and it is becoming a more frequent topic of research. Passionate love is the type of love linked most frequently with sexual desire, and indeed, desire and passion seem to go together. Recent research on the ways in which people view the links between love and sex has resulted in four themes that characterize how people view these links: (1) that love is the most important thing; (2) that love comes before sex; (3) that sex is a way of showing love; and (4) that sex can decline. The declining of sex is especially strongly related to decreasing satisfaction with a relationship.

Men tend to sexualize situations more then women do, and many reasons have been proposed for this, including evolutionary ones. Date rape occurs when a woman is sexually assaulted by a man with whom she is romantically involved, and it causes trauma for the victim and sometimes for the perpetrator.

When considering people's sexual relationships, it is important to remember that sexuality is not confined simply to those who are young, white, beautiful, and heterosexual. Gay and lesbian couples, couples of different races and cultures, couples who are aging, and couples who have physical disabilities and illnesses are all included among those who have rich and satisfying sexual lives. Sex is a great positive force, but it is also an area of risk and thus an area requiring trust. The risks of acquiring STIs and STDs must be balanced with trust of one's partner and the unfolding of the sexual process; sexual relating therefore requires ongoing communication and ongoing negotiation for most couples.

A final comment: The increase of sexual freedom that has occurred over recent decades, particularly for women, is part of an emphasis on the individual. Yet the increase in individual freedom and rights does not appear to have brought about an increase in sexual satisfaction and general well-being. That is likely the case, at least in part, because individualism in the extreme moves away from relatedness, which is at the core of sexuality and at the core of our human need to belong. To the extent that sexuality is more relational and less individual, it is likely to be more satisfying.

Key Terms

Sex (p. 98)
Sexual attitudes (p. 99)
Sexual desire (p. 105)

Sexual frequency (p. 98)
Sexual satisfaction (p. 103)

Suggested Reading

Christopher, F. S. (2001). *To dance the dance: A symbolic interactional exploration of premarital sexuality.* Mahwah, NJ: Lawrence Erlbaum.

Christopher, F. S., & Sprecher, S. (2000). Sexuality in marriage, dating, and other relationships: A decade review. *Journal of Marriage and the Family, 62,* 999–1017.

Laumann, E. O., Gagnon, J. H., Michael, R. T., & Michaels, S. (1994). *The social organization of sexuality: Sexual practices in the United States.* Chicago: University of Chicago Press.

Regan, P. C., & Berscheid, E. (1999). *Lust: What we know about human sexual desire.* Thousand Oaks, CA: Sage.

Rossi, A. S. (Ed.). (1994). *Sexuality across the life course.* Chicago: University of Chicago Press.

Sprecher, S., & Regan, P. C. (2000). Sexuality in a relational context. In C. Hendrick & S. S. Hendrick (Eds.), *Close relationships: A sourcebook* (pp. 217–227). Thousand Oaks, CA: Sage.

6

Communication and Relational Maintenance

Relationship Story

The Party

Nick and Elaine were running late, as usual. The party had started half an hour before, and while Nick paced the floor in irritation, fiddling with his car keys, Elaine was still putting the finishing touches on her makeup and holding up various earrings, trying to decide which ones she liked best. Nick got more and more agitated, finally walking into their bathroom, surveying Elaine, and saying sarcastically, "If you take *any* longer to get ready, there will be no point in our going at all—the party will be over!" Elaine flushed, put on the earrings that she had picked out originally, and grabbed her purse. "I'm ready," she said.

They got into the car without speaking and silently wound their way out to the highway; they had to drive nearly all the way across town to the party. It was a quiet ride, far different from the old days, when their

115

twin girls were along and they were all going somewhere together. Then, the car was never quiet; there was fighting or giggling or both from the back seat. But now the kids were 17 and had destinations of their own, so family trips were few. And so Nick and Elaine's trips, like their life together, seemed to get quieter—and emptier. Sometimes, the past seemed much more fun than the present, which often appeared to consist mostly of Nick's increasingly successful career.

Elaine knew she should have gotten ready for the party earlier, but she just kept putting it off and finding other things to do. This was an important occasion for Nick; it was the first department party since he had been awarded his big grant, so it would be an opportunity for people to congratulate him and for him to bask in the sunshine of success. He had worked hard for it, Elaine knew. Oh, did she ever know!

As a biochemistry professor, he spent endless evenings and weekends in the lab, just continuing the crazy schedule he'd had as a graduate student, when Elaine had first met him. Back then, she thought his intense commitment to his work was attractive—even sexy. He seemed so intelligent and so serious. She just knew he was going to be a famous chemist some day. Elaine supported his single-minded commitment to his work as a central part of his personality. So when they got married, at first, she didn't even mind the fact that he wasn't home very much. She didn't expect him to be. She had her own work as an occupational therapist to keep her busy, and much of her nonwork time was spent trying to create a pretty apartment that Nick would enjoy coming home to (when he finally did come home).

Then Elaine got pregnant with the twins and decided to quit her job. Nick found his first academic position, and they traded in their cozy apartment for a small house. Elaine was so busy taking care of the girls and trying to decorate the little house that she didn't miss Nick during those long hours in the lab—at least, not too much. He was good with the girls when he was home, but he often seemed a little distracted, as though his mind was somewhere else. And there was always that barely concealed impatience to get back to the lab. Sometimes Elaine could break through that impatience—when they were making love, for instance, or sometimes when they took the twins to the park or to the beach. At those times, Nick would seem fully there.

Elaine tried once or twice to talk with Nick about his long hours at work, asking if he couldn't spend more time at home. But he would resist, sometimes defensively and sometimes with unarguable logic about how he had to work that hard in order to get ahead. And he always withdrew from her for awhile after those talks. Elaine learned that a part-time husband was better than no husband at all, and she stopped asking him to be around more. She just built her life and the girls' lives to include Nick when he was at home and to work just fine when he wasn't around.

Nick drove purposefully and crisply, the way he did almost everything. He was irritated about being so late for the party, but that really wasn't all of it. He was irritated with Elaine for dragging her feet about going to this party when she knew how much it meant to him. Maybe it was only a department party to her, but to him, it was a chance for him to finally feel as though he belonged. He was a successful biochemistry professor, but it was only with the recent award of his big grant that he finally felt like one of the "in" group.

Nick wished his father could see him now—how successful he was. But then again, his father probably wouldn't be that impressed. He never thought Nick would amount to anything. He couldn't understand why Nick didn't go into one of the construction trades, like all the other men in the family. He always thought that Nick's endless education and fooling around in a laboratory with chemicals was kind of a "sissy thing." Nick never felt that he could please his father.

That made it all the more important when he met Elaine. He was a graduate student in biochemistry, and she was an occupational therapy student. Right from the beginning, when they had just dated a couple of times, Nick felt Elaine's support for what he was trying to do with his life, for his goals and ambitions. She seemed to understand how important it was for him to be the very best biochemist that he could be. She was always attentive when he talked about his work, and her intelligence, good looks, and supportive and caring personality all combined to make her the most special woman he had ever met. He couldn't imagine life without her, so when he proposed marriage to her, he was elated that she accepted.

Then it became even more important for him to succeed because now he had someone to work for besides himself. And when the twins were born, he had even more responsibilities. He wanted to be the kind of father for them that he himself had never had—a father who would provide for them financially but, even more, who would believe in them and support them in what they did. He remembered how tiny they were when he and Elaine brought them home from the hospital; he felt such an overwhelming love for them and a commitment to take care of them. He promised himself that he would never let them down, and he tried to keep that promise over the years.

Becoming a successful biochemistry professor took a lot of time away from his family life with Elaine and the girls. But he felt he was doing it for them—at least in part. Along the way, it seemed as though Elaine and the twins got used to him being gone so much. They were always glad to have him home, but their lives somehow seemed to move on without him. Once in awhile, he felt guilty about his long hours, but then he would push the guilt aside and just keep on working.

It helped him feel less guilty when Elaine started getting into her artwork. Rather than seek employment as an occupational therapist when the girls got older, she took some painting classes and discovered that she had real talent. Her specialty was portrait painting, especially of children. Not surprisingly, her first subjects were the twins, but as soon as people saw those paintings, they overwhelmed Elaine with work. She had commissions booked for months ahead, and she was even going to have her first show at a local art gallery—a collection of portraits of twins and triplets. In fact, she was working on one of those portraits earlier this evening, when she should have been getting ready for the party. Even though he was angry with her, Nick realized again how proud he was of Elaine. She was finding her talents and following her passions, just as he was.

Nick felt himself soften. How could he be angry with Elaine for simply doing what made her happy? Without saying a word, he reached over for her hand, which was lying there on the car seat, resting lightly on her purse. She let his hand rest on hers, but she didn't make any move to reciprocate. She really wasn't surprised to feel his hand on hers. He would occasionally reach out in some way after they had a disagreement, even when it wasn't his fault—like tonight. She knew that his irritation was justified, and she really wasn't sure why she didn't want to go to the party.

In truth, her negative attitude wasn't really about the party at all. It was about them— Nick and Elaine—and what was missing for her in their relationship and their life together. And somehow, it was all symbolized by this party. Elaine didn't know what she would do if she didn't have her art. Her artwork fed her and sustained her. Some of her happiest times were when she was painting or when she was sharing her work with other people. She was excited about her upcoming show. And she knew Nick was proud of her, even though he hadn't said very much about it to her.

Nick stopped the car; they were there. Lights were blazing in the brick colonial, and it looked like virtually everyone in the department had turned out for this annual event. Elaine and Nick got out and walked up to the front door, entered without knocking, and sought out the hosts. They saw people they knew holding glasses of wine and soft drinks, eating from the buffet table and making small talk. They finally located Bob, the host and the chair of the department, who welcomed them and congratulated Nick again on obtaining his big grant. "So predictable," thought Elaine. "Finally," thought Nick. They wandered into the kitchen, where the bar was set up on the kitchen table. Nick poured wine for both of them, and then Elaine told Nick to feel free to circulate and talk to people; she'd take care of herself. Elaine wandered out onto the patio, where some people were talking about the latest scandal at the university and others were discussing chemistry. Elaine saw a couple of women she had known for years and talked with them for awhile.

Then she moved off and just stood there silently, trying to decide what to do next, when she felt someone come up beside her and stand a little too close. She turned and there was Nick. "How are you doing?" he asked her. "Fine. I just spent some time talking with Mary and Anne about children's summer camps, and I thought I'd take a breather and maybe get a little more wine. What about you?" "Oh, I talked with Bob about the grant and with Dale about the new book he's writing, and I guess I thought I'd take a break too. The party is fine, but . . . (he lowered his voice) . . . it's just the same old thing." Nick put his arm around Elaine's waist and gave her a squeeze. "How about developing a headache?" "What?" she said. Then she got it! "As a matter of fact, my head is really starting to throb," she said. Nick leaned over and whispered in her ear, "You're wonderful! I'll tell Bob that I'm sorry, but you're just not feeling well."

They made their way back through the house, with Nick offering brief apologies to the host. Then suddenly they were out the door and walking toward their car through the balmy summer evening, holding hands and trying not to laugh until they were safely in the car. But as soon as they got in and closed the door, they burst into laughter. It had been a long time since they had laughed like that. And they couldn't remember how long it had been since they'd done something even slightly impulsive, like leave a boring party. All of a sudden, they realized that they were starving, so they stopped at a little restaurant on the way home to get a sandwich. As they sat across the table from each other, Nick looked over at Elaine, who was reading her menu, and he blurted out, "You know, you're really beautiful." Elaine flushed with pleasure and smiled, looking him squarely in the eye. "I love you" she said. And with that came, perhaps, a new beginning in their relationship.

■ ■ ■

Questions to Consider in Reading This Chapter

- How did Nick's childhood experiences with his father affect his choice of a relationship partner?
- Think about one negative nonverbal communication and one positive nonverbal communication between Elaine and Nick the night of the party.
- How could Elaine tell Nick that she wishes he would spend more time at home? If she did tell him, how do you think Nick would respond?
- What would happen if Nick told Elaine how proud he is of her?
- What could Elaine and Nick do to nurture their relationship on a daily basis?

What Do We Know about Communication and Relational Maintenance?

Elaine and Nick are not unusual. Their story is told and retold every day in relationships that start out with wonderful expectations of a future together and evolve over the years into spoken and unspoken disappointments and accusations. Questions of "Why did you?" and "Why didn't you?" fill the conversations of many partners who once thought that simply being together would guarantee living happily ever after. What is different about Nick and Elaine's story is that it has a happy ending—at least, for the evening in question.

This chapter looks at communication, both verbal and nonverbal, as well as other behaviors that maintain relationships and allow such happy endings to occur. General ideas about relationship maintenance will be addressed first, setting the stage for a discussion of communication, one of the most significant components of relationship initiation and maintenance.

Definitions of Relational Maintenance

It is not enough for human beings to connect with one another; they must also maintain that connection. What does it mean to *maintain* a relationship? Is maintenance a process of relationship partners performing certain activities, or is it the ongoing nature of the relationship itself?

The answer to both these questions appears to be yes, as relationship maintenance consists of several different things. Dindia (2000) has articulated in detail various definitions of **relational maintenance.** First, relational maintenance, or just *maintenance,* may refer simply to a relationship that continues. Its sheer existence defines it. Second, maintenance can refer to a relationship that not only continues but is stable. Third, maintenance can refer to continuity, stability, and satisfaction. Fourth, maintenance can involve all the above conditions being met plus the quality of being "in good working condition" (p. 288). Thus, maintenance at the first level may refer merely to a relationship's existence, whereas at the fourth level it refers to behaviors undertaken actively to renew and repair a relationship.

Truly maintaining a relationship in healthy and satisfying condition requires ongoing relational work, since a variety of forces always affect relationships. Some of those forces, such as having shared hopes and goals, pull partners toward each other, whereas other forces, such as facing career demands, push partners away from each other. Duck (1994) refers to "relational maintenance as a shared meaning system" (p. 45), thereby emphasizing the importance of communication and also the human tendency to make sense of and create meaning in one's world as a central aspect of relational maintenance. Relationship maintenance involves a number of processes and behaviors, discussed in some detail in the following section.

Strategies for Maintaining Relationships

There are likely as many strategies for maintaining relationships as there are persons in relationships, but one organized system or typology of strategies was developed by Stafford and Canary (1991). These authors considered how maintenance strategies might vary according to whether a relationship involved dating, serious dating, being engaged, or being married, and they used several methods to collect information. With that information, Stafford and Canary developed five relational maintenance strategies that have become widely used in research on maintenance: *assurances* (expressing commitment, faithfulness, love); *network* (involvement with social networks); *openness* (disclosure and other communication); *positivity* (being upbeat and cheerful); and *tasks* (sharing household chores). Research by Canary, Stafford, and Semic (2002) has affirmed the importance of *ongoing* use of these maintenance strategies for relationship well-being. For example, "One cannot rely on a chore done last month to have a positive impact on one's partner" (p. 403).

Based on Stafford and Canary's (1991) strategies, it would seem that more emotional strategies, such as having open communication and expressing love, would be the most powerful maintenance strategies. Dainton and Stafford (1993), however, found that sharing tasks (a very everyday sort of behavior) was the maintenance behavior most frequently mentioned by participants. As Duck (1994) commented, "Relational maintenance contains two elements, not one; the first is strategic planning for the continuance of the relationship; and the second is the breezy allowance of the relationship to continue by means of the everyday interactions and conversations that make the relationship what it is" (p. 46). A dozen roses given by a husband to his wife on her birthday may be a dramatic *assurances* maintenance behavior, but working together every evening to clean up after the family's dinner may actually be a much more powerful, if less glamorous, *tasks* maintenance behavior. In the Relationship Story, Elaine and Nick did some fairly dramatic assurances and openness behaviors during and after the party because they had been neglecting some of the more routine but perhaps even more important behaviors, such as task sharing.

Relationship maintenance may operate somewhat differently for different types of couples. For example, Weigel and Ballard-Reisch (1999), using Fitzpatrick's (e.g., 1987) couples typology, found that couples who were classified as *traditional* (traditional gender roles, sharing, dependence on each other) and as *independent* (more equal gender roles, flexibility of the relationship) used more and varied maintenance behaviors than couples classified as *separate* (value individual freedom, less oriented toward sharing). And the use of particular maintenance behaviors was related differently to partners' perceptions of the quality of their relationship for the different types of couples. In other words, different maintenance strategies worked for different couple types. Each relationship, or shared meaning system, is unique.

The personality characteristics of the individual partners are also influential in relationship maintenance. Bradbury and Fincham (1988) observed that immediate relational experiences, as well as more stable circumstances such as partners' personality traits, can affect a relationship. Personality characteristics such as being outgoing have been associated with positive relationship functioning (e.g., Karney & Bradbury, 1995), whereas characteristics such as being neurotic have been associated with negative relationship functioning (e.g., Sanderson & Kurdek, 1993). Thus, relational maintenance is affected by what the partners bring to the relationship, such as personality characteristics and previous life experiences, as well as current and immediate partner behaviors, such as communication.

Minding is another approach to the issue of relational maintenance. The process of "minding the relationship" has been articulated most completely by Harvey and Omarzu (1997), who characterize *minding* as "a package of mutual self-disclosure, other forms of goal-oriented behavior aimed at facilitating the relationship, and attributions about self's and other's motivations, intentions, and effort in the relationship" (p. 224). Self-disclosure and related forms of communication are a central part of this concept, yet in Harvey and Omarzu's view, minding is about much more than disclosure/communication. Minding involves a high level of caretaking, staying close to, renewing attachment with, and, in general, attending to one's partner. At its best, minding is also a relationship behavior, one that requires both partners to be involved actively with one another. Trust, for example, is not the same thing as minding, but it is built in a relationship through the minding process. Minding may be love in action. Nick and Elaine had not been minding their relationship, and it showed! Minding may be one of the constructs that best illustrates the idea that a relationship and all that goes into it is a process, rather than an event. A successful relationship is built over time, through many behaviors and interactions.

Also related to the minding concept is the process of *relationship awareness,* defined by Acitelli (1993) as "a person's thinking about interaction patterns, comparisons, or contrasts between himself or herself and the other partner in the relationship" (p. 151). It involves both thinking a lot about the relationship itself and also tending to think in relationship terms, such as "we" and "us," rather than individual terms, such as "I" and "you."

Communication

Communication, both verbal and nonverbal, forms the bedrock of close, personal relationships, including romantic relationships. Thus, it follows that theory and research on communication have provided much of the basis for the study of close relationships (e.g., Andersen & Guerrero, 1998). Since research on relational communication is too vast to be detailed here, selected findings on communication and relationships will be presented.

Burleson, Metts, and Kirch (2000) propose that interpersonal communication, examined very broadly, can be divided into the **strategic/functional** and the **consequential/cultural** approaches. The *strategic approach* assumes that communication is goal oriented and to some degree intentional. This approach is characterized by words such as *goals, intentions, strategies, tactics,* and *plans.* Elaine and Nick may have had good communication as a goal or intention for their marriage, but they had few actual strategies for attaining that goal. The *consequential approach* emphasizes that communication, whether intentional or unintentional, creates a context within which a relationship can thrive or wither. Words characterizing the consequential approach are *codes, rituals,* *roles,* and *rules.* For Nick and Elaine, their unintentional rituals and roles had become increasingly either negative or disconnected as far as their communication was concerned. Their context or atmosphere was allowing their marriage to wither.

The strategic/functional and consequential/cultural approaches are made up of various components. For example, the strategic perspective emphasizes the relationship tasks accomplished by communication, including instrumental, relationship maintenance, and interaction management tasks (Burleson et al., 2000). *Instrumental tasks* focus interactions and include such things as requesting or offering information and providing social support. *Relationship maintenance* tasks include defining rules for the relationship and handling conflict. Finally, *interaction management* addresses the "how-to" tasks involved in developing adequate conversation between relationship partners.

These communication skills all require motivation, skill, and both verbal and nonverbal action. Although it might seem that motivation, skill, and action would be related to greater relationship positives, such as satisfaction, the outcomes are not that simple. Burleson and Denton (1997) found that in happy marriages, the wives' communication skills were positively related to the husbands' marital satisfaction, whereas in unhappy marriages, some of the wives' skills were negatively associated with the husbands' satisfaction. This double-edged sword of communication is evident to any therapist who has counseled a couple in which one partner was especially good with words. For example, lawyers are trained to do battle with words, to use words as weapons. In their relationships, lawyers can be either eloquent, using their skills to communicate clearly and lovingly with their partner, or argumentative, putting their partner on the witness stand in front of the judge or therapist while they act as the prosecuting attorney.

The consequential/cultural approach acknowledges that communication essentially defines a relationship (Wood, 2000). All relationships of a certain type—for example, engaged partners—share particular characteristics, yet each individual relationship also has its own individual feel and style. Partners construct relationship stories about such events as how they fell in love; share their own relationship language with special nicknames and words for activities such as sex; enjoy interaction routines such as having morning coffee together; and establish rituals such as spending every anniversary having dinner at a certain restaurant. Partners also develop relationship *norms,* which refer to things as they are, and relationship *rules,* which refer to how things should be (Burleson et al., 2000). For instance, a couple might set the rule that they will use direct communication to solve problems, while the couple's norm, or typical behavior, might be that they tend to communicate indirectly, trying to avoid conflict.

Whether one views communication through the strategic/functional lens or the consequential/cultural lens, *communication* provides the meaning system for an intimate relationship. As detailed in earlier chapters, communication is a central feature of how people define *friendship* (Cole & Bradac, 1996), is one of the factors by which people determine that a friendship is truly close (Parks & Floyd, 1996), and is embedded in how relationship partners (Pasch et al., 1997) and others (Wortman & Dunkel-Schetter, 1987) provide social support. One central aspect of communication is self-disclosure.

Self-Disclosure

Self-disclosure is only one aspect of the general communicational meaning system, but it is a very significant aspect. Self-disclosure can refer, in general, to telling someone else about oneself—one's feelings, attitudes, experiences, and so on. But in the context of a close relationship (and in the current chapter), self-disclosure concerns intimate, even risky information that we share with another. To *tell* about ourselves means that we simply offer facts—age, gender, place of birth, and so on. To *disclose* about ourselves means that we drop our social mask, cease the careful editing of our words, and share some of our innermost thoughts and feelings with another person. *Telling* merely requires that two people literally speak the same language, whereas *disclosing* requires that two people figuratively speak the same language. One goal of self-disclosure may be to tell the other person who we really are, another may be to elicit personal disclosures from the other person and thus deepen the intimacy of our relationship, and another may be just to unload a secret that has become too heavy for us to bear alone. Whatever our reasons for disclosing, this behavior can be immensely powerful.

One of the first social scientists to study disclosure was Sidney Jourard (1964), who believed that holding and hiding our innermost thoughts and feelings led to a major disconnection within ourselves and between us and others. He felt that withholding disclosure could have serious negative emotional and physical consequences for individuals and for their relationships and that offering disclosure was healing. In many ways, he has been proven right, as we will discuss in the section on wellness.

Theoretical Approaches

One important theoretical perspective on disclosure was developed by Altman and Taylor (1973) within the larger theory of social penetration. *Social penetration theory* (discussed in Chapter 2) is a comprehensive theory of relationship development that involves verbal and nonverbal communication as well as aspects of interpersonal perceptions and the physical environment. The theory views progressive involvement in a relationship as beginning with the general breadth of such things as self-disclosure and continuing to a greater depth of disclosure as the relationship progresses. This notion of progression in one direction was revised to allow more attention to how disclosure and other relationship aspects occur in cycles (e.g., Altman, Vinsel, & Brown, 1981). The **dialectical** nature of disclosure—that is, that a pull toward openness and away from closedness/privacy is followed by a pull toward privacy and away from openness/enmeshment—has offered one useful lens through which to view self-disclosure (e.g., Altman et al., 1981). Thus, it is now believed that self-disclosure provides different functions in different situations, that it ebbs and flows both within and across relationships and over time. In the Relationship Story, Elaine and Nick apparently disclosed a great deal to each other early in their relationship but then moved too far in the opposite direction and appeared to stop disclosing much, if anything, about how each of them felt.

Dindia (1997) notes that self-disclosure *"is a life-long/relationship-long process*, a process that changes as individuals and relationships change" (p. 411; italics in original). Although she acknowledges that self-disclosure has been studied typically as a personality characteristic of an individual or as a behavior enacted by relationship partners, she proposes that disclosure be thought of as a *transactional process*. This means that the very process of self-disclosure requires a person who discloses, a person to whom the disclosure is offered, and the transaction/interaction between them. And every transaction/interaction modifies to a greater or lesser degree both the individual persons involved and the relationship between them. The idea that self-disclosure and relationships are "mutually transformative" has also been espoused at length by Derlega et al. (1993).

This perspective underlines the developmental, as opposed to the strictly situational or so-called snapshot, nature of relationships. The developmental perspective is like a continuous video of a relationship over time, whereas the snapshot or action view of disclosure (Dindia, 1997) is like a series of single pictures. Most of the research methods currently used in social science may only capture a relationship at one point in time; even so, the ultimate vision of the relationship process should not be constrained by method, since relationships are dynamic, evolving entities, always in process (Duck & Sants, 1983).

Self-disclosure can consist of information offered about oneself—"I think . . . ," "I feel . . . ," "I have experienced . . . ,"—in relation to the outside world or to the relationship itself. There is an immediacy to disclosures that relate to the partner and relationship, especially to the present moment. Such relational self-disclosures provide information to the partner and are also a metaphor for the closeness of the relationship. "Thus, superficial SD [self-disclosure] communicates the relational message, 'we are strangers'; intimate SD communicates the relational message, 'we are friends'" (Dindia, 1997, p. 417).

Research on Self-Disclosure

Research on self-disclosure has been organized around three basic areas, including (1) individual differences in self-disclosure, (2) self-disclosure in close relationships, and (3) self-disclosure and illness/wellness (Berg & Derlega, 1987).

Women and men have been reputed to differ in self-disclosure, with women disclosing more, and indeed, women tend to disclose more intimately to women friends than men disclose to men friends (Derlega et al., 1993). However, Dindia and Allen (1992), in their meta-analysis of disclosure and gender, found only modest gender differences in self-disclosure.

Consistent with these findings is research by Burleson and his colleagues (Burleson, Kunkel, Samter, & Werking, 1996), who assessed women's and men's ratings of the relative importance of affective, emotion-based communication skills versus instrumental, task-oriented communication skills in both friendships and romantic relationships. Although men and women differed slightly, in that women rated affective skills more highly than men rated them and men rated instrumental skills more highly than women rated them, overall, both women and men rated "affectively oriented skills as more important than instrumental skills" (p. 201). So, how a conversation feels may at times be more important than whether a specific problem gets solved.

Reciprocity of self-disclosure has to do with the matching, giving and receiving, of self-disclosure between partners, both in terms of intimacy level and positivity/negativity. Reciprocity is important because it is related to attraction, although Erber and Erber (2001) suggest that attraction *follows from,* rather than *precedes,* matching of self-disclosure. Reciprocity seems to be more important in acquaintanceships than in friendships and long-term romantic relationships, where self-disclosure is more variable and flexible (Derlega et al., 1993; Morton, 1978).

Disclosure between long-term partners, such as spouses, is driven by much more than a perceived need to reciprocate. Disclosure may decrease over the lifetime of a relationship (e.g., S. S. Hendrick, 1981), but the rate of decrease may slow after the couple's early years together, much as it does for sexual frequency (i.e., declining sharply at first but much more gradually after that). This is likely part of what happened to Nick and Elaine, who communicated much more early in their relationship than they did after many years of marriage. Self-disclosure is typically a positive factor in relationships, contributing to relationship satisfaction (Meeks, Hendrick, & Hendrick, 1998) and relationship continuation (Sprecher, 1987).

Prager's (2000) model of relational intimacy (discussed in Chapter 4) includes self-disclosure as one of three central components. The other two components are positive affect or emotion and listening/understanding by the partner. In this view, self-disclosure is an indispensable aspect of intimacy but not the *whole* of intimacy. In research that deepens current understanding of the role of self-disclosure in intimacy, Prager and Buhrmester (1998) examined the role of self-disclosure, positive affect, and partner listening/understanding in contributing to need fulfillment (or having one's personal needs met for such things as acceptance, validation, and belongingness). Several interesting findings emerged. First, the researchers found that overall, the intimacy components of self-disclosure, positive affect, and listening/understanding were, indeed, related to need fulfillment for both women and men, but they also found "that intimacy's contribution to need fulfillment is greater than the sum of the contributions of its component parts" (p. 455). In other words, needs are more fulfilled when all three intimacy components are present. Self-disclosure, however, was a relational positive even when the other components, such as positive affect, were not present. Self-disclosure appeared to mediate or actually soften negative interactions, so that if couples having negative interactions do more, rather than less, self-disclosing, they will do better. The authors also found that frequency of communication between partners may be less important than the intimacy of the communication.

It is important to remember, however, that there are individual preferences for disclosure, and these preferences become apparent in relationships. For example, Fitzpatrick (1987) points out that different couple types may prefer different self-disclosure styles. Fitzpatrick has identified three couple types, mentioned earlier in this chapter in connection with maintenance strategies: *Traditionals* tend to have high self-disclosure, primarily about positive things; *independents* have high willingness to disclose both positives and negatives; and *separates* have little self-disclosure about anything. These couple types also vary on other relational dimensions besides self-disclosure, as noted earlier.

Self-disclosure has also been linked to actual physical well-being. Jourard (1964) believed that nondisclosure led to estrangement from others as well as to actual physical illness. He understood that secrets have a way of "growing" in the dark of silence and becoming larger and larger barriers to good health. Research has proven Jourard to be correct. In studying the relationship between self-disclosure and traumatic or stressful life events, Pennebaker (1990) found that "excessive holding back of thoughts, feelings, and behaviors can place people at high risk for both major and minor diseases" (p. 14). In an extensive program of collaborative research, Pennebaker found that the disclosure of traumatic life events—whether through writing in a journal, talking with a friend or romantic partner, or through a form of religious confession—contributed to an increase in immune system functioning and a decrease in visits to health care providers. So, selective disclosure can positively influence health.

Pennebaker (1990) did not, however, advocate indiscriminate disclosure. On the contrary, he urged care and wisdom in how one confides/discloses, since disclosure of trauma may also reveal some stigma about the discloser (e.g., she was the victim of incest; he is HIV positive) (see also Dindia, 1997). Some self-disclosures can change the nature of the relationship between the discloser and listener or can even come back to haunt the discloser. Thus, self-disclosing must be done carefully in order to ensure that so far as possible, its effects are positive and not negative for the discloser or the listener.

The awareness of the risks of disclosure points the way toward consideration of the dialectical nature of the disclosure process.

The Dialectical Aspects of Self-Disclosure

As observed earlier, there is a dialectical aspect to self-disclosure in that as relationship partners move from autonomy toward closeness and then move from closeness toward autonomy, their disclosures follow suit. Baxter and Montgomery (1996) have detailed the many research findings concerning the usefulness of self-disclosure and the importance of being open to others, yet they also point out the value of *less* or even *no* disclosure. For example, (1) surface talk, as contrasted to deep disclosure, is the substance of everyday interaction, (2) surface talk helps maintain an acquaintanceship network, (3) withholding disclosure can be a form of discretion, and (4) withholding disclosure allows needed privacy in relationships. These authors underscore the validity of both those who promote self-disclosure and those who promote privacy, noting that neither perspective fully characterizes all relationships; both perspectives characterize different relationships and even the same relationship at different points in time. The back and forth, yin and yang, dialectical nature of disclosure is shown in everyday close relationships.

Some research (Finkenauer & Hazam, 2000) indicates that disclosure and non-disclosure are both important for relationship satisfaction and that each is important under different conditions. Although a general personal tendency to disclose (dispositional disclosure) was not related to relationship satisfaction for married persons, more specific disclosures of thoughts and feelings to one's partner based on a specific context were positively related to satisfaction. In the Relationship Story, neither Elaine nor Nick seemed to operate as high dispositional disclosers, but when Nick told Elaine that she was beautiful and Elaine in reply told Nick that she loved him, those contextual disclosures were timely and meaningful. Nondisclosure can also be useful. Finkenauer and Hazam (2000) found that people's selective nondisclosure or avoidance of difficult issues in the relationship was positively related to satisfaction. However, beliefs that one's partner was actually keeping secrets was strongly and negatively related to disclosure.

Self-disclosure is an important part of communication, as noted earlier, but it is typically considered to be within the verbal arena of communication. Also important is the nonverbal arena.

Nonverbal Communication

Although much of the communication that occurs in relationships is verbal—what partners do and don't say to each other—the day-in and day-out time spent in relationships is as much occupied with **nonverbal communication,** or what partners actually do. Keeley and Hart (1994) have organized nonverbal behaviors into sets of rules, messages, and behaviors called *codes,* and these codes are in turn divided into dynamic (changing) and static (unchanging) nonverbal codes. *Dynamic codes* can and do change during dyadic interaction and include body language (posture, body orientation, eye contact), touching behavior, and space or interaction distance (known as *proxemics*). *Static nonverbal codes* include such things as physical appearance. Although both types of codes influence relationships, the dynamic codes are particularly powerful. "If there is a discrepancy between verbal and nonverbal channels, nonverbal channels are focused on more often and believed" (p. 141). Nonverbal behaviors both influence positivity and intimacy in a relationship and indicate how much positivity and negative there is, and they are likewise linked to control issues (Montgomery, 1988).

How one uses his or her body in a relationship may be more informative about positivity and intimacy than what he or she says. If a wife reaches out to touch her husband lovingly and he pulls away, that message is worth a thousand words. When Nick put his hand over Elaine's in the car and she did not respond, that was an ambiguous message; she neither reciprocated the affectionate gesture nor pulled away. Later, in the restaurant, when Nick told Elaine she was beautiful, she flushed and also smiled. This combination of nonverbals was not ambiguous; it indicated pleasure.

Facial expressions are also highly communicative. Ekman, Friesen, and Tomkins (1971) suggest that six facial expressions display *basic emotions* and serve as the basis for most other expressions: surprise, happiness, sadness, fear, disgust, and anger.

Eye contact is another powerful form of body language. Norms for gaze and eye contact vary across cultures and across types of relationships. Various theoretical approaches address questions of how eye contact is balanced between intimacy and distance. For example, Argyle and Dean (1965) propose an *equilibrium model of intimacy,* in which a comfortable balance exists between eye contact and interaction distance. If one partner increases his or her eye contact, the other partner might well increase his or her interaction distance (move farther back) in order to maintain balance or *equilibrium.* On the other hand, if one partner increases eye contact and the other partner wants to increase the intimacy level of the relationship, he or she may maintain or even decrease interaction distance.

Because nonverbal behaviors are essential ways of expressing emotion, they can be used positively, in the service of building relational intimacy and trust, or negatively, to reinforce control and dominance (Keeley & Hart, 1994). Ironically, the behaviors that can express the greatest caring, such as caressing during lovemaking, can also express the greatest violence, such as hitting and other physical abuse.

The negative aspects of nonverbal behavior will be discussed again in other chapters in the contexts of conflict, abuse, and breakup. At this point, it is important to remember that "nonverbal behaviors are indicative of quality communication. Research indicates that people pay close attention to nonverbal behaviors as indicators of the health of their relationships" (Keeley & Hart, 1994, p. 161).

Communication has been discussed from a number of directions, including meta-perspectives (strategic/functional and consequential/cultural), self-disclosure's powerful role in communication, and the importance of nonverbal communication. The discussion will now look more practically at how communication functions on a day-to-day basis in relationships and how it corresponds with relationship satisfaction.

Day-to-Day Communication

The *shared meaning systems* referred to by Duck (1994) are created, in large measure, by partners' sharing of their similarities and dissimilarities (Monsour, 1994). Research is relatively consistent in showing that similarities foster attraction and other positive characteristics of relationships, yet no two partners are ever similar in every way. The ways in which partners handle dissimilarities is thus very significant. Partners' recognition of their similarities, whether actual or simply perceived, leads to further communication and assumptions of further commonalities (Monsour, 1994). Yet inevitably, communication

reveals dissimilarities as well as similarities. And "accurate understanding of the similarities and differences between oneself and a relational partner lays the groundwork for
building intimacy in a relationship" (p. 128).

One communication approach to handling couples' differences is the *demand/
withdraw* communication pattern (e.g., Jacobson & Christensen, 1996). In this situation,
one partner attempts to engage the other in communication typically intended to bring
about some change in the relationship, and the partner on the receiving end withdraws or
avoids the communication interaction, also avoiding conflict and possible relationship
change. This pattern has been described as *gendered* in the sense that in heterosexual
couples, women are more likely to do the demanding/seeking change, whereas men are
more likely to do the withdrawing/resisting change.

The issue is less directly about gender than it is about desired change, however. In
recent research, when married couples were asked "to discuss an issue about which the
husband wanted the wife to change and an issue about which the wife wanted the husband to change . . . wives demanded and husbands withdrew during discussions of her
issue, whereas husbands demanded and wives withdrew during discussions of his issue"
(Klinetob & Smith, 1996, p. 945). In other words, when he wanted change, he pushed
and she backed away. When she wanted change, she pushed and he backed away.

What is communicated, how it is communicated, and how it is received and responded to are all important aspects of ongoing communication processes. Reis and
Shaver (1988) emphasize the reciprocal, or back-and-forth, nature of communication in
the intimacy process. They provide a model in which, using our Relationship Story as an
example, Nick's goals, motives, and fears are disclosed or expressed emotionally (i.e.,
communicated) to Elaine, who has her own goals, motives, and fears. She then understands Nick's communication through her own *interpretive filter* and responds to Nick.
Nick understands Elaine's response through his own interpretive filter, and the process
continues. It is very interactive and can be improved or derailed at any point. "Intimacy
is a dynamic process whose operation is best observed in the pattern of communication
and reaction between two people" (p. 383). This interactional view of intimacy is very
consistent with the interactional view of disclosure, discussed earlier.

One reason that communication patterns and styles are of such intense interest to
relationship scholars is that communication is important for relational quality and satisfaction. First of all, there are communication variables that positively influence satisfaction. For example, in an exploration of communication, conflict, and love, Meeks et al.
(1998) found that people's perceptions of their partner's ability to take their perspective
(an aspect of empathy that is conveyed through communication) was positively related to
both satisfaction and love. Game-playing love and hostile conflict tactics were negatively related to satisfaction.

Still other research has shown that communication skills training, which can be
taught in a number of settings—from premarital education to marital enrichment to marital therapy—has a positive impact on relationships (Cole & Cole, 1999). Other research
has questioned the value of specific aspects of communication (e.g., active listening) in

situations of marital conflict (Gottman, Coan, Carrere, & Swanson, 1998). Interestingly, however, this very research found that other communicational behaviors—such as a softened, rather than harsh, escalation of conflict by a wife and a husband's willingness to accept influence from his wife—were both linked with marital happiness and stability. And still other research has linked active listening skills to improvement of the relational environment (Cole & Cole, 1999).

Communication tactics can function very differently for couples, not only depending on the couple, as noted earlier, but also depending on the context. For instance, it has been taken for granted that interrupting someone is impolite. Daigen and Holmes (2000) have assessed the function that communication interruptions performed in particular interactions for 78 married or cohabiting couples. Although there were several functions expressed by interruptions, the bottom-line finding relevant to relationship satisfaction was that interruptions used to indicate *agreement* were positively related both to how the partners reacted emotionally to their conversation and to their current satisfaction. But interruptions employed to indicate *disagreement* were negatively related to affect and satisfaction. All interruptions are obviously not created equal.

Negative interruptions—and more generally, negative communications—have the potential to hurt partners and impair relationship functioning. Vangelisti and Young (2000) have sought to answer questions regarding hurtful communication messages and if such messages have the same impact on people whether the messages are perceived to be intentional or unintentional. When people believed that someone had been intentionally hurtful to them during an interaction, they were less satisfied with their relationship with that person, felt less close to that person, and in general experienced a "distancing effect" (p. 393) from that person. When people had a hurtful interaction they thought was not intentional, they didn't experience these negative relational effects. Vangelisti and Young's research underlines the importance of context in assessing how communication behavior impacts a relationship. Whether the behavior is positive or negative, whether it seems intentional or unintentional, whether it is directed at the partner or someone else— all these factors are related to the behavior's impact on the relationship. For some suggestions on effective communication, see the Up Close box on page 132.

It is apparent that aspects of communication are related to satisfaction with a relationship and that communication in all its forms is an essential building block of maintaining a relationship. Before concluding this discussion of the various methods of relationship maintenance, however, it is important to consider briefly the issue of relationship satisfaction itself.

Relationship Satisfaction

Relationship satisfaction is a relatively new concept and recent phenomenon, since historically, marriages were either arranged by families or based on convenience, with limited alternatives (Levinger, 1997). However, "amid today's greatly increased alternatives,

Guidelines for Effective Communication

The following strategies are suggested for effective communication in a romantic relationship:

- Assure your partner of your affection.
- Be open about your feelings.
- Be positive and cheerful.
- Pay attention to your partner; mind the relationship.
- Think in relational terms, such as "we," instead of individual terms, or "you" and "me."
- Balance self-disclosure with privacy.
- Make it a rule not to keep secrets.
- Keep your nonverbals positive (e.g., don't frown or roll your eyes).
- If you want more intimacy, increase your eye contact.
- Take your partner's perspective.
- Only interrupt your partner to agree with him or her.
- Be a good listener.

decreased social constraints, and heightened pair instability . . . it matters far more how well two partners are pleased with the quality of their relationship" (p. 3).

So, what is *relationship satisfaction?* This term is typically used to refer to people's subjective feelings about their relationship. This is in contrast to *relationship adjustment,* which has been viewed as comprising the more objective characteristics and behaviors in a relationship (S. S. Hendrick, 1995). Fletcher, Simpson, and Thomas (2000) propose that satisfaction is only one of six relationship quality components that are different and rather specific indicators of overall relational quality but can be combined into an overall construct called *relationship quality.* The additional components are commitment, intimacy, love, passion, and trust, all of which are discussed in this volume.

Taking a somewhat different perspective, Karney and Bradbury (1995) have developed a model of relationship quality and stability, in which satisfaction also plays an important role. They propose that a truly comprehensive approach to predicting quality requires the analysis of multiple, interrelated influences on quality. These influences or predictors include enduring vulnerabilities, such as personality characteristics; stressful events; and adaptive processes, which refer to various coping strategies and skills used by the relationship partners. From this viewpoint, relationship quality is clearly a multidimensional construct.

A more global view of relationship quality is that proposed by Fincham, Beach, and Kemp-Fincham (1997), who suggest that relationship quality is essentially two dimensional, with both positive and negative relationship quality being important to a couple. Partners can either be high or low on positive quality or negative quality. Thus, partners with high positive quality and low negative quality would be happy; those with high positive quality and high negative quality would be ambivalent; those with high negative quality and low positive quality would be distressed; and those with low positive and low negative quality would be indifferent.

What most people are interested in, however, is not definitions or complex models but rather the utility and meaning of *satisfaction*. What makes satisfaction important is that it can be linked with whether relationships actually continue or end. For example, in one study of dating couples, couples lower in satisfaction and other specific qualities were more likely to break up (S. S. Hendrick et al., 1988). Satisfaction can be considered a sort of "barometer" of a relationship's well-being—not the only barometer, of course, but an important one (Karney & Bradbury, 1995).

The research on gender differences in relationship satisfaction provides mixed results. Looking at marriage specifically, we can ask, "Are wives happier than husbands, or are husbands happier than wives?" Surveys have shown that men seem to profit more from marriage than do women, at least in terms of such dimensions as physical health and well-being (Cutrona, 1996), and some time ago, sociologist Jesse Bernard (1972) referred to "his marriage" and "her marriage" as different experiences of the same marriage, based on gender and gender roles. Most research indicates, however, that women and men experience similar levels of satisfaction in relationships (e.g., Clements, Cordova, Markman, & Laurenceau, 1997), although the factors contributing to satisfaction may sometimes differ slightly between women and men. For same-sex couples, predictors of satisfaction as well as satisfaction levels are very similar to those for heterosexual couples (Peplau & Spaulding, 2000).

It is not surprising that satisfaction is related to many, if not all, of the emotions and behaviors that operate in partnered relationships. For example, the presence of passionate love and the absence of game-playing love are positively related to satisfaction (S. S. Hendrick et al., 1988), as are perceived perspective-taking ability of a partner and the avoidance of hostile and aggressive forms of conflict (Meeks et al., 1998). Satisfaction is also related to partners' attachment styles (secure styles for both partners is optimal) (Feeney et al., 2000) and to such things as relationship commitment. In fact, Rusbult (e.g., Rusbult & Buunk, 1993) proposes that commitment is more important than satisfaction in terms of relational outcome. A number of approaches to measuring satisfaction exist, with short and easy-to-administer measures being the most useful for routine clinical situations. One such measure is Hendrick's (S. S. Hendrick, 1988; S. S. Hendrick, Dicke, & C. Hendrick, 1998) Relationship Assessment Scale (RAS), displayed in a modified form in the following Up Close box (see page 134). As an interesting exercise, take the RAS once in regard to your current or most recent romantic relationship and again for your ideal relationship. Compare your results to see how closely your current relationship fits your ideal one.

Relationship Assessment Scale

For each question, circle the answer that best describes your current romantic relationship. After you have answered all the questions, add up your score. The higher your score, the more satisfied you are. (Note that the maximum possible is 35 and the lowest is 7.)

1. How well does your partner meet your needs?

    1 = *Poorly*   2   3 = *Average*   4   5 = *Extremely well*

2. In general, how satisfied are you with your relationship?

    1 = *Unsatisfied*   2   3 = *Average*   4   5 = *Extremely satisfied*

3. How good is your relationship compared to most?

    1 = *Poor*   2   3 = *Average*   4   5 = *Excellent*

4. How often do you wish you hadn't gotten in this relationship?

    1 = *Very often*   2   3 = *Average*   4   5 = *Never*

5. To what extent has your relationship met your original expectations?

    1 = *Hardly at all*   2   3 = *Average*   4   5 = *Completely*

6. How much do you love your partner?

    1 = *Not much*   2   3 = *Average*   4   5 = *Very much*

7. How many problems are there in your relationship?

    1 = *Very many*   2   3 = *Average*   4   5 = *Very few*

Total Score _____

Summary and Conclusions

Relational maintenance refers to a wide variety of behaviors that facilitate a relationship's success and survival. Having the same view of the relationship, or a shared meaning system, is related to maintenance. Five strategies for maintaining relationships include assurances, network involvement, openness, positivity, and sharing tasks. Minding and relationship awareness are two additional maintenance strategies that involve cognitive and affective focus on the partner and the relationship.

Communication is central to relationship maintenance and can be divided into strategic/functional and consequential/cultural approaches. The former concentrates on intentional behaviors, whereas the latter is more concerned with the culture of the relationship. Different types of couples may rely on different maintenance and communication strategies in expressing their relational cultures.

Self-disclosure is an important form of communication and refers to honestly telling someone else about one's intimate feelings and experiences. Self-disclosure may be broader and more general at the beginning of a relationship but gradually becomes deeper as a relationship continues, according to social penetration theory. Relational partners have many opposing or dialectical needs, such as the needs for openness/disclosure and closedness/privacy. Disclosure, like other relational phenomena, changes over the course of a relationship; it is a process. Men and women differ only moderately in disclosure. Along with positive affect and listening/understanding by a partner, self-disclosure has been viewed as one of three components of intimacy. Finally, the disclosure of traumatic events, though risky, may be a pathway toward greater physical and mental health. Both communication and intimacy are interactive processes in relationships.

Nonverbal communication is very powerful, and if verbal and nonverbal messages differ, it is the nonverbal message that is likely to be believed. Body language, facial expressions, and eye contact are all key aspects of nonverbal communication.

Partners' handling of both similarities *and* dissimilarities has implications for relationship success. When partners want relational change, they tend to push for it, and when they want things to remain as they are, they tend to back off. This sequence of behaviors is called demand/withdraw. Although interrupting a partner can be viewed as negative, interruptions that show agreement are positively related to partners' emotion and current satisfaction. Hurtful communications are less problematic when they are seen as unintentional, as opposed to intentional.

Maintenance, including communication, is important for relationship satisfaction, which typically refers to people's subjective feelings about their relationship. Relationship satisfaction, quality, and commitment are all related to relationship health.

Key Terms

Consequential/cultural (p. 122)
Dialectical (p. 124)
Minding (p. 122)
Nonverbal communication (p. 128)

Relational maintenance (p. 120)
Relationship satisfaction (p. 131)
Self-disclosure (p. 124)
Strategic/functional (p. 122)

Suggested Reading

Cole, C. L., & Cole, A. L. (1999). Marriage enrichment and prevention really works: Interpersonal competence training to maintain and enhance relationships. *Family Relations, 48,* 273–275.

Harvey, J. H., & Omarzu, J. (1998). Minding the close relationship. *Personality and Social Psychology Review, 1,* 224–240.

Meeks, B. S., Hendrick, S. S., & Hendrick, C. (1998). Communication, love, and relationship satisfaction. *Journal of Social and Personal Relationships, 15,* 755–773.

Pennebaker, J. W. (1990). *Opening up: The healing power of confiding in others.* New York: Morrow.

Prager, K. J., & Buhrmester, D. (1998). Intimacy and need fulfillment in couple relationships. *Journal of Social and Personal Relationships, 15,* 435–469.

7 Conflict and Abuse

Relationship Stories

The Flame of Anger

Antonio slammed the door! The sound reverberated through the apartment. Maria was in the kitchen, taking dishes out of the dishwasher to keep herself focused so that she wouldn't yell something after him—or worse yet, start crying. Just because Antonio had a temper tantrum didn't mean she had to have one, also!

Maria brushed back her long, black hair as she fought to keep her emotions in check. She and Antonio had only been engaged for a year, but she had known him for almost six years, since they met in high school. She was short and curvy, with big brown eyes and a smile to light up a room. He was tall, with wavy dark hair and an easy, comfortable, joking style. They met in math class their junior year. She sat in front of him, and he'd poke her in the back with the eraser end of his pencil whenever the teacher wasn't looking. At first she ignored him. He was an athlete, and she didn't typically like athletes. She was a serious student with college on her mind. But his persistent teasing led to talking, and talking to dating, and then they became a couple. They went together for several years before they felt ready to make the commitment to get engaged and then live together.

Usually, Maria and Antonio got along very well; both were warm and expressive and very much in love with each other. But every once in awhile, when things didn't go the way Antonio thought they should, he would have a major "meltdown," as Maria referred to it. Whether he was mad at Maria for something—or just mad, in general—he would yell and slam doors and generally let his feelings be known. Sometimes, he would storm out of the house, as he had this morning. Maria didn't worry about him doing something dangerous with his anger. She knew that this morning he would get into his car, put in a CD, and mellow out on his way to work. He didn't translate his anger into "road rage" or anything destructive like that. He just liked to make noise!

A simple conversation is what started the particular argument this morning. Antonio told Maria that he wanted to get tickets for a concert next week; one of his favorite bands was coming to town for a one-night gig. Then Maria had to remind him that they already had plans for that evening. They were going to her parents' house to celebrate her mother's birthday. That was when Antonio hit the roof, talking about how they needed to put their own wishes first once in awhile and stop always doing what their families expected them to do. Finally, he stormed out of the house, saying, "Fine, we'll go to your mother's birthday dinner, but this concert is a once-in-a-lifetime event!" His final words drifted after him as he left, the door slamming behind him.

Maria had never really gotten used to Antonio's way of expressing anger. It's not that she didn't show anger herself. She definitely did! She could raise her voice and be very clear about her feelings, and occasionally, when she was very upset, she might even break into tears. But she never got angry in quite the way Antonio did. He was just like the rest of his family: high tempered and volatile. When his family—his parents, his two brothers, and Antonio—would get in a family argument, no one could get a word in edgewise. Especially not Maria. Everyone talked at the same time, interrupting each other, gesturing furiously, determined to have the last word or at least the loudest word. Maria always felt out of place at these times and would usually go to another room or take a walk outside. Amazingly, these arguments didn't seem to bother Antonio's family. By the time she got back from her walk, they were usually talking and laughing and drinking wine. No big deal!

Maria's family was different. If conflict meant a group debate to Antonio's family, then it meant quiet problem solving to Maria's family. Her parents, her older sister, and Maria tried to talk calmly about a situation and work toward a solution, without letting emotions get out of hand or having anyone's feelings get hurt. That was the way Maria learned to handle disagreements and conflicts, and when she and Antonio developed a romantic relationship, she expected they would handle their conflicts as problems to be solved. Not so! The first time they had an argument—now, she couldn't even remember what it was about—he got angry during a movie and got up and left the theatre. She followed him to his car and they got in, driving along in silence until he dropped her off at home without a word. Of course, he called her the next day as though nothing had happened. To him it was simple: Get angry, blow up, and get over it. But it wasn't that simple to Maria. She was slower to get angry but also much slower to get over it. This morning, she was sure she would hear from him once he got to work and had a chance to simmer down. He might call to apologize, but more likely, he'd just call.

Maria didn't understand why Antonio had to make such a big deal out of things that were not life or death situations. It was just a concert, after all. She had tried to talk with Antonio about his temper because the problem wasn't just that *she* had to deal with him when he was being difficult. She was actually worried about him—that his emotional intensity would have health consequences, like high blood pressure (which ran in his family) or some other health problem, especially as he got older. But Antonio always blew her off. "Maria, that's just the way I am. I get mad and show my feelings, but then I get over it. I don't destroy things, and I don't hold grudges. What's the problem?"

No problem, thought Maria, except that it takes us a lot longer to solve problems if we have to wait for Antonio to react and have a meltdown, then get over it, and then start to work on whatever the issue is. Why can't we just work on the issue in the first place? She loved Antonio, but she sometimes found him tiring. He was just a lot to deal with! She was starting to wonder if they would *ever* be able to handle conflict constructively. Then suddenly the phone rang, and she picked it up. It was Antonio.

■ ■ ■

The Big Chill

The house was eerily quiet as Peter fixed himself some lunch. Usually on a Saturday, the CD player was going, and he and Lisa were doing chores, running errands, taking care of 2-year-old Ethan, and filling the little house with sounds of family life. But not today. Today, the house was silent and cold—strange to have it feel cold in the middle of July. Ethan was taking his nap, and Lisa had gone to the grocery store.

Peter and Lisa had had a disagreement that morning. It wasn't a huge fight; they had simply disagreed about the timing of their visit to the new child care center where they were thinking about sending Ethan three days a week, starting in September. Both of them realized what an important step they were taking, but Lisa was a lot edgier about it than Peter was. So when he suggested changing the time of their visit from Monday morning to Wednesday afternoon, her face clouded over and she simply said, "Fine. I'll rearrange my schedule." She didn't argue with him. The only reason he knew that she was upset was that she had become very quiet, and he felt a distinct chill in the air.

This wasn't unusual. Lisa sometimes would talk about what she perceived to be a conflict and would even argue her position. But more often, she would simply "shut down."

It could last from an hour to a day to several days. Peter never really knew how long it would take for things to get back to normal. He just waited it out.

Peter thought back to the time when he and Lisa had first met. He was new in town, working for a computer company. He was recently divorced and ready to begin a new life in a new city. Soon after he arrived in town, Joanne, a woman he worked with, wanted to introduce him to Lisa, a friend of hers and her husband Tom's. Lisa turned out to be slender and blond, with a cool elegance that seemed in sharp contrast with her work for the county as a counselor for at-risk families. Peter and Lisa met on a blind date, when Joanne and Tom arranged for the four of them to go out to dinner.

Once Peter and Lisa met and started talking and getting to know one another, Tom and Joanne might as well have been eating dinner at another restaurant! But they just shrugged their shoulders, secretly very pleased that the blind date was going so well. Meanwhile, Lisa and Peter talked intensely about everything in their past and present lives. Each had been married before and was childless, and each was looking for someone with whom they could have something more than just a superficial relationship. It seemed that they might just have found what they were looking for.

An intense courtship, wedding, and starting a family followed that blind date in short order. Ethan's birth was a joy for both of them. Lisa's decision to return to work only part time and stay home to care for Ethan was a financial sacrifice, but it was a choice that both Lisa and Peter felt totally committed to. Peter was a very involved father, and he spent a lot of time with Ethan. Life was good.

In fact, the only thing that really bothered Peter was the way Lisa handled conflicts or sometimes even small disagreements. He never knew quite how she would react. Sometimes, it was okay—they could talk a problem through. But at other times, when they even started to disagree, Lisa would get icily quiet, the way she did this morning. Peter hated being shut out, and he wasn't used to this way of handling conflict. His first marriage had been very different; he and his ex-wife had survived some serious shouting matches. The family in which he grew up was different still. His parents were quiet people who seldom disagreed. On those rare occasions when they did, either they came to a compromise or his father tended to make the final decision. Peter and his younger sister were encouraged to settle sibling conflicts by talking, rather than fighting. He still remembered the time when he was 10 and his sister was 8, and during a fight, she slapped him on the back so hard that his mother could see the handprint. His sister got sent to her room and never tried that tactic again.

But Lisa was an only child, so she had never had to negotiate—or fight—with a sister or brother. Her parents were older when she was born, and they always tried to "reason" with her. In fact, she seemed to have grown up having things her own way, as long as what she wanted seemed reasonable. Because they agreed on so many things, Peter had not realized that he and Lisa had fundamentally different styles of handling conflict. Then, after Ethan was born, life got more complicated, and there were more things to negotiate. Household chores, work hours, childrearing approaches, child care, and a thousand other things all had to be worked out.

It still didn't happen too often—Lisa's shutting down and shutting him out—but when it did, it always unnerved him a little. It was as if his wife were someone he didn't fully know. He wished he knew what to do or how to make things better. Peter looked down at the sandwich that he had just made for his lunch; he didn't even remember making it. As he heard the back door open, he turned. Lisa walked into the kitchen, arms full of grocery bags, tears streaming down her face. "Peter, we need to talk," she said. And so they talked

■ ■ ■

Questions to Consider in Reading This Chapter

- Is it better to express anger and get it out, the way Antonio does, or to try to manage it calmly, as Maria does?
- Like Peter, have you ever been surprised by the way that your romantic partner has handled (or not handled) conflict?
- Does conflict between relationship partners necessarily mean that they have relationship problems?
- How do you handle conflict? Do you explode, avoid, try to problem solve, or use some combination of those behaviors?

What Do We Know about Conflict and Abuse?

As we consider the couples in the two Relationship Stories, it is likely much easier to view Maria and Antonio as having **conflict.** Lisa and Peter seem to be having some communication problems, but would we actually label it "conflict?"

Brickman (1974) defines *conflict* as existing "in situations in which parties must divide or share resources so that, to some degree, the more one party gets, the less others can have" (p. 1). This definition does fit Antonio and Maria: She wants to go to her mother's birthday dinner; he wants to go to the concert. But it is less appropriate for the struggles of Peter and Lisa. Their dilemma may be captured better by Peterson's (1983) definition of *conflict* as "an interpersonal process that occurs whenever the actions of one person interfere with the actions of another" (p. 365). This means essentially that whenever two people in a relationship want different things, there is some uneasiness or difficulty, which can be termed *conflict*.

The Basics of Conflict

The Structure of Conflict

Conflict can also be put into a structure, sometimes envisioned as a series of stages: beginning, middle, and end. For example, Peterson (1983) views conflict as having a *beginning stage,* in which conflict is initiated by some event or behavior and then responded to either by engagement (i.e., attempting to deal with the conflict; more like Maria and Antonio) or avoidance (more like Lisa and Peter). Engagement or avoidance continues to be at issue in the *middle stages* of conflict, where partners can avoid, at least temporarily; negotiate and solve the problem; or escalate and increase the conflict level without really getting anywhere. According to Peterson, the conflict *termination stage* can have any one of several outcomes: separation or withdrawal; domination, in which one person wins; compromise, in which each person gives a little; integrative agreement, in which a solution is found that satisfies both persons' needs; and structural improvement, or long-term change in the relationship.

Operationalizing these strategies in Maria and Antonio's situation, *separation* involves avoidance of the issue, and this is, to some extent, what happened when Antonio stormed out of the house. A *domination* strategy would mean a win/lose situation, so the couple would either go to the birthday dinner (Maria wins) or the concert (Antonio wins). *Compromise* might mean that Maria and Antonio would go to the birthday dinner for a little while and then go late to the concert. An *integrative agreement* might mean that Antonio and Maria would take Maria's mother out for a lovely birthday lunch but would then be free to go to the concert. A *structural improvement* in the relationship would have less to do with this particular issue than with how the couple handles such issues, so it might involve their seeking counseling to help them handle conflict better or to establish their own rules for conflictual discussion (e.g., Antonio won't yell; Maria won't cry).

It is helpful to understand that conflict has overarching definitions and at least reasonably predictable stages because there are many causes of conflict.

Causes of Conflict

There are almost as many causes of conflict as there are people in conflict situations. Therapists often used to say that couples seeking counseling were arguing about money, sex, or in-laws, but that is an extreme simplification. In fact, couples argue about each other's personality qualities, children, in-laws and other family, friends, money, jobs, time, where to live, how to spend time, activities, who does the chores, who gets the remote, religion, politics, what movie to see, what car to buy, and the list goes on and on. Different things matter to different people, so couples may argue about different things.

There are also different *levels* of causes of conflict. For example, partners may argue about specific behaviors ("You never cook"), norms for behavior ("You don't do your share of the household work"), or personal dispositions ("You're irresponsible") (Peterson, 1983). Gottman (1994) notes that there are many causes of conflict, but he states that "much more important than having compatible views is *how* couples work out their differences" (pp. 23–24; italics in original). Most conflicts are solvable, but they may at times be solved by "agreeing to disagree" and then moving on.

Processes of Conflict

Attributional Approaches

An **attribution** is an inference or judgment made about why a particular event occurred. People make attributions for their own and others' behavior by perceiving the behavior and then making inferences about it. Attribution is really a meaning-making behavior, in which we try to assign causes for things and thereby make sense of our world and the people in it, including ourselves and our partners.

When making judgments about our own behavior, we tend to attribute causality to something about the situation, referred to as a *situational attribution*. When judging someone else's behavior, however, we tend to attribute causality to something about the person, referred to as a *dispositional attribution*. That means that if we are late in meeting our partner for dinner, we say, "I got caught in traffic," but if our partner is late in meeting us for dinner, we say, "You're always late; you're so slow." Also, there is a tendency to attribute better motives to our own behavior than to others' behavior. For example, research by Schutz (1999) that involved interviews with 25 married couples found that "even in non-distressed close relationships accounts of conflict [were] distorted in a self-serving manner. Both partners tended to emphasize their own needs and hurt feelings, and to refer to aspects that excused or justified their own behavior. Each partner also tended to blame the other for initiating the conflict, to describe the partner's behavior as irrational and incomprehensible, and to refer to prior negative partner behavior" (p. 193). So, Lisa may have made the attribution that when Peter wanted to change their appointment, he was being inconsiderate of her plans. Peter, on the other hand, might simply have thought that a Wednesday afternoon would be a less hectic time to visit a day care center than a Monday morning.

The reason that the concept of attribution is so important to the study of conflict in relationships is that while specific events or behaviors can cause routine conflict in a relationship, the attributions we make about the causes of those conflicts can lead to much more severe and profound conflict. As discussed throughout this chapter, *how we think about conflict* has as much or more importance than *what we do about it*. If we think negatively about our partner, making negative attributions during conflict, we are likely to smolder and get more and more upset. Then we may approach our partner negatively or, perhaps worse, respond negatively when our partner approaches us positively. (See Gottman [1994] for many more examples.) Making negative attributions tends to make conflict resolution more difficult and is linked to lower satisfaction (Fincham & Bradbury, 1993). As you read the rest of this chapter, underline the word *attribution* every time it occurs, just to highlight the importance of attribution processes.

Exchange Approaches

Exchange theory (discussed in Chapter 3) is based on marketplace notions of rewards and costs (Blau, 1964), accompanied by outcomes (rewards minus costs) and comparison levels (essentially seeing how well one's outcomes compare to others' outcomes, especially a partner's outcomes). In fact, Kelley (1979) suggests that romantic relationships can be evaluated in terms of each individual partner's rewards and costs as well as the couple's joint rewards and costs.

Linked to exchange theory is *equity theory* (e.g., Walster et al., 1973), which emphasizes fairness in human relations and the desire by most partners to have equivalent outcomes (rewards minus costs). These concepts become particularly significant in conflict situations, in which partners have opposing, or at least different, desires. During a conflict, it becomes important that partners experience more rewards than costs in the relationship and thus have positive outcomes, and it is equally important that both partners feel a sense of equity in their outcomes. It is also important that a couple be able to think in terms of "we" as well as "I" (Acitelli, 1993). If each person wants what is best for his or her partner and the relationship, as well as what is best for himself or herself, then the couple is more likely to be able to handle conflict constructively. In both of the Relationship Stories, it is likely that the rewards exceed the costs and that the couples have the potential to handle conflict more constructively.

Grote and Clark (2001) assessed responses from 181 married couples over time—specifically, during the transition to first parenthood (i.e., birth of the first child)—and tried to develop a model of the relationship between marital distress and perceptions of fairness/unfairness. Most research has emphasized perceptions of unfairness in a relationship leading to relationship distress; however, Grote and Clark considered the possibility that the *reverse* occurs: that relationship distress may lead to perceptions of unfairness. Their results indicated "that the oft-reported findings in the literature that there is a link between perceptions of unfairness and low relationship quality probably result sometimes from low quality leading to perceptions of unfairness, sometimes from perceptions of unfairness leading to low relationship quality, and sometimes from both" (p. 290).

While these conclusions may not seem surprising, they illustrate how attribution theory and exchange theory may both work in relationships, particularly during conflict. For example, relationship partners may assess what they are getting from their relationship (rewards) and what they are giving to the relationship (costs) and compute the difference. If their outcomes are either low positive or negative, or are considerably lower than their partner's outcomes, that may lead to relationship distress. Or if partners are distressed due to sleep deprivation and other stresses following the birth of a child, for example, then the most distressed person is likely to examine the rewards and costs in the relationship and perceive that things are unfair and that he or she is coming up short. He or she may then make negative attributions about the partner's behavior. The most distressed person is likely to view the partner's failure to do a fair share of the work as dispositional (i.e., an aspect of the partner's personality), and he or she may even generalize the negative evaluation to other qualities or behaviors of the partner. Those negative attributions then feed back to the relationship distress and increase it, creating what Bradbury and Fincham (1992) have referred to as a *spiral of negativity*.

Although relationship theorists often try to develop their own theories to the exclusion of others, it is more useful to view each theory as contributing a necessary but not sufficient piece to the puzzle of relationships.

The Pluses and Minuses of Conflict

Conflict has often been viewed as something negative; however, it is a natural part of human behavior and can be used constructively or destructively. Conflict is not, in and of itself, negative. As discussed in earlier chapters, relationships are exemplars of *dialectical processes* (e.g., Baxter & Montgomery, 1996), in which needs for such things as connection with others pull against needs for such things as autonomy or separateness from others. Erbert (2000) used multiple methods to explore the conflicts of 25 marital couples and determine the extent to which dialectical contradictions were played out in their conflicts. He found that dialectical issues were indeed important and that the autonomy-versus-connection and openness-versus-closedness contradictions were most important during conflict. So, dialectical processes are clearly significant during conflict.

Yet the conflict inherent in a dialectical contradiction is also inherent in relationships more generally and does not depend on a particular conflictual event or behavior. In other words, it may be that conflict/change versus peacefulness/stability is itself a dialectical process in relationships (e.g., Duck & Wood, 1995; Gottman, 1993a). Erber and Erber (2001) discuss the relatively recent emphasis on conflict as both positive and negative, referring to *constructive conflict* as "transformational" in its ability to reinvent relationships in an improved form. (This is similar to Peterson's [1983] notion of *structural improvement*.) The Erbers also recognize the difficulties inherent in *destructive conflict,* however, which can involve hostile communications and escalating conflict and can lead to the ending of a relationship.

Although this chapter will explore destructive conflict in couple relationships in some detail, it is important to consider briefly how conflict is naturally expressed in other close relationships—for example, those between parents and children and those between friends.

Conflict in Families and Friendships

Parents versus Children

This title, *Parents versus Children,* was adopted very consciously because although parents and children typically have loving relationships and interactions, even in the happiest of families, there is sometimes a sense of "us versus them" on the parts of both the children and the parents. Scholars have often taken a *unidirectional perspective* toward parent/child conflict, emphasizing the effect of parental behavior on children, but more recently, the *bidirectional approach* has been explored to emphasize "how children influence parents as well and how both parties influence each other" (Canary, Cupach, & Messman, 1995, p. 53). Just as parents shape children's behavior (conflict and otherwise), so do children shape their parents' behavior. Consider how each of the partners in the Relationship Stories was influenced by his or her parents' and family's ways of handling conflict.

Conflict between children and parents occurs early on, with children as young as 18 to 24 months showing some knowledge of the rules governing conflict. Throughout the early childhood period, children develop more and more sophistication about how to enact, justify, and manage conflict. Children are incredibly observant, and they develop their knowledge of conflict management from their own experiences with their parents as well as from their parents' interaction, their siblings' interaction, and so on (Canary et al., 1995).

Although conflict skills are developed initially in early childhood and become more sophisticated throughout the later childhood years, it is during adolescence that parent/child conflict takes center stage. Canary and his colleagues (1995) detail a number of theoretical perspectives on adolescent development in regard to conflict, and the overall theme seems to be that the biological changes of puberty, as well as cognitive and emotional maturing, urge the adolescent toward greater autonomy. This drive toward autonomy causes fluctuations in the parent/adolescent relationship, as the parents struggle to adjust to their child's changes. Previous family rules and patterns become accentuated during this period, so that if the parents have been firm and flexible in dealing with the child during earlier years, it is more likely that conflict will be resolved satisfactorily. If, however, the parents have been inconsistent or overly rigid in their parenting style, adolescent autonomy seeking can cause a crisis in the parent/adolescent relationship.

In referencing the work of Paikoff and Brooks-Gunn (1991), Canary et al. (1995) note that both adolescents and their parents have developmental tasks during this period. Adolescents need to increase their autonomy while also taking others'—particularly parents'—expectations into account. Parents need to maintain their parental roles while also respecting their child's increasing autonomy and accepting that he or she is simply not going to do everything that the parents wish. This is really not so different from the accommodations that long-term partners, such as spouses, need to make with each other.

Friendships

As discussed earlier in this volume, having friendships is an important way to satisfy the need to belong. Moreover, the nature of friendships is relatively unique in that these relationships are voluntary. No contracts or legal obligations enforce friendships, so the mutuality found in them is in a sense chosen, one interaction at a time. Interestingly, this aspect of choice means that conflict in friendships must be handled more delicately than often occurs in the family.

As children learn to handle conflict within the family, they also gain experience in handling conflict in friendships, wherein conflict also can be constructive or destructive

(Canary et al., 1995). Four-year-olds may disagree about who gets to play with a particular toy or who gets the biggest cookie at snack time. During adolescence, a time when friendship is especially important (Collins & Laursen, 2000), conflict with friends seems to be less negative and less intense than that with family (Canary et al., 1995). But it is present, nevertheless, with reported conflict increasing as a friendship deepens and becomes more rewarding (Fehr, 1996). Friends *do* get angry and have arguments with one another.

Adolescents and young adults learn to differentiate between relatively minor conflicts and more important ones (Canary et al., 1995), and reasons for conflict in friendships are similar to those for other close relationships, including dismissing behavior, annoying behavior, and so on. Betrayal of trust is a significant cause of conflict in friendships and romantic relationships (Baxter, Mazanec, Nicholson, Pittman, Smith, & West, 1997; Fehr, 1996). Friends may handle conflict by discussing it and working through it, but often conflict is avoided, sometimes to the detriment of the relationship's continuation.

One reason conflict in friendships has not been studied more frequently is that conflict in family and romantic, particularly marital, relationships has been of central interest to relationship scholars.

Conflict in Romantic and Marital Couples

As noted earlier, conflict is present in most partnered relationships and may even be necessary as part of the dialectical processes that occur in interaction. So, conflict is less of an "if" question for couples and more of a "why and how" question.

Conflict occurs at different rates for different couples but can range from one *per week* or so for couples who are nondistressed to one or more conflicts *per day* for distressed couples (Canary et al., 1995). Just as with friendships, the deeper the relationship becomes, the greater the interdependence between partners and the greater the potential for both pleasure and conflict (e.g., Braiker & Kelley, 1979). As Sprecher and Felmlee (1993) found in studying couples, "Intense feelings of love in the initial stages of a relationship suggest that individuals are highly emotionally invested in the relationship, which may increase the likelihood of subsequent conflict" (p. 123). Knowledge of these findings would likely have reassured Maria, who worried about the conflicts that she and Antonio experienced.

Qualities of Distressed Couples

Extending the earlier discussion on attribution, for couples who are distressed, partners tend to make more negative attributions about each other and to attribute negative behaviors to more dispositional and stable causes. They are also likely to assess a partner's negative behavior as "global, . . . negative in intent, selfishly motivated, and blameworthy" (Fincham, Beach, & Nelson, 1987, p. 71). Ironically, distressed couples also have a tendency to disregard a partner's positive behaviors, viewing them as due to temporary, situational factors. For nondistressed partners, however, the processes are reversed, in that a partner's positive behaviors are seen as enduring and his or her negative behaviors as temporary. Cross-cultural findings offer additional information on partner interaction. As noted by Halford, Hahlweg, and Dunne (1990), "the most outstanding feature of un- happy couples is their inability to terminate negative interaction, particularly in nonverbal communication. . . . In contrast, happy couples manage to deescalate such a process or re- frain from starting it at all" (p. 499). Lisa and Peter were happy in their relationship, so even if they didn't always handle conflict well, their conflict didn't keep spiraling.

Another problem for distressed couples is that they tend to be less clear in their communication than are nondistressed couples. Noller and Venardos (1986) found that when partners with high or moderate adjustment communicated with each other, they tended to be flexible in their assessments of the communication, sometimes confident that they had interpreted a partner's communication correctly and other times less confident about their own interpretations. These partners tended to be reasonably accurate in these assessments, as well. However, poorly adjusted partners were equally confident about all their interpretations of partner communications, whether they were right or wrong. "Thus, couples low in marital adjustment are both less accurate in their communication than are other couples and also less aware of that lack of accuracy" (p. 40).

Recent findings by Sillars and his colleagues are consistent with a variety of earlier research (Sillars, Roberts, Leonard, & Dun, 2000). In their research with 118 married couples, they found that spouses tend to evaluate their own behavior more positively than their partner's behavior and that in more serious conflicts and in distressed couples, partners are very subjective and also somewhat hostile. Thus, the negative communica- tion cycle escalates and further entrenches the conflict. Negative evaluations/attributions are again related to conflict.

Approaches to Handling Conflict

Yet another perspective on the process of conflict was developed by Rusbult and her col- leagues (e.g., Rusbult & Zembrodt, 1983). To the dimension of *engagement/avoidance* (also called *activity/passivity*) of conflict discussed earlier, they added the dimension of *constructiveness/destructiveness*. They crossed the two dimensions, thereby creating four different quadrants that represent four different approaches to relational conflict: (1) **exit** (leaving the conflict and the partner, active and destructive); (2) **voice** (engaging the part- ner in problem solving, active and constructive); (3) **loyalty** (avoiding conflict but re- maining committed to the partner, passive and constructive); and (4) **neglect** (avoiding/ ignoring both the conflict and the partner, passive and destructive). The negative strate- gies, such as exit and neglect, have been shown to be more powerful negative influences on relationship success than the positive strategies have been shown to be positive influ- ences on relationship success (Rusbult, Johnson, & Morrow, 1986). Such findings are consistent with other research showing that relational negatives are more powerful than relational positives (e.g., Gottman, 1994; Meeks et al., 1998).

Another way of understanding couples conflict, presented by Christensen and his colleagues (e.g., Heavey, Christensen, & Malamuth, 1995; Sagrestano, Christensen, & Heavey, 1998), is called the **demand/withdraw** cycle (discussed briefly in Chapter 6). In this sequence of events, one of the partners, typically the woman/wife, is seeking change from her partner and enacts the demand behavior. The partner on the receiving end, typically the man/husband, resists the request for change/demand and pulls back from his partner, thereby enacting the withdraw behavior. Canary et al. (1995) discuss the explanations that have been made for the demand/withdraw cycle, most notably that either women are more relationally sensitive and competent in communication and therefore more attuned to needs for relationship change or that women seek more relationship change than men do because women are typically underbenefited in marriage, as compared to men. Considerable research has explored the demand/withdraw cycle, and indeed, it appears that the cycle has less to do with relational sensitivity than with who desires change in the relationship. In other words, when women want change in a heterosexual relationship, they tend to demand and their male partner withdraws; however, when men want change in a relationship, they demand and their female partner withdraws (e.g., Klinetob & Smith, 1996; Sagrestano et al., 1998). The importance of this cycle is its link to relationship satisfaction because when a partner demands or withdraws, that can cause conflict and resulting relationship dissatisfaction (e.g., Heavey et al., 1995).

Roberts (2000) has attempted to sort out some of the complexities of communication, conflict, and distress in a study of married couples, noting that all withdrawing is not the same. In other words, is withdrawal more negative when it comes from husbands as opposed to wives? Is angry withdrawal from an interaction as emotionally negative for a partner as withdrawal in order to avoid conflict? What Roberts found was that each of these questions can be answered *no*. Wives' withdrawal from intimacy was predictive of greater marital distress by husbands, but the reverse was not the case. What predicted marital distress for wives, however, was hostile responding by husbands. So in fact, wives reacted negatively to hostility, as Maria did to Antonio, and husbands reacted negatively to withdrawal, as Peter did to Lisa. As Roberts points out, this pattern contradicts the stereotype in the relationship literature that women demand, men withdraw, and women get distressed.

The pattern is even more complicated, however, because withdrawal in the form of conflict avoidance on the part of the husband may sometimes, but not always, be problematic for the wife. "A wife may react positively to her husband's conflict-avoiding behaviors if the alternative is hostile responsiveness. . . . On the other hand, if her husband is unlikely to engage in hostile behavior, his conflict avoidance may undermine her positive feelings about the relationship" (p. 704). Indeed, still other research (Caughlin & Vangelisti, 2000) emphasizes the degree to which demand/withdraw issues have less to do with gender than with the particular characteristics of the individual partners and their relationship. It is difficult to know how showing hostility or withdrawing will impact any given couple having any given conflict. Thus, it is probably wise to use strategies other than hostility and withdrawal during conflict. To better understand your own way of handling conflict, consider the questions in the Up Close box on the next page.

Handling Conflict

Think of a conflict that you have had recently with a romantic partner, a friend, or a family member. Consider these questions:

- What were your reactions?
- Did you assume that you were completely in the right?
- Did you make any attributions about the other person? If so, what kinds of attributions did you make?
- Did you tend to blame the person or the situation?
- Did you discuss the issue calmly, or did you use harsh words and hostility?
- Was your relationship better or worse after the conflict?

Now, think about how conflict was handled in your family when you were growing up.

- How does this influence the way you handle conflict now in your relationships?
- Are you satisfied with the way you handle conflict? If not, how would you like things to be different?

Scholar and relationship researcher John Gottman (1993b) has emphasized couple differences in conflict styles, proposing a typology of couples based on both their approach to conflict and their overall marital stability. From longitudinal research with couples, Gottman described three stable couple types: *avoiders*, *validators*, and *volatiles*. Avoiders tended to be very patient and let time solve the issue or let the issue fade; confronting conflicts was not something that appealed to them. (Note that a *couples* strategy of avoiding conflict is very different from having one partner demand and the other avoid/withdraw.) Validators were supportive and problem solving in their approach, with moderation a key to their success. Finally, volatiles had lots of positive emotions and lots of negative emotions; they battled with drama and made up passionately. The two unstable couple types were the *hostile* couples and the *hostile/detached* couples. The former engaged in very negative conflict, while the latter added emotional distancing to their negative conflict style. As Gottman points out, it is not the simple occurrence of conflict that is positive or negative for a relationship but how the conflict is handled. The reason that the couples in the Relationship Stories were having problems handling conflict was not so much that one partner's approach was better than another's but that the partners had different approaches.

Gottman (1994) has also proposed that a key to relationship success is the ratio of positive to negative affective experiences and events in the relationship. He believes that if a couple can maintain five positives for every one negative in their relationship, then the relationship will remain stable and healthy. The notion of positives outweighing negatives is very consistent with exchange theory (i.e., rewards should outweigh costs in a satisfying relationship) and with previous research showing that marital satisfaction could be predicted from the number of times a couple had intercourse minus the number of arguments they had during a 35-day period of time (Howard & Dawes, 1976). Whether the ideal ratio is 2 to 1 or 5 to 1 or 10 to 1, it is clear that positives must outnumber negatives in a relationship if it is to survive and prosper.

Relational Power

Power is related to virtually all aspects of heterosexual close relationships but particularly to conflict. "The major proportion of marital power has historically been seen to reside with husbands rather than with wives" (S. S. Hendrick & C. Hendrick, 1992, p. 186). Although some people would argue that women have had greater power in the family setting, their power is only one of the five kinds of social power proposed by French and Raven (1968), and it is the least powerful one: *referent power* (power associated with attractiveness and liking). Men have traditionally had more of the other four types of power: *reward power* (ability to reward), *coercive power* (ability to punish), *legitimate power* (power based on authority), and *expert power* (power based on knowledge). Although resources such as money and professional prestige have been linked to power (as discussed in Chapter 10), women with high resources still may not have high power.

As a group in society, men have had more power than women have had. And this power has made a difference in relationships. Winter, Stewart, and McClelland (1977) looked at husbands' motivation for power and found that the greater the power motive for the husband, the lower the wife's career achievement. McAdams (1988) has discussed a variety of research linking higher power motivation in men with higher rates of breakup and divorce.

But power is usually not all one way in a relationship. Men may experience a relative lack of power in intimate relationships in such areas as communication, where women often are more comfortable with the process. And husbands who try to initiate sex with their wives and are refused, no matter how tactfully, may feel anything but powerful.

An extended discussion of power is beyond the scope of this chapter, but it is important to be aware of how power is distributed in a relationship if one wants to understand how conflict is handled. For example, research (e.g., Heavey et al., 1995) has indicated that the demand/withdraw sequence occurs when one partner wants change (demands) and the other partner does not (withdraws). The outcome of this sequence is likely to look very different, depending on whether it is the less powerful partner or the more powerful partner who wants the change.

Handling Conflict Constructively

As emphasized several times, the occurrence of conflict is much less important than the way in which the conflict is handled. Gottman (1994) has proposed four conflict warning signs that he calls the "Four Horsemen of the Apocalypse." These warnings are presented here because either avoiding them or handling them constructively becomes an important strategy for conflict resolution. The first warning sign is *criticism,* which Gottman differentiates from simple complaining or objecting to a specific behavior. Namely, criticism is bigger and more inclusive; it tends to involve attacking the person, rather than the behavior. And cross-complaining—wherein one partner complains and rather than respond to the complaint, the other partner complains about something else—is a recipe for unproductive conflict. The second warning sign is *contempt,* which involves devaluing and dismissing the partner. The third warning sign is *defensiveness,* or being unwilling to acknowledge any fault on one's own part, and the fourth sign is **stonewalling,** a form of complete withdrawal from the interaction and the partner and perhaps the most destructive of the four "horsemen."

To combat these four warning signs, Gottman (1994) has proposed four conflict management strategies: calming down, being nondefensive, validating one's partner, and practicing positive conflict management. If one is calm, then everything else will follow more easily. If one is nondefensive and validates his or her partner, then one's criticism will be reduced and he or she will not be in danger of either stonewalling or being contemptuous of his or her partner.

Other research rounds out the picture of conflict management. For example, Thompson and Bolger (1999) assessed negative emotion, often involved in conflict, in couples in which one partner was preparing to take a major professional examination: the bar exam. These authors found that although the feelings of anxiety and depression felt by the individuals who were preparing to take the exam were picked up on by their partners and resulted in the partners also feeling anxious, depressed, and less pleased with the relationship, this *emotional transmission* decreased over the month preceding the exam. In other words, although the examinees became increasingly depressed and anxious, their partners were less and less negatively affected as the examination drew closer. It was as though the partners could make the attribution that "It's not about me; it's about the bar exam" and not overreact to the negative emotions.

Other findings in the same research (Thompson & Bolger, 1999) showed that "the partner's support became increasingly effective in preventing a rise in distress during the same period. This suggests that partners were especially attentive to the examinee's needs when stress was greatest" (p. 46). These findings are consistent with still other research showing that when relationship partners believed that their partner's position in a conflict was legitimate, they were more willing to listen to the partner (Klein & Lamm, 1996). Of course, Gottman (1994) would point out the need to be calm and nondefensive in order to listen to the partner's position in the first place. So, accepting the legitimacy of one's partner's point of view and being willing to make allowances when he or she is

Strategies for Handling Conflict

In order to handle conflict more effectively, try using some of the strategies listed below. They are based on the findings of research discussed in this chapter, suggestions a therapist would give, and common sense.

- Try to avoid conflict when you're tired or hungry.
- Be prepared to compromise.
- Deal with a specific issue, not accumulated problems or someone's bad mood.
- Focus on the issue—don't get distracted.
- Talk in a neutral place (NOT the bedroom).
- Give yourselves time—don't rush it.
- Keep a sense of humor.
- Fight fair; no name-calling.
- Don't start an argument on a holiday.
- Try not to be defensive. (This is a hard one!)
- If the conflict is going poorly, take a time-out.
- Don't interrupt your partner unless it is to agree with her or him.
- Listen carefully to your partner.
- Look at your partner when he or she is speaking.
- Don't dominate the discussion.
- Be creative in trying to find solutions to conflicts.

going through a stressful period are other effective conflict management techniques. The Up Close box above offers some specific strategies for handling conflict.

Conflict is an interesting and complex phenomenon that is likely to generate even more research in years ahead. Cupach (2000) has highlighted several ways in which conflict should be examined, noting that capturing the essence of conflict is far more than assessing one issue at one point in time. Conflict in a relationship may be a one-time issue but is equally often the tip of a relational "iceberg." It is also important to embed the study of conflict within the study of other relational behaviors. To what extent do such things as communication and social support moderate conflict? Finally, how can the causes and solutions of conflict be considered at multiple levels: intrapersonal, interpersonal, social network, and societal? In addition, it would be particularly useful to study relational conflict using the couple, rather than the separate partners, as the unit of analysis (Ridley, Wilhelm, & Surra, 2001). Conflict is a basic aspect of many couple relationships, and if handled well, it can even keep the relationship strong (Gottman, 1994).

Abuse in Relationships

Although they are being considered in the same chapter, *conflict* and *abuse* are not the same thing. Conflict is frequent in relationships and, if handled appropriately, can aid relationship growth. Abuse is very different. The issue of abuse, both physical and sexual, is a profound concern for relationship researchers, people in relationships, and society as a whole. The topic of abuse will be considered only briefly in this chapter; comprehensive reviews can be found elsewhere (e.g., Christopher & Lloyd, 2000; Johnson & Ferraro, 2000; Lloyd & Emery, 2000a, 2000b).

Relationship *abuse/violence/aggression* (terms used interchangeably in this chapter) can be both verbal and behavioral. Even so, it is the *behavioral* aspects—restraint or force—that command most attention. Definitions of *violence* are complex and subject to interpretation. To some people, a push or shove constitutes violence, but to others, it does not. Breaking a partner's nose, however, is likely to be rated as violence by nearly everyone. Depending on the definition, physical or sexual aggression may occur in up to half of all intimate relationships (Lloyd & Emery, 2000a). In fact, millions of women are assaulted seriously each year by their intimate male partners (Straus & Gelles, 1990). Abuse occurs in dating, cohabiting, and marriage relationships (Lloyd & Emery, 2000b).

Johnson and Ferraro (2000) make the point that abuse is not a unitary phenomenon. They differentiate among four patterns of abuse between relational partners: (1) **common couple violence,** in which both partners participate and that typically does not escalate; (2) **intimate terrorism** (also called *patriarchal violence* [Johnson, 1995]), which involves a heavy element of control; (3) *violent resistance,* in which one partner, typically the woman, resists the domination of the other partner, typically the man; and (4) *mutual violent control,* a relatively rare pattern in which both partners are controlling and violent (Johnson & Ferraro, 2000). These authors also note that whereas common couple violence may be equally exercised by women and men and women may more frequently display violent resistance, men are nearly always the perpetrators of intimate terrorism.

In addition to the different types of violence, there are also different types of perpetrators of violence and different relational contexts for violence (Johnson & Ferraro, 2000). For example, Holtzworth-Monroe (2000) has extended an earlier typology of violent men to include *family-only batterers,* who are the least violent and exhibit no psychopathology; *dysphoric/borderline batterers,* who exhibit more severe violence and are emotionally unstable and dependent on the partner; *generally violent/antisocial batterers,* who are the most violent and are violent inside and outside the family; and *low-level antisocial batterers,* who are in between the family-only and antisocial groups. Similar findings by Jacobson and Gottman (e.g., 1995) have delineated battering men who are emotionally wrought up even as they are violent and another group who are cool and calm as they harm their partners.

Although most attention has been given to marital violence, in fact, violence occurs in dating, cohabiting, and same-gender (lesbian and gay male) relationships and in all ethnic, racial, and socioeconomic groups. Thus, a full exploration of violence in intimate relationship increasingly needs to take these contextual differences into account.

Causes and Correlates of Abuse

Relationship violence originates with an individual, is carried out in a relational context, and is embedded within a culture and society. Beginning at the most general level, it is not surprising that relational abuse is so prevalent when violence is daily fare in all the media, including the evening news. American society is, in many ways, a violent society. The particular dynamic of men abusing women is as old as recorded history. Male dominance has been endorsed by prevailing cultures, by religious authorities, and even by British common law. The phrase *rule of thumb* developed out of British law that said a wife should be disciplined by being beaten with a stick no thicker than her husband's thumb (Langley & Levy, 1977). Gender issues are explored in greater detail in Chapter 10, but at this point, suffice it to say that there is no way to separate gender from much of the abuse that occurs. As noted earlier, women and men may be equally violent in common ways, but men are the ones who enact the controlling, escalating violence.

Beyond the social climate, various relational factors have been linked to violence. Christopher and Lloyd (2000) note that dynamics of power and dominance, deficits in social skills, conflict in everyday interactions, and marital distress are all related to violence. Recent research with dating couples also has shown that relationship factors such as commitment may reduce the occurrence of violence (Gaertner & Foshee, 1999). In this research, the longer the relationship continued, the more likely violence was to occur, yet an increase in commitment reduced the likelihood of violence.

Individual factors involved with violence may include sociodemographic factors (e.g., being age 30 or under, living in poverty), social stress, individual power needs, use of alcohol, and growing up with violence, a phenomenon that is called the *intergenerational transmission of violence* (Christopher & Lloyd, 2000; Erber & Erber, 2001). All these factors are related to but not necessarily predictive of violence, in that most people who are under 30, who are poor, or who consume alcohol are not violent. In terms of the issue of transmission, Johnson and Ferraro (2000) point out that research, in fact, shows that parental violence offers very little predictive value for violence, and other scholars also question the levels of violence transmission (Kaufman & Zigler, 1993). Research by Simons, Lin, and Gordon (1998) found that "although frequent exposure to corporal punishment increased the risk of dating violence, this was not the case for interparental aggression, which did not predict dating violence" (p. 467).

Lloyd and Emery (2000a) have proposed a multilevel analysis of violence, specifically of aggression against women, that is based on seven propositions, or "working observations." This approach is worth discussing in some detail because it exemplifies some of the newer, more complex, and nuanced approaches that Johnson and Ferraro (2000) believe will offer the most fruitful future theoretical development on the topic of violence.

Lloyd and Emery's (2000a) first proposition is that "Most women believe that aggression will never happen in their intimate relationships" (p. 504). This means that when aggression occurs, women are invariably taken by surprise and may have difficulty even labeling the behavior as abuse. Proposition two says that "Aggression is not always accompanied by relational distress or dissatisfaction" (p. 505). Indeed, partners in relationships in which physical aggression is present may still report relationship satisfaction. Marshall and her colleagues (Marshall, Weston, & Honeycutt, 2000) found that in abusive relationships, men's positive behaviors toward their women partners, such as demonstrating caring and happiness, mediated the women's reported relationship quality. Thus, some of the effects of the abuse seemed to be lessened by the positivity, and this result held across types of relationships (dating, cohabiting, married) and ethnic groups.

Lloyd and Emery's (2000a) third proposition is that "The discourses of intimate relationships and aggression are critical components of the larger context surrounding intimate aggression" (p. 506). Prevailing discourses (i.e., social language) concerning intimate relationships include (1) the idea that there is true equality between men and women, (2) romance, in which partners are supposed to "forgive and forget," and (3) notions of sexuality in which women are supposed to comply with men's sexual desires. These discourses all contribute to women's powerlessness in the face of abuse. Added to these are the discourses of aggression, such that (1) the aggressor is excused, (2) the victim is blamed, (3) discussion of the definition of aggression hides the severity of the problem, and (4) myths and methodological problems combine to further hide the extent to which aggression occurs in an intimate context.

Proposition four states that "The intersection of aggression with interpersonal communication enhances our understanding of the dynamics of aggression" (Lloyd & Emery, 2000a, p. 510). Central to understanding aggression is analyzing communication patterns, which have been shown to differ between aggressive and nonaggressive relationships, with the latter exhibiting more negative attributions, poorer communication skills, greater volatility, and the like. "Control is a key dynamic in intimate aggression" (p. 513) is proposition five. Themes here are reminiscent of M. P. Johnson's (1995) definition of *patriarchal violence* and include (1) domination of an argument, (2) domination of both the woman and the relationship, (3) keeping the woman in the relationship, and (4) possessiveness and a sense of ownership of the woman.

Lloyd and Emery's (2000a) proposition six is that "A sense of betrayal and self-blame are pervasive effects of experiencing aggression" (p. 516). Because a woman's beliefs about her partner and relationship are embedded in her view of relationships in general and her overall world view, the trauma of abuse rocks the very foundation of a woman's sense of self and sense of her world. Because of society's messages to women that they are sexual gatekeepers and relationship maintainers, when things go wrong in relationships, women often blame themselves.

Finally, Lloyd and Emery's (2000a) seventh and final proposition is that "Victims of physical and sexual aggression are silenced in multiple ways" (p. 517). Women may have difficulty finding words for their experience, they may fear the reactions of family and friends, or they may believe the prevailing social discourse that calls intimate abuse something other than *abuse*. Whatever the case, women are often silent about their experiences. It is perhaps less surprising that so many women keep silent than that more and more women are becoming willing to speak.

Consequences of Abuse

Although men who suffer physical and emotional abuse are impacted negatively, more of the research references women victims, and indeed, women typically suffer more serious consequences (Johnson & Ferraro, 2000). The physical consequences are many and include broken bones, concussions, visual and hearing impairments, and so on. Of course, the ultimate physical consequence is the victim's death. Indirect effects may include increased health risk behaviors of victims, such as smoking and drinking. Emotional aftereffects include "lowered self-esteem and sense of well-being; heightened mistrust of men; greater social isolation, stress, depression, and withdrawal; and symptoms associated with posttraumatic stress disorder" (Christopher & Lloyd, 2000, p. 333). The effects of a woman's abuse on her children may include greater aggression and delinquency, as well as psychological effects such as anxiety, lowered self-esteem, and depression (Johnson & Ferraro, 2000). Women also suffer serious interference with employment, often reducing them to poverty and even homelessness (Johnson & Ferraro, 2000). The impact is endless (Walker, 1994).

Given the severe consequences just described, the inevitable question is "Why do women stay?" As Johnson and Ferraro (2000) point out, they don't! Many, if not the majority, of women in these situations do leave the abusive relationship. The leaving process may take several attempts, however, and patience on the parts of others in the victim's support system, including advocates in women's shelters, is imperative. The point is, women are resilient and work hard to cope with abuse, sometimes by leaving and sometimes by getting the abuse to end.

The decision to leave is not simple and involves a number of considerations. Choice and Lamke (1999) have integrated components of four theories relevant to stay/leave decisions into a single framework. The victim asks two major questions: "Will I be better off?" involves an assessment of the costs and benefits of the relationship, and "Can I do it?" involves an assessment of a woman's resources for and barriers to leaving the relationship. Results of a study of 126 persons who experienced violence in their serious dating relationships indicated that "Will I be better off?" is the key question. This research is consistent with other research (Marshall et al., 2000) in that consideration of positives as well as negatives is necessary when puzzling out women's stay/leave decisions. Perhaps if relationship rewards are reduced *or* if relationship violence escalates, then a woman may be more likely to leave an abusive relationship (DeMaris, 2001; Kirkwood, 1993).

Relationship breakup is not the only solution to relational abuse. Some abusive partners respond positively to therapy and anger management and other strategies, and some women are themselves able to negotiate a stop to the abuse (Johnson & Ferraro, 2000). But often, violence extends to the bedroom, and a discussion of relationship violence cannot overlook sexual aggression and abuse.

Sexual Aggression

Sexual violence is typically considered under the topics of marital rape and date rape. *Marital rape* is a fairly recently developed term, and some people may still not believe that marital rape can exist, arguing that if two people are married, they automatically have sexual rights to each other. But in fact, the law does now recognize the existence of marital rape. Even though the prevalence is very hard to track, it is estimated that marital rape occurs in from 10% to 15% of marriages (Christopher & Lloyd, 2000). Research by DeMaris (1997) indicated that violent husbands have more sex with their wives than nonviolent husbands, and some of those sexual encounters may be forced. One of the strongest predictors of a woman's general fear in her intimate relationship is having been forced to have sex (DeMaris & Swinford, 1996). Wives often keep these sexual assaults to themselves, fearing that if they draw attention to the rapes, they will be beaten, their children will find out about the sexual violence, or they will be abdicating their so-called wifely duty to serve their husband's sexual needs (Christopher & Lloyd, 2000).

Date rape (also discussed in Chapter 5) was once thought to be rare, but that is no longer the case. Approximately 50% of a college sample reported disagreements about the level of sexual intimacy in dating relationships (Byers & Lewis, 1988), and 15% of all college women are likely to have experienced unwanted intercourse (Koss & Cook, 1993). Although consistent figures are hard to pinpoint, a significant number of dating couples experience sexual aggression. Researchers have attributed at least some date rapes to sexual miscommunication between partners (Shotland, 1989), and other research has pointed out how the stereotype that women often say "no" sexually when they mean "yes" has influenced attitudes toward both victims and perpetrators in date rapes (e.g., Muehlenhard, 1988).

Yet other research speaks to the range of factors involved in sexual coercion in dating relationships, including social attitudes (e.g., rape-supportive myths, such as women "asking for it"), gendered dating roles (men as commanding and women as dependent), peers (members of some all-male groups are likelier to coerce women), dating experiences (use of alcohol, male power and privilege), and individual male characteristics (Christopher & Lloyd, 2000). For example, sexually coercive men appear to be more sexually active in all areas, including earlier sex and more frequent sex with more partners, and to believe more in male power and the inherent adversarial nature of sexual relationships between women and men. Interestingly, sexually coercive women (who are fewer in number and exert less coercive behaviors with partners) appear to have many of these same individual characteristics, such as the view of heterosexual relationships as essentially adversarial (Christopher & Lloyd, 2000; Johnson & Ferraro, 2000).

Sexual aggression is not synonymous with other physical aggression in intimate relationships because there is only partial overlap between the two types of violence (between 37% and 40%, as discussed in Christopher and Lloyd [2000]). However, many of the dynamics—such as aggression, power, and control—are the same.

Summary and Conclusions

Conflict occurs in virtually all relationships and involves two people having different or competing goals, which may interfere with one another. Conflict occurs in stages, with the option to engage the partner and the issue or to avoid the partner and the issue existing at each stage. Attributions, or inferences made about a behavior or event, occur frequently during conflict, as people try to make sense of the situation. Exchange theory frames relationships in marketplace terms and is concerned with the rewards and costs that occur in relationships. Equity theory is linked to exchange theory and is concerned with the fairness of outcomes or rewards minus costs. Perceptions of unfairness may lead to reduced relationship quality, or the reverse may occur. Conflict may be a necessary dialectical process in relationships that balances needs for change with needs for stability. Conflict occurs throughout the lifespan and begins with parent/child conflict. Conflict also occurs in friendships. If children learn to handle conflict well with parents and friends, they are likely to have better conflict management strategies when they enter romantic relationships.

Couples who are distressed have greater conflict, more negative attributions, and less flexibility in communication. Negativity can spiral. People may respond to conflict using any of four strategies: exit, voice, loyalty, and neglect. The demand/withdraw response involves one person requesting/demanding change and the other person withdrawing. This process has less to do with gender than with who wants the change. Couples may handle conflict in different ways yet be very stable. These include validating, volatile, and avoiding couples. Hostile and hostile/detached couples are conflictual and unstable. In a stable relationship, more positives than negatives occur, ideally at a ratio of at least 5 positives to 1 negative. Relational power is very much involved with how relational conflict is handled. There are many constructive ways to handle conflict, including being nondefensive, listening to one's partner, trying to problem solve rather than win, and so on. Relationship partners who make allowances for each other during times of stress can handle conflict better. It is necessary to consider conflict within the whole relationship context, rather than as an isolated behavior.

Physical and sexual abuse occur in many intimate relationships. Both women and men may be abusive, but men's abuse of women typically produces more severe injuries. Abuse is not new and is related to social factors such as a society that supports male power, interpersonal factors, and individual factors. It is not clear how much violence may be transmitted to children who grow up in abusive homes. Some scholars view abuse as emerging largely from a gendered and patriarchal society. Abuse has negative consequences for the victim, the children involved, the abuser, and society as a whole. Sexual aggression occurs in approximately 40% of physical abuse situations. Women often must leave their relationships in order to be safe, but other alternatives may work on occasion.

Key Terms

Attribution (p. 143)
Common couple violence (p. 154)
Conflict (p. 141)
Demand/withdraw (p. 149)
Exit (p. 148)

Intimate terrorism (p. 154)
Loyalty (p. 148)
Neglect (p. 148)
Stonewalling (p. 152)
Voice (p. 148)

Suggested Reading

Canary, D. J., Cupach, W. R., & Messman, S. J. (1995). *Relationship conflict.* Thousand Oaks, CA: Sage.

Christopher, F. S., & Lloyd, S. A. (2000). Physical and sexual aggression in relationships. In C. Hendrick & S. S. Hendrick (Eds.), *Close relationships: A sourcebook* (pp. 331–343). Thousand Oaks, CA: Sage.

Johnson, M. P., & Ferraro, K. J. (2000). Research on domestic violence in the 1990s: Making distinctions. *Journal of Marriage and the Family, 62,* 948–963.

Kirkwood, C. (1993). *Leaving abusive partners: From the scares of survival to the wisdom for change.* Newbury Park, CA: Sage.

Lloyd, S. A., & Emery, B. C. (2000a). The context and dynamics of intimate aggression against women. *Journal of Social and Personal Relationships, 17,* 503–521.

Lloyd, S. A., & Emery, B.C. (2000b). *The dark side of courtship: Physical and sexual aggression.* Thousand Oaks, CA: Sage.

8 *Breakup, Divorce, and Bereavement*

Relationship Story

He Never Saw It Coming

As he pulled his car into the driveway, George was surprised that the house was dark. It was not like Brenda to be out in the evening, and besides, she hadn't mentioned anything about having plans. Of course, he hadn't talked to her since Monday, when he left to go to Atlanta for the big sales meeting. He had been very busy for the last few days and simply hadn't found time to call her. Now that the kids were in college, he didn't feel the need to check in when he was away. As he parked in the garage and pulled his briefcase and suit carrier out of the trunk, he noticed that Brenda's car was gone. "She probably left me a message," he thought. Walking through the mudroom and laundry room, into the spacious kitchen of their suburban home, George didn't really notice anything out of

place, until he started to put his briefcase down on the kitchen counter. It was then that he
saw the note:

George,

*I am sorry. I wish I could have talked with you, but I tried, and it never seemed to
work. So many times, I said, "George, we need to talk about our marriage," and you
would say, "Our marriage is fine." I would say, "But things have changed," and you
would respond, "Of course they've changed. The kids are away at college." Then
we'd go on like that for awhile, and I'd finally give up. I gave up so many times that
I almost gave up on myself. I finally realized that I don't need antidepressants any
more—I need a divorce! I am leaving you, George. I have spoken with an attorney,
and she suggests that you get an attorney as soon as possible. I have taken all my
clothes and books and some of the furniture and a few other things. For the most part,
I took things that I didn't think you'd miss. I have not told the kids. They won't be
coming home until spring break, which is about a month away, so I figured that would
give us enough time to plan the best way to tell them. I think we should be together.
They will be upset, I suppose. We have never fought very much, so they probably
didn't know anything was wrong. But I think they'll be okay; at least, I hope so.
I suppose this will all surprise you, even though it shouldn't. I tried to tell you, but
you wouldn't listen. If you need to talk to me, you can call me at work.*

Brenda

George was stunned. He pulled a kitchen chair out from the table and sat down. He
had no idea that this was coming. He had assumed that Brenda would have kept dinner warm
for him and that they would sit down at the kitchen table and talk a little about how each
of their weeks had gone at work. Then they'd run through the schedule for the weekend:
Saturday chores; dinner with their good friends, the Smiths, on Saturday evening; church
on Sunday. But she wasn't here. Brenda wasn't here. She had left him!

George kept repeating this to himself so that he could begin to take it in, but it still
didn't make sense to him. He got up and walked through the house, turning the lights on as
he went. The living room looked like it always did, until he noticed that Brenda's small
armchair and ottoman, the one she liked to sit in to read in the evenings, was gone. A large
fake plant filled in the space where it had been. He checked the dining room; it looked intact
until he noticed that the glass hutch was empty. Brenda had taken the set of china that had
belonged to her grandmother. As he entered the family room/den, he noticed immediately
how bare the bookshelves appeared. Obviously, Brenda had taken all her books, and there
had been no way to fill in that space. He went upstairs, first checking the kids' rooms and
noting that everything seemed to be in place. As he walked into the master bedroom and
turned on the overhead light, he felt his stomach drop. The doors to Brenda's closet were

opened, and all he could see were bare shelves and empty space. When he went into the master bathroom, he could see that none of her things remained—lotions, nail polish, bathrobe. Nothing was left. When he walked back out into the bedroom, he noticed two things missing: Brenda's pillow and the pictures of the children when they were small, which had hung on the wall for many years. George sat down again, this time on the edge of the bed, and he put his head in his hands and began to cry.

Brenda checked the restroom mirror to be sure she looked all right. She knew that she was simply avoiding what was next: the big meeting with George and their lawyers, in which they were going to try to work out the financial details of the divorce in terms of the house, the savings account, the retirement plans, paying for the kids' college tuition, and all the shared economic commitments and obligations that they had. She wasn't exactly worried about the meeting—she knew that it would be civilized—but she dreaded it and felt sad about it. Divorce was an option that she had considered for a long time, but only when she could not see any other options—only when she recognized that in keeping her marriage, she was losing her mental and physical health—did she take that step and leave George. She never thought it would turn out that way.

When she and George first met in an undergraduate psychology class, she immediately thought he was attractive. He was intelligent and always one of the first students to raise his hand in response to the professor's questions. And when he asked her out, she said yes without thinking twice. They dated for a year before George proposed, and again, she said yes without thinking twice. They had a lot in common. He was great "marriage material," and she was sure that she loved him. As the years went by and their careers developed—hers much more slowly than his because of the years she stayed at home when the children were small—they always seemed to have goals they wanted to reach, like buying their first house, achieving a little bit of financial security, and, at the top of the list, being good parents.

It took awhile for Brenda to realize that although they shared those goals, how they set about achieving them was very different. Brenda loved their first house, which was in a neighborhood of small, tract homes, with kids playing in every yard, but George was always restless for something better. Brenda thought that the way to get financial security was to keep driving their old cars and building up their savings, while George worked long hours to meet and exceed sales quotas so that he could bring in more income. They were both devoted parents, but George left a lot of the day-to-day parenting to Brenda. He'd get to some of the school programs and soccer games, but he knew that if he couldn't make it, he could count on her to be there and represent both of them.

The gaps between them widened into chasms as the children got older, but as each kid went off to college—first, Brian and then two years later, Gina—George never seemed to notice how distant he and Brenda had grown. Brenda got more and more lonely, trying to talk with him about their relationship but never getting through. She even had a brief affair with a man at work, but she felt so guilty that she broke it off abruptly. She developed arthritis symptoms and began taking several medications. She tried talking to her closest friends, and while she appreciated their support, it didn't really help. Brenda grew more and more desperate. Then finally, soon after a hollow Christmas season, in which she seemed merely to go through the motions, she decided that she had to get out of her marriage. And the rest, as they say, was history.

It was almost time for the meeting. Brenda pushed open the door of the restroom and walked out into the corridor. She made her way to her lawyer's office and was ushered into a stark conference room. This is it, she thought.

As George got off the elevator and walked toward Brenda's lawyer's office, he straightened his tie and stood up a little straighter, as though he were getting ready to go into battle. He knew the meeting would probably go all right, but he was dreading it, nevertheless. He met his lawyer in the reception area of the office, and the two of them were shown into the conference room. Brenda and her lawyer were already there, chatting quietly.

Brenda's lawyer got the meeting underway. As they sat around the table, Brenda and George made small talk while the lawyers compared versions of the divorce agreement. It was straightforward—split down the middle for all the assets, including the house. George agreed to continue paying tuition and expenses for the children until they finished college. He and Brenda had made a comprehensive list of most of the furnishings in the house, and each had initialed the items he or she wanted. For the most part, they didn't have any conflicts, since they wanted different things. George kept more of the furniture because Brenda didn't have room for most of it in her townhouse, but she took the bulk of the kitchen items and some family memorabilia. Brenda got the antique desk, and George got the big-screen television.

The meeting seemed to be going well. Then Brenda's lawyer spoke up: "I see that in the listing of assets, you did not include any retirement accounts. Is there some reason for that?" George's lawyer responded immediately, saying, "George's retirement account is his alone and is exempt from the division of property." Brenda's lawyer came back directly: "The most recent changes in federal legislation open retirement accounts up to inclusion in property settlements. Therefore, Brenda requests half of George's retirement account, since virtually all of the money has been earned during the time of their marriage."

George hit the roof! "You can't take my retirement—that would be like cutting off my arm! I have earned that all by myself, and it is NOT part of this settlement!" Then Brenda got angry. "Who do you think helped make it possible for you to earn all that money and build up that retirement account, anyway? Who cooked your meals and washed your clothes and raised your children while you were becoming Salesman of the Year? If you want, I'll take half of your retirement account, and you can have half of mine." Of course, George knew that even if they took this approach, he would get much less out of the arrangement than Brenda would, so he resisted, as did his lawyer. The two lawyers suggested that since there was no rush for the divorce, they might adjourn the meeting, let George and Brenda think about their respective positions, and then meet again in a couple of weeks. Everyone agreed to that, but Brenda and George walked out of the room not speaking to or looking at each other. The lawyers stayed behind to confer.

As they stood waiting for the elevator, George said, "Brenda, it's not *just* the money. It's the principle of the situation. I earned that money and built up that retirement, and I think it is mine." Brenda replied, "George, for me, it's not just the principle of the situation. It's also the money. We have *both* worked hard all these years, and I don't regret that. But the way we chose to handle things meant that you built up a large retirement account, and I have only really started to build mine in the past few years. I don't see why I should suffer financially just because I worked inside the home and you worked outside the home." The elevator arrived, and they both got in and rode down silently to the lobby. Eventually, Brenda and George agreed on a two-thirds to one-third split of George's retirement, with George keeping the larger share. But that wasn't the most difficult thing they had to do. No, the most difficult thing was talking to the kids.

Gina and Brian were heading up on spring break, so they weren't calling home too often. They figured they could just catch up with their parents when they got home. Both kids were undergraduates at the large state university a few hundred miles from their home. On the few occasions when they did call, however, they were surprised to find their dad at home and their mom "out." She called them back awhile later, and neither one of them thought too much about it. It was early Friday evening when they drove in the familiar driveway, unloaded their suitcases and dirty laundry, and walked in through the back entry area into the kitchen. Brenda and George were sitting at the kitchen table, talking and drinking coffee, and they looked up, startled, when they heard Gina and Brian come in. There were greetings and hugs all around, and then Brenda said, "We need to talk to you about something."

■ ■ ■

Questions to Consider in Reading This Chapter

- Has anyone in your family gotten divorced? If so, how were you told about the divorce? How did you react?
- Have you ever been totally surprised by a partner's breaking off a relationship with you? Did your partner give you clues along the way that you somehow missed?
- How distressed were you about the breakup? How did you get over it?
- Have you ever been jealous of a partner?
- Have you ever been unfaithful to a partner or had a partner be unfaithful to you?

What Do We Know about Breakup, Divorce, and Bereavement?

Relationship **loss** is often equated with divorce, which is certainly a compelling issue for many people today. Yet loss can come in many forms. The ending of even a nonmarital romantic relationship (i.e., dating, being engaged, cohabiting) can bring tremendous emotional pain. And while it is less common for young people now than in earlier centuries, the loss of a partner through death can still occur at any age.

Thus, this chapter considers relationship losses that occur through relationship breakup, divorce, and death. These types of losses differ, yet there are many thematic similarities among them. Two kinds of behaviors/events that often create relationship problems and may be linked to breakups or divorce are jealousy and infidelity. These topics will be addressed initially.

Causes of Relationship Disruption

Jealousy

Jealousy is a largely negative emotion, multidimensional in its complexity (Pfeiffer & Wong, 1989). In a romantic relationship, it is precipitated by the fear of losing someone who is cared about and valued. Jealousy is different from *envy,* which has to do with wanting something that someone else has. Although some researchers believe that envy and jealousy are essentially two subtypes of the same emotion constellation, the two are, in fact, different in composition and intensity (Erber & Erber, 2001). Jealousy is more profound and relates to fears of an intruder upsetting one's relationship with another person.

Although the focus here is on jealousy in romantic, partnered relationships, jealousy also occurs in family relationships (a child who is jealous of a new sibling; a parent who is jealous of a new son- or daughter-in-law) and friendships (someone's best friend develops another close friendship). It is even possible to be jealous of a partner's job or hobby, if that activity consumes his or her time, energy, and emotion.

Buunk and Dijkstra (2000) have reviewed the relevant research and outlined three different types of jealousy: (1) *reactive/emotional* jealousy, a negative emotional reaction to a partner's actual or imagined involvement with someone else; (2) *anxious/cognitive* jealousy, obsessive anxiety and thinking about a partner's involvement; and (3) *preventive/suspicious* jealousy, an unprovoked response to a partner's possible slight interest in someone.

People may be differentially susceptible to jealousy, depending on their personality characteristics as well as their relational situations. For example, lower self-esteem (especially in women), emotional dependency, and similar qualities are related to greater jealousy (Buunk, 1995; Buunk & Dijkstra, 2000). Sharpsteen and Kirkpatrick (1997) found that attachment style was relevant for the experience of jealousy. Participants who were secure in attachment style were more likely to express their anger, whereas anxiously attached persons were more likely to withhold their anger. Avoidant participants blamed the third party, rather than the partner. Knobloch, Solomon, and Cruz (2001) found that both attachment anxiety and intimacy were related to emotional jealousy, whereas relational uncertainty was related to cognitive uncertainty, again underlining the individual and relational layers of jealousy.

Women and men both have the capacity for jealousy, but they may differ in what makes them jealous and how they react to jealousy. Women tend to react with greater jealousy when they believe their partner has been emotionally unfaithful to them as opposed to sexually unfaithful, whereas for men, the opposite is true: Sexual unfaithfulness arouses greater jealousy (Buss, Larsen, Westen, & Semmelroth, 1992). The evolutionary perspective on these differences says that men are more concerned with certainty of paternity, so they are more threatened by a partner's sexual unfaithfulness. Women, however, are supposedly more concerned about a man's continued provisioning of offspring, so they are concerned about emotional unfaithfulness.

This gendered view of reactions to jealousy has been challenged by DeSteno, Bartlett, Braverman, and Salovey (2002), who argue that how a question about sexual unfaithfulness versus emotional unfaithfulness is asked will produce gender differences or no gender differences. If asked in certain ways, both men and women will say that sexual unfaithfulness causes more upset and jealousy than emotional unfaithfulness.

Women tend to cope with jealousy by doubting themselves, believing that they are somehow inadequate (Buunk, 1995), and women also "are more inclined than men to endorse aggressive action against . . . rivals" (Buunk & Dijkstra, 2000, p. 327). Even so, it is known that more men than women commit violent crimes due to jealousy. Perhaps this discrepancy is linked to Johnson's (1995) theory of relationship violence, in which women and men are equally likely to enact low-level violence in a relationship but men are much more likely to enact serious, dangerous violence.

Coping with jealousy is difficult, and strategies likely need to be tailored to the individual. Three broad approaches to coping were listed by Buunk and Dijkstra (2000) in their review of jealousy research, including reconsidering the situation, avoiding the partner, and communicating with the partner. However, serious jealousy responses are probably best addressed through therapeutic work. One major cause of jealousy is a romantic partner's real or suspected involvement with another partner.

Infidelity

The involvement of one partner in a romantic dyad with a third person has generally been referred to as unfaithfulness or **infidelity.** But in recent years, scholars have tried to demoralize the behavior by using such terms as *extradyadic relationships* (Buunk & Dijkstra, 2000), *extradyadic involvement* (Wiederman & Hurd, 1999), and *extrarelationship involvement* (Boekhout, Hendrick, & Hendrick, 2000).

The terms may change, but the behavior remains remarkably the same. Estimates of infidelity range from 50% of married men and 25% of married women (Kinsey, Pomeroy, & Martin, 1948) to 8% to 14% of surveyed participants (Treas & Giesen, 2000). In surveying college-student daters, Wiederman and Hurd (1999) found that approximately 40% of women and 45% of men had engaged in extradyadic dating, and Boekhout (1997) reported that 44% of women and 59% of men stated that they had been either emotionally or sexually unfaithful at least one time while they were in a committed relationship. Online infidelity has even begun to be a problem (Young, Griffin-Shelley, Cooper, O'Mara, & Buchanan, 2000).

It is interesting that such large numbers of people report their unfaithfulness, since "a majority of respondents in most Western countries consistently disapprove of extramarital relationships under all circumstances" (Buunk & Dijkstra, 2000, p. 318), including approximately 85% of Americans, according to Pestrak, Martin, and Martin (1985). Attitudes are a little less critical for those in dating, cohabiting, and gay male relationships, but nevertheless, infidelity is frowned upon.

Given the contrast between people's attitudes and behaviors, a number of theories have been proposed to explain infidelity. These theories reflect individual, relational, and social levels of explanation. At the *individual level,* it has been proposed that people with various personality problems or with insecure attachment styles are more likely to engage in extrarelationship involvement (Buunk & Dijkstra, 2000), and it has been related to sexual sensation seeking (Wiederman & Hurd, 1999) and more permissive sexual attitudes (Treas & Giesen, 2000). At the *relationship level,* infidelity has been related to a game-playing love style (Wiederman & Hurd, 1999) and has been hypothesized to be related to lower commitment, based on interdependence theory (Buunk & Dijkstra, 2000). At the *social level,* infidelity has been related to less religious involvement and to the acceptance of cohabitation as an alternative to marriage (Treas & Giesen, 2000).

Evolutionary psychology explains infidelity by emphasizing men's and women's reproductive strategies. Men, either consciously or not, want to impregnate as many women as possible, and women want to mate with the best possible partner, regardless of whether that partner is the main provisioner of their young. This theory also discusses concealed ovulation (women), mate guarding (men), and mate poaching (Buss, 1995; Schmitt & Buss, 2001).

Women and men show some differences in infidelity, differing less in the rates of infidelity than in the reasons for it (Prins, Buunk, & Van Yperen, 1993). Women who have affairs are more likely to be dissatisfied with their current relationship, whereas for men, relationship satisfaction/dissatisfaction is not a motivator. This was certainly the case for Brenda in the Relationship Story. And women focus more on the emotional aspects of an affair, whereas men focus more on the sexual aspects (Glass & Wright, 1992). Liu (2000) found that whereas women were less likely to engage in extramarital sex the longer they had been married, men's extramarital involvements were U-shaped—that is, higher at the beginning, lower in the middle, and higher again after 25 or 30 years of marriage.

People justify infidelity in four primary ways, according to Glass and Wright (1992). These include (1) the need for sexual variety, (2) the need for emotional intimacy, (3) love (receiving love/falling in love), and (4) extrinsic motivations, such as getting even with one's partner.

One of the most difficult aspects of infidelity is its after-effects, or coping with the lack of faithfulness by a partner. Roloff, Soule, and Carey (2001) have studied people's responses to relational transgressions, with infidelity as one of five categories of transgressions. They found that people who were transgressed against often remained in a relationship after transgression, sometimes because of fear of losing the partner (which led to negative reactions, such as considering revenge on him or her) or because of emotional involvement (which led to positive reactions, such as attempts to repair the relationship).

Afifi, Falato, and Weiner (2001) have assessed people's reactions to infidelity based on how they found out about their dating partner's unfaithfulness. The method of discovery did affect the reaction. When the unfaithful partner voluntarily disclosed the infidelity to his or her partner, the relationship was impacted the least. When the person found out about the partner's infidelity because he or she got suspicious and confronted the partner, the relationship was impacted somewhat more. The relationship suffered the most, however, when the person either caught the unfaithful partner in some demonstration of infidelity or when the person found out about the infidelity from a third party, such as a friend.

Infidelity clearly impacts relationships. Charny and Parnass (1995) obtained information from practicing therapists about their clinical experiences with married couples in which one partner was unfaithful. According to those practitioners, in over half the situations, extramarital relationships had negative effects on the primary relationship. Kaslow (1993) documented several severely negative relationship/family outcomes due to infidelity, including family disruption and even suicide. Fidelity is important, since sexual exclusivity is positively related to emotional satisfaction with sex for both women and men (Waite & Joyner, 2001).

Some marriages survive infidelity, but others do not. Shackelford (1998) discusses research indicating that across over 150 cultures, infidelity was the most frequently stated reason for divorce. And in some cultures, infidelity, especially by women, elicits an extreme reaction. "A sexual infidelity by a woman, either actual or suspected, is the leading cause of wife battering and wife homicide" (p. 135).

Relationship Breakup

Relationship breakup comes in many forms, with divorce being one important subtype. General information about breakup will be considered first in this section, followed by an examination of divorce.

Although George expressed complete surprise at the breakup of his marriage to Brenda, from her point of view, he should have known it was coming. He likely simply missed or ignored the cues that Brenda was unhappy and that their relationship was in trouble. What causes relationships to get into trouble in the first place?

Factors Involved in Breakup

Duck (1982) proposes that three major categories of events or behaviors are related to relationship **breakup.** The first category is *pre-existing doom*. How many of us have known a couple whom we looked at and simply shook our heads, saying, "They'll never make it"? Perhaps the partners are ill matched in terms of temperament, style, interests, background, and so on, or perhaps one partner abuses drugs or alcohol. Most of us have seen relationships that we thought were doomed from the beginning. Duck's second category is called *mechanical failure/process loss*. Here, partners either do negative things, such as nag, complain, or try to control, or fail to do positive things, such as communicate well, offer social support, and act lovingly. This is probably the category most relevant to the breakdown of George and Brenda's marriage. The third category is *sudden death* and includes "a partner's adultery, betrayal of trust, or deception, and instances of personal renunciation" (p. 7). Here, a failure of ethics, such as infidelity, devastates the relationship.

Kurdek's (1991) research with lesbian and gay couples who had broken off long-term romantic relationships found that the five reasons given most frequently for breakup were frequent absence, infidelity, lack of love, mental cruelty, and sexual incompatibility. In terms of Duck's (1982) categories, whereas infidelity certainly fits into the "sudden death" category, the others appear to be "mechanical failure/process loss" issues, although lack of love could be an aspect of "pre-existing doom." Gottman's (1993b) research indicated that when the ratio of relational positives to negatives falls below 5 to 1, a relationship is at risk.

Levinger (e.g., 1979a, 1979b) has taken a holistic view toward relationship breakup, concerned not only with the forces of attraction that bring people together (what could be termed *rewards* in an exchange framework) but also the relationship negatives that pull people apart (what could be termed *costs* in exchange theory). In addition, he has noted the barriers or restraining forces—such as social pressure to stay together, children, and economics—that affect the more straightforward reward/cost balance. For example, two couples who have been married for eight years might have equal rewards and costs in terms of how the partners relate to each other. But suppose one couple has two children, share in a part-time consulting business, and own one home in the city and a cabin in the mountains, whereas the other couple has no children, no shared property, and separate jobs. The first couple will clearly have many more barriers to breakup than will the second couple. It is likely that both their children and economic issues provided the strongest barriers to Brenda and George's breakup.

Still another perspective—one long observed by marital therapists—was taken by Felmlee (1995), who found that the very qualities that can be attractive in a partner initially can later be interpreted differently and eventually lead to breakup. (See the discussion of "fatal attractions" in Chapter 2.) She found that some of the qualities that attracted people to romantic partners did not cause problems later. For instance, "if a person was initially attracted to a partner's 'smile' or 'good looks,' it is doubtful that a person would later say she or he disliked a partner's smile or looks" (p. 306). But qualities that expressed either excitement or being different were more likely to cause problems. Thus, what seemed like intense caring or interest at one point in time could look like dependency or even jealousy later on. Similarly, having an air of confidence might be appreciated early on but seem like arrogance or even dominance at another point in the relationship. It is not clear that such qualities would be extreme enough to qualify as Duck's (1982) pre-existing doom, but they were problematic, nevertheless.

Arriaga (2001) found that beyond a particular quality of an individual or a relationship leading to a breakup, *variability* of those qualities, specifically relationship satisfaction, was related to relationship breakup. "Individuals who exhibited greater fluctuation in their repeated satisfaction ratings were more likely to be in relationships that eventually ended. . . . Individuals with fluctuating levels of satisfaction also reported relatively lower commitment" (p. 754). Thus, maintaining a consistently positive attitude toward one's partner, although very hard to do, is optimal for relationship survival.

Even a brief survey of the literature on relationship breakup makes it apparent that there is no single cause of such an outcome. Individual personality attributes, as well as the characteristics of a relationship, may lead to breakup for some couples but not others. A partner who is quite dependent on a relationship, whose important needs are being satisfied, and/or who sees fewer options for other relationships may stay in a relationship that appears to be seriously deficient (Drigotas & Rusbult, 1992). Even infidelity is not a "sudden death" event for all couples.

Stages of Relationship Dissolution

The question of *how* a relationship dissolves is linked to but not identical with that of *why* it dissolves. Duck (1984) proposes five stages of relationship dissolution and the remediation and repair processes that accompany those stages. The first stage is *breakdown,* in which one partner experiences dissatisfaction with the relationship. The dissatisfaction may not be severe, but it is enough to alert the individual to the need to improve communication and increase intimacy, for example. Events in this stage are definitely reparable, and in fact, virtually all relationship partners experience relational frustration and a sense of "We can do better." A key to effective relational repair in this stage is a sense that the relationship just isn't working as well as it could and should be but that neither partner is necessarily at fault (p. 173).

If relational repair does not work, the person moves into the *intrapsychic phase*, in which his or her partner becomes more clearly the source of dissatisfaction. In this period, the person may think obsessively about the partner and even monitor the partner's behavior, just waiting for him or her to do something annoying: "Oh, she's nagging me about my being a slob again" or "If he grabs the remote one more time, I'll scream." Considerable relational focus occurs, but it is virtually all in the person's mind—unknown, or at least unspoken, to the partner. We can imagine that Brenda spent a lot of time in this phase.

In the next phase, the *dyadic phase,* both partners become involved in dealing with one or both of their dissatisfactions. This is a risky time that requires skilled negotiation, if repair, rather than continuing disintegration, is to occur. If Brenda had spoken more urgently or if George had listened more carefully, perhaps their marriage could have been salvaged.

If the partners can't repair the relationship, they move to the *social phase.* Here, the partners are concerned about dealing with their separate and joint social networks—family, friends, colleagues, and so on—as well as with their own needs for social support from these people and from new network members, such as a therapist.

The final phase, called the *grave-dressing phase,* is the time after the breakup when accounts of the relationship are formed, revised, and then reformed into a final account. That account finally is laid to rest, allowing the persons involved to move on with their lives (see also Weber & Harvey, 1994).

Of course, the breakup process is not typically a tightly ordered progression that moves from stage to stage. In fact, Battaglia and her colleagues (Battaglia, Richard, Datteri, & Lord, 1998) assessed the breakup process extensively and found that it has a cyclical pattern, in which such phenomena as "lack of interest" and "acting distant" may occur and reoccur several times during the course of a breakup.

Emotional Consequences of Breakup

As it becomes increasingly clear that a relationship is not going to survive, there are a number of emotional consequences for both partners. In a longitudinal study of couples, Sprecher and Felmlee (1993) found that for couples who broke up, ambivalence and conflict increased over time, whereas maintenance behaviors and love decreased. Since a breakup is a process that occurs over time, rather than a single event, it is likely that the effects of a breakup can be felt during the course of relationship decline, quite some time before the partners actually dissolve their relationship (Amato, 2000).

Breakup is never easy, but it is even more difficult under certain conditions. For example, people in breakup situations who were preoccupied with their relationships, reflecting anxious/ambivalent attachment, as compared to respondents who endorsed other attachment styles, were more likely to report that their partners had initiated the breakup and that they were feeling more negative and having more difficulty adjusting to the breakup (Barbara & Dion, 2000). And Robak and Weitzman (1998) found that young adults who had experienced the loss of a love relationship reported considerable grief. If marriage had been discussed, the grief was even greater, although in this case, respondents' families were more likely to take the grief seriously and not disenfranchise or invalidate it. Too often, people underestimate the seriousness of a breakup because a couple was "only dating," yet many of the grief reactions of a dating breakup are similar in tone to those of a marital breakup.

Most of the research on breakups has looked at the consequences of the breakup itself. Frazier and Cook (1993) were among the first researchers to examine the consequences of breakup at two different times: immediately after the breakup and some time after the event. Using a retrospective technique, they asked people to recollect how they felt at the time of a recent breakup (within the past six months) and how they felt at the current time. Frazier and Cook found that variables representing commitment and involvement—including higher satisfaction, feeling closer to one's partner, and perceiving fewer relationship alternatives—were all related to people feeling greater stress at the time of the breakup. But these variables were not particularly related to recovery from the breakup or to the person's current emotional adjustment. Coping variables were related in different ways to breakup stress, recovery, and current adjustment, with lack of control related to greater stress and less recovery although not lower adjustment. Still wanting to be in a relationship with one's ex-partner was related to more stress and less recovery and adjustment. Social support was related positively to recovery, and lower self-esteem was related to more stress and less recovery and current emotional adjustment. One of the most important findings in this study was the relatively low correlation between initial distress and later recovery. This finding means that people who experience great emotional distress at the time of a breakup are not necessarily going to have a harder time in recovering from the breakup and in getting on with their lives.

Sprecher, Felmlee, Metts, Fehr, and Vanni (1998) also used a retrospective design to assess a number of variables that possibly influenced people's initial reaction to a breakup and their reaction a year or so after the breakup. These authors found that distress was higher at the time of a breakup if someone had worked harder to initiate the relationship in the first place, if the relationship was of longer duration and elicited higher satisfaction and commitment, and if someone was left for another person. Individual factors such as a fearful attachment style, wherein people may be afraid of abandonment, were also predictive of breakup distress. So, it was again affirmed that a number of factors, both individual and relational, contribute to the stress experienced when a relationship ceases. This research also showed, however, that these same factors did not predict current upset. Here, only original commitment, length of relationship, and a fearful attachment style predicted continuing distress. Some persons seemed to recover from the breakup completely and others only partially (Sprecher et al., 1998).

In other research, Sprecher (1994) asked the question "Do relationship partners who have broken up view their breakup in the same way?" As with so many relationship questions, the answer seemed to be both yes and no. Ex-partners did not report similar emotional reactions to the breakup, and indeed, "significant and negative correlations were found for three negative emotions: guilt, resentment, and loneliness" (p. 208). What partners did seem to agree on was which partner initiated and controlled the breakup and the reasons the breakup occurred. Partners reported experiencing both positive and negative emotions after breakup, and women and men did not differ appreciably in their reactions.

Relationship partners experience a number of reactions before, during, and after a breakup, and many of these reactions are negative. Uncomfortable feelings tend to lessen over time, and some may be shared by partners, while others may not. Breakup is not easy, but it happens to nearly everyone at one time or another. One very special type of breakup is divorce.

Divorce

While marriage rates have declined in the United States for the past 50 years, **divorce** rates have increased (Teachman, Tedrow, & Crowder, 2000). It is estimated that about half of recent first marriages will end in divorce, that one of every six adults in the United States will experience two or more divorces, and that one out of three children will live in a household with a stepparent some time during their child or adolescent years (Amato, 2000). Although the divorce rate appears to have leveled off in recent years (Teachman et al., 2000), it was one of the major social changes of the twentieth century, since in the midnineteenth century, only about 1 in 20 marriages ended in divorce (Amato, 2000).

It is natural to wonder what caused the rate of divorce to increase so dramatically, but there is no one answer to that question. There are certain trends, however. For instance, the trend of more women being employed and freed from complete economic dependence on men has likely made some contribution to divorce. Also, couples who wed at young ages are more likely to break up than those who wed when older (S. S. Hendrick & C. Hendrick, 1992a), and divorce is more common earlier in a marriage, particularly in the first couple of years (Bumpass, Sweet, & Castro Martin, 1990). In addition, there are factors that predict romantic breakup that also predict divorce (e.g., incompatibility, jealousy, infidelity). In spite of the many barriers to divorce that may exist (Levinger, 1979a, 1979b), divorce occurs frequently.

Gottman's work is central to the study of marital interaction, generally (e.g., Gottman & Notarius, 2000); marital conflict, more specifically; and the trajectory toward divorce. As also discussed in Chapter 7 on conflict, Gottman (1993a, 1993b) describes four conflictual behaviors as particularly corrosive for couples: criticism, leading to contempt, leading to defensiveness, leading to stonewalling. These behaviors occur in a spiral of negativity, or what Gottman terms a *process cascade* (1993a, p. 62). In addition, Gottman and Levenson (2000) suggest that stonewalling is a particularly male response to conflict and particularly upsetting for both partners. If these behaviors escalate and if the ratio of positives to negatives falls below 5 to 1, then divorce is more likely (Gottman & Notarius, 2000).

Pasley, Kerpelman, and Guilbert (2001) have expanded Gottman's model of factors leading to marital instability to include a strong emphasis on gender as part of the relational context. They provide a plausible explanation of how central gender is to human identity and how marital partners confirm or disconfirm each other's identities, including gender identities. They explain how disconfirmation, or *identity disruption,* can lead to negativity, which can, in turn, lead to distancing, congruent with Gottman's model.

Other models have also been proposed to explain the pathway toward divorce. Huston, Caughlin, Houts, Smith, and George (2001) have described several of these models, including (1) the concept that people marry wearing "rose-colored glasses" and then become disillusioned as the relationship continues; (2) the concept that people may deal poorly with emerging stresses over the years and erode the quality of their relationship; and (3) the concept that couples early in their courtship display both the positive and negative personal and interpersonal themes that will characterize their relationship. This latter model is not exactly the same thing as Duck's (1982) notion of pre-existing doom, but it is similar.

Huston et al. (2001) followed a large group of couples from the time of their wedding to approximately 13 years postwedding. Although the research was understandably complex, the authors' bottom-line conclusion was that couples who divorced early in the marriage had substantial problems early in the relationship, probably representing a case of Duck's (1982) pre-existing doom. Another group was idealistic early on but became disillusioned as time went by and finally divorced. Couples who stayed together were not uniformly happy. Indeed, some accepted ongoing conflict as part of the deal, and others had their needs met through children, friends, and work rather than by their spouse. Of course, others stayed married and were happy doing so.

What was, in some ways, most significant about this research was that "differences in the intensity of newlyweds' romance as well as the extent to which they expressed negative feelings toward each other predicted (a) whether or not they were happy 13 years later (among those who stayed married) and (b) how long their marriage lasted prior to separation (for those who divorced)" (Huston et al., 2001, p. 237). This research underlines the importance of positive relationship qualities and interaction from the very beginning of a relationship, and it also demonstrates the value of longitudinal research, or research over time.

The importance of positives was also emphasized by Gottman and Levenson (2000), who explored predictors of divorce in a sample of couples followed for approximately 14 years. The researchers focused on positive emotion and negative emotion as comprising two models for predicting breakup. By coding videotapes of the partners' conflict and affect in interaction, which were made when the couples had been married for an average of five years, the researchers found that positive affect and negative affect served as predictors of divorce at different times in the life of the relationship. Negative affect predicted early divorce (average of 7.4 years following marriage). However, the lack of positive affect predicted later divorce (average of 13.9 years following marriage). These findings were quite similar to those of Huston et al. (2001). Negatives predicted early divorce, lack of positives predicted later divorce, and interactions observed relatively early in the relationship could forecast later relational outcomes.

Of course, the reality is that it is impossible to really forecast divorce for a particular couple. Although divorce may occur early in a marriage, for example (Bumpass et al., 1990), satisfaction is usually higher at that time. In fact, some research indicates that satisfaction is high early and later in relationships but drops during the middle years (Rollins & Cannon, 1974; Weishaus & Field, 1988). Some of the drop in satisfaction is associated with having children (Gottman & Notarius, 2000). Parenthood is both rewarding and stressful.

Again, there is no simple formula for predicting or avoiding breakup other than to avoid being in a relationship in the first place. But there are some documented warning signs for relationship breakup, as outlined in the Up Close box that follows.

Theoretical Approaches to Divorce

Bohannan (1970, 1984) has developed a conceptual framework of divorce that acknowledges its complexity by including six different types of divorce. The first is *legal divorce,* which refers to the formal process of dealing with attorneys and the courts. The second, *economic divorce,* is typically intertwined with the first and refers to the distribution of assets and decisions about property, support payments, and the like. The third is *emotional divorce,* which involves the sadness and the letting go of someone who was once loved a great deal. As noted elsewhere, "Ironically, emotional and economic divorce may overlap as partners begin to split up their joint possessions and relinquish the memories and the relationship 'history' that some of the possessions may represent" (S. S. Hendrick & C. Hendrick, 1992, p. 202). This overlap was evident in Brenda and George's meeting with their attorneys. The fourth type of divorce is the *community divorce* (akin to Duck's [1984] social phase of breakup). Here, friends, family, and co-workers must be dealt with, not only in the sense of informing these people of the impending breakup but also learning to relate to them as two separate individuals rather than as a couple unit. The fifth type of divorce occurs only for those couples who have children and is called the *co-parental divorce.* Here, parents who are no longer relating as marital partners must relate as parenting partners. It is important to recognize that parents' ability to handle co-parenting, no matter what the actual custody arrangements might be, is key to children's successful adjustment after divorce. George and Brenda are working hard at this type of divorce. The final type of divorce is *psychic divorce,* which may occur several years after all the other types of divorce are concluded or at least settled. At this point, the final goodbyes occur, the accounts are concluded, and the emotional resolution is accomplished. Brenda and George are a long way from this type of divorce. Most important in Bohannan's approach is the awareness that divorce is not a single event; it is multidimensional and multilayered.

One perspective on divorce that is mentioned frequently is the *selection perspective* (e.g., Amato, 2000; Bloom, Asher, & White, 1978), which says essentially that some people have personality problems, emotional disorders, or other types of disabilities that predispose them to unsuccessful marital experiences. Given that so many marriages end

Warning Signs of Breakup

Although there are no *absolute* predictors of whether a particular couple will stay together or break up, research has shown that there are particular risks for breakup. Here are selected risks, largely drawn from the current chapter:

- Excessive jealousy
- Infidelity or other betrayal
- Lack of love
- Partners who are poorly matched
- Nagging; trying to control
- Ignoring one's partner
- Defensiveness
- Not communicating
- Criticism
- Sexual incompatibility
- Stonewalling, or being difficult or evasive
- Too many negatives relative to positives
- Too much negative emotion; too little positive emotion
- Not respecting one's partner

in divorce in current U.S. society, the selection perspective may not be a particularly useful stance.

There have been a number of theoretical approaches to the divorce process (e.g., family systems theory, attribution, interdependence), and they are reviewed in some detail elsewhere (Amato, 2000; Fine, 2000). Amato (2000) acknowledges the politically laden territory of divorce research, with people on one side of the debate insisting that divorce destroys the two-parent family, eventually eroding society as a whole, and people on the other side of the debate insisting that divorce is simply one pathway, albeit a stressful one, for changing and perhaps improving family life. This might be referred to as the *moral perspective* on divorce. There is also a *temporal perspective* that either views divorce stress as short term (a crisis model) or views divorce as having long-term effects (the chronic strain model) (Amato, 2000).

Against this polarized backdrop, Amato (2000) proposes a *divorce-stress-adjustment perspective* (p. 1271), which attempts to look objectively at the research on the consequences of divorce for adults and children. This approach is consistent with other approaches (e.g., Fine, 2000) that accept divorce as a stressful event that impacts people differentially. The effects of divorce on both the adults and children involved are of intense interest to virtually everyone.

Consequences of Divorce for Adults

Research indicates that divorce impacts people's physical health at least initially (Bloom et al., 1978), although some research does not confirm tight linkages between health problems and divorce (Burman & Margolin, 1992). Emotional well-being is also negatively impacted (Fine, 2000), as is one's sexual well-being (Laumann et al., 1994). Divorce has economic consequences, as well. Income is lowered, especially for women (Barber & Eccles, 1992; Kitson & Morgan, 1990).

Amato (2000) notes that research in the 1990s was consistent with that of the 1980s in showing that "the divorced are worse off than the married in multiple ways" (p. 1274). However, Fine (2000) cites research indicating that these negative effects reduce substantially over time.

Amato (2000) also underscores the helpful effects of certain relational and sociodemographic factors on divorce stress. Remarriage is one of the most positive actions a divorced person can take, since emotions, economics, and parenting are all likely to improve when one has a supportive partner. Other helpful factors include more education, better employment, and being the partner who initiated the divorce.

Consequences of Divorce for Children

Children are impacted strongly by their parents' divorce but may experience different reactions depending on their age at time of divorce (Santrock & Sitterle, 1987). For instance, preschoolers and early school-age children may be fearful and confused and may blame themselves for the divorce. Older children and adolescents may have less fear and more anger, and they may feel torn between their loyalties to both parents.

Whether divorce occurs in early childhood or later in life does not appear to make major differences in later outcomes for children (Furstenberg & Kiernan, 2001). Children from divorced families, as compared to those from intact families, appear to have more conduct problems, lower academic success, less social competence, and lower self-esteem, but the differences are small (e.g., Amato, 2000). Simons and his colleagues (Simons, Lin, Gordon, Conger, & Lorenz, 1999) have examined adjustment problems in boys and girls from divorced and intact families and found that boys' aggressive and violent behavior (externalizing behavior) increased after divorce because the father became less involved in parenting and the mother became depressed, reducing the effectiveness of her parenting. And boys from divorced families were more depressed than other boys, no matter what the quality of parenting. Girls appeared less affected and were not different from girls of intact families, if mothers were able to do quality parenting. However, it is clearly important for children, especially boys, to have father involvement. Father absence is significant (McLanahan, 1999), and indeed, father love is extremely influential "on children's and young adults' social, emotional, and cognitive development and functioning" (Rohner & Veneziano, 2001, p. 382).

It does appear that parenting and other home life issues are important to children's adjustment, but these factors are important no matter what the family structure. For example, Deater-Deckard and Dunn (1999) compared children from single-mother, stepmother, stepfather, and nonstep families and found that "the predictive links between . . . various multiple risk factors and adjustment were similar, rather than different, across the four family types considered" (p. 61).

Although the negative effects of divorce have been documented extensively, there is also evidence that divorce can have beneficial effects on children under some conditions. For example, when children are freed from living in a high-conflict environment, they show improved functioning after divorce, although negative effects can occur if parental conflict has been low (Booth & Amato, 2001; Hetherington, 1999). And recent research indicates that divorce mediation is helpful to divorcing parents and their children (Emery, Laumann-Billings, Waldron, Sbarra, & Dillon, 2001).

While some research indicates that the after-effects of divorce continue to impact children well into adulthood (Amato, 1999; Booth & Amato, 2001), other research indicates that young adults from divorced families do not differ in critical ways from young adults whose parents remained married. Hayashi and Strickland (1998) surveyed young adult college students from both divorced and intact families and compared them on several dimensions related to their current romantic relationships. The groups did not differ on secure attachment or other positive relational dimensions. Students who grew up with at least one accepting (e.g., nurturant) parent or parent-substitute and who were encouraged to be independent reported feeling more secure in their current romantic relationships than did those students who experienced their parent or parent-substitute as rejecting and overprotective.

Other research has also found virtually no differences in romantic relationship attitudes between young adult children from divorced and intact families (S. S. Hendrick, C. Hendrick, Shoemaker, & Inman-Amos, 1995). Burns and Dunlop (1998) conducted a longitudinal study of adolescents whose parents divorced and found that in young adulthood, their close relationships did not differ in quality from those of young adults whose families were intact. However, Jacquet and Surra (2001) found that young adults (especially women) whose parents had divorced had less satisfaction and trust and more conflict and ambivalence in their romantic relationships than did respondents from intact families. Yet the differences between the groups were small.

Even though there is no neat consensus on the immediate and long-term impacts of divorce on children and adults, the extensive body of research on divorce indicates that "divorce benefits some individuals, leads others to experience temporary decrements in well-being that improve over time, and forces others on a downward cycle from which they might never fully recover" (Amato, 2000, p. 1282). George and Brenda earnestly hoped that their children would recover from the divorce. It is important to try to understand that no two divorces and no two people are alike. Thus, achieving a greater understanding of the diversity of divorce—and indeed, the diversity of family structures—will likely improve the availability of coping resources for divorced, remarried, and single-parent families (Fine, 2000). In addition, it is possible that the growing interest by relationship researchers in studying forgiveness (Fincham, Paleari, & Regalia, 2002; Finkel, Rusbult, Kumashiro, & Hannon, 2002) will result in knowledge that can actually help preserve relationships.

No study of relationship loss would be complete without an acknowledgement of loss through death, and that topic is considered briefly in the following section.

Bereavement

Bereavement is a vast topic, and excellent reviews of it are available (e.g., Stroebe, Stroebe, Hansson, & Schut, 2001). Although the focus here is on bereavement due to the death of a relationship partner, it is wise to keep a broader definition in mind. Harvey and Hansen (2000) describe *bereavement* as "a process associated with major losses that, at both conscious and unconscious levels, is ongoing to different degrees throughout much of our lives" (p. 360). The loss experience is different for each person, although qualitative similarities that have been documented.

Bereavement typically involves feelings of separation anxiety, grief, and mourning. It has been placed by some theorists within an attachment perspective (e.g., Raphael & Dobson, 2000); indeed, some have found that aspects of anxious attachment were related to coping difficulties after loss (Field & Sundin, 2001). Feelings of loss and loneliness, as well as crying and sadness, are all part of the process. Grieving becomes less intense after the first year for most people, and grief that continues for a prolonged period has been termed *chronic grief* (Raphael & Dobson, 2000). Grieving that includes anger, severe depression, and uncontrollable intrusive memories of the deceased and that continues well beyond what might be considered a normal grieving period has been described as *complicated mourning* or *pathological grief* (e.g., Horowitz, Bonanno, & Holen, 1993). Ambivalence toward the deceased, past relationship conflict, and unresolved emotional issues are thought to be related to more difficult adjustment to bereavement (Field, Hart, & Horowitz, 1999). Nolen-Hoeksema, McBride, and Larson (1997) extended earlier work with bereaved persons to gay men in committed relationships whose partners had died, concluding that a constructive working through of one's grief involves neither avoidance of the emotional issues nor dwelling on them.

Bereavement has a number of physical effects, including decreased effectiveness of the immune system (Raphael & Dobson, 2000). Social effects include disruptions of social status and social structure, increased loneliness and social isolation, and a loss of the meaning of life (Hansson & Hayslip, 2000). Although many of these effects are temporary and are resolvable if people engage in the necessary "grief work," bereavement is a physical, psychological, and emotional stressor.

Much of the existing research focuses on widows, rather than widowers, because women are more likely to outlive their spouses, are less likely to remarry, and are more likely to spend their later years alone (Hansson & Hayslip, 2000). Younger, as opposed to older, women have somewhat different experiences of widowhood (Levinson, 1997), as the younger women are more likely involved in childrearing and all its accompanying responsibilities. Levinson (1997) describes a three-stage model for young widows' recovery from loss. The first stage includes simple survival from day to day, adjusting to the major life changes that have occurred. The second stage involves initial integration of the loss and beginning attempts to reorganize the widow's life along new lines, such as redecorating the house, widening her social network, and engaging in her first intimate relationship. Although this first relationship may not last, it facilitates her movement into the next stage, which is one of renewal. "As a result of the first relationship ending, the young widow frequently experiences internal, intrapsychic change that is reflected in aspects of her sense of self. . . . The adjustment process is completed when a new structure of meaning occurs" (pp. 284–285). At this point, the young widow may enter into a new relationship and build a new life, whereas the older widow may accommodate her existing life to her loss.

Although older widows may address bereavement differently than younger widows, they may be equally or more successful. Older persons may have a more diversified self-concept, more experience at handling stressors, and better balance between the social support that is needed and the social support that is available (Hansson & Hayslip, 2000; Harvey & Hansen, 2000). In comparing grief and coping in persons over 65 and in their 20s, Barnes and her colleagues (Barnes, Harvey, Carlson, & Haig, 1996) found that older persons showed more positive adaptations to the loss of loved ones than did younger persons on several dimensions. Thus, age may be a risk factor for some elements of coping with loss (Hansson & Hayslip, 2000), but it is also a positive resource.

Recovering from loss and completing active bereavement is a process that an individual must go through, but the context in which the individual engages the process is crucially important. Support from and active involvement with family and friends over the months and years following a partner's death helps the surviving partner to stay engaged with life and satisfies the need to belong. Responsiveness by both the health and mental health systems can allow the bereaved person to get needed help earlier in the grieving process. Counseling is useful for some people, and self-help groups provide a special type of support.

Bereavement has some overlap with relationship breakup and divorce in the feelings of sadness and loss. But as Harvey and Hansen (2000) note, divorce—and by implication, breakup—allows partners time to engage each other in a new way, perhaps over a period of years, and even rework old issues and resolve them in better fashion. Death does not provide such an option. Bereavement is unique among the loss experiences in its finality. Complete the exercise in the Up Close box on page 182 to help you explore your own loss experience.

Exploring a Loss Experience

Everyone has the experience of losing someone he or she loves, perhaps through a broken friendship, a family disruption, a relationship breakup, a divorce, or a death. Think of a loss that you have experienced personally: You may have had a painful romantic breakup, your parents may have gotten divorced, or you may have lost a friend through a misunderstanding. Think about this loss experience. Remember when you first became aware of the loss.

- What time of day was it?
- Where were you?
- How did you feel?
- Did you feel sad? Angry?

Now take a pen and paper or sit down at your computer and begin writing a letter to the relationship partner you lost, the friend who got angry with you, or your parents who got a divorce. First, say hello to him or her and then tell what you remember about the loss event. Describe how you felt at the time. Ask him or her questions that you might have never asked or never gotten answered. Tell this person about any long-term effects that you have had from the loss of your relationship with him or her. Then write down what you wish had happened instead of what did happen and your thoughts about how things might be different now if the loss experience had never happened. Finally, tell this person what you would like him or her to know about your current life and how you are doing. Then say goodbye and sign the letter.

Put your letter away for a few days, and then get ready to take it out and reread it. Before you actually reread the letter, make sure that you have at least one person you can talk with about it, should you need to do that. This exercise can be informative and even healing, but it can also be upsetting.

Summary and Conclusions

Relationship loss can involve the breakup of a romantic relationship, a divorce, or even a death. Jealousy is an emotion that has negative effects on relationships. It is typically caused by a person's fear that he or she is going to lose a romantic partner to someone else. Although some people view jealousy and envy as the same thing, jealousy involves a fear of loss whereas envy involves wishing to have something that someone else has. Both women and men experience jealousy but may respond to it differently. Infidelity is a behavior that is frowned on by much of Western society but engaged in by many people. It occurs when someone in an intimate relationship becomes sexually involved with a third person. Typically, women are unfaithful due to relationship dissatisfaction, but men are motivated more by the sexual experience itself. Infidelity can be a serious relationship stressor but does not inevitably lead to relationship breakup.

Relationships break up for many reasons, including pre-existing problems, breakdown of relationship processes, and important negative events, such as infidelity. When relationship interaction becomes defensive and dismissive and the ratio of positives to negatives falls below 5 to 1, a couple is more likely to break up. There are both costs and benefits to relationships as well as barriers to breakup. Sometimes, what attracts someone to a partner is ultimately what turns him or her off to that partner. A breakup is a process, rather than an event, and it may involve individual thinking, relational negotiation, social network, and final account-making stages. People may react to breakup with great emotional turmoil, but given time, self-esteem, and social support, they are likely to recover well. In many cases, the more serious the relationship, the more difficult the breakup. Partners do not seem to have similar reactions to breakup.

Divorce, or the legal dissolution of a marriage, has become more common in the United States over the last several decades. Some research on divorce emphasizes negative interaction between partners, and other research indicates that interaction very early in the relationship can forecast later relationship outcomes. Negative interaction may predict early divorce, whereas lack of positive interaction may predict later divorce. There are many aspects to divorce, including economics, emotions, dealing with children, and so on, and many of these aspects overlap. Adults may react to divorce with physical and emotional distress, and women are virtually always worse off economically after divorce. Children are impacted negatively in many ways, and although continued effective parenting by the mother (if she is the custodial parent) can make a great positive difference, the father's involvement is extremely important, also. Remarriage may be positive for both adults and children. Research does not indicate large differences between adults who were the children of divorce and adults whose parents stayed married. Discussion of divorce has become politicized, with some people claiming that divorce erodes the whole of society and other people claiming that divorce is simply one more lifestyle choice. In fact, divorce has positive effects for some people, short-term negative effects for other people, and continuing negative effects for others.

Bereavement occurs when a loved one dies, and this chapter focused on the death of a relationship partner/spouse. This type of loss has emotional, physiological, and social effects and requires major life adjustments. Grief that has many negative emotional components and that lasts much longer than is customary is called *pathological grief* or *complicated mourning*. Age is a risk factor for dealing with bereavement, since older people may have more problems, but older people also may have more resources for dealing with those problems. Women who are younger when widowed are more likely to reorganize their lives and then move on to other intimate relationships, whereas older widows are more likely to simply reorganize their lives. In recovering from bereavement, as in recovering from breakup or divorce, it is important to stay engaged with other people and with life in general.

Key Terms

Bereavement (p. 180)   **Infidelity** (p. 167)
Breakup (p. 170)   **Jealousy** (p. 166)
Divorce (p. 174)   **Loss** (p. 166)

Suggested Reading

Amato, P. R. (2000). The consequences of divorce for adults and children. *Journal of Marriage and the Family, 62,* 1269–1287.

Buunk, B. P., & Dijkstra, P. (2000). Extradyadic relationships and jealousy. In C. Hendrick & S. S. Hendrick (Eds.), *Close relationships: A sourcebook* (pp. 317–329). Thousand Oaks, CA: Sage.

Duck, S. W. (1984). A perspective on the repair of personal relationships: Repair of what, when? In S. W. Duck (Ed.), *Personal relationships 5: Repairing personal relationships* (pp. 163–184). New York: Academic Press.

Fine, M. A. (2000). Divorce and single parenting. In C. Hendrick & S. S. Hendrick (Eds.), *Close relationships: A sourcebook* (pp. 139–152). Thousand Oaks, CA: Sage.

Hetherington, E. M. (Ed.). (1999). *Coping with divorce, single parenting, and remarriage.* Mahwah, NJ: Lawrence Erlbaum.

Stroebe, M. S., Stroebe, W., Hansson, R. O., & Schut, H. (Eds.). (2001). *Handbook of bereavement research: Consequences, coping, and care.* Washington, DC: American Psychological Association.

Relationship Story

Painting the Baby's Room

Becky and Chris had a dilemma: Becky wanted to paint the baby's room yellow, and Chris wanted to paint it green. They both had agreed a long time ago that the standard pink and blue was *not* what was going in their new baby's room, so they figured they wouldn't have any trouble agreeing on what color they did want and how everything should look. Were they ever wrong! And of course, they had to paint before they could do anything else. Becky and Chris knew this was only a temporary setback, and they were actually very glad to be in the position of having to make a decision about what color to paint the baby's room.

You see, Becky and Chris had been wanting this baby for a very long time. They had first met in college—in a chemistry lab—and they had hit it off right away. They found that they shared similar backgrounds and held

185

similar beliefs in terms of religion and politics. Becky had grown up in an intact family, and Chris had spent most of adolescence in a remarried family after a parental divorce, but both were close to their parents, stepparents, and brothers and sisters. They began dating and essentially were together from that time on.

After college graduation, Becky went to seminary and then began her career as a hospital chaplain, and Chris worked as an architect. They had a loft in the city and spent several years furnishing it the way they liked, building their careers, traveling, and generally living like any young couple just starting their life together. Of course, life wasn't problem free, but the job issues and health concerns weren't major.

The biggest problem they faced during those early years was learning to really listen to each other. Early on, Chris was more outgoing and confident than Becky and sometimes seemed almost to run the relationship. Then every so often, Becky would blow up, saying, "Chris, you don't ever listen to me! You always act like you know best. I'm sick of it! Stop trying to run things." Chris was invariably surprised by Becky's outbursts, sometimes lashing back, sometimes apologizing, and sometimes just walking around feeling confused by it all. But as time went on and with the help of a therapist, they worked on their relationship and got to the point where each partner felt listened to by the other. They felt that through their years together, they had learned how to do a better and better job of sharing power in the relationship, not to mention finances, housework, and so on.

As time went on, their careers were going well and they bought their first house. Their parents had been hinting about becoming grandparents for a long time, and several of their siblings had children, whom Chris and Becky loved to play with. Quite a few of their friends had also started having kids. Pretty soon, Becky and Chris decided that they were ready for children, but nothing happened. They started to get impatient and then very anxious about the whole thing, but the more Becky tried to get pregnant and didn't succeed, the more they both wanted a baby.

This was a hard time for both of them. No matter where they went, they saw babies. Their families and friends made tactful inquiries, and it became increasingly difficult for Becky and Chris to talk about their difficulties getting pregnant. Sometimes, they even found themselves arguing about whether having a baby was worth all the stress and anguish they were going through. They always decided that it *was* worth it! Then finally, they went through extensive infertility testing. It was almost a relief to finally find out that due to a variety of medical problems, a pregnancy was *very* unlikely for them. At least they knew. But it was a tough blow! Becky and Chris simply held each other and cried, grieving for the baby that they were never going to have.

As months went by, Chris and Becky slowly moved past their grief at not being able to conceive a baby and began talking about the whole issue of parenthood from a different perspective. They had both been intent on having their "own" child, but as they thought past the biological issues of having a child who looked like them and had their mannerisms, they realized that what they really wanted, individually and as a couple, was to be parents. They wanted a baby and child to love and raise, whether he or she was their biological child or not. The thought of adoption was new to them, however, and they did a lot of thinking and talking with each other before they talked with anyone else or attempted to learn more about the adoption process.

Chris and Becky talked with their parents and found a level of support that surprised them. Their parents all talked about the joys and stresses of raising children, but no one said anything negative about adoption. Their siblings were equally supportive, as were most of their friends. One Caucasian/Hispanic couple they knew had adopted a biracial (African American and Hispanic) infant, so they talked with that couple about the adoption process as well as the special issues accompanying biracial adoption. The couple explained that some people feel strongly that African American children should be raised in the African American community and that Native American children should be raised only in the Native American community. Other people believe that loving parents are all that is required in an adoptive family.

As they explored adoption from a number of different angles, Becky and Chris got an education about some of the political and legal issues surrounding the adoption process. Becky's chaplain training helped them in talking with the various adoption counselors and agencies as they explored private adoptions, religious agency adoptions, government agency adoptions, and even foreign adoptions. They also began exploring adoption websites and found that the Internet represented a whole new source of information.

After several months of searching, they realized that for them, there were several areas of concern. In particular, they were concerned with the potential for health and physical problems of a baby who may have been born in poverty and raised in a government orphanage. They knew that they could deal with many of these potential problems, but they did not want to get themselves into a situation with a baby that had so many problems that Becky and Chris would be overwhelmed and unable to cope.

The waiting time was also a problem for them. Adoption could sometimes take years! It didn't take as long with a private adoption, but private adoption didn't always have as many legal protections as other forms of adoption, which worried Becky and Chris. They didn't want to "fall in love" with a baby and then have the birth mother turn around and reclaim the child.

Chris and Becky were educated, knew how to deal with bureaucracies, and had financial resources, but the adoption process still seemed overwhelming at times. Cost was a huge factor. It would cost thousands of dollars. Could they afford it? The time involved was another factor. It might take several years, and the waiting would be very difficult. Finally, after pondering long and hard, they decided to go ahead. It was right after New Year's that they decided to work with a religious social service agency that had an office in their hometown, and they agreed to pursue the adoption of a Chinese baby. Their baby would be a girl, and they were told that the wait would be one to two years.

Once they made the decision, they immediately felt that a weight had been lifted off their shoulders. No matter what happened from here on, they both felt that together, they had made the right decision. That was how they found themselves in the paint section of their local hardware chain store on a Saturday morning in July, trying to decide what color of paint to buy—together.

Fortunately for them, they were in one of those stores where salespeople actually try to be helpful, so Aretha, the motherly saleswoman working in the paint department, seemed genuinely interested in their dilemma. As they told her their story, her face lit up and it became clear that she was taking them on as a "project." "My kids are grown now," she said, "but I remember that decorating that first nursery for that first baby was a wonderful time in my life. And now there are all sorts of things that make decorating easier and more fun. Let me show you what we have." Well, an hour later, Becky and Chris emerged from the store with a cartload full of stuff and a plan for how they were going to decorate the baby's room. The plan of yellow walls and a yellow-and-green border gave each of them something of what they wanted and sounded perfect for a baby's room. As they worked over several weekends, they saw the room take shape, and they got more and more excited. Even though they knew it could be a long time before their baby arrived, they wanted to be ready.

Then, in early November, the call that they were waiting for finally came! Becky was at the hospital doing paperwork when their caseworker called and said their baby had been born. Becky immediately called Chris. "They have a baby for us!" she exclaimed. "It is a girl, and she will be arriving in about 3 or 4 weeks. They'll call us when they know the arrival time for sure." That night, Chris and Becky called their family and close friends to tell them the exciting news and then sat staring at each other across the kitchen table, too excited to sleep. They were going to have a baby! The next few days passed quickly as they made final arrangements for child care, secured a pediatrician, bought baby clothes and diapers and formula, and got everything ready that they could possibly think of. Then they waited around for the phone to ring—and finally it did. An agency adoption worker from China was bringing their baby girl to the United States, and they would be arriving at the airport next Tuesday.

It was already Thursday, and Becky and Chris couldn't contain themselves. They called everyone—again—and told them the news. Then they watched the clock. The hours ticked by, the calendar pages rolled over, and finally it was Tuesday. The plane was due at 5:00 P.M., but they got to the airport at noon because they just couldn't wait any longer. They walked around the airport for awhile and then ate (or tried to eat) lunch. They walked some more, watching planes arrive and take off, realizing that one of those planes was bringing someone who would change their lives.

At 4:00, Becky and Chris went down to the gate where the plane was due to arrive, and they saw several young couples—childless couples—waiting and looking as eager, hopeful, and frightened as they looked. They began talking to one of the couples, and soon the whole group of six couples was talking together as though they had known each other for years. All of them were waiting for the same plane, and all of them were welcoming Chinese baby girls into their families. Becky and Chris were the only lesbian couple in the group, but otherwise, all of the couples were in pretty much the same situation. Oh, they had different jobs and families and lifestyles, but they all very much wanted to be parents.

Talking helped pass the time, and soon, someone said, "There's the plane!" They all fell silent and watched the plane taxi toward the gate, straining forward as though they could hurry it up through sheer force of will. Finally, the plane was at the gate, the passageway was opened, and the first passengers started to deplane. The very first people off the plane were the social service workers carrying babies, each worker with a tag on her shirt showing the last name of the family that the baby was promised to. As Chris and Becky watched a young, black-haired woman wearing a tag with their name walk out into the terminal, they rushed up to her and told her who they were. Then they got their first look at their new little daughter. It was love at first sight.

■ ■ ■

Questions to Consider in Reading This Chapter

- Were you sympathetic to Becky and Chris as you saw their story unfold? Have you ever known a couple dealing with infertility? Have you ever known someone who was adopted? If you do, what were those experiences like?

- How do you feel about multiracial adoptions? Do you believe that children should be raised within their own racial or cultural groups, or do you think that loving parenting is all that matters?

- Do you have any friends who are gay or lesbian? Are those friendships any different from your friendships with persons who are heterosexual?

- Did your feelings about Becky and Chris change when you found out they were a lesbian, rather than a heterosexual, couple?

What Do We Know about Diverse Relationships?

One of the underlying themes or premises of this book is that relationships, including families, come in many different forms—in diverse shapes, sizes, colors, and configurations. Although much of society's attention, and the attention of social scientists, has been on the young, white, heterosexual couple who is married or moving toward marriage, the reality of relationships in Western society and the wider world paints a much broader picture (e.g., Teachman et al., 2000).

Although the full breadth of relationship and family forms cannot be covered in this chapter, the chapter will address four major areas of diverse relationships and acknowledge that this is just the tip of the relationship "iceberg." The chapter will discuss remarried relationships, gay and lesbian relationships, multicultural/multiracial relationships, and cohabitation while also recognizing that more attention needs to focus on partners dealing with illness and disability (e.g., Lyons, Sullivan, Ritvo, & Coyne, 1995), families coping with poverty (Seccombe, 2000), and other groups with special needs.

Conceptualizing Relationships

"The ideal traditional family form includes one man and one woman, co-residing and legally joined in a permanent and sexually exclusive first marriage, who have children" (Scanzoni, Polonko, Teachman, & Thompson, 1989, p. 13). Yet if we go to a grocery store or a mall anywhere in North America, it is apparent that young, white, attractive, affluent couples are not all that we see; in fact, they are in the minority. We see Hispanic, African American, Asian, and many other couples. We see male and female pairs who may be just friends or who may be gay or lesbian couples. We see older couples walking very slowly and overweight couples with overweight children. We see families, and they do not wear T-shirts that say "Intact Family" or "Remarried Family." We can't tell a remarried family by looking at one. So, if our stereotypical couple is not the prevailing norm, and in fact never was (Coontz, 1992), then how do we define a *romantic, partnered relationship?*

Scanzoni and his colleagues (Scanzoni et al., 1989) define such a relationship as a **sexually based primary relationship** "if the persons define sexual exchanges or interdependence as a legitimate element/expectation for their type of relationship (whether or not they are currently engaged in sexual activity)" (p. 47). Such a relationship also requires diverse exchanges/interactions, frequent interactions, intensity of interactions, and duration of the impact of the interactions. Thus, the relationship is defined, in large measure, by its ongoing processes (e.g., aspects of interaction and communication), rather than by its socially defined structure (e.g., a married couple, a dating couple, a heterosexual couple). Such a perspective gives definitional control to those who enact the relationship or observe it, rather than to the greater society.

Although this chapter concentrates on types of relationships, rather than transcendent processes, it nevertheless considers several relational forms that have been set apart from the more traditional form of relationship in that they have sometimes been looked down on (e.g., lesbian and gay relationships, multicultural/multiracial relationships) and have sometimes been overlooked (e.g., remarried relationships, cohabiting relationships). As Duck and Wood (1995) note, "Because knowledge about a broader range of relationship phenomena increases awareness of variations in form, meaning, and substance, it cultivates appreciation of the pluralism characteristic of relationship life" (p. xi).

The Up Close box that follows will help you explore your own attitudes and experiences in your relational culture. The first focus of this chapter is remarried families.

Remarried Families

Today, about half of the marriages that occur in the United States are *remarriages* for one or both partners (Coleman, Ganong, & Fine, 2000), and many of these remarriages involve children. In fact, about one-third of the children in the United States will spend part of their growing-up years in a remarried family (Ganong & Coleman, 2000). Although remarriage rates have decreased slightly overall in recent decades, especially for women,

Examining Your Relational Culture

As proposed elsewhere in this book, every close relationship is, in some sense, a cross-cultural relationship. Everyone grows up in a particular family, at a particular time, in a particular place, within a particular culture. Some of you will identify with one or more of the groups of people discussed in this chapter: remarried families; gay and lesbian couples and families; multiethnic and multiracial couples; and cohabiting couples. But others of you will identify with some other group or groups.

Take a look at your current relationship partner (if you have one) and at your network of friends and family, as well. Think about the following:

- What kinds of diversity are represented in these relationships? Are different ethnicities, races, and religions represented? What about diversity of interests, personalities, and styles?
- How are the people in your network similar to and different from you and from each other? How are these differences handled? Do you find these differences annoying, enriching, or perhaps both annoying and enriching at different times?
- What is your general attitude toward differentness?

half or more of all divorced women remarry (Teachman et al., 2000). And many of these women have children in their remarriages (Coleman et al., 2000).

If so many people are involved in remarriages and **remarried families,** then why is so much written about families in general and so little, relatively speaking, about remarried families? Ganong and Coleman (2000) propose that remarried families do not fit the traditional stereotype of what a family should be, so they have been given less attention than traditional intact families. "The cultural ideal of the private nuclear family is basically a European model that ignores cultural/historical family patterns of African Americans, Native Americans, Latinos, and other groups of families. This nuclear family model is associated with a moral natural imperative, and other family forms are considered to be immoral or (at best) less moral" (p. 157). Yet most people probably know someone who is in a remarried family, considering that a substantial proportion of the U.S. population is involved in one.

Remarried families have been considered within three broad frameworks, according to Ganong and Coleman (2000). First, there is the *incomplete institutionalization* framework, which is consistent with the quotation above and views remarried families as "partial families," without the norms, rules, and structures that serve to keep an intact (meaning "not divorced") family functioning. A second framework is that remarried families are *deviant families* that have negative attributes. Both these perspectives take the traditional intact family as the normal family and view all other family arrangements as being different and inferior. The third framework views remarried families as *reconstituted nuclear families,* or re-creations of the original nuclear families, but without non-residential parents, noncustodial visits, and so on. It is, in some sense, a denial of the *re-* in *remarriage* (e.g., Ganong & Coleman, 2000). None of these perspectives views the remarried relationship and family as simply one of many variations in how people "do" relationships and families.

Courtship in Remarriage

Although divorce is seen as typically preceding remarriage, there are, in fact, other pathways to consider. One such pathway is having been widowed, which is more common among the elderly. Yet a third path is not having been married before but having had children who will join their parent in a new relationship (Ganong & Coleman, 1994). Depending on the pathway taken, the challenges for the people involved may be somewhat different. The emphasis in this chapter, however, is on postdivorce remarriage.

The average length of time between divorce and remarriage is a bit less than four years, but nearly one-third of people remarry within a year after divorce (Coleman et al., 2000). Many of the courtship dynamics discussed in earlier chapters are a part of the courtship that leads to remarriage but with a few big differences. First, partners in remarriage are typically older (by about a decade) than partners in a first marriage. Second, one or both partners have been married previously, so a substantial amount of experience is brought to the new relationship. Third, when children are involved, the remarriage is a "package deal" of parent and child/children; an instant family is created, which must be taken into account. Other differences include the higher percentage of people who cohabit before remarriage, greater pragmatism in a remarriage than a first marriage, and fewer background similarities between partners in a remarriage (Ganong & Coleman, 1994).

Relationship Quality in Remarriage

According to Coleman et al. (2000), "Findings are mixed regarding differences in marriage quality between individuals in first marriages and in remarriages" (p. 1291). Some research has found lower relationship quality for remarried couples, and other research has found no difference between remarried and first-married couples. Relationship problems occur on individual, relational, and social levels (Ganong & Coleman, 1994) for remarried couples, just as they do for first-married and nonmarried couples.

But remarried couples with children face greater complexities, just in terms of the number of relationships that must be managed. Children may be unhappy about the remarriage and may try to undermine the relationship, and partners may differ on child-rearing approaches. Because of their prior relationship experiences and greater maturity, partners in remarriages are more likely to share decision making equally than are first-marriage partners (Ganong & Coleman, 2000).

Women have more power in remarriages than in previous marriages, and therefore the new marriage is typically more equitable or balanced. Allen and her colleagues (Allen, Baucom, Burnett, Epstein, & Rankin-Esquer, 2001) found that remarried women reported greater autonomy in several areas than did first-married women. Buunk and Mutsaers (1999) asked remarried women and men to answer a series of questions concerning how they felt about their current marriage and to answer the same questions for their previous marriage "for the period in their former marriage when they did not yet expect that it would end in divorce" (p. 126). Respondents generally felt that their current marriage was more equitable than their previous one, and this finding was especially marked for women.

In spite of the positive aspects of remarriage, remarriages, especially those with stepchildren, break up at a higher rate than do first marriages. According to Booth and Edwards (1992), reasons for this higher breakup rate include the lack of support and structure for remarriage, the greater willingness of people who have been divorced to divorce again, and the smaller pool of potential partners for remarriage than for first marriage. The smaller pool of partners thus offers a greater opportunity for mismatches or "pre-existing doom" (Duck, 1982).

The occurrence of conflict—and more particularly, the handling of conflict—is centrally important in remarriage. Coleman, Fine, Ganong, Downs, and Pauk (2001) analyzed qualitative interviews of remarried family members to determine major areas of conflict and to uncover conflict resolution approaches in remarried families. They found that stepfamily conflict is rather predictable and occurs over particular issues. The families in their research "experienced strife over resources, loyalty conflicts, control over and responsibility for children, or disputes with extended family members and nonresidential parents. These disagreements appeared to be the manifestation of the underlying issue of *negotiating the boundaries around and within the stepfamily*" (Coleman et al., p. 71; italics in original). Family members used a wide variety of conflict resolution strategies; some were successful, and some were not. Conflict sometimes went unaddressed, but at other times, it was the basis for positive change in the family. Bray (1999) found conflict to be more predictive of the adjustment of children in remarried than in first-married families. Conflict is a normal part of relationships, and remarried families are not an exception.

Baxter, Braithwaite, and Nicholson (1999) were interested not just in conflict but in many other processes that go on as a remarried family develops. These authors employed an interview approach in which they asked 53 people from different remarried families, both parents and children, to look back at their blended family and identify significant events or turning points as the remarried family developed the feel of a family. The researchers identified 15 types of turning points, of which five were most dominant: (1) celebration of special events and holidays, (2) conflict, (3) changes in household composition, (4) family crises, and (5) family member quality time. They found that families followed different trajectories in their development, varying in such things as length of time to develop as a family, emotional turbulence, conflict, and so on. They also found that parents and children often agreed in their views of the family. Consistent and clear views of family members' roles, particularly the roles of stepparents, as well as efforts by stepparents to seek and maintain affectionate relationships with stepchildren also contributed to increased family resiliency and reduced family stress (Fine, Coleman, & Ganong, 1999). It is important to note that stepchildren—particularly adolescents— impact stepparents, just as stepparents impact stepchildren (Anderson, Greene, Hetherington, & Clingempeel, 1999).

Children in Remarried Families

Much of the research published on remarried families deals with what happens to the children in these situations. The findings are similar to those from research on the children of divorced families, because in many cases, they are the same children.

Research has focused on topics such as academic achievement and completion, psychological adjustment, and behavior problems, and the results have typically shown lower achievement and higher rates of difficulties (e.g., Bray, 1999). As Coleman et al. (2000) note in their review of relevant research published during the 1990s, "Although the findings ranged widely, most researchers reported that stepchildren were similar to children living with single mothers on the preponderance of outcome measures and that stepchildren generally were at greater risk for problems than were children living with both of their parents. However, most researchers also found that the differences between stepchildren and children in first-marriage families were small" (p. 1292). A number of models have been proposed to explain why children in remarried families display problems, examining such factors as accumulated stress due to disruption of the original family, parent and stepparent involvement and interaction with children, and the selection approach discussed earlier (Coleman et al., 2000). It has also been suggested that the problems displayed by children in remarried families are not due to the remarriage but to the divorce that preceded it (Anderson et al., 1999).

Most children in stepfamilies do as well as children in first-marriage families; if this were not so, the research would show much greater differences between the two groups of children. Nevertheless, remarried families have many complex tasks to accomplish, and society needs to be more supportive of these families. Dispensing with such myths as "the wicked stepmother" and "the instant family" and accepting that this family form has both unique stresses—such as managing relationships among children, parents, and stepparents—and unique possibilities—such as providing a rich and diverse family life with extended family and stepfamily—will result in a better social context for remarried families.

Lesbian and Gay Relationships

A substantial number of people seek romantic partners of the same gender. Estimates of the percentage of the U.S. population who identify their sexual orientation as **gay** or **lesbian** range from 10%, as stated by Kinsey's research (Kinsey, Pomeroy, & Martin, 1948;

Kinsey, Pomeroy, Martin, & Gebhard, 1953), to approximately 1.5% for lesbians and nearly 3% for gay males (Laumann et al., 1994).

It is important to recognize that the numbers of people who identify themselves as gays and lesbians are likely to be underreported, since the lack of societal support for same-gender relationships keeps many lesbians and gays from "coming out" and self-identifying as homosexual (Huston & Schwartz, 1995). Indeed, Eldridge and Gilbert (1990) found that of the employed lesbians in their study, over one-third were completely "closeted" in their work settings. Such lack of disclosure increases stress for lesbians and gays (Huston & Schwartz, 1995), and in fact, parental and family support is extremely important to gay and lesbian couples (Demo & Allen, 1996).

Courtship and Maintenance

In spite of being stigmatized by society and sometimes by their own families, gays and lesbians have been able to form satisfying intimate relationships, as was the case with Becky and Chris in the Relationship Story. It is estimated that the majority of gay men and lesbian women are in romantic relationships, many of which are long term (Peplau & Spalding, 2000). Historically, gay men often sought casual, impersonal sex. But since the mid-1980s, the proliferation of HIV (human immunodeficiency virus) and the resultant spread of AIDS (acquired immune deficiency syndrome) has led to more careful partner selection and a greater emphasis on fidelity among gay males (Huston & Schwartz, 1995). This trend may be reversing for young, especially African American gays, however (Levine, 2001).

Romantic partners in homosexual couples meet in many of the same ways that heterosexual partners meet, such as through introductions from people in their social networks. Courtship patterns are also similar to those for heterosexual couples in terms of dating "scripts," although lesbians more often incorporate friendship and gay males more often incorporate sexual contact into their beginning romantic relationships (Peplau & Spalding, 2000). Moreover, physical attractiveness is more sought after by gay than by lesbian partners, similar to gendered patterns in heterosexual couples (Peplau & Spalding, 2000).

Power issues are typically worked out more equitably for gay and lesbian couples than for heterosexual couples. However, earning capacity confers power on gay male partners, as it does on heterosexual male partners, while other issues, such as having one's children from a previous relationship, may increase power for a lesbian partner (Huston & Schwartz, 1995). When same-sex partners cohabit, household responsibilities are not assigned according to a traditional and gendered division of labor, but there are still issues of negotiation (Berzon, 1988; Huston & Schwartz, 1995).

Many similarities exist between same-gender couples and heterosexual couples. Kurdek and Schmitt (1986), for example, found that heterosexual, lesbian, and gay male couples were similar in love and liking for a partner and satisfaction with the relationship, and Adler, Hendrick, and Hendrick (1987) found that heterosexual and gay men endorsed similar love and sex attitudes. Haas and Stafford (1998) found that lesbian and gay couples used many of the relationship maintenance strategies that have been established for heterosexual couples, including sharing tasks, communication, and spending time together. These same-sex couples also relied even more heavily on supportive networks than did heterosexual couples. In addition, lesbian and gay couples described the importance of having a gay/lesbian supportive environment for their relationship and also highlighted their sense of being similar to heterosexual couples, except for traditional gender stereotypic behaviors (Haas & Stafford, 1998). Indeed, in a longitudinal study, Kurdek (1998) found that gay, lesbian, and heterosexual couples did not differ in relationship satisfaction at any point in time.

Lesbian and gay couples are further similar to heterosexual couples in that they also have problems with conflict, jealousy, violence, and the like. In surveying areas of conflict for lesbian, gay, and heterosexual couples, all of whom were living together and without children, Kurdek (1994) found the three groups to be very similar. They reported equally frequent conflict in four major areas: intimacy, personal distance, personal flaws, and power. In addition, power and intimacy were the top two conflict areas for all three couple types and were correlated negatively with relationship satisfaction.

Jealousy, a source of difficulty for heterosexual couples, is also a problem for gay and lesbian couples, particularly because of the higher rate of nonmonogamy for gay males (Blumstein & Schwartz, 1983). In heterosexual couples, women have been shown to be more jealous of a male partner's emotional involvement and men have been shown to be more jealous of a female partner's sexual involvement, but the reverse was true for gay and lesbian couples in one study (Dijkstra, Groothof, Poel, Laverman, Schrier, & Buunk, 2001). "Whereas gay men more often than lesbian women chose a mate's emotional infidelity as the most upsetting event, lesbians more often than gay men chose a mate's sexual infidelity as the most upsetting event" (p. 41).

As with conflict and jealousy, relationship violence is also an issue for homosexual couples. As more gays and lesbians admit to being victims of relationship violence, rates of such abuse appear to be similar for homosexual and heterosexual relationships (Huston & Schwartz, 1995).

Relationship Breakup

Rates of breakup for lesbian and gay couples are somewhat higher than those for heterosexual couples (Peplau & Spalding, 2000), and the reasons for breakup are both similar to and different from those for heterosexuals. Kurdek (1998) found in a longitudinal study of married, lesbian cohabiting, and gay cohabiting couples that all were similar in the links among five dimensions of relationship quality, including autonomy, barriers to leaving, constructive problem solving, equality, and intimacy. The couples were also similar in two dimensions of relationship outcome: the trajectory of relationship satisfaction and relationship outcome itself. Thus, many aspects of relationship functioning were similar across the three couple types. However, the couples differed in other ways. Lesbian partners reported more autonomy, more equality, more intimacy, fewer barriers to leaving, and more frequent relationship dissolution than did married partners. Gay partners, more than married partners, reported greater autonomy along with fewer barriers to and more frequent occurrence of dissolution.

Kurdek (2001) has noted that considerable research has established the similarities between homosexual and heterosexual couples in how their relationships function and concluded that lesbian and gay couples should be compared with each other, rather than with heterosexual couples. Based on longitudinal findings, Kurdek found few differences between gay and lesbian couples in such qualities as enduring traits, appraisals and beliefs, and conflict resolution. Lesbian couples reported higher equality between partners and slightly more social support from friends than did gay couples. (Remember that Chris and Becky had an active support network.) The predictors of relationship dissolution were similar for both types of couples, with low intimacy and low equality predicting later dissolution, and higher conflict and lower relationship quality early in the study also predicting dissolution.

Gottman and his colleagues (discussed in Smith [2001]) found that homosexual couples may handle conflict episodes in a more positive and equitable manner than heterosexual couples do, but they may have more difficulties repairing relationships after conflict is over. Thus, Gottman and others are offering workshops geared to teaching gay and lesbian couples even more effective strategies for managing and recovering from conflict (Smith, 2001).

Finally, there is one area in which homosexual and heterosexual couples differ greatly: the recognition of their grieving after the loss of a romantic partner through breakup or death. Because society denies the legitimacy of a gay or lesbian relationship, mechanisms for dealing with the end of that relationship, whether signing divorce papers or planning a funeral, are typically not available to the surviving partner (Huston & Schwartz, 1995; Peplau & Spalding, 2000). In addition, depending on how open the partners were with their relationship, a lesbian or gay person may not even be able to grieve openly and gather support from others after losing a partner.

Children in Gay and Lesbian Families

As the acceptance of gay and lesbian (and to a lesser extent, bisexual) relationships has increased, it has become apparent that gay and lesbian families, as well as lesbian and gay relationships, must be considered. Although romantic partners may also be considered a family, this discussion will refer to lesbian and gay parents who have children, both residential and nonresidential. These children were either "born or adopted in the context of heterosexual marriages that later dissolved when one or both parents came out as gay or lesbian" or "were born or adopted after parents had affirmed lesbian or gay identities" (Patterson, 2000, p. 1055).

It is important to recognize the diversity *within* types of diverse families, since no two families are exactly alike. Some research (Patterson, 2000) has compared divorced lesbian mothers to divorced heterosexual mothers and found few differences between them in either individual psychological health or parenting practices, except that lesbian mothers have greater fears about losing custody of their children. A comparison of divorced gay fathers with heterosexual divorced fathers in the same research also indicated high similarity. Although more and more lesbian and gay couples are choosing to become parents through adopting or having biological children, there is little research about these couples and their resulting families. What might be assumed is that the drive toward parenting is extremely high in such couples, given the obstacles they must overcome on the road to parenthood. Becky and Chris's intense desire to become parents is representative of many lesbian and gay couples.

Because of the prevalence of societal negativism toward gay and lesbian relationships, there has been considerable focus on comparing the children of gay and lesbian parents to the children of heterosexual parents in areas of children's sexual identity, individual development, and ability to relate to others. It was previously assumed that the children of homosexual parents would somehow be disadvantaged, relative to the children of heterosexual parents. However, research has found few differences between the two groups (Patterson, 2000). Namely, the children in both groups were similar in personal development, including intelligence and self-concept, and in social relations, such as relationships with peers. And in terms of sexual identity, there did not appear to be a relationship between the parents' sexual identity and the children's sexual identity.

Overall, "considering the children of lesbian and gay parents, the available evidence suggests that they learn to tolerate and value diversity, to develop considerable empathy for others, to follow their own feelings about sexuality and intimacy and to redefine the very foundations (i.e., that a person can have only one mother or one father) upon which notions of families are based" (Demo & Allen, 1996, p. 432).

Multicultural/Multiracial Relationships

If we were to read a book on relationships 50 years from now, we would likely find it to be very different from this one in terms of content. Research on relationships and families in the United States, as well as the books that summarize such research, will likely reflect a population that is almost equally balanced between white non-Hispanics and people of color (25% Hispanic American, 14% African American, and 8% Asian American) (McLoyd, Cauce, Takeuchi, & Wilson, 2000). The increase in population among people of color will come from both increased fertility and increased immigration among various groups.

Families of Color

Although the ultimate focus of this section is on **multicultural relationships** and **multiracial relationships,** it is important to understand some basic findings relevant to partnered and family relationships within the various racial/ethnic groups and the research that compares two or more groups. For example, African Americans, Hispanic Americans, and Asian Americans differ in rates of marriage and divorce. Declining marriage rates for African American women (Crowder & Tolnay, 2000) coupled with higher divorce rates for African American married couples mean that more African American families will be single-headed families, typically led by women (McLoyd et al., 2000). Moreover, Michael et al. (2001) note that African American women and men may differ in their sexual attitudes, with women much less likely than men to have a recreational attitude toward sexuality.

The situation is somewhat different for Hispanic American families—often differentiated into Cuban American, Mexican American, and Puerto Rican groups—where rates of female-headed households are almost twice as common among Puerto Rican families than among the other two groups. Asian American families, in contrast, typically have children later and have fewer children. And among this group, mothers have more education, are more likely to have been born outside the United States, and have fewer nonmarital births (McLoyd et al., 2000).

Research on Hispanic American families has tended to emphasize the notion of male *machismo,* or male dominance of the household (from which the word *macho* has been derived), as well as female submissiveness and self-sacrifice, but McLoyd et al. (2000) have pointed out that this is a narrow and distorted picture. These authors found that both Hispanic Americans and African Americans were more likely than European Americans to endorse traditional male gender roles, but they also had more positive attitudes toward working wives. African American husbands were also more active than other husbands in sharing household work with their wives. Although some research has shown similarities between Mexican American and European American married couples in love attitudes, sexual attitudes, and relationship satisfaction (Contreras et al., 1996), other research has indicated lower satisfaction in African American couples (McLoyd et al., 2000). Differences in economic resources, as well as differential acceptance by society, account for stresses within families of color, yet such variables in and of themselves do not necessarily explain all group differences.

Gaines (1995) takes the position that prevailing cultural values—such as *familism* in Hispanic families and *collectivism* in African American families—offer useful lenses through which to examine relationships and families. *Familism* refers to "a set of values . . . which prioritizes the welfare of one's immediate and extended family by biology and marriage" (p. 64), and *collectivism* refers to "an orientation toward the well-being of the entire ethnic group" (p. 69). These values move beyond the *deficit perspective* that has so often influenced researchers of cultural minorities—namely, that if a person or a group is not white and heterosexual, then that person or group is deficient.

Cultural and Racial Comparisons

Research on close relationships has focused largely on comparisons of African American and European American dating and married couples and with some interesting results. Sanderson and Kurdek (1993) compared African American and white, largely college-student dating couples on a number of indices of relationship quality. The authors were largely interested in determining the usefulness of three different models in predicting relationship commitment and satisfaction: (1) the *interdependence model,* in which happy partners perceive more rewards and fewer costs in their relationships; (2) the *individual differences model,* in which happy partners are those with positive personality characteristics such as expressiveness; and (3) the *problem-solving model,* in which happy partners solve problems well. What Sanderson and Kurdek found was that all three models, particularly the interdependence one, predicted both commitment and satisfaction similarly for both African American and white couples.

Several studies comparing African American and European American married couples have been based on a longitudinal sample of couples recruited at the time of their marriage in the Detroit area, which is referred to as the *First Years of Marriage* or *Early Years of Marriage* study. For example, Ruvolo and Veroff (1997) examined respondents' (153 African American couples, 160 white couples) ratings on 12 personal characteristics of both their partner in reality and their ideal for their partner. The characteristics ranged from gentleness to impatience. Although greater real/ideal discrepancies (the farther the real partner was from the ideal partner) were related to lower marital well-being for both wives and husbands, no racial differences were found in these relationships. In research that looked at other characteristics of this same sample (161 African American couples, 155 white couples) at different points in time, Ruvolo (1998) found that general happiness and marital well-being were positively related for both individuals and their partners. For example, reports of well-being at one point in time predicted partners' reports of well-being at a later point in time. Again, no racial differences were found.

Acitelli, Douvan, and Veroff (1997) studied various conflict processes in the same sample (approximately 115 African American and 120 white couples), and they did find some differences based on race. For example, they found that wives' understanding of their husbands' constructive actions was *positively* related to wives' and husbands' marital well-being for African American couples but *negatively* related to well-being for white couples. Acitelli et al. offered several possible explanations for the latter findings. Even so, it is interesting that the findings for African American couples were directly in line with what had been predicted and with what might seem logical, in that greater understanding equaled greater well-being.

In yet another study based on this sample, Timmer, Veroff, and Hatchett (1996) examined the relationship of 115 African American and 136 white couples' marital happiness to their ties with family members. A number of comparisons were made between the couple groups, with most of them showing racial similarities rather than racial differences. For example, "blacks and whites felt similarly close to their parents and in-laws, although on average black husbands claimed to be closer to their families than did white husbands" (p. 345). One of the differences noted by the authors was that white couples more often argued over issues pertaining to extended family, whereas black couples visited their families more often but also perceived fewer family members who could help if needed. The authors concluded that beyond various structural factors, such as economic status, African Americans value family ties particularly strongly.

This valuing of the extended family sounds less like the collectivism that Gaines (1995) ascribed to African American families and more like the familism he ascribed to

Hispanic American families. Nevertheless, it is consistent with the proposition that African American couples, as well as other couples of color, may have a greater awareness that the immediate nuclear family functions best when it is embedded in a supportive familial and cultural network (see also McLoyd et al., 2000).

Adelmann, Chadwick, and Baerger (1996) examined marital quality in a large sample of white and African American adults, based on interviews conducted with a sample that approximated a nationally representative sample of households in the United States (p. 369) in the 48 contiguous states. The sample for the Adelmann et al. analyses consisted of 333 African American respondents (183 women, 150 men) and 1,097 white respondents (619 women, 478 men). Assessing both positive (satisfaction and interdependence) and negative (discord and negative behavior of the spouse) aspects of marital quality, plus a number of family structural variables, Adelmann et al. found that whites and African Americans had similar *patterns* of marital quality but different *levels* of marital quality. In other words, the same things contributed to marital well-being for both groups; however, African Americans showed somewhat lower levels of the positive aspects and somewhat higher levels of the negative aspects than whites did. It is important to note, however, that the groups differed only slightly, even though the differences were statistically significant. Both groups were well above average on the positive aspects of marital quality and well below average on the negative aspects. In fact, given that the African American respondents reported having more children, more parental strain, more financial strain, and lower income than the white respondents, it is probably surprising that the marital quality differences were not greater. Other research has indicated higher divorce rates for African Americans than for whites but reduced risk of divorce as education increased (Orbuch, Veroff, Hassan, & Horrocks, 2002).

Interethnic/Interracial Couples

Research on interracial and intercultural couples is in its beginning stages, and much more such research will be conducted over the next decades. In a study of attachment and other relationship processes, Gaines, Granrose, and their colleagues (1999) assessed 103 heterosexual interracial couples. One of the most interesting findings was that the majority of individuals reported themselves to be securely, rather than insecurely, attached to their partner, a finding that the authors note was "taken for granted in studies of . . . intraracial couples . . . but also runs counter to stereotypes of individuals who date and marry across racial lines as psychologically unhealthy" (p. 103).

In another study, this time involving 91 interracial couples, Gaines, Rios, et al. (1999) found that men and women "exchanged affection and respect at significant levels" (p. 103). Although it might seem perfectly reasonable that women and men in interracial relationships would be respectful of and affectionate with each other, it is important to remember that partners in these relationships may face harassment and even physical attack by some outsiders who do not approve of interracial/intercultural dating or marriage (Gaines & Liu, 2000).

In an attempt to undercover people's attitudes and biases about interracial/inter-cultural dating and friendship, Garcia and Rivera (1999) conducted a study with college students, who were asked to fill out questionnaires and evaluate couples on a number of characteristics based on their photographs. The couples had the following partner combinations: both partners Hispanic; both partners African American; or racially mixed couples (African American male/Hispanic female; Hispanic male/African American female). Garcia and Rivera found that couples who were described as "at the friendship stage" were evaluated more positively than couples described as "engaged." In addition, couples in which both partners were of the same race were viewed more positively. The authors noted "that perceivers, at least those from the college population, seem to rely on stereotypes when forming impressions about racially similar and dissimilar couples" (p. 82).

Of course, it is one thing to record people's perceptions of interracial/intercultural couples and quite another to assess people who are actually in these relationships. Shibazaki and Brennan (1998) sought to do the latter in their survey of college students, some of whom were involved in interethnic relationships and some of whom were in same-ethnic relationships. Although the two groups were similar on a number of variables, such as satisfaction and perceived approval of the relationship by parents and friends, they differed on others, such as self-esteem and perceived approval of the relationship by the general public. People in interethnic relationships had slightly (although significantly) lower self-esteem than did people in the other group and perceived less approval of their relationship by the general public. The authors concluded "that same- and inter-ethnic relationships are largely similar, and similar dynamics may characterize both kinds of relationships. . . . Myths surrounding inter-ethnic romance, however, may create difficulties for individuals in such relationships" (p. 255).

The issue of self-esteem was further explored by Gurung and Duong (1999) in a sample of college students in interethnic and same-ethnic relationships. Of the 131 undergraduates, 58 were in same-ethnic and 73 in mixed-ethnic relationships. After comparing the groups on individual characteristics—including self-esteem, clarity of self-concept, and ethnic identity, as well as relational characteristics such as satisfaction, commitment, and expectations of the partner—the authors found no group differences on either set of characteristics. Thus, self-esteem was just as high for people in mixed-ethnic relationships as for those in same-ethnic relationships. (This finding is clearly somewhat different from that of Shibazaki and Brennan [1998].) The groups were also similar in other ways, such as preferred attributes in partners.

Although more work is needed in order to clarify the exact nature of the similarities and differences between people in mixed-ethnic/mixed-racial and same-ethnic/same-racial relationships, it appears that, once again, people are more similar than different. Ultimately, when considering multicultural and multiracial relationships, it will be important to accept the many similarities found across ethnic and racial groups—including people considered to be white/Caucasian/white non-Hispanic/European American—to explore the differences when they occur, to recognize that *difference* does not mean *deficit,* and to welcome the lessons that all cultures and races have to teach about how to build healthy relationships and families.

Cohabiting Couples

Because so many of the characteristics common to cohabiting couples are discussed in other chapters of this book, and even in other parts of this chapter, this section addresses only briefly some of the demographic information and research findings solely about cohabiting couples. (For an extended review, see Seltzer [2000].)

By 1997, there were estimated to be 4.1 million cohabiting couples in the United States, and rates of **cohabitation** continue to rise for both young adults and older adults (Seltzer, 2000). For younger people, this is due to the delay of marriage, but for older persons, it may also be influenced by increasingly tolerant attitudes toward cohabitation. This lifestyle form still receives less approval in the United States than in many other countries (although some countries consider cohabitation to be completely unacceptable). In the United States, cohabitation rates have increased for African Americans, Hispanic Americans, and European Americans and for people at all education levels (Seltzer, 2000).

One of the difficulties with nonmarital cohabiting is that such a relationship has no legal status in the event of an illness or breakup. Much like gay and lesbian couples, cohabiting partners have few legal protections, even though some states, more than others, consider cohabiting relationships legitimate. "The substantial variation across states in the availability of domestic partnership registration, the eligibility rules, and the benefits and responsibilities of registration demonstrates public disagreement about the meaning of cohabitation and its place in the U.S. kinship system" (Seltzer, 2000, p. 1262).

For some couples, cohabitation is just one point on the continuum that runs from dating to marriage, but for others, it is the way the relationship is ultimately defined. Cohabitation would seem to offer couples the opportunity either to decide that they cannot live together or to work out their differences, thus allowing greater marital success in the long run, but that is not the case. Couples who cohabit before marriage are more likely to get separated or divorced than couples who do not cohabit (DeMaris & Rao, 1992). Cohan and Kleinbaum (2002) found that "spouses who cohabited before marriage demonstrated more negative and less positive problem solving and support behaviors compared to spouses who did not cohabit" (p. 180). The differences between the groups were small, however, and both groups were functioning well.

Another misconception about cohabiting couples is that they are young and carefree, but in fact, nearly half of cohabiting households include children (Seltzer, 2000). More older couples are also considering cohabiting, given the complex issues that often accompany marriage or remarriage in later life.

One area in which cohabiting couples look different from married couples is in their greater equality: greater sharing of household responsibilities, comparable commitments to work responsibilities, and lesser conformity to traditional gender roles (Blumstein & Schwartz, 1983; Seltzer, 2000). Cohabiting couples may experience greater freedom from societal expectations about what women and men should do in relationships, but it is equally possible that people who are less interested in conforming to society's gendered expectations are those who choose to cohabit.

As Seltzer (2000) points out, whether people cohabit because they can't afford to get married, because they want a less gendered lifestyle than offered by traditional marriage, or because they want a trial period before committing to marriage, a greater variety of people are cohabiting for a greater variety of reasons, and society needs to understand rather than evaluate them. In commenting about a committed couple who were living together but were unmarried, Rabbi Judy Shanks (2001) notes, "A sanctified relationship derives not only from formal vows, but from two partners creating and sustaining a covenant based on love, trust, mutual respect, and deep and lasting joy in their friendship and intimacy" (p. 96).

Summary and Conclusions

Partnered relationships come in many forms, although the most popular and widely researched form is the marital relationship. Some scholars have defined relationships as *sexually based primary relationships,* trying to underline the idea of using processes, rather than structure, as a way to define a relationship.

The remarried family represents one couple form that involves marital partners, at least one of whom has been married before. A remarried family includes children from one or both partners' previous marriages. This family form is not new, but it has become much more common in recent decades. Remarried couples often have shorter courtships than first-marrieds, are older than first-marrieds, and (especially for women) seek greater equality in their relationships. Remarried partners are as satisfied in their marriages as are first-married partners, but remarriages break up at a higher rate than first marriages. This likely occurs because of the greater complexity of remarried families and the greater number of conflicts to be resolved and relationships to be managed. Most children in remarried families do as well as children in first-married families, but problems may occur that are similar to those that follow divorce. If the remarried family's immediate and extended family and friend network—including people such as noncustodial parents and grandparents, stepgrandparents, and so on—is both civilized and supportive, a remarried family can thrive.

Lesbian and gay couples may face considerable social ostracism as they attempt to develop and maintain their intimate relationships. Many of the courtship dynamics of lesbian and gay couples are similar to those for heterosexual couples, including positive factors such as love and more problematic factors such as conflict. Gay and lesbian couples typically work out power issues more equitably than heterosexual couples do, and household tasks are also shared more equally. Issues such as infidelity (particularly for gay couples) and relationship violence also occur in same-gender couple relationships. Breakup rates are somewhat higher for homosexual than for heterosexual couples, in part, because there are typically fewer barriers to relationship dissolution, such as a legal marriage agreement, joint property, or children. Research has indicated few differences between lesbian and gay couples, except for higher reported equality and somewhat higher reported social support from friends for lesbian than for gay couples. More and more gay and lesbian couples are deciding to have or adopt children, so society should expect to see more lesbian and gay families in the future.

The demographics of the U.S. population are changing, and by the mid-2000s, about half the population will likely be people of color, including African Americans, Hispanic Americans, and Asian Americans. It is important to understand similarities and differences among various cultural and racial couples, families, and groups as well as how multi-/interethnic and multi-/interracial couples and families function. For example, the concept of *machismo* may have been overrated in its importance in Hispanic families. Although African American couples report lower relationship satisfaction than couples in other ethnic groups, African American husbands are more active than husbands in other ethnic groups in sharing in household work. Longitudinal research with African American and European American married couples, beginning when the couples were newlyweds, found many similarities and only a few differences between them. For example, African American couples perceived less conflict with extended family. Other research found similar patterns but different levels of marital quality for European American and African American couples. Some research has found lower self-esteem for partners in multiethnic/multiracial relationships than for partners in interethnic/interracial relationships, but other research has not found these differences in self-esteem. It may be that societal attitudes toward people in multiracial/multiethnic relationships are more negative than are the feelings held by the people actually in the relationships. In fact, relationship processes are very similar for couples in which both partners are from the same racial or ethnic group as for those in which the partners are from different racial or ethnic groups.

It has become much more common for couples of all ages to live together without being married. This may be due to people choosing to delay marriage or to actively decide on cohabitation rather than marriage. Cohabiting couples may be very committed to each other, but they do not have the legal and other bonds and protections that married couples have. When cohabiting partners marry, they are somewhat more likely to divorce than are partners who have not lived together.

Overall, remarried couples, lesbian and gay couples, multicultural and multiracial couples, cohabiting couples, and married couples are more similar than different. All represent unique aspects of the diversity of relational and family life in today's world. As society becomes more supportive and less condemning of diverse couple types—recognizing the positive aspects of diversity—it is likely that benefits will accrue to all couples.

Key Terms

Cohabitation (p. 203)
Gay (p. 194
Lesbian (p. 194)
Multicultural relationships (p. 198)

Multiracial relationships (p. 198)
Remarried families (p. 191)
Sexually based primary relationship (p. 190)

Suggested Reading

Berzon, B. (1988). *Permanent partners: Building gay and lesbian relationships that last.* New York: Plume.

Coleman, M., Ganong, L., & Fine, M. (2000). Reinvestigating remarriage: Another decade of progress. *Journal of Marriage and the Family, 62,* 1288–1307.

Coontz, S. (1992). *The way we never were: American families and the nostalgia trap.* New York: Basic Books.

McLoyd, V. C., Cauce, A. M., Takeuchi, D., & Wilson, L. (2000). Marital processes and parental socialization in families of color: A decade review of research. *Journal of Marriage and the Family, 62,* 1070–1093.

Scanzoni, J., Polonko, K., Teachman, J., & Thompson, L. (1989). *The sexual bond: Rethinking families and close relationships.* Newbury Park, CA: Sage.

Gender

Relationship Story

The Laundry

Della heard the phone ringing in the kitchen, but she let the answering machine take it. She heard Jerome's warm, lazy voice, now edged with irritation, on the line. "Della, if you're there, pick up. Della, pick up. Della!" Finally, he left a brief message for her to call him and hung up.

Della made no move to get the phone; she just kept trying to focus on her accounting book. She had a midterm coming up tomorrow, and she wanted to be prepared for it. Accounting was not her favorite class, but she needed to pass it in order to stay on track for her business degree. She didn't want to talk to Jerome now—and maybe not for awhile. She had really *needed* to talk with him two days ago, after they had a big argument about the laundry, but then, Jerome said he was too busy studying for his chemistry exam. Well, now she was busy, and he could just wait!

The truth was, Della didn't know what to say to Jerome. The argument about the laundry and everything that followed had put her mind in turmoil. She had thought for a long time that she knew where she and Jerome were going with their relationship, but now she wasn't sure. Della had been in love with Jerome for almost two years. They met in a psychology class their sophomore year, and now, they were both seniors in college and still together. When they first saw each other in class, they had this feeling that they had met before. It turned out that they hadn't ever met but that they were both from the same large southern city and amazingly even knew some of the same people.

The more they got to know each other, the more they seemed to have in common. Both of them were quiet—but not too quiet—and the oldest kids in their families. They came from similar families and shared similar values, and although they didn't agree about everything, they agreed about the really important things, like faith and ethics for dealing with people. They were both very committed to school (Della was a business major, and Jerome planned to go to physical therapy school), and they each worked part time to pay for expenses.

They sure had different living styles, however. Jerome lived in a small house near the university, along with two male roommates. They mowed the yard during the warm weather because the landlord drove by occasionally and didn't want the neighbors complaining, but they only cleaned up the inside of the house when they were going to have a party or when someone's parents were coming to visit. Then, there would be a mad rush to vacuum and dust, wash the dishes, clean the bathroom, carry out weeks' worth of trash, and do loads of laundry (or stuff dirty clothes in the closets or under the beds). When that happened, Jerome would sometimes ask Della to come and help them out because she was so organized. She would usually go over and lend a hand, unless she needed to study for an exam or had to be at work. Jerome was right—she was organized!

Della, in contrast, lived by herself in a one-bedroom apartment. She had tried living in the dorm and then tried sharing an apartment with roommates, but she didn't like living with other people, except maybe her family. Her current apartment wasn't elaborate, but she had a few of her favorite things around, and she always kept the place neat and clean. Jerome came over a lot because he said that he liked her place better than his; it was certainly easier to study there than at home with his two roommates. In fact, it was Jerome's coming over a few days ago that had started the current crisis in their relationship.

The fight had happened on the previous Saturday afternoon. Della had been reading her sociology book; in fact, she had been reading about gender roles and their impact on women's and men's behavior. Jerome walked in, carrying some books and hauling a plastic trash bag over his shoulder. She looked up and said, "Hi, what've you got there?"

"I brought my laundry over," he said.

"Oh, okay. The machines are in the next building. You just—"

"Aren't you going to go with me and help me?" he interrupted.

"Why?" she answered.

Jerome looked at her impatiently. "I have a lot of laundry to do; I haven't washed any clothes for two weeks. And besides, I have a chemistry exam that I really need to study for."

"Excuse me, is there a sign on my door that says 'maid service'?" Now Della was ticked off!

Jerome responded with a hurt look on his face. Then he threw down his books and headed out the door to the apartment complex's laundry room, saying "I'll be back" over his shoulder as the door slammed shut.

When he came back awhile later, he got a soda from the refrigerator and came into the living room. He sat down in a chair across from where she was sitting, studying. He said, "Della, I just don't understand. We're almost engaged. Why wouldn't you want to help me with my laundry? I mean, I guess this isn't a big deal to you, but it is to me. Why even get married if we're not going to help each other out?"

Della put down her book and looked Jerome squarely in the eye. "Listen, this is not just about your laundry. When we first started dating, we pretty much kept things separate. You took care of your stuff, and I took care of mine. Then when you guys were having that Halloween party last year, you needed to clean up the house all of a sudden, and you asked me to come over and help. And so I did. Then you started calling me whenever you three needed to clean, and sometimes you even sounded a little ticked off when I was busy studying or had to go to work. Lately, you've been over here at least three nights a week, and sometimes you expect me to cook for you. Hello? I'm not going to start helping you with your laundry, because if I do, pretty soon I'll be doing it all myself!"

Jerome just kind of sat there, not knowing what to say. That's not the way *he* saw things at all. He loved Della, and they had talked about getting engaged sometime before they graduated. If he got accepted into physical therapy school back home, then she would move there with him and get a job. Eventually, they would get married. It was as simple as that. It wasn't like he never did anything for her! He always made sure her car was running well, and if she had to work extra late, he would drive her to work and then pick her up after, just to make sure she was safe. She really seemed to appreciate the things he did, and she always thanked him. Wasn't that what being in a relationship meant—that people did things for each other?

The conversation just kind of drifted along, until both Della and Jerome decided they needed to study. They studied and then went out for something to eat, after Jerome got his clean clothes out of the laundry room dryer. They didn't talk anymore about the problem that night. Then, the next day, Della called Jerome and wanted to talk some more. But Jerome had a chemistry exam the next day and said, "I can't talk about it now. I just won't ask you to help me with my laundry again, that's all."

"That's not the point," said Della.

"Well, I have to study. I'll call you tomorrow." Click.

The next day, after the chemistry test, Jerome called Della, but she didn't answer. Then he remembered that she had to work that afternoon and evening, so he figured she would call him when she got home. He settled into watching *Monday Night Football* and forgot that he was expecting her to call. After the game, he realized that she hadn't called, but he shrugged it off and went to bed. After classes were over the next day, he called her again. "Della, if you're there, pick up. Della, pick up. Della!"

At this point, Jerome got in his truck and drove over to Della's apartment. He walked up to the apartment and knocked on the door. He had a key, but somehow he didn't want to use it today. The door opened, and there stood Della, looking at him with an expression of irritation. He said, "You didn't answer your phone, so I just came over to see if you were home. I want to talk with you."

"If I'd wanted to talk to you, I would have answered my phone. But as long as you're here, come in."

Jerome started talking almost as soon as he got in the door. "I don't understand what is going on. We need to talk about this. We had an argument—and I'm still not sure exactly what it was about—and now it seems like you're not speaking to me. What gives?"

"I wanted to talk with you about this on Sunday, but you were too busy studying for your chemistry exam. So I decided that I was too busy to talk with you. But the fact is, we weren't just fighting about your laundry, in case that's what you think. We were fighting about gender roles, and power, and entitlement, and being taken for granted, and all kinds of other things. So Jerome, do you want to get married and have kids some day?"

"What are you saying, woman? You know we've talked about getting married, and you know we've talked about having kids. Why are you asking me this?"

"Well, then, who is going to take care of those kids?"

Jerome sat silent for a moment; he didn't have an answer for that question. He had never thought about it before. "I don't know. Maybe you'll take care of them. Or we'll do the day care thing. I'll help, too. Why are you asking me this now?"

"Jerome, you and I have spent a lot of time together. We've said we love each other, we've had sex, and lately we've been talking about getting married and even having children. But we've never talked about how we're going to do all this. Oh, I know that we both want careers, but how do we do the rest of it? Who does the housework? Who does the laundry? Who stays home and takes care of the kids, or do we use child care or day care? Do we take turns, do we split things in half, or do you expect me to do most of the work because I'm a woman? I don't know how you feel, because we've never talked about it. I'm not even sure I know how *I* feel, much less how *you* feel! All I know is that when you walked in with your laundry the other day, something in me just snapped! I was furious with you, but I didn't know why."

Jerome didn't know why exactly, but he was beginning to get some ideas. He remembered that when his twin brother and sister were little, his mom stayed at home with them. She did virtually all the child care and housework, and his dad worked to provide financially for the family. Things were hard, but they got along all right. Then when the twins got older, his mom went back to work and his dad started doing the cooking and some of the housework. His mom seemed to be happier, and his dad—once he got used to cooking—seemed relieved to have two people bringing in income. These were the kinds of thing he and Della needed to talk about.

"Della, I don't know about power and entitlement and all that other stuff you mentioned, but I do know that we need to talk about these things. I don't know how I feel about a lot of this. And I understand that you don't necessarily know how you feel, either. So we need to think a lot and talk a lot more. But I do know two things: I love you. And I'm going to do my own laundry!"

■ ■ ■

Questions to Consider in Reading This Chapter

■ Are you a woman or a man?

■ Did you automatically take a side in the conflict between Della and Jerome? Do you think your gender has anything to do with the way you viewed this situation?

■ How did housework and child care get done in your family while you were growing up? How do they get done in your current living situation?

■ Do you believe men and women are naturally suited to do different kinds of things, including housework and child care?

What Do We Know about Gender?

What is **gender?** Is gender about biology, personality, or behavior? West and Zimmerman (1987), in a now-classic discussion of gender, might say that it is all of these things and none of these things. They stated that individual characteristics might impact gender but that gender is not "a property of individuals." Rather, *gender* is "an emergent feature of social situations: both as an outcome of and a rationale for various social arrangements and as a means of legitimating one of the most fundamental divisions of society" (p. 126). These authors distinguished between *gender* and *sex* in some interesting ways.

The **sex** of an infant is most often determined by inspection of his or her genitals at birth and on rare occasions by chromosomal typing. Most often, an infant is clearly identified as male or female and therefore assigned to a *sex category,* male or female. A person's sex category is displayed to society through various *identification displays,* such as particular hairstyles and dress codes for women versus men. For example, men typically don't wear lace, ruffles, or skirts, although there are exceptions. Beyond simply being assigned to a sex category based on biological (i.e., genital) criteria, people learn many sophisticated actions, such as how to manage emotions, cognitions, and behaviors in ways that conform to society's dictates and expectations for their sex category. The sum total of all of these activities can be called *gender.* In the beginning, there is sex and sex category, but everything after that is gender.

Origins of Gender and Gender Differences

West and Zimmerman (1987) elaborated on these issues in a variety of ways, but their central thread remained the idea that gender is not something we *are* but rather something we *do.* And we cannot *not* do it! Since gender accompanies sex category, and since sex/sex category is something we carry with us everywhere (a *master status variable;* Laumann et al., 1994), gender, like sex, is always with us. Even *undoing* or *redoing* gender is easier said than done, since society holds us accountable for our gendered behavior.

This **accountability** can result in punishment if we do not accommodate to the expectations for our gender. For example, because men are supposed to be strong, a man who cries in public may be labeled "overly emotional" or "weak." Because women are supposed to be expressive and supportive, a woman who makes decisions based on logic and who appears unemotional may be labeled "cold and unfeeling." The prices paid for such accountability failures may be subtle, but they are real, nevertheless. The "weak" man or the "cold" woman may fail to get promoted at work, may be less well liked by co-workers, or may be labeled as "odd."

The idea that gender is something we do, rather than something we are, is extremely important in the context of intimate relationships, and it provides an underlying theme for this chapter. For example, in the Relationship Story, if Della had agreed to help Jerome with his laundry, do you think she would have been "doing gender?"

Feminist scholars have pointed out that we not only do gender but we do it with a purpose. Wood (1995) noted this when she described feminist scholarship as focusing on "how gender is systematically reproduced . . . in ways that naturalize arbitrary social arrangements and inequitable roles and opportunities for women and men" (p. 104) and further that "gender is socially constructed, valued, and used to sustain inequality" (p. 105). Wood's goal was to highlight intersections of feminist scholarship and relationship scholarship, and in doing this, she emphasized the active, interactive, process aspects of gender. Like gender itself, some feminist research is thus shaped around *process* rather than *content* (see also Fox & Murry, 2000). (For a complete discussion of contemporary theory and research on gender, see Worell [2001].)

Evolutionary and Social Structural Approaches

Recent research and theory relevant to gender concerns sex differences in how humans behave and (1) whether such differences originated in *evolved dispositions* that are different for women and men, as proposed by some evolutionary theorists such as Buss

(1995), or (2) whether such differences have developed from men's and women's relative positions in the *social structure* (Eagly & Wood, 1999).

Eagly and Wood (1999) take the position that although a social structural approach to sex differences is compatible with much of evolutionary theory, it is not compatible with the more narrow approach taken by Buss (1995) and others, who have focused a considerable amount of their work on mate selection (e.g., Kenrick & Trost, 1993), discussed in more detail in Chapter 2. Eagly and Wood (1999) argue that women's and men's "physical sex differences, in interaction with social and ecological conditions" (p. 412), resulted in a complex division of labor at an early point in human history that allowed men greater status and power in the roles that they assumed, whether primitive hunter or twenty-first-century business executive, and women lesser status and power, whether primitive gatherer or twenty-first-century homemaker.

This perspective contrasts somewhat with the evolutionary approach, articulated at some length by Buss (1995), which places sex differences more squarely within biology than within culture. Of course, evolutionary psychologists do not deny the importance of culture (Kenrick & Trost, 1993), just as social structure adherents do not deny the importance of evolutionary processes (Eagly & Wood, 1999). But it is the relative importance of biology versus culture that makes evolutionary psychology and social structural perspectives come down somewhat differently on the issue of gender as something we do rather than something we are.

For example, if mate selection strategies have a primarily biological basis, so that men seek attractive women (because such women will presumably produce healthier offspring), and women seek men who have money and status (because such men will presumably be better providers for potential offspring), then modern sociocultural pressures on women to attend constantly to their appearance and men to attend constantly to their achievement have greater legitimacy. By the same token, if mate selection strategies have been influenced strongly by power and status, with men seeking trophy partners and women seeking economically advantaged partners, then changing power differences between men and women should lead to modifications of stereotyped mate selection strategies.

And indeed, Eagly and Wood (1999) make this case. In many ways, this whole discussion is simply the current expression of the old nature/nurture debate. If nature makes us what we are, then we're stuck: Gender is something we *are*. If nurture, or learning, makes us what we are, then we're potentially unstuck: Gender is something we *do*. Of course, nature and nurture interact in forming who and what we are, and behaviors are not fixed but *emergent* (Travis, 2001). Even so, "either/or" modes of thinking still exist.

The evolutionary psychology approach has been less than popular with many feminist theorists, although accusations that the perspective is sexist are denied vehemently (e.g., Kenrick, 1995). Yet it is difficult for many gender scholars to be reassured that evolutionary perspectives actually affirm women. For example, while some evolutionary scholars accord women more, rather then less, power—as in the proposition that women control sexual access (e.g., Kenrick, 1995)—other evolutionary theorists present a destructive behavior such as rape as part of men's evolutionary heritage, suggesting that men are creatures who will employ any means at their disposal to impregnate women and thereby increase their genetic fitness (Thornhill & Palmer, 2000). To be sure, these latter theorists do not promote rape as something positive, but they do present it as something natural. As LaFrance (2001) notes, however, "By declaring that rape is the direct and simple result of evolution, . . . this book may be less a solution than a part of the problem" (p. 379). (For an additional critique, see de Waal [2002].) Interestingly, anthropologist Sarah Hrdy (1999) affirms that rape is not common at all in primates.

It is apparent that although evolutionary psychology scholars do not necessarily seek to be adversaries with gender scholars who have a social structural bent, each group is wary of the other. Yet both perspectives can contribute to our understanding of gender as well as other aspects of relationships.

Still another lens has been held up to the gender area by Maccoby (1990), who has examined gender and social interaction from a developmental point of view. Maccoby argues that sex differences in social interaction in relationships are only apparent when males and females are interacting. Girls and boys or women and men are unlikely to display obvious differences when tested individually or even when observed in same-sex groups, but they do show differences when observed with other-sex peers. Maccoby summarizes these differences in terms of boys' "rough-and-tumble play styles" (p. 515) and inclination toward competition and dominance and girls' greater reliance on cooperation, reciprocity, social facilitation, communication, and so on.

Although Buss (1999) used Maccoby's 1990 paper to bolster his case for "the evolutionary theory of a sex difference in motivation to gain dominance or status" (p. 353), Maccoby proposed no such explanation for girls' and boys' differing interaction styles. It is likely that a social structural interpretation of Maccoby's observations would conclude that both family and society reinforce boys' dominance-striving and girls' social facilitation behaviors, beginning at very early ages. In fact, social structural theory would even predict such findings.

Benevolent Sexism

Discussions of gender have changed in recent decades as gender roles have changed to some degree, such that there are more women in the workforce and more men involved in family work. Lesbian and gay individuals and couples have also played a role in blurring traditional gender role lines. Indeed, many people might argue that the old forms of doing gender have changed and that women are more advantaged and well thought of now than they have ever been. In fact, overall attitudes toward women are very positive; this is known as the *"women are wonderful" effect* (Glick & Fiske, 2001, p. 110). Yet women are economically and politically disadvantaged across virtually all cultures and historical time periods, including the present.

Glick and Fiske (2001) characterize the quality of holding positive attitudes toward women while also endorsing a negative status for women as **benevolent sexism.** These authors have gone to some length to document the existence of benevolent sexism in both men and women. Although **hostile sexism** (i.e., having negative attitudes toward women) also exists, it is benevolent sexism—patriarchy concealed within protection and chivalry—that is "disarming." As these authors conclude, "Not only is it subjectively favorable in its characterization of women, but it promises that men's power will be used to women's advantage, if only they can secure a high-status male protector" (p. 111). It is the seeming goodwill of benevolent sexism that makes it seductive to both women and men. Namely, it gives women some protection and idealization, and it soothes men's guilt for having higher status and more benefits. "Women who endorse benevolent sexism are more likely to tolerate, rather than challenge, sexist behavior when the sexist's motivation can be interpreted as being protective" (p. 111).

While *hostile sexism* can be more readily seen as creating a prison for women, *benevolent sexism,* which provides a "golden cage," is often looked on more benignly. Yet a cage and a prison are much the same.

Implications of Gender

This section has set the stage for the discussion of gender as it is embodied and enacted in women's and men's relationships. It is important to stay focused on the question "Is gender something we *are* or something we *do?"*

If gender is part of the sex package and is something we are, then perhaps it is something that we are stuck with. Perhaps Maccoby's (1990) discussion of boys' aggressive play styles and girls' supportive play styles merely reflects the realities of inborn gender differences. If men inevitably have higher status than women, perhaps benevolent sexism is as good as it gets. On the other hand, if gender is something we do and is thus only moderately related to sex and sex category, then perhaps it can change. Perhaps the social structure that has fostered hostile and benevolent sexism can evolve into one that will foster equality. Maccoby (1990) states that she does not have an answer to the "why" of women's and men's differences in social styles but that finding such an answer "is important if we are to adapt ourselves successfully to the rapid changes in the roles and relationships of the two sexes that are occurring in modern societies" (p. 519).

As you read the rest of the chapter, consider the implications of gender as something you *are* versus gender as something you *do*. The Up Close box on the next page will help you become more aware of your own gender-related behaviors.

Sex or Gender? Women's Sexual Plasticity

The topic of relational sexuality is considered in detail in Chapter 5, and some readers may wonder why the topic of women's sexual **plasticity** was not discussed there. The answer is simple: The current dialogue about plasticity is much more profoundly concerned with gender than it is concerned with sex. See if you agree with this statement after reading the rest of this section.

"Doing Gender"

Consider the perspective that gender is not something you *are* but something you *do*. Take one day during the week and write down everything (or almost everything) that you do. Then go back and analyze all of your actions, identifying each one that was "doing gender." Review your final list and decide whether, overall, you "do gender."

Here are some examples of the behaviors of a young, married, working woman with no children. Each of her "doing gender" behaviors is indicated with a checkmark.

Woke up when alarm went off—pushed snooze—finally got up

Made coffee

Had quick breakfast

Showered

✓ Put on makeup and did hair

Got dressed for work

✓ Made bed

Drove to work

✓ On way to work, dropped husband's shirts at laundry

Going into work, held door open for man carrying boxes

✓ Listened to male co-worker's personal problems

✓ At lunch, bought birthday card for mother-in-law

One Set of Propositions on Plasticity

Are women more sexually malleable, persuasible, and flexible than men? Is women's sexuality less direct, less biologically driven than men's sexuality? Roy Baumeister (2000) would answer yes to both of these questions. In a lengthy scholarly article, Baumeister has summarized considerable research, much of it interdisciplinary, that purports to show that women differ from men in having greater *erotic plasticity*, which he defines as "subject to situational, social, or cultural influences regarding what types of partners and what types of sexual activities one would desire and enjoy" (p. 348). He proposes that women have greater sexual/erotic plasticity than men do and that if this is indeed the case, three predictions can be made: "(a) Individual women will exhibit more variation across time than men in sexual behavior, (b) female sexuality will exhibit larger effects than male in response to most specific sociocultural variables, and (c) sexual attitude-behavior consistency will be lower for women than men" (p. 347).

To support his first proposition—that women will vary more than men in their sexual behavior—Baumeister (2000) cites studies showing, for example, that men masturbate more consistently throughout their lives, that women's attitudes become more permissive as a function of dating experience, and that women, more than men, are likely to have sex with both men and women than to have only same-gender or other-gender partners. Finally, Baumeister points out that more women than men in prisons engage in homosexual activity (50% for women compared to 30% to 45% for men).

To support his second proposition—that women are more influenced by social and sexual variables—Baumeister (2000) cites data indicating that such factors as education, religion, culture, and family and peer influences all affect women's sexual behavior more than men's. For example, more educated women have more liberal sexual attitudes yet maintain their virginity until an older age. (This is not true for men.) In addition, greater education is related to greater same-gender sexual activity and more consistent contraception in an extramarital affair for women. And women are more likely to be influenced by friends' attitudes toward sex than are men.

To support his third proposition—that women are less consistent than men in sexual attitudes and behavior—Baumeister (2000) employs a variety of research results: for example, noting that women, more than men, were likely to express negative attitudes toward casual sex but then engage in casual sex anyway. He also cites research showing that while men and women expressed about equal rates of positivity toward the idea of same-gender sex, men who had positive attitudes were much more likely to have engaged in such behavior within the past year than were women.

While Baumeister's (2000) main focus is on establishing the reality of women's sexual plasticity, not on trying to determine why such plasticity might occur, he nevertheless offers three theories of possible causes: (1) the greater power and strength of men may coerce or at least facilitate flexibility of sexual responses from women; (2) women's sexual "scripts" are flexible, such that women typically say no to most sexual proposals and shift to yes in only selected cases (presumably because of their need to invest sexually very carefully); and finally, (3) women have a relatively milder sex drive. Baumeister notes that any or all of these causes might be possible.

Responses to Those Propositions

Throughout his discussion, Baumeister (2000) seems to lean in the direction of offering evolutionary, sociobiological explanations for women's supposed greater plasticity, or by contrast, men's supposed greater fixedness. But invited commentaries on his article have disagreed with him on a number of points. Hyde and Durik (2000), for example, contend that an evolutionary explanation is in error and that a multidimensional social structural explanation offers a better fit for women's erotic plasticity. Andersen, Cyranowski, and Aarestad (2000), on the other hand, argue that Baumeister relies too little on evolutionary explanations of women's sexuality, noting a probable interaction of both biological processes and social/interpersonal factors in shaping men's and women's sexualities.

Both commentaries make clear points about why Baumeister's (2000) thesis of women's erotic plasticity is as much or more about gender than it is about sex. First, Hyde and Durik (2000) point out that the whole question of women's so-called great sexual plasticity frames the issue as one of men's behavior being the sexual norm or standard and women's behavior as then deviating from the norm. For example, the question could have been framed as "Why is *men's* sexual behavior *less flexible* than women's?" and all the same research studies could have been applied. These authors also criticize Baumeister for dismissing a sexual double-standard as one possible explanation for women's and men's sexual differences, citing research that shows that a version of the sexual double-standard is still alive and well.

Andersen et al. (2000), while coming from a somewhat different empirical research perspective, also underline some gender-based issues, noting that Baumeister (2000) "downplayed areas in which the genders are, in fact, quite similar in their sexual attitudes, behaviors, and responses" (Andersen et al., 2000, p. 381). Perhaps more importantly, these authors draw attention to some of Baumeister's conclusions regarding the potential controllability of women's sexuality, as when he states that "from the point of view of society, the gender difference in erotic plasticity suggests that it will be more productive and effective to try to control female than male sexuality. . . . A society that needs a change in sexual behavior in order to survive or flourish would do better to target its messages and other pressures at women rather than men because of the greater difficulty in changing the sexual desires and habits of men" (Andersen et al., 2000, p. 369).

As Andersen et al. (2000) highlight, it can be a short distance from *discussing* the control of women's sexuality to *proposing* the control of women's sexuality, and social scientists must be aware that research can be misinterpreted and used in ways the researcher had never intended or even imagined. In fact, women's sexuality has been controlled historically, whether women were stoned to death for committing adultery, had their external genitalia sown shut to maintain virginity, or were advised not to wear provocative clothing so as not to provoke men into raping them.

Baumeister and his colleagues (Baumeister, Catanese, Campbell, & Tice, 2000) argue that he was not taking any kind of moral or political position but simply presenting social science research. However, it is likely that he could have made the same points without ever wading into the murkiness of controlling women's sexuality. If, indeed, gender is something we *do*, rather than something we *are*, all those involved in the discussion of women's sexual plasticity are *doing* a lot of gender!

Other Views on Sexual Plasticity

Consistent with the discussion of sexual plasticity is Peplau's (2001) presentation of a way to rethink women's sexual orientation. Although the concept of women's sexual plasticity is one cornerstone of Peplau's article, she seems less interested in proving why plasticity is or is not so than in using the concept to look more broadly at women's choices of sexual partners. "The key point is that at least some women are capable of variation and change, and this plasticity appears to be more characteristic of women than of men" (p. 10). She uses sexual plasticity to explain many women's sexual attraction both to men and to other women as "part of a much broader pattern in which sexual behavior serves diverse social and emotional functions among both primates and humans" (p. 12). Although Peplau does not restrict sexual plasticity to women, she focuses on women particularly, arguing for more attention by scholars across a range of disciplines to move beyond a focus on sex acts and sexual orientation to *relationship orientation.* The nature of Peplau's argument, as well as the data she uses to reinforce her argument, make it appear that, at least to some measure, Peplau is attempting to *undo* gender.

Overall, the current debate about women's supposed sexual plasticity appears to be only moderately related to issues of sexuality. It has much more to do with *who* is saying *what* about *which* women and *why*. If men scholars try to make the case that women's sexuality is more flexible than men's sexuality, that may not be problematic, particularly if women scholars are saying many of the same things. If men also raise the possibility of society controlling women's sexuality, even if they do not advocate that this should occur, then controversy will be more likely.

Clearly, questions of gender in society are complex and have yet to be sorted out fully. They are equally puzzling and interesting in intimate relationships. The next section addresses some of the ways in which gender is expressed in partnered relationships.

Gender and Relational Beliefs and Behaviors

Gender has been an important factor in the study of close relationships, whether the purpose is to examine how gender roles are enacted in relationships or to consider how the sexes differ or don't differ on various relationship dimensions. The following section comments briefly on gender similarities and differences in relationships, whereas a later section discusses the doing of gender in ongoing intimate relationships.

Although the *research* on heterosexual relationships often shows no, few, or small differences between women and men, *published work* in the social sciences tends to emphasize differences. As Canary and Emmers-Sommer point out (1997), "Differences appear informative, interesting and meaningful . . . so researchers often emphasize these in interpreting findings and explain away the similarities" (p. 12). However, subscribing to either of the extreme positions—*many* sex differences or *no* sex differences—can lead to missing the point about how men and women really behave in relationships. Because of the complexities and inconsistencies in the literature on gender roles, relationship researchers have chosen to focus much of their energy on simple sex differences and similarities in relationships.

Relational Beliefs

Fitzpatrick and Sollie (1999) were interested in how people's general beliefs and gender-related beliefs about relationships would impact relationship commitment and investment, key components of the investment model (e.g., Rusbult, 1983). Specifically, they assessed *unrealistic gendered beliefs,* which view men and women as having different and essentially incompatible relationship needs (the idea that women and men come from "different planets"), and *unrealistic relationship-specific beliefs* (the idea that relationship partners should be able to read each other's minds). Based on responses from over 250 participants, these authors concluded that women and men did not differ in either unrealistic gender beliefs or unrealistic relationship beliefs, although women were more committed and the like to their partners.

Fitzpatrick and Sollie (1999) concluded that these beliefs functioned differently for men and women, however. For women, having unrealistic beliefs about either gender, or relationships more generally, meant that they were less committed to their partner and also affected other aspects of their attitudes—for example, feeling their relationship was less than ideal. For men, neither kind of unrealistic belief was associated with commitment. These findings were not unexpected, given that women, more than men, are expected to be finely attuned to their relationships, including being aware of even small negatives, whereas men may be "more romantic and more accepting of their partner" (p. 864).

Another study explored gender roles (Vogel, Tucker, Wester, & Heesacker, 1999) in couples' conversations about either intimacy in the relationship or an ordinary, nonintimate topic. There was also a control condition: The authors took the perspective that traditional gender roles occur more because specific situational contexts promote certain behaviors, rather than because biology or ingrained personality traits drive the behaviors. What they found was that the topic of discussion, intimate or nonintimate, made a big difference in men's and women's endorsement and enactment of more traditional gender roles. In the "intimate" conversation condition, both women and men endorsed more traditional gender roles (for their own sex, not for each other) and also enacted more traditional gender role behavior. This result did not occur in the "nonintimate" topic conversation. Thus, the authors concluded that the specific *situation* cued specific gender role behavior.

An analogy to the results of this study is the frequent occurrence of men and women who function nontraditionally in the workplace—where say, he is a supportive co-worker and she is a task-oriented manager—but who go home to very traditional roles—where he repairs the cars and she listens to the kids' problems.

Relational Cultures and Climates

As noted earlier, men and women can be thought of as coming from different planets or merely from two different apartments in the same building. Another way to put it is that women and men may come from two different *relational cultures.*

Vangelisti and Daly (1997) propose that women and men do not differ in culture so much as in experiences within the culture. In a study of men's and women's standards or values for relationships (e.g., privacy, reliability, and emotional attachment), these authors found that women and men did not differ in the standards they thought were important in a romantic relationship but did differ in how well they thought the standards were being met in their own relationship. Women felt "their standards were being met less fully than did men" (p. 203). Thus, both sexes *wanted* the same things in their relationships, but men, more than women, felt they were *getting* what they wanted.

A study by Acitelli, Rogers, and Knee (1999) found that women, in general, spent more time thinking positively about their romantic relationships than men did. But women and men were similar in how thinking positively about the relationship and also seeing oneself as part of a couple, or having a *couple identity,* influenced relationship satisfaction. Men and women thus exhibited substantial similarities, even though women appeared to track their relationships more closely than did men.

Just as thinking about one's relationship positively and thinking about oneself as part of a couple may contribute to satisfaction, so, too, does one's attitude or focus (i.e., on oneself versus someone else) make a difference. Harter and her colleagues (Harter, Waters, Pettitt, Whitesell, & Kofkin, 1997) compared people who described themselves and their relationship partners as (1) focused primarily on the self, (2) focused primarily on the other person, or (3) balanced in their focus, referred to as *mutuality.* Not surprisingly, people who described both themselves and their partners as "mutual" felt the most honest/authentic and validated in their relationships. Gender stereotypes for heterosexual relationships would expect that dominant, self-focused men would be paired with subordinate, other-focused women. Indeed, more women (18.9%) than men (14.4%) identified as "other-focused," whereas more men (13.4%) than women (12.1%) identified as "self-focused." Yet these differences were not great, especially for the "self-focused" group. And the relational outcomes for these pairings did not differ by sex. "Not only did self-focused *males* with other-focused *female* partners report only moderate levels of validation and true self behavior, but the same pattern was obtained for self-focused *females* with other-focused *male* partners" (p. 162; italics in the original). The interaction style and focus of the person made more difference than his or her sex.

These notions about focus on oneself versus one's partner are not unrelated to social support, in that other-focused individuals might be expected to be more supportive of their partners than self-focused individuals. As noted in an earlier chapter, some research and much conventional wisdom suggests that women provide more social support than men do—or at least that men and women provide different kinds of support. Yet some of these assumptions are being rethought.

Goldsmith and Dun (1997), for example, assessed college women's and college men's verbal responses to seven scenarios involving another person who was distressed and required social support. Although the men's responses to the situations were shorter than the women's responses and the women said more about both their emotions and actions to solve the problem, the men and women did not differ in the proportion of talk devoted to action versus emotion or in denying the problems or the person's feelings about them. The authors concluded that it is not useful to view men and women as coming from different cultures regarding social support and suggested that "we might be better served by examining how *shared* beliefs and practices within a particular culture provide both men and women with situationally variable responses" (p. 335; italics in the original).

In considering how men and women might differ in the links between relational quality and self-esteem in both marriage and same-sex friendship, Voss, Markiewicz, and Doyle (1999) discovered that women and men are similar in how they view their spouse as a friend. The quality of that friendship, along with marital adjustment, was related to self-esteem similarly for both sexes. Women tracked more conflict/disagreement than men did, but conflict was similarly detrimental to self-esteem for both women and men. Finally, women were more likely to rate their spouse and friend similarly on key dimensions, whereas men typically differentiated between spouse and friend, rating spousal friendship more highly than same-sex friendship on various dimensions. Once again, women and men were found to be similar in aspects of close relationships although not exactly the same.

Women and men have also exhibited similarities in areas of intimacy, love, and conflict. Prager (2000) has described *intimacy* as having three components: self-disclosure, positive affect, and listening/understanding. For *self-disclosure,* sex differences sometimes are shown and sometimes not. When they do occur, women typically disclose more, but the differences are small (Dindia & Allen, 1992). *Positive affect* is valued by both women and men. "For example, both women and men seek emotional expression, social support, trust, and spending time with a close same-sex or other-sex friend" (S. S. Hendrick, 2001, p. 636). As was apparent in the Relationship Story, both Della and Jerome valued positive emotions. Positive affect implies a relative lack of negative affect, which can have negative implications for relationships. Some couples are high in both positive and negative affect, however (Gottman, 1993b).

Previous research (e.g., Gottman & Levenson, 1988) has proposed that men become more aroused physiologically in a negative way (e.g., increased heart rate) during relationship conflict and thus tend to avoid conflict interactions. More recently, however, Kiecolt-Glaser and her colleagues (Kiecolt-Glaser et al., 1996) have shown that wives, *more than husbands,* experience negative arousal, such as increased levels of stress hormones. Other research is consistent with these findings, confirming that while being married is related to better physical health for both men and women, the effect is stronger for men. In addition, marital conflict is linked to more negative health outcomes for women. (See Kiecolt-Glaser and Newton [2001] for an extended discussion of this topic.)

Prager's (2000) third component of intimacy, *listening/understanding,* is important both to men and women. For example, Meeks et al. (1998) found men and women to be similar in their self-reported perspective-taking ability, and perceived empathy and perspective-taking ability for oneself and one's partner predicted relationship satisfaction similarly for women and men.

In the area of love, also, men and women share many similarities, although this has not always been the case. Men and women have differed traditionally on several love styles, with men more endorsing game-playing love and women more endorsing friendship and practical love (C. Hendrick & S. S. Hendrick, 1986). But more recently, fewer sex differences have been observed in love styles, except for that known as *Agape* (see Chapter 4). Men, more than women, say that they are altruistic in their love styles (S. S.

Hendrick & C. Hendrick, 2002). In addition, women and men are quite similar in how certain relationship constructs, such as love attitudes and sexual attitudes, are related to each other. In one study, S. S. Hendrick and C. Hendrick (1995) found that the relationships between love and sex were very similar for men and women, with game-playing love related to permissive sexuality and passionate love related to idealistic sexuality. Thus, once again, there is a pattern of predominant similarities between women and men.

The genders seem very similar in the positive areas that have been considered thus far, but what about the more problematic area of power and control? That topic is the focus of the following section.

Power and Control

Power and control in close relationships exist against the traditional backdrop of men having more power in the general society and women having more power in homelife decisions. Falbo and Peplau (1980), in some now-classic research, examined the power strategies used by women and men in homosexual and heterosexual couples. Although homosexual men and women did not differ, heterosexual women and men used different strategies. Heterosexual women reported using more indirect, nonnegotiating strategies, whereas heterosexual men reported using direct, negotiating ones.

Research by Howard, Blumstein, and Schwartz (1986) also examined power strategies and found that both women and men tended to use weaker power strategies (e.g., manipulation, supplication) when dealing with a man. "Men elicit perceived manipulation and supplication from both female and male partners" (p. 107). Much of this research on power assumes that men have more power and use more powerful tactics, but that may depend on the situation. Sagrestano (1992) found that when men and women were put in the same experimental situations, they did not differ in their use of power strategies, and Steil and Weltman (1992) had similar results. Tannen (1994) also pointed out that power cannot be determined in a particular interaction on the basis of such things as directness or indirectness of communication. "The interpretation of a given utterance, and the likely response to it, depends on the setting, on individuals' status and their relationship to each other, and also on the linguistic conventions that are ritualized in the cultural context" (p. 34).

There are other ways to view power besides seeing it in a gendered context. For instance, according to the *principle of least interest,* "the person who feels less dependent on the other holds more power" (Canary & Emmers-Sommer, 1997, p. 75). Consistent with this perspective is research by Solomon and Samp (1998) on the *chilling effect,* or the impact that greater power by one partner has on the other partner's willingness to confront or deal with difficult issues. These authors had research participants read scenarios of hypothetical problems they could potentially encounter with their partners. Men, more than women, said their partner would likely respond to confrontation with physical or symbolic aggression, and men also tended to minimize the severity of the problem. Women, more then men, reported that they were not likely to confront their partner about the problems. For both men and women, however, perceiving that a partner had more power in the relationship caused the individual to rate problems as less severe and also to withhold complaints and avoid confrontation. Perceiving that a partner has greater power in the relationship really does appear to have a chilling effect for both genders.

Finally, power and self-disclosure have been studied in dating and married couples. Murstein and Adler (1995) found that women and men did not differ in how powerful they perceived themselves to be. Dating partners, both women and men, who perceived themselves as powerful were more likely to disclose their own accomplishments. Overall, women in the study were more disclosing of feelings than were men. The authors concluded, "Within the restrictions of our limited sample, power, as we defined it, seems to be independent of gender" (p. 207).

The literature on power and gender is mixed, with some studies finding gender differences—typically with men being more powerful—and other studies finding no gender differences. Yet an examination of the research on families and household work reveals some inequities in what women do and what men do, even though there is a rhetoric of equality in the couples (Knudson-Martin & Mahoney, 1998). Why might this be the case? *Entitlement* has been proposed as one answer.

Entitlement

Steil, McGann, and Kahn (2001) define **entitlement** "as a set of attitudes about what a person feels he or she has a right to and can expect from others both as an individual and as a member of a social group" (p. 404). It appears that in the work environment, men have more power than women overall and are more rewarded. (Women earn only 76 cents for each dollar made by men [Steil et al., 2001].) Yet women do not seem upset about such underbenefiting, and the same pattern exists in the home.

No matter what their work or career involvements might be, women in heterosexual, two-parent families typically do the majority of both housework and child care (Coltrane, 2000). And many studies have indicated that women do not report feeling disadvantaged by such responsibilities. In fact, because of gendered roles, women often assume that they will need to carry most of the household burdens, and they may even get some satisfaction from "doing gender" this way. Based on the Relationship Story, it appears that Della is not someone who is willing to be disadvantaged or at least is struggling with the issue.

One explanation for women's and men's relative contentment with how work and home responsibilities are divided up is that men have a greater sense of entitlement than women do (Steil et al., 2001). Even though some research has indicated that college-age men and women do not differ in entitlement (Bartsch, 2001), clinical observations have shown that men behave in entitled ways more often than women, particularly in family settings. One solution to the entitlement issue might be to have men *decrease* their entitlement level, but a more practical solution might be for women to *increase* theirs. "For women to improve their outcomes relative to men, they must adjust their identity from that of nurturer to that of conurturer and coprovider . . . and they must negotiate from a base of entitlement rather than deserving" (Steil, 2000, p. 409).

If women were to gain in entitlement, particularly in the area of family work, it would be interesting to see how couple and family life might change for both genders. These issues of family work and gender will be discussed in the following section.

Gender and Family Work

No discussion of gender in contemporary romantic relationships can overlook the arena of *family work*. Most relevant research on this topic has been conducted with heterosexual couples/families; information more fully reflecting today's society will emerge as gay and lesbian couples and families become more visible.

Issues of gender and work exist in all types of families, including so-called traditional nuclear families, in which the wife stays at home with children and the husband works full time outside the home as the sole economic provider for the family. Yet much of the current social science research has focused on families in which both partners work outside the home. Indeed, in 1997, it was reported that over 78% of women with children between the ages of 6 and 17 were employed outside the home (Perry-Jenkins, Repetti, & Crouter, 2000).

In the late 1980s and early 1990s, discussions of family work focused on such things as career and relationship issues for dual-career couples (S. S. Hendrick & C. Hendrick, 1992), comparisons of women employed outside the home with those not so employed, and examinations of role strain in employed couples (e.g., Bolger, DeLongis, Kessler, & Wethington, 1989). Discussions of gender and work were also framed within power and equity perspectives. (See Canary and Emmers-Sommer [1997] for a discussion.) More recently, however, in a review of work and family research from the 1990s, Perry-Jenkins et al. (2000) have highlighted four themes that provide connections among the previous literature, current practice, and future directions for family work research.

The first theme is concerned with the effects on children of *maternal employment*. As with research on divorce, this topic has resulted in considerable controversy. Reanalyses of earlier findings that had noted both positive effects and negative effects of maternal employment on child care have indicated that "neither early maternal nor paternal employment status, nor the timing and continuity of maternal employment, were consistently related to child outcomes" (p. 983). As will be discussed, this conclusion does *not* mean that children are unaffected by certain aspects of parental employment, but it does mean that "mothers working" is not synonymous with "children suffering."

Children are affected by parents who *overwork* as well as by those who are *under-employed* (Perry-Jenkins et al., 2000), due in part to the quality of child care. High-quality child care, along with involved parenting, bodes well for children's development. In turn, poor-quality child care, lack of involved and stable parenting, and lack of adequate super-vision of adolescents after school can lead to problems in school and in other areas. Perry-Jenkins et al. note that future research should "include a wider range of child 'outcomes,' including children's own perceptions of their mothers' and fathers' work" (p. 984).

The second theme discerned from Perry-Jenkins et al.'s (2000) review, *workplace quality,* involves the idea of socialization in the workplace. Basically, if the work envi-ronment is enriching—providing parents with opportunities to have autonomy, to prob-lem solve, to work with congenial people, and so on—then adults will feel better about themselves and do better at parenting. What is apparent is that links between work and family roles are not simple.

The third theme is exceptionally important and concerns *occupational stress* and how it affects families (Perry-Jenkins et al., 2000). *Job stress* involves objective factors about the workplace, such as physical environment, and *personal stress* involves subjec-tive reactions to those factors. Stress can also be either long term or short term. Many studies have not shown direct links between work stress and family outcomes because individual and interpersonal characteristics, such as marital quality, intervene. For exam-ple, Hammer, Allen, and Grigsby (1997) studied *crossover effects* in married couples, or how each partner's work/family conflicts affected the other partner. There were substan-tial crossover effects for both wives and husbands, with greater work involvement in-creasing conflict and more flexible work schedules reducing conflict. Garrido and Aci-telli (1999) also found that for couples, the greater the number of hours worked outside the home, the lower the woman's relationship satisfaction. And the relationship between hours worked and satisfaction was stronger for women who were higher in relational identity—that is, tending to think in terms of "we," rather than "you" and "me."

Although scholars sometimes emphasize the differences between men and women in their experiencing of home and work, the fact is, there are some similarities, too. Milkie and Peltola (1999) found that "women and men report similar levels of success and kinds of work-family tradeoffs" (p. 476). Different factors were found to contribute to a sense of imbalance for each gender—namely, working longer hours and having less marital happiness were unbalancing for men, whereas having less marital happiness and making sacrifices at home were unbalancing for women. Nonetheless, men and women seemed to cope with equal levels of strain.

Still other couples deal with work/family stress by doing what Becker and Moen (1999) refer to as "scaling back." Middle-class, dual-earner couples used three principal strategies to balance work and family, while giving special attention to family: (1) placing limits by limiting both hours and expectations for promotion; (2) designating who had a true career (which required greater commitment) and who had a job (which allowed greater flexibility); and (3) trading off, whereby one person at a time had a career. These solutions were shown to be gendered, with women more often making career compromises than men. However, one-third of those "placing limits" and one-third of those who had "the job" (while the partner had "the career") were men. So, while it may be happening slowly, some of the gendered role behaviors are changing.

The fourth theme from Perry-Jenkins et al. (2000) is concerned with *multiple roles* and the idea that having a number of roles can be related to greater mental health. It is not just a matter of how many roles a person has but how he or she experiences those roles, his or her choices about the roles he or she assumes, whether the roles are equal or hierarchical, and so on. Two people may have approximately the same number of roles yet experience the roles quite differently.

Gender and Housework

One of the key issues in the study of work/family balance has been the gendered nature of household work and child care. Women's traditionally greater responsibility in the home has been widely documented. More recently, however, the picture has become more complex, at least for two-parent families.

Wilkie, Ferree, and Ratcliff (1998) sampled 382 two-earner families and found that husbands averaged 38% of *domestic* work hours and wives averaged 62%. For *paid* work hours, husbands averaged 56% and wives averaged 44%. In this same study, husbands were more likely to feel that housework was shared fairly in the family, and wives were more likely to feel that paid work was shared fairly. Feeling empowered was important and helpful for both genders, but husbands' preferences appeared to prevail more so than did wives'. Interestingly, both genders were more likely to feel that the work balance was unfair to them when they put in extra hours in atypical areas (i.e., paid work for women, housework for men). As noted earlier, among couples who scaled back their work involvement in order to devote more time to family life, the husband made the career sacrifice in one-third of the cases (Becker & Moen, 1999). Although traditional gender role attitudes linger, balance in work/family responsibilities seems to be growing. Remember that in the Relationship Story, Jerome recalled how his parents had tried to share family work and paid work.

In some studies (e.g., Hammer et al., 1997), men actually reported more involvement in the family than women reported and sometimes more involvement in paid work, as well. Yet women often reported greater stress in managing or juggling family and work responsibilities. Reasons for these findings could include such things as women having greater anxiety about managing their roles, men reporting greater involvement but women actually working more, or some other reasons not yet identified.

Risman and Johnson-Sumerford (1998) interviewed 15 couples whom they termed *postgender* because of their egalitarian responses to managing paid and household work. Couples seemed to take four routes to these nontraditional relationships, including *dual-career,* in which both partners were interested in career growth and parenting;

Up Close   *Examining Gender Roles*

Think about the family in which you grew up. How was family work accomplished? Make a list of 10 to 15 chores that were regularly done, perhaps including making meals, doing laundry, providing child care, vacuuming, and anything else from mowing the lawn to taking the kids to the doctor. Then next to each work item, write down the person who typically did that chore. If several people did the chore, put down all their names. Now take a pen of a different color and write down for each chore the person that you think should do the chore in your current or future household.

The goal here is to see how family work was managed in the family in which you grew up and how you would like such work to be managed in your current or future household. Do you want things to be the same as they were when you were growing up? Do you want them to be different? Why? In terms of household/family work, how are you "doing gender?" How are you "undoing gender?"

dual-nurturer, in which both partners put home and family before career; *posttraditional,* in which partners had tried traditional gender roles and did not like them; and *external forces,* including situations in which the husband got laid off so the wife became the primary breadwinner or the wife became ill so the husband took on the housework. "No single pattern emerged in terms of these couples' relationships except that in nearly every couple both partners mentioned in separate interviews that their spouse was their very best friend, irreplaceable, and precious. The relationships of these couples seem embedded within the framework of a valued, intimate companionship" (p. 35).

Some growth in nontraditional relationships might be expected, since nontraditional parents tend to have children with less traditional gender role attitudes (Booth & Amato, 1994). Read the Up Close box above to help you explore how work is or was handled in your family.

Gender and Income

One final gender-related issue relates to how married women's income from paid work may influence relational variables such as satisfaction. It has traditionally been assumed that a woman's earnings might threaten a man's sense of self. Is that the case?

Rogers and DeBoer (2001) found that increases in wives' income—both absolute increases and increases in the proportion of the family income produced by the wife—was related to greater marital happiness for women. And while men's happiness did not decrease when women's income increased, their well-being did go down when their wives started contributing a greater proportion of the family income. Perhaps a perceived threat to their provider role impacted these men negatively.

Brennan, Barnett, and Gareis (2001) had congruent findings. In examining partners' marital role quality and changes in women's earnings for paid work, these authors found that women's improved earnings did not impact their marital quality. For men, however, when their wife's salary was increasing relative to the man's own salary *and* when salary was particularly important to and rewarding for the man, marital quality was impacted negatively. This is consistent with the idea that the breadwinner role is very important to many men.

Interestingly, a finding not highlighted by Brennan et al. (2001) but that seems relevant was that "wives reported feeling more subjectively rewarded by their salaries than did their husbands" (p. 175). Wives also earned as much or more than their husbands in 31.5% of the 300 couples in the sample. Thus, breadwinning may be important for both spouses in dual-earner families.

Gender, Work, and the Future

Although we cannot be absolutely sure of where we are in terms of how our society views women, men, and household work, we can be fairly sure that we are not at the same place we were a few decades ago. Barnett and Hyde (2001) make a compelling case that the old theories of gender and work no longer fit current societies, especially industrialized Western societies. These authors describe three theories that they say are no longer sufficient to describe current behavior: (1) the sociological theory that men should earn the living and women should raise the children; (2) the psychoanalytic theory that women and men are essentially different and that women achieve a full adult identity only when partnered with a man; and (3) the sociobiological/evolutionary theory that to be reproductively successful, men must be aggressive and competitive in acquiring resources and women must be nurturing and care for offspring. Each of these theories implies that men and women are functionally very different and that the so-called natural order requires a distinct separation of roles and tasks, the traditional gendered "separate spheres." Of course, this whole idea of women staying at home and men going out in the workforce is a very middle-class notion, since poor and working-class women have virtually always had to work outside the home.

Barnett and Hyde (2001) point out that research does not support the beneficial effects of "separate spheres." Rather, "study after study has demonstrated that women and men who engage in multiple roles report lower levels of stress-related mental and physical health problems and higher levels of subjective well-being than do their counterparts who engage in fewer roles" (p. 784). Thus, these authors present four basic premises, which have been and will likely continue to be tested in research.

The first premise is that engaging in multiple roles is generally beneficial to both men and women. The second premise is that playing multiple roles is thought to be beneficial because experiencing positive outcomes in some roles can make up for experiencing negative outcomes in other roles; for example, getting a promotion at work may balance out the stress of having an illness in one's extended family. The third premise is that the benefits of engaging in multiple roles are not universal but occur under certain conditions; in other words, having too many roles may be as problematic as having too few roles. And the sheer quantity of roles is much less important than the experienced quality of those roles. Finally, the fourth premise is that psychological gender differences are not, in general, large or immutable; women and men are not forced by their natures into highly differentiated roles. Barnett and Hyde (2001) view their perspective as open, flexible, and expansionist, but they wisely caution that it is also a time-bound, culture-bound perspective.

It is important to remember that every perspective is influenced by the time period and culture in which it is produced. Thousands of years ago, our human ancestors might have assumed that men enacting hunting, securing meat, and women enacting gathering, securing nuts and grains, comprised the natural order. And in fact, without both men's hunting and women's foraging, humans likely would have starved. Thus, issues of gender and work in our current society are complicated, fluid, and worthy of respectful inquiry.

Summary and Conclusions

Gender can be considered to be the attitudes and behaviors that accompany a particular sex category, which is based on assignment to a biological sex (female or male). Gender can be thought of as something we *are* or as something we *do*. The evolutionary psychology perspective emphasizes biological bases for current behavior and seems to lean more toward gender as something we *are*. Social structural perspectives emphasize social and cultural influences on behavior and seem to lean more toward gender as something we *do*.

Many aspects of gender research are somewhat controversial. Sexism can be benevolent and involve positive attitudes toward women but support negative status for women, or sexism can be hostile and primarily involve negative attitudes toward women. The question of sexual plasticity—whether women are more sexually/erotically flexible than men—has become one of considerable interest. Some researchers believe that sexual plasticity has a biological basis, whereas others believe the basis is more socio-cultural. The issue of controlling women's sexuality is definitely controversial.

Women and men in intimate relationships display both gender differences and gender similarities. For example, the genders do not differ in having unrealistic gender beliefs or relationship beliefs; in tending to exhibit more gender-stereotypic behaviors when discussing an intimate topic with relational partners; in evaluating standards deemed as important in a relationship; in having a couple identity; in being self-focused versus other-focused in relationships; in displaying action versus emotion in a social-support situation; or in viewing a marital partner as a friend. Men and women are also similar in having needs for positive affect; in experiencing problematic outcomes from negative affect (although the negative effects seem stronger for women); in demonstrating perspective-taking abilities; in using power strategies (when on a level playing field); in experiencing a chilling effect from a partner's power; and in perceiving themselves as powerful. For the most part, men and women display similar love styles and sexual attitudes, as well. However, research is unclear on whether men have a greater sense of entitlement or whether the genders do not differ in this area. It has been proposed that women should become more entitled, rather than men becoming less entitled.

Women have traditionally performed more household work and child care than men have, but these behaviors are changing. Children are affected by aspects of parental employment, but maternal employment per se is not negative for children. Parents who have high workplace quality may be able to parent more effectively. Paid work and family work can produce stress in marital partners, and each partner's stress affects that person plus his or her partner. Men and women have many similar needs at work and home, yet there are also differences. Women are more likely to make career compromises such as scaling back, and men and women are closer to equal sharing of home work and paid work they have been previously. Couples and families use many different strategies to manage all the responsibilities involved in family and work life. Women's income has traditionally been thought to be threatening to men's egos, but research has indicated that, for the most part, women's income is perceived positively by both wives and husbands. Engaging in multiple roles, in which women and men do both family work and paid work, is thought to be beneficial in many ways.

Perhaps the most accurate thing that can be said about gender and gender roles in our society is that we have taken real steps but we have not yet arrived.

Key Terms

Accountability (p. 212)
Benevolent sexism (p. 214)
Entitlement (p. 224)
Gender (p. 211)

Hostile sexism (p. 215)
Plasticity (p. 215)
Sex (p. 211)

Suggested Reading

Barnett, R. C., & Hyde, J. S. (2001). Women, men, work, and family: An expansionist theory. *American Psychologist, 56,* 781–796.

Eagly, A. H., & Wood, W. (1999). The origins of sex differences in human behavior. *American Psychologist, 54,* 408–423.

Peplau, L. A. (2001). Rethinking women's sexual orientation: An interdisciplinary, relationship-focused approach. *Personal Relationships, 8,* 1–19.

Perry-Jenkins, M., Repetti, R. L., & Crouter, A. C. (2000). Work and family in the 1990s. *Journal of Marriage and the Family, 62,* 981–998.

Steil, J. M., McGann, V. L., & Kahn, A. S. (2001). Entitlement. In J. Worell (Ed.), *Encyclopedia of women and gender* (pp. 403–410). San Diego, CA: Academic Press.

West, C., & Zimmerman, D. H. (1987). Doing gender. *Gender & Society, 1*(2), 125–151.

Epilogue

The first part of the Epilogue revisits some of the Relationship Stories presented throughout the book, illustrating how the stories might continue in the future. Based on what you have learned in this book, think about how each relationship is progressing and suggest ways these people can continue to improve their relationship. The second part of the Epilogue draws a contrast between a life with and without connected relationships and offers some thoughts about the various choice points that couples encounter in their relationships.

The Relationship Stories Continued

Chapter 2
Attraction and Relationship Development

The Relationship Stories that begin this chapter describe the first dates of three different couples. Nora and Tomas were college students who met at work. They really enjoyed their first date, talked a lot about their backgrounds and interests, and found that they had much in common. After that first date, they continued to see each other. Their relationship was fostered by their similarities and by their ability to communicate those similarities. Because of their willingness to talk about themselves, both as individuals and as a couple, their commitment kept growing stronger. They didn't agree on everything, but they could talk about almost everything, so they almost never got stuck in a conflict. They were always able to settle things by compromise or by agreeing to disagree.

Because Nora and Tomas met at work and had the same type of job, they started out their relationship viewing one another as equals. Thus, they never enacted stereotyped gender roles, such as protective male/dependent female. Nora was independent from the start—in fact, that was one of the things that Tomas found attractive—and they handled their relationship and their lives as equals. Gender issues weren't absent from their lives, of course, but they experienced their relationship as occurring between two people, rather than a man and a woman.

- What are the strengths and weaknesses of Nora and Tomas's relationship?
- How will it likely continue to develop?
- Is it likely to become permanent? Why or why not?

233

James and Keisha met in the dorm dining room, and James was immediately impressed with Keisha's proud body language. Their first date wasn't too successful because Keisha had just gotten out of a long-term relationship and was wary of starting a new one. But James decided to give it one more try and invited Keisha to a party that a friend was having. At the party, James was much more outgoing than Keisha had expected—he had a great sense of humor—and Keisha relaxed a little.

They had a good time and continued to go out together, finding that their best dates occurred when they were part of a group of couples, rather than just by themselves. They became strongly physically attracted to each other, and sex was a big part of their relationship. They liked each other a lot, but they didn't seem to have much to talk about sometimes. And if a conflict came up, they tended to ignore the issue, rather than try to deal with it. They both knew that they needed to improve their communication, but neither one did anything about it. They just kind of drifted along.

- How might Keisha and James improve their relationship?
- What is likely to happen to their relationship?
- How is this relationship different from that of Nora and Tomas?

Alicia and Dan met on a blind date that involved attending a basketball game and then going out to eat. They were introduced by people they knew—Alicia's sister and her boyfriend—which is often a great way to begin a relationship. Alicia and Dan found that they had a lot in common and enjoyed each other's company. They continued to date, often going out with Alicia's sister and her boyfriend. They introduced each other to their families and friends rather early in the relationship, and thus, their social networks were influential in their developing relationship.

Alicia always tended to be overcommitted to school and work, and Dan sometimes got frustrated because she didn't seem to have time for him or for their relationship. But he would let her know his feelings, and after some arguing, she would usually admit that she had once more gotten herself into too many activities. For awhile, Alicia would slow down her pace and have more time for Dan, but then the cycle would begin all over again.

- Do you think Alicia and Dan will stay together? Why or why not?
- Who will have to change the most for the relationship to succeed?
- Should a person have to change in order to make a relationship successful?

Chapter 3
Friendship and Social Support

Two different types of friendship were presented in these Relationship Stories. Erin and Mike had been friends since childhood, and even though they were now in college, they promised each other that they would be friends forever. Because theirs was a cross-sex friendship, they always had to contend with other people's questions about whether it was really a friendship or a romantic relationship instead.

After graduating from college and even marrying other people, Erin and Mike continued to stay in touch. Eventually, they and their spouses met for a "reunion/get-acquainted" weekend and found that they all got along very well and enjoyed spending time with each other. They recognized that some of the communication and problem-solving skills that Erin and Mike had learned in their friendship had helped them to be more understanding, communicative, and effective marital partners. After several other such get-togethers, Erin and Mike and their spouses agreed to be friends forever!

- How would you feel if your relationship partner was involved in a long-term friendship like Erin and Mike's?
- Do you think such cross-sex friendships are usually possible? Why or why not?

Jonelle and Tamika's friendship began because of the environmental factor of being assigned to each other as roommates. It continued because their individual personality styles were compatible, although dissimilar. And it deepened when one of them had to depend heavily on the other during the crisis situation surrounding Jonelle's biking accident.

The two young women remained roommates during college, continuing to support each other even as their lives moved increasingly in different directions. They eventually graduated from college and got jobs in different cities. They tried to keep in contact with each other through e-mails and phone calls, but that contact decreased over time. Even so, they realized how much they had learned from each other about how to be a good friend, how to support someone when it was needed, and how to receive as well as give the gift of friendship.

- What specific things did Tamika and Jonelle do during the crisis incident to deepen their friendship?
- Which of these behaviors were the most important, in your opinion?
- What is important to *you* in forming friendships? Why?

Chapter 4
Romantic Love

This chapter opened with the story of Sandy and Joe. Sandy was a breast cancer survivor, and Joe was a high school teacher and sometimes basketball coach. They had two small children and a supportive extended family and friendship network. They loved each other deeply, but their love was severely tested—and strengthened—by the cancer experience.

Much of the research on love focuses on passionate types of love, but from the beginning, Joe and Sandy experienced more of a secure attachment and friendship-oriented kind of love. They were still romantic and sexual with each other, however, and they believed that their love deepened over time. They didn't believe that they should have to choose between passionate and companionate love; they believed they could have both. More generally, they had a communal relationship, in which Joe was called on to give more to Sandy than she could possible return. But they simply accepted that as the way things had to be. Although Sandy is now in remission from her cancer, she and Joe both know that the future does not have any guarantees. And they are sure that they would have had an even tougher time without the support of their wonderful family and friends.

It is easy to make Sandy and Joe sound more like saints than real people, but in fact, they have personal faults and occasional difficulties. They don't handle conflict well, both preferring to avoid problems rather than attempt to settle them. And while they communicate a great deal about their children and dealing with Sandy's cancer, they are less likely to talk about their own individual needs and their feelings about each other. Thus, their relationship continues to grow stronger in some ways but not in others.

- How do you think you would handle having a partner who is seriously ill, perhaps even dying?
- What could Sandy and Joe do differently to make their marriage better?

Chapter 5
Relational Sexuality

Noah and Katherine, the couple whose story opened this chapter, met at the wedding of some mutual friends and were immediately attracted to each other. As their relationship developed, they became sexually involved and their physical attraction to each other remained an important part of their relationship, even after they were married and their son was born. Neither of them was overly concerned when they realized how much having a baby had severely curtailed their sex life. In fact, Katherine's purchase of the red nightgown was less about jump-starting their sex life than showing Noah that she was as interested in him as ever.

Both Katherine and Noah kept their marriage as their highest emotional priority. They tried to call each other from work during the day, and they made sure that they took time to sit and talk with each other every evening. They even started getting a babysitter and going out on a "date" at least once every couple of weeks. They knew that it was easy for new parents to put their own relationship on the back burner while the baby was front and center.

Katherine and Noah did not get caught up in traditional gendered behavior. Both did a lot of child care and both worked outside the home, so they seemed able to take each other's perspective more easily than is true for many couples. And they worked at keeping the passion in their relationship alive.

- How are Noah and Katherine taking care of their relationship?
- What additional strategies could you suggest to them?

Chapter 6
Communication and Relational Maintenance

Nick and Elaine, a married couple with teenage children, were the focus of this Relationship Story. They began their relationship with love and hope, but in recent years, they had drifted apart. What rescued their marriage on the night of the party was their willingness to be honest about what they wanted. They took very active steps that evening to talk with each other, listen to each other, and appreciate each other. They began to realize that they were at a time in their lives when many of their early individual and couple goals had been achieved.

What had been missing for awhile—and what they began to work to regain—was communication and the intimacy that it can produce. Remember that intimacy requires positive emotion, a sense of being listened to and understood by one's partner, along with self-disclosure. And intimacy was in short supply in Nick and Elaine's marriage for quite a long time. But after the night of the party, they began to really devote time and effort into putting intimacy back into their relationship. And it was none too soon!

- How likely is it that Nick and Elaine will be able to continue this rediscovered intimacy in their relationship?
- What advice would you give them on ways to keep their marriage vital and satisfying?
- What techniques do you use to keep channels of communication open?

Chapter 7
Conflict and Abuse

The stories in this chapter were about two young couples who handled conflict in their relationships in very different ways. Maria and Antonio were a young couple, engaged and living together. When they had a conflict in deciding whether to go to a concert by Antonio's favorite band or to help Maria's family celebrate her mother's birthday, Antonio stormed out of the house and Maria felt very sad. Although Antonio telephoned Maria a short time later to suggest a compromise, Maria listened quietly but really didn't feel any pleasure about the resolution of their conflict. She was depressed about Antonio's anger. She thought he had overreacted, and for his part, Antonio thought that Maria had overreacted to his overreaction. As time went on, Antonio learned to tone down his anger a little and Maria learned to shrug off his sometimes explosive reactions. They didn't surprise her anymore. Yet Maria and Antonio continued to feel stuck in their pattern of relating to each other.

- Knowing what you do about relationship conflict, what are some of this couple's problems? For example, is either of them guilty of criticism, contempt, defensiveness, or stonewalling?
- Do you think abuse is a possibility for them?
- Do you think they will stay together? Why or why not?

Peter and Lisa had a very different style for handling conflict in their marriage. They were a bit older than Antonio and Maria, and it was the second marriage for each of them. They had a little boy, whom they both adored. Most of the time, they agreed about things. But when they didn't, Peter was inclined to be at least moderately direct in handling conflict and Lisa often withdrew and became cool and distant. After their most recent conflict, when Lisa walked into the house with the groceries, tears streaming down her face, Peter was astonished! She was usually calm and collected; this was one of the first times he had seen her so very upset. In sentences punctuated by sobs, Lisa told Peter that the icy, withdrawn style she had for dealing with conflict made her feel disconnected and lonely—and miserable. She knew they couldn't stop having occasional conflicts; that was part of any marriage. But she wanted to change the way in which she responded. Peter realized that, in some ways, life would be more difficult if he and Lisa had more open conflict, but he felt strongly that that was the way to go.

- What will be the biggest obstacles for Lisa and Peter as they try to alter their approach to handling conflict?
- What are the strengths of their relationship?
- Is Lisa moving from a "loyalty" approach to conflict toward a "voice" approach?
- Will she succeed in changing? Why or why not?

Chapter 8
Breakup, Divorce, and Bereavement

Brenda and George, a middle-aged married couple with two college-student children, were getting a divorce. When they and their respective lawyers met to discuss the divorce settlement, conflicts arose. They finally worked out a settlement, but the task remained of telling their young adult children that they were getting a divorce. They gently told their children about what was happening, and while the kids were surprised, they seemed to handle the news fairly well. George and Brenda were very civilized and cordial in their interactions, so their children did not have to deal with parental conflict and hostility. Brenda and George made every effort to reassure their kids that they would be loved and supported and that their lives would not change drastically. In the process of dealing constructively with the kids, Brenda and George realized that they could work together as a team and even cultivate a level of friendship.

At first, George was lost, living by himself, but then he began to build a life. He realized that he had to cut back on work and travel, something Brenda had asked him to do for years. Brenda found it peaceful to live by herself but lonely. Now, she and George see each other occasionally, usually going out to dinner about once a month. When they get together, they talk about their work, the kids, and what they are doing. It almost feels to them as if they are starting all over, building a friendship.

- What were some of the factors that led to Brenda and George's divorce?
- Did any of those factors change after the divorce? If so, which ones?
- What are some possible outcomes for George and Brenda's developing postdivorce relationship?

Chapter 9
Diverse Relationships

Chris and Becky, the subjects of this Relationship Story, met, fell in love, and established a life together. Along the way, they decided they wanted to have children. Unable to conceive a child and after a great deal of consideration and soul-searching, they decided to adopt a baby. At the end of the story, they had just been introduced to their new baby girl, who had come all the way from China.

It is both central yet peripheral to their story that Becky and Chris are a lesbian couple. It is *central* in that they are less typical of the population at large than are the partners in a heterosexual couple. This means that they must put forth extra effort in much of what they do, including undergoing medical interventions such as fertility testing; being able to serve as each other's next of kin in case of a medical emergency; making legal arrangements for the ownership of their house and the adoption of their daughter; and deciding how open they can be about their relationship in their respective workplaces. That they are a lesbian couple is *peripheral* in that their love and commitment for each other is not based on sexual orientation and their family and friends are completely supportive of them as a couple, and now as a family of three. Both Chris and Becky's parents are proud and involved grandparents, and their friends, both heterosexual and homosexual, provide a supportive social network.

With the arrival of their daughter, Becky and Chris are learning about parenthood: sleep deprivation, feeding schedules, diaper changes as well as the joys of seeing an infant change and grow almost before their eyes. They have both kept their jobs outside the home, and although they believe they have excellent child care, they are trying to be equally involved with caring for the baby in the evenings and on weekends.

- Think about the new parents you have known. How are Becky and Chris similar to and dissimilar from those people?
- What special challenges might a homosexual couple have in raising a child?

Chapter 10
Gender

This chapter presented the story of Della and Jerome, a college-student couple who were dating seriously and considering marriage. They are working on gender issues in their relationship, inspired in part by an assignment in a course that Della took, which had the students interview their parents (or whoever raised them) about *how* work was divided up in the family and *why*. Della and Jerome worked on the assignment, learning a lot about their parents in the process. For example, Jerome learned that when his mother had stayed at home with his younger twin sister and brother, both of his parents had felt that the work she was doing was important. But life had been hard for her, nevertheless. She was very outgoing and enjoyed being out in the work world; she got lonely being at home all day. And as much as her husband said he wanted to help her, he was tired when he came home from work and wanted to relax. It had been difficult for them to view their roles as equal, as much as they wanted to, so she became the homemaker and he the provider. Both of them had felt more comfortable in later years, when their roles were more shared. For her part, Della had been raised by two parents who managed a small business, so she had grown up with everybody in the family helping with the business and everyone in the family helping out at home. Her models for how gender is done were thus somewhat nontraditional.

The more Della and Jerome have talked with each other, the more they have realized that their values on gender issues are very similar. But those values sometimes don't translate into behavior. So they are trying to apply what they have learned from their parents and from their discussions with each other and are now much more conscious of how they behave in the relationship. They have decided that it is less important that Jerome always does his own laundry or that Della takes her own car in for a tune-up than that it is to have general equity and fairness in the relationship. And every day seems to bring them a new lesson in what equity and fairness mean!

- How would you suggest to Della and Jerome that they handle issues of gender in their relationship?
- Do you think they will manage these issues successfully? Why or why not?
- If they marry, will they go back to traditional ways of "doing gender?"

This overview of Relationship Stories has shown how some relationships have continued and questioned whether other relationships will be able to. Strategies have been considered for how the people in these relationships might maintain and improve their relationships. The next section will discuss the human need for belonging and connection that has been emphasized throughout the book and how we can make choices to strengthen or weaken our human connections.

Connections and Choice Points

Imagine the following:

> You live alone and take your college courses through a combination of distance-learning (Internet-based courses) and correspondence courses. You work part time in a job that involves minimal contact with people, including co-workers. You and your co-workers do not even know each other's first names. You may attend a "virtual" religious service, sports event, or concert or movie, but you never actually attend these events with other people. When you shop for groceries and other items, the transactions are completed by automatic scanners. You order all your clothes via the Internet. If you go to the doctor or dentist, you fill out the forms online, go to an office where you are put through a scanner, and then receive a written report. Any actual treatment is provided by someone you have never seen before and will never see again. You bank and pay all your bills by mail or Internet. You have no contact with your family; in fact, you do not even remember having a family. And you have no close friends or casual acquaintances. You have no romantic partner and never expect to have one.

- If you are able to truly put yourself in the world just described, how do you feel?
- What are your reactions to having little, if any, human contact?
- Is it beyond your ability to even imagine such a world?
- Could you enjoy living in such a world?

If, as this book has proposed, people have a fundamental need for belonging, for connection with other people, then this world of isolation just described will seem foreign and unappealing. We all may have days when we would just like to be left alone, but those days occur within the context of ongoing relational connections. Our connections with other people are so much a part of our daily lives that we sometimes hardly notice them. We see people at school and at work, deal with people as we proceed through our daily lives, communicate with our families, go out with our friends, and spend time with our intimate partners. We have casual relationships and close relationships, and through these relationships, we are connected with others.

These connections, which we so often take for granted yet without which we would be so bereft, deserve our time and attention. A great deal of knowledge has been accumulated about relationships—some of it, contained in this book—and it can be used to improve and enrich our relationships. Even so, enriching our close relationships ultimately involves much more than taking a course or reading a book. It involves making frequent conscious choices about what we will or will not ask of ourselves and our relational partners.

In a romantic relationship, for example, partners make many important choices at different times in the life of the relationship. Some of these choice points occur early in the relationship. For instance, when partners first meet, they can choose whether even to speak to each other, whether to begin a relationship. If a relationship is started, then at some point, the partners will choose whether to become a couple. Part of this choice may involve becoming sexual with each other, and another aspect may involve exclusivity. Will the partners continue to date other people, or will they be exclusive? If the latter, will exclusivity include sexual faithfulness? Taking off one's rose-colored glasses and seeing a partner's faults realistically can become a choice point in whether to continue the relationship.

Later on in the relationship, the couple encounters decisions about cohabiting, getting married, and /or establishing a lifetime partnership. Career issues may become important and need to be addressed. Will both partners have careers? If yes, will both careers have equal priority? What about relocating? Is each partner willing to move in order to benefit the other person's career, or must both people be professionally advantaged by a move? To have children or not—and then when and how many—can be another significant choice point for couples. Around this time, partners may also encounter lifestyle and value choices. How will child care and housework be accomplished? How will gender issues be handled? Will the partners decide that money and material possessions are important, unimportant, or somewhere in between? Decisions about religious/ spiritual values and leisure time can also represent choices, and important choices can also occur around issues of involvement with family and friends—how much, how often, how intimate? How integrated into a social network will the couple or family be?

Much later in a relationship, the couple confronts decisions about how to handle illnesses and other family crises, when and where to retire, and so on. And even more new decisions arise as to how involved to be with adult children, grandchildren, and others in the social network.

Other choices confront couples throughout the life of a relationship, particularly choice points about whether to communicate about virtually everything or to have some topics that are off-limits and whether to avoid conflict or to engage conflict. And if conflict is to be engaged, will the partners talk quietly to solve problems or hold emotionally charged shouting matches? And always, there are choice points regarding how much and what kinds of social support the partners may offer to each other.

Certainly, there are many major and very obvious choice points in romantic relationships, but there are many more minor, almost indiscernible ones. The smaller choices come so quietly that they hardly seem like choices at all—but they are. For example, we can spend time with our partner if we have any time left over after school and work, or we can make spending time with our partner our first priority. Either option is a choice. If something in our relationship has been bothering us, we can be completely open with our partner or we can hold back our feelings. Again, either option is a choice. If our partner has a big test coming up, we can either offer to do his or her share of the household chores or we can just ignore the issue. Either option is a choice.

As we become aware of the many relational choices that we make every day, we can consciously shape our relationships for better or for worse. Every day offers opportunities to make good choices and bad choices. Most of us will make *both* kinds of choices as we live out our relational lives. Do what you can to make mostly good choices.

Glossary

Accountability An evaluation of a person's behavior in terms of its appropriateness for his or her gender (as used in Chapter 10). (p. 212)

Affect Another word for *emotion,* such as sadness or happiness. (p. 24)

Anxious Refers to a style of attachment reflecting ambivalence, or both closeness and distance at the same time. (p. 5)

Archival Refers to a type of research in which existing information—such as census data, legal records, and personal letters—is examined. (p. 14)

Attachment An emotional bond toward someone that may be reciprocal. (p. 4)

Attribution An inference or judgment about the cause of a particular event or behavior; concerned with making sense of the world. (p. 143)

Avoidant Refers to a style of attachment reflecting independence and a lack of emotional involvement. (p. 5)

Benevolent sexism Holding positive attitudes toward women yet endorsing negative status for them. (p. 214)

Bereavement The process of dealing with loss, particularly the death of a loved one; involves grieving that may be *uncomplicated* or *complicated.* (p. 180)

Breakup The dissolution of a romantic relationship; often involves sadness and anger on the parts of the former partners. (p. 170)

Cohabitation A living arrangement in which adults, either homosexual or heterosexual, in a romantic, partnered relationship live together but are not married. (p. 203)

Commitment In regard to relationships, refers to the intention to remain in the relationship; there are several types or facets of commitment. (p. 40)

Common couple conflict A type of interpersonal violence that is not terribly severe, that involves both relational partners, and that does not escalate. (p. 154)

Communal Refers to a type of relationship in which one person gives to another without expecting to get something back; the giving is based on the recipient's needs. (p. 52)

Companionate love A type of love characterized by shared values, affection, stability, and a strong emphasis on friendship; can be present for people who have been in relationships for a relatively short time or a relatively long time. (p. 79)

Conflict The interpersonal process that results when two people have different and competing goals or wishes. (p. 141)

Consequential/Cultural Refers to a communication approach that emphasizes the culture of the relationship and considers such things as interaction routines, rituals, and norms for behavior. (p. 122)

Demand/Withdraw Refers to a style of handling conflict in which one partner wants change and enacts the request (or *demands*) and the other partner wants to maintain the status quo and enacts the avoidance (or *withdraws*). (p. 149)

Dialectical Refers to the idea of opposing (or complementary) needs and forces in relationships, such as the need for disclosure and the need for privacy. (p. 124)

Divorce The legal ending of a marriage; includes many aspects, including financial, logistical, and emotional ones. (p. 174)

Entitlement One's attitudes about what he or she feels he or she has a right to expect. (p. 224)

Equity Refers to an approach concerned with fairness of outcomes in situations, including relationships; people generally prefer equitable relationships. (p. 51)

Exchange Refers to an approach in which one person gives to another and expects to get something equivalent in return; this is often based on what the giver might hope to get in return. (p. 50)

Exit One of Rusbult's four conflict responses; refers to an active and destructive approach that involves leaving the conflict and the partner. (p. 148)

Experimental Refers to a type of research in which comparisons are conducted under controlled conditions. (p. 14)

Friendship A voluntary, affectional relationship, usually without romantic implications; friendships are important throughout the lifespan. (p. 49)

Gay Refers to men who are romantically and sexually attracted to relationship partners who are also men. (p. 194)

Gender The entire set of situations and behaviors linked to a person's sex category. (p. 211)

Hostile sexism Holding negative attitudes toward women and their status. (p. 215)

Infidelity A behavior in which one partner in an intimate relationship (typically, a marriage) becomes sexually or emotionally involved with a third person. (p. 167)

Internal working model A cognitive and emotional structure or template of a relationship or an aspect of a relationship that provides a blueprint for future relationships. (p. 5)

Intimacy Emotional closeness in a relationship; according to one typology, includes partner disclosure, positive emotion and an absence of conflict, and feeling understood by the partner. (p. 86)

Intimate terrorism A type of interpersonal violence in which one partner controls, abuses, and terrorizes the other. (p. 154)

Jealousy A negative feeling precipitated by the fear of losing one's romantic partner to someone else; a multidimensional emotion. (p. 166)

Lesbian Refers to women who are romantically and sexually attracted to relationship partners who are also women. (p. 194)

Loss A general feeling of sadness due to having someone or something that one values taken away. (p. 166)

Love A general term that refers to emotional connection with and affection for another person; can be felt for friends, family members, and romantic partners. (p. 75)

Love styles A typology of love attitude constellations that includes six major types: Eros (passionate love), Ludus (game-playing love), Storge (friendship love), Pragma (practical love), Mania (possessive, dependent love), and Agape (altruistic love). (p. 82)

Loyalty One of Rusbult's four conflict responses; refers to a passive and constructive approach that involves commitment to the partner but avoidance of the conflict. (p. 148)

Matching hypothesis The idea that people seek romantic partners who are similar in level of physical attractiveness. (p. 30)

Minding A multidimensional concept that describes the need to give ongoing attention to oneself, one's relational partner, and the relationship itself. (p. 122)

Multicultural relationships Relationships in which people from different cultural/ethnic backgrounds are romantically involved (as used in Chapter 9). (p. 198)

Multiracial relationships Relationships in which people from different racial backgrounds are romantically involved (as used in Chapter 9). (p. 198)

Neglect One of Rusbult's four conflict responses; refers to a passive and destructive approach that involves avoidance of both the conflict and the partner. (p. 148)

Nonverbal communication A type of communication encompassing essentially all communication that is not verbal, including such things as body orientation, eye contact, touch, interaction distance, and so on. (p. 128)

Observation A type of research in which researchers watch participants and document what they see. (p. 13)

Passionate love A type of love characterized by physiological arousal, intense emotional feeling, and a desire for union with the partner; like companionate love, can be present for people who have been in a relationship for a relatively short time or a relatively long time. (p. 79)

Perceived support The support that someone *feels* he or she has received. (p. 63)

Plasticity Refers to women's sexual flexibility regarding attitudes, behaviors, and choices of partners (as used in Chapter 10). (p. 215)

Positive illusions Partners' positive beliefs about each other, which may or may not be based on fact. (p. 38)

Prototype An approach to defining a particular concept (in Chapter 4, the concept of love) in terms of its best example or set of features. (p. 80)

Proximity Refers to being close together in spatial or geographic terms; a positive factor in initial attraction. (p. 27)

Relational maintenance All of the behaviors, such as communication, that partners enact to nurture their relationship. (p. 120)

Relationship satisfaction A subjective sense of well-being and contentment with one's close relationship. (p. 131)

Remarried families Families that include two partners, at least one of who has been married before and who brings a child or children to the remarriage. (p. 191)

Romantic attachment A behavior that involves closeness to and bonding with a romantic partner; there appear to be four adult attachment styles, including secure, preoccupied, dismissing, and fearful attachment. (p. 76)

Secure Refers to a style of attachment reflecting a stable and positive emotional bond. (p. 5)

Self-disclosure Communicating one's inner feelings, thoughts, and experiences to another person; is rather intimate and goes beyond superficial information. (p. 124)

Self-report A type of research in which participants provide information about themselves through such means as questionnaires and interviews. (p. 12)

Sex The biological designation of maleness or femaleness (p. 211); also, sexual activity, including but not limited to sexual intercourse. (p. 98)

Sexual attitudes Attitudes, typically favorable or unfavorable, toward various sexual practices and behaviors; see the section Attraction as an Attitude in Chapter 2. (p. 99)

Sexual desire A sexual wishing or wanting for another person; a yearning for sexual union with someone. (p. 105)

Sexual frequency Typically refers to the number of times a particular sexual behavior occurs within a specified time period; the behavior typically assessed is sexual intercourse and the number of times it occurs for someone each week or month. (p. 98)

Sexual satisfaction One's contentment with and appreciation for aspects of his or her sexual life; may be experienced in regard to a particular sexual behavior, to one's sexual partner, or to one's whole sexual relationship. (p. 103)

Sexually based primary relationship A partnered relationship that is defined in terms of relationship processes, such as commitment and sexual involvement, rather than in terms of social structure, such as marriage. (p. 190)

Similarity Refers to being alike on one or more dimensions; an important factor leading to attraction. (p. 25)

Social network The constellation of persons, both friends and family, who are considered to be close associates and who can typically be counted on for help. (p. 55)

Social penetration A theory of relationship development in which self-disclosure is a primary aspect. (p. 36)

Social support Being responsive to another person and fulfilling his or her needs in both ongoing situations and occasions of crisis. (p. 62)

Stonewalling A dysfunctional response to conflict that involves complete unyieldingness and withdrawal from the partner; contains elements of both the exit and neglect responses. (p. 152)

Strategic/Functional Refers to a communication approach that emphasizes the intentional, goal-oriented, instrumental aspects of communication. (p. 122)

Voice One of Rusbult's four conflict responses; refers to an active and constructive approach that involves problem solving with the partner. (p. 148)

References

Abbey, A. (1982). Sex differences in attributions for friendly behavior: Do males misperceive females' friendliness? *Journal of Personality and Social Psychology, 42,* 830–838.

Acitelli, L. K. (1993). You, me, and us: Perspectives on relationship awareness. In S. Duck (Ed.), *Individuals in relationships* (pp. 144–174). Newbury Park, CA: Sage.

Acitelli, L. K., Douvan, E., & Veroff, J. (1997). The changing influence of interpersonal perceptions on marital well-being among black and white couples. *Journal of Social and Personal Relationships, 14,* 291–304.

Acitelli, L. K., Rogers, S., & Knee, C.R. (1999). The role of identity in the link between relationship thinking and relationship satisfaction. *Journal of Social and Personal Relationships, 16,* 591–618.

Acker, M., & Davis, K. E. (1992). Intimacy, passion and commitment in adult romantic relationships: A test of the triangular theory of love. *Journal of Social and Personal Relationships, 9,* 21–50.

Adams, R. G., & Blieszner, R. (1994). An integrative conceptual framework for friendship research. *Journal of Social and Personal Relationships, 11,* 163–184.

Adelmann, P. K., Chadwick, K., & Baerger, D. R. (1996). Marital quality of black and white adults over the life course. *Journal of Social and Personal Relationships, 13,* 361–384.

Adler, N. L., Hendrick, S. S., & Hendrick, C. (1987). Male sexual preference and attitudes toward love and sexuality. *Journal of Sex Education and Therapy, 12*(2), 27–30.

Afifi, W. A., Falato, W. L., & Weiner, J. L. (2001). Identity concerns following a severe relational transgression: The role of discovery method for the relational outcomes of infidelity. *Journal of Social and Personal Relationships, 18,* 291–308.

Afifi, W. A., & Faulkner, S. L. (2000). On being 'just friends': The frequency and impact of sexual activity in cross-sex friendships. *Journal of Social and Personal Relationships, 17,* 205–222.

Ainsworth, M. D. S., Blehar, M. S., Waters, E., & Wall, S. (1978). *Patterns of attachment: A psychological study of the Strange Situation.* Hillsdale, NJ: Erlbaum.

Allen, E. S., Baucom, D. H., Burnett, C. K., Epstein, N., & Rankin-Esquer, L. A. (2001). Decision-making power, autonomy, and communication in remarried spouses compared with first-married spouses. *Family Relations, 50,* 326–334.

Allen, K. R., & Walker, A. J. (2000). Qualitative research. In C. Hendrick & S. S. Hendrick (Eds.), *Close relationships: A sourcebook* (pp. 19–30). Thousand Oaks, CA: Sage.

Altman, I. (1975). The environment and social behavior: Privacy * personal space * territory * crowding. Monterey, CA: Brooks/Cole.

Altman, I., & Taylor, D. A. (1973). *Social penetration: The development of interpersonal relationships.* New York: Holt, Rinehart & Winston.

Altman, I., Vinsel, A., & Brown, B. B. (1981). Dialectic conceptions in social psychology: An application to social penetration and privacy regulation. In L. Berkowitz (Ed.), *Advances in experimental social psychology* (Vol. 14, pp. 107–160). New York: Academic Press.

Amato, P. R. (1999). Children of divorced parents as young adults. In E. M. Hetherington (Ed.), *Coping with divorce, single parenting, and remarriage* (pp. 147–164). Mahwah, NJ: Erlbaum.

Amato, P. R. (2000). The consequences of divorce for adults and children. *Journal of Marriage and the Family, 62,* 1269–1287.

Andersen, B. L., Cyranowski, J. M., & Aarestad, S. (2000). Beyond artificial, sex-linked distinctions to conceptualize female sexuality: Comment on Baumeister (2000). *Psychological Bulletin, 126,* 380–384.

Andersen, P. A., & Guerrero, L. K. (1998). *Handbook of communication and emotion: Research, theory, applications, and contexts.* San Diego: Academic Press.

Anderson, E. R., Greene, S. M., Hetherington, E. M., & Clingempeel, W. G. (1999). The dynamics of parental remarriage: Adolescent, parent, and sibling influences. In E. M. Hetherington (Ed.), *Coping with divorce, single parenting, and remarriage* (pp. 295–319). Mahwah, NJ: Erlbaum.

Argyle, M., & Dean, J. (1965). Eye contact, distance, and affiliation. *Sociometry, 28,* 289–304.

Aries, E. (1996). *Men and women in interaction: Reconsidering the differences.* New York: Oxford University Press.

Aron, A., Dutton, D. G., Aron, E. N., & Iverson, A. (1989). Experiences of falling in love. *Journal of Social and Personal Relationships, 6,* 243–257.

Aron, A., & Westbay, L. (1996). Dimensions of the prototype of love. *Journal of Personality and Social Psychology, 70,* 535–551.

Aron, E. N., & Aron, A. (1996). Love and expansion of the self: The state of the model. *Personal Relationships, 3,* 45–58.

Aronson, E., Willerman, B., & Floyd, J. (1966). The effect of a pratfall on increasing interpersonal attractiveness. *Psychonomic Science, 4,* 227–228.

Arriaga, X. B. (2001). The ups and downs of dating: Fluctuations in satisfaction in newly formed romantic relationships. *Journal of Personality and Social Psychology, 80,* 754–765.

Barbara, A. M., & Dion, K. L. (2000). Breaking up is hard to do, especially for strongly "preoccupied" lovers. *Journal of Personal and Interpersonal Loss, 5,* 315–342.

Barbee, A. P., & Cunningham, M. R. (1995). An experimental approach to social support communications: Interactive coping in close relationships. *Communication Yearbook, 18,* 381–413.

Barber, B. L., & Eccles, J. S. (1992). Long-term influence of divorce and single parenting on adolescent family-and work-related values, behaviors, and aspirations. *Psychological Bulletin, 111,* 108–126.

Bargh, J. A., & Chartrand, T. L. (1999). The unbearable automaticity of being. *American Psychologist, 54,* 462–479.

Barnes, M. K., Harvey, J. H., Carlson, H., & Haig, J. (1996). The relativity of grief: Differential adaptation reactions of younger and older persons. *Journal of Personal and Interpersonal Loss, 1,* 375–392.

Barnett, R. C., & Hyde, J. S. (2001). Women, men, work, and family: An expansionist theory. *American Psychologist, 56,* 781–796.

Bartholomew, K. (1990). Avoidance of intimacy: An attachment perspective. *Journal of Social and Personal Relationships, 7,* 147–178.

Bartsch, N. (2001). Gender role, entitlement, disclosure, and silencing the self: Factors in romantic relationships. Unpublished manuscript, Texas Tech University, Lubbock, TX.

Battaglia, D. M., Richard, F. D., Datteri, D. L., & Lord, C. G. (1998). Breaking up is (relatively) easy to do: A script for the dissolution of close relationships. *Journal of Social and Personal Relationships, 15,* 829–845.

Baumeister, R. F. (2000). Gender differences in erotic plasticity: The female sex drive as socially flexible and responsive. *Psychological Bulletin, 126,* 347–374.

Baumeister, R. F., & Leary, M. R. (1995). The need to belong: Desire for interpersonal attachments as a fundamental human motivation. *Psychological Bulletin, 117,* 497–529.

Baumeister, R. F., & Wotman, S. R. (1992). *Breaking hearts: The two sides of unrequited love.* New York: Guilford.

Baumeister, R. F., Catanese, K. R., Campbell, W. K., & Tice, D. M. (2000). Nature, culture, and explanations for erotic plasticity: Reply to Andersen, Cyranowski, and Aarestad (2000) and Hyde and Durik (2000). *Psychological Bulletin, 126,* 385–389.

Baumeister, R. F., Wotman, S. R., & Stillwell, A. M. (1993). Unrequited love: On heartbreak, anger, guilt, scriptlessness, and humiliation. *Journal of Personality and Social Psychology, 64,* 377–394.

Baxter, L. A., & Erbert, L. A. (1999). Perceptions of dialectical contradictions in turning points of development in heterosexual romantic relationships. *Journal of Social and Personal Relationships, 16,* 547–569.

Baxter, L. A., & Montgomery, B. M. (1996). *Relating: Dialogue and dialectics.* New York: Guilford.

Baxter, L. A., Braithwaite, D. O., & Nicholson, J. H. (1999). Turning points in the development of blended families. *Journal of Social and Personal Relationships, 16,* 291–313.

Baxter, L. A., Mazanec, M., Nicholson, J., Pittman, G., Smith. K., & West, L. (1997). Everyday loyalties and betrayals in personal relationships. *Journal of Social and Personal Relationships, 14,* 655–678.

Becker, P. E., & Moen, P. (1999). Scaling back: Dual-earner couples' work-family strategies. *Journal of Marriage and the Family, 61,* 995–1007.

Berg, J. H., & Derlega, V. J. (1987). Themes in the study of self-disclosure. In V. J. Derlega & J. H. Berg (Eds.), *Self-disclosure: Theory, research and therapy* (pp. 1–8). New York: Plenum.

Bernard, J. (1972). *The future of marriage.* New York: World.

Berscheid, E. (1988). Some comments on love's anatomy: Or whatever happened to old-fashioned lust? In R. J. Sternberg & M. L. Barnes (Eds.), *The psychology of love* (pp. 359–374). New Haven, CT: Yale University Press.

Berscheid, E., & Meyers, S. A. (1996). A social categorical approach to a question about love. *Personal Relationships, 3,* 19–43.

Berscheid, E., & Walster, E. (1978). *Interpersonal attraction* (2nd ed.). Reading, MA: Addison-Wesley.

Berscheid, E., Dion, K., Walster, E., & Walster, G. W. (1971). Physical attractiveness and dating choice: A test of the matching hypothesis. *Journal of Experimental Social Psychology, 7,* 173–189.

Berzon, B. (1988). *Permanent partners: Building gay and lesbian relationships that last.* New York: Plume.

Bettor, L., Hendrick, S. S., & Hendrick, C. (1995). Gender and sexual standards in dating relationships. *Personal Relationships, 2,* 359–369.

Blau, P. M. (1964). *Exchange and power in social life.* New York: Wiley.

Bleske, A. L., & Buss, D. M. (2000). Can men and women be just friends? *Personal Relationships, 7,* 131–151.

Blieszner, R. (2000). Close relationships in old age. In C. Hendrick & S. S. Hendrick (Eds.), *Close relationships: A sourcebook* (pp. 85–95). Thousand Oaks, CA: Sage.

Blieszner, R., & Adams, R. G. (1992). *Adult friendship.* Newbury Park, CA: Sage.

Bloom, B. L., Asher, S. J., & White, S. W. (1978). Marital disruption as a stressor: A review and analysis. *Psychological Bulletin, 85,* 867–894.

Blumstein, P., & Schwartz, P. (1983). *American couples.* New York: Morrow.

Boekhout, B. (1997). Extrarelationship involvement: Perceptions, disclosures, and consequences. Unpublished manuscript, Texas Tech University, Lubbock, TX.

Boekhout, B., Hendrick, S. S., & Hendrick, C. (2000). *The loss of loved ones: The impact of relationship infidelity.* In J. H. Harvey & E. D. Miller (Eds.), *Loss and trauma: General and close relationship perspectives* (pp. 358–374). Philadelphia: Brunner-Routledge.

Bohannan, P. (1984). *All the happy families: Exploring the varieties of family life.* New York: McGraw-Hill.

Bohannan, P. (Ed.). (1970). *Divorce and after.* Garden City, NY: Doubleday.

Bolger, N., Delongis, A., Kessler, R. C., & Wethington, E. (1989). The contagion of stress across multiple roles. *Journal of Marriage and the Family, 51,* 175–183.

Boon, S. D. (1994). Dispelling doubt and uncertainty: Trust in romantic relationships. In S. Duck (Ed.), *Dynamics of relationships* (pp. 86–111). Thousand Oaks, CA: Sage.

Boon, S. D., & McLeod, B. A. (2001). Deception in romantic relationships: Subjective estimates of success at deceiving and attitudes toward deception. *Journal of Social and Personal Relationships, 18,* 463–476.

Booth, A., & Amato, P. R. (1994). Parental gender role nontraditionalism and offspring outcomes. *Journal of Marriage and the Family, 56,* 865–877.

Booth, A., & Amato, P. R. (2001). Parental predivorce relations and offspring postdivorce well-being. *Journal of Marriage and the Family, 63,* 197–212.

Booth, A., & Edwards, J. N. (1992). Starting over: Why remarriages are more unstable. *Journal of Family Issues, 13,* 179–194.

Bowlby J. (1958). The nature of the child's tie to his mother. *International Journal of Psychoanalysis, 39,* 350–373.

Bowlby, J. (1969). *Attachment and loss: Vol. 1. Attachment.* New York: Basic Books.

Bowlby, J. (1973). *Attachment and loss: Vol. 2. Separation: Anxiety and anger.* New York: Basic Books.

Bowlby, J. (1980). *Attachment and loss: Vol. 3. Loss.* New York: Basic Books.

Bradbury, T. N., & Fincham, F. D. (1988). Individual difference variables in close relationships: A contextual model of marriage as an integrative framework. *Journal of Personality and Social Psychology, 54,* 713–721.

Bradbury, T. N., & Fincham, F. D. (1989). Behavior and satisfaction in marriage: Prospective mediating processes. In C. Hendrick (Ed.), *Close relationships* (pp. 119–143). Newbury Park, CA: Sage.

Bradbury, T. N., & Fincham, F. D. (1992). Attributions and behavior in marital interaction. *Journal of Personality and Social Psychology, 63,* 613–628.

Braiker, H. B., & Kelley, H. H. (1979). Conflict in the development of close relationships. In R. L. Burgess & T. L. Huston (Eds.), *Social exchange in developing relationships* (pp. 135–168). New York: Academic Press.

Bray, J. H. (1999). From marriage to remarriage and beyond: Findings from the developmental issues in stepfamilies research project. In E. M. Hetherington (Ed.), *Coping with divorce, single parenting, and remarriage* (pp. 253–271). Mahwah, NJ: Erlbaum.

Brennan, R. T., Barnett, R. C., & Gareis, K. C. (2001). When she earns more than he does: A longitudinal study of dual-earner couples. *Journal of Marriage and the Family, 63,* 168–182.

Brickman, P. (1974). Rule structures and conflict relationships. In P. Brickman (Ed.), *Social conflict.* Lexington, MA: D. C. Heath.

Brock, D. M., Sarason, I. G., Sarason, B. R., & Pierce, G. R. (1996). Simultaneous assessment of perceived global and relationship-specific support. *Journal of Social and Personal Relationships, 13,* 143–152.

Bumpass, L., Sweet, J., & Castro Martin, T. (1990). Changing patterns of remarriage. *Journal of Marriage and the Family, 52,* 747–756.

Burleson, B. R., & Denton, W. H. (1997). The relationship between communication skills and marital satisfaction: Some moderating effects. *Journal of Marriage and the Family, 59,* 884–902.

Burleson, B. R., & Goldsmith, D. J. (1998). How the comforting process works: Alleviating emotional distress through conversationally induced reappraisals. In P. A. Andersen & L. K. Guerrero (Eds.), *Handbook of communication and emotion: Research, theory, applications, and contexts* (pp. 245–280). San Diego: Academic Press.

Burleson, B. R., Kunkel, A. W., Samter, W., & Werking, K. J. (1996). Men's and women's evaluations of communication skills in personal relationships: When sex differences make a difference—and when they don't. *Journal of Social and Personal Relationships, 13,* 201–224.

Burleson, B. R., Metts, S., & Kirch, M. W. (2000). Communication in close relationships. In C. Hendrick & S. S. Hendrick (Eds.), *Close relationships: A sourcebook* (pp. 245–258). Thousand Oaks, CA: Sage.

Burman, B., & Margolin, G. (1992). Analysis of the association between marital relationships and health problems: An interactional perspective. *Psychological Bulletin, 112,* 39–63.

Burns, A., & Dunlop, R. (1998). Parental divorce, parent-child relations, and early adult relationships: A longitudinal Australian study. *Personal Relationships, 5,* 393–407.

Buss, D. M. (1988). Love acts: The evolutionary biology of love. In R. J. Sternberg & M. L. Barnes (Eds.), *The psychology of love* (pp. 100–117). New Haven, CT: Yale University Press.

Buss, D. M. (1995). Evolutionary psychology: A new paradigm for psychological science. *Psychological Inquiry, 6,* 1–30.

Buss, D. M. (1994). *The evolution of desire.* New York: Basic Books.

Buss, D. M. (1999). *Evolutionary psychology: The new science of the mind.* Boston: Allyn & Bacon.

Buss, D. M., & Barnes, M. (1986). Preferences in human mate selection. *Journal of Personality and Social Psychology, 50,* 559–570.

Buss, D. M., Larsen, R. J., Westen, D., & Semmelroth, J. (1992). Sex differences in jealousy: Evolution, physiology, and psychology. *Psychological Science, 3,* 251–255.

Buss, D. M., & Schmitt, D. P. (1993). Sexual strategies theory: An evolutionary perspective on human mating. *Psychological Review, 100,* 204–232.

Buunk, B. P. (1995). Sex, self-esteem, dependency, and extradyadic sexual experiences as related to jealousy responses. *Journal of Social and Personal Relationships, 12,* 147–153.

Buunk, B. P., & Dijkstra, P. (2000). Extradyadic relationships and jealousy. In C. Hendrick & S. S. Hendrick (Eds.), *Close relationships: A sourcebook* (pp. 317–329). Thousand Oaks, CA: Sage.

Buunk, B. P., & Mutsaers, W. (1999). Equity perceptions and marital satisfaction in former and current marriage: A study among the remarried. *Journal of Social and Personal Relationships, 16,* 123–132.

Byers, E. S., Demmons, S., & Lawrance, K. (1998). Sexual satisfaction within dating relationships: A test of the interpersonal exchange model of sexual satisfaction. *Journal of Social and Personal Relationships, 15,* 257–267.

Byers, E. S., & Lewis, K. (1988). Dating couples' disagreements over the desired level of sexual intimacy. *Journal of Sex Research, 24,* 15–29.

Byrne, D. (1969). Attitudes and attraction. In L. Berkowitz (Ed.), *Advances in experimental social psychology* (Vol. 4, pp. 35–89). New York: Academic Press.

Byrne, D. (1971). *The attraction paradigm.* New York: Academic Press.

Byrne, D. (1997). An overview (and underview) of research and theory within the Attraction paradigm. *Journal of Social and Personal Relationships, 14,* 417–431.

Byrne, D., & Nelson, D. (1965). Attraction as a linear function of proportion of positive reinforcements. *Journal of Personality and Social Psychology, 1,* 659–663.

Call, V., Sprecher, S., & Schwartz, P. (1995). The incidence and frequency of marital sex in a national sample. *Journal of Marriage and the Family, 57,* 639–652.

Canary, D. J., Cunningham, E. M., & Cody, M. J. (1988). Goal types, gender, and locus of control in managing interpersonal conflict. *Communication Research, 15,* 426–446.

Canary, D. J., Cupach, W. R., & Messman, S. J. (1995). *Relationship conflict.* Thousand Oaks, CA: Sage.

Canary, D. J., & Emmers-Sommer, T. M. (1997). *Sex and gender differences in personal relationships.* New York: Guilford.

Canary, D. J., Stafford, L., & Semic, B. A. (2002). A panel study of the associations between maintenance strategies and relational characteristics. *Journal of Marriage and Family, 64,* 395–406.

Cash, T. F., & Derlega, V. J. (1978). The matching hypothesis: Physical attractiveness among same-sexed friends. *Personality and Social Psychology Bulletin, 4,* 240–243.

Cate, R. M., Huston, T. L., & Nesselroade, J. R. (1986). Premarital relationships: Toward the identification of alternative pathways to marriage. *Journal of Social and Clinical Psychology, 4,* 3–22.

Cate, R. M., Levin, L. A., & Richmond, L. S. (2002). Premarital relationship stability: A review of recent research. *Journal of Social and Personal Relationships, 19,* 261–284.

Cate, R. M., & Lloyd, S. A. (1988). Courtship. In S. Duck (Ed.), *Handbook of personal relationships: Theory, research and interventions* (pp. 409–427). New York: Wiley.

Cate, R. M., & Lloyd, S. A. (1992). *Courtship.* Newbury Park, CA: Sage.

Caughlin, J. P., & Vangelisti, A. L. (2000). An individual difference explanation of why married couples engage in the demand/withdraw pattern of conflict. *Journal of Social and Personal Relationships, 17,* 523–551.

Charny, I. W., & Parnass, S. (1995). The impact of extramarital relationships on the continuation of marriages. *Journal of Sex and Marital Therapy, 21,* 100–115.

Cho, W., & Cross, S. E. (1995). Taiwanese love styles and their association with self-esteem and relationship quality. *Genetic, Social, and General Psychology Monographs, 121,* 283–309.

Choice, P., & Lamke, L. K. (1999). Stay/leave decision-making processes in abusive dating relationships. *Personal Relationships, 6,* 351–367.

Christopher, F. S. (2001). *To dance the dance: A symbolic interactional exploration of premarital sexuality.* Mahwah, NJ: Erlbaum.

Christopher, F. S., & Lloyd, S. A. (2000). Physical and sexual aggression in relationships. In C. Hendrick & S. S. Hendrick (Eds.), *Close relationships: A sourcebook* (pp. 331–343). Thousand Oaks, CA: Sage.

Christopher, F. S., & Roosa, M. W. (1991). Factors affecting sexual decisions in the premarital relationships of adolescents and young adults. In K. McKinney & S. Sprecher (Eds.), *Sexuality in close relationships* (pp. 111–133). Hillsdale, NJ: Erlbaum.

Christopher, F. S., & Sprecher, S. (2000). Sexuality in marriage, dating, and other relationships: A decade review. *Journal of Marriage and the Family, 62,* 999–1017.

Clark, M. S., & Mills, J. (1979). Interpersonal attraction in exchange and communal relationships. *Journal of Personality and Social Psychology, 37,* 12–24.

Clark, M. S., Mills, J., & Powell, M. C. (1986). Keeping track of needs in communal and exchange relationships. *Journal of Personality and Social Psychology, 51,* 333–338.

Clements, M. L., Cordova, A. D., Markman, H. J., & Laurenceau, J.-P. (1997). The erosion of marital satisfaction over time and how to prevent it. In R. J. Stemberg & M. Hojjat (Eds.), *Satisfaction in close relationships* (pp. 335–355). New York: Guilford.

Cohan, C. L., & Kleinbaum, S. (2002). Toward a greater understanding of the cohabitation effect: Premarital cohabitation and marital communication. *Journal of Marriage and Family, 64,* 180–192.

Cole, C. L., & Cole, A. L. (1999). Marriage enrichment and prevention really works: Interpersonal competence training to maintain and enhance relationships. *Family Relations, 48,* 273–275.

Cole, T., & Bradac, J. J. (1996). A lay theory of relational satisfaction with best friends. *Journal of Social and Personal Relationships, 13,* 57–83.

Coleman, M., Fine, M. A., Ganong, L. H., Downs, K. J. M., & Pauk, N. (2001). When you're not the Brady Bunch: Identifying perceived conflicts and resolution strategies in stepfamilies. *Personal Relationships, 8,* 55–73.

Coleman, M., Ganong, L., & Fine, M. (2000). Reinvestigating remarriage: Another decade of progress. *Journal of Marriage and the Family, 62,* 1288–1307.

Collins, W. A., & Laursen, B. (2000). Adolescent relationships: The art of fugue. In C. Hendrick & S. S. Hendrick (Eds.), *Close relationships: A sourcebook* (pp. 59–69). Thousand Oaks, CA: Sage.

Coltrane, S. (2000). Research on household labor: Modeling and measuring the social embeddedness of routine family work. *Journal of Marriage and the Family, 62,* 1208–1233.

Contreras, R., Hendrick, S. S., & Hendrick, C. (1996). Perspectives on marital love and satisfaction in Mexican American and Anglo couples. *Journal of Counseling and Development, 74,* 408–415.

Cooper, A., & Sportolari, L. (1997). Romance in cyberspace: Understanding online attraction. *Journal of Sex Education and Therapy, 22,* 7–14.

Coontz, S. (1992). *The way we never were: American families and the nostalgia trap.* New York: Basic Books.

Correia, K. M. (2000). Suicide assessment in a prison environment: A proposed protocol. *Criminal Justice and Behavior, 27,* 581–599.

Crowder, K. D., & Tolnay, S. E. (2000). A new marriage squeeze for black women: The role of racial intermarriage by black men. *Journal of Marriage and the Family, 62,* 792–807.

Cunningham, M. R., & Barbee, A. P. (2000). Social support. In C. Hendrick & S. S. Hendrick (Eds.), *Close relationships: A sourcebook* (pp. 273–285). Thousand Oaks, CA: Sage.

Cunningham, M. R., Roberts, A. R., Barbee, A. P., Druen, P. B., & Wu, C. H. (1995). "Their ideas of beauty are, on the whole, the same as ours": Consistency and variability in the cross-cultural perception of female physical attractiveness. *Journal of Personality and Social Psychology, 68,* 261–279.

Cupach, W. R. (2000). Advancing understanding about relational conflict. *Journal of Social and Personal Relationships, 17,* 697–703.

Cupach, W. R., & Comstock, J. (1990). Satisfaction with sexual communication in marriage: Links to sexual satisfaction and dyadic adjustment. *Journal of Social and Personal Relationships, 7,* 179–186.

Cupach, W. R., & Metts, S. (1991). Sexuality and communication in close relationships. In K. McKinney & S. Sprecher (Eds.), *Sexuality in close relationships* (pp. 93–110). Hillsdale, NJ: Erlbaum.

Cupach, W. R., & Metts, S. (1995). The role of sexual attitude similarity in romantic heterosexual relationships. *Personal Relationships, 2,* 287–300.

Cutrona, C. E. (1996). *Social support in couples.* Thousand Oaks, CA: Sage.

Cutrona, C. E., Hessling, R. M., & Suhr, J. A. (1997). The influence of husband and wife personality on marital social support interactions. *Personal Relationships, 4,* 379–393.

Cutrona, C. E., & Suhr, J. A. (1992). Controllability of stressful events and satisfaction with spouse support behaviors. *Communication Research, 19,* 154–176.

Cyranowski, J. M., & Andersen, B. L. (1998). Schemas, sexuality, and romantic attachment. *Journal of Personality and Social Psychology, 74,* 1364–1379.

Daher, D. M., & Banikiotes, P. G. (1976). Interpersonal attraction and rewarding aspects of disclosure content and level. *Journal of Personality and Social Psychology, 33,* 492–496.

Daigen, V., & Holmes, J. G. (2000). Don't interrupt! A good rule for marriage? *Personal Relationships, 7,* 185–201.

Dainton, M., & Stafford, L. (1993). Routine maintenance behaviors: A comparison of relationship type, partner similarity and sex differences. *Journal of Social and Personal Relationships, 10,* 255–271.

Davis, J. L., & Rusbult, C. E. (2001). Attitude alignment in close relationships. *Journal of Personality and Social Psychology, 81,* 65–84.

Davis, K. E., & Latty-Mann, H. (1987). Love styles and relationship quality: A contribution to validation. *Journal of Social and Personal Relationships, 4,* 409–428.

Deater-Deckard, K., & Dunn, J. (1999). Multiple risks and adjustment in young children growing up in different family settings: A British community study of stepparent, single mother, and nondivorced families. In E. M. Hetherington (Ed.), *Coping with divorce, single parenting, and remarriage* (pp. 47–64). Mahwah, NJ: Erlbaum.

DeGarmo, D. S., & Forgatch, M. S. (1997). Confidant support and maternal distress: Predictors of parenting practices for divorced mothers. *Personal Relationships, 4,* 305–317.

DeLamater, J. (1989). The social control of human sexuality. In K. McKinney & S. Sprecher (Eds.), *Human sexuality: The societal and interpersonal context* (pp. 30–62). Norwood, NJ: Ablex.

DeMaris, A. (1997). Elevated sexual activity in violent marriages: Hypersexuality or sexual extortion? *Journal of Sex Research, 34,* 361–373.

DeMaris, A. (2001). The influence of intimate violence on transitions out of cohabitation. *Journal of Marriage and the Family, 63,* 235–246.

DeMaris, A., & Rao, K. V. (1992). Premarital cohabitation and subsequent marital stability in the United States: A reassessment. *Journal of Marriage and the Family, 54,* 178–190.

DeMaris, A., & Swinford, S. (1996). Female victims of spousal violence: Factors influencing their level of fearfulness. *Family Relations, 45,* 98–106.

Demo, D. H., & Allen, K. R. (1996). Diversity within lesbian and gay families: Challenges and implications for family theory and research. *Journal of Social and Personal Relationships, 13,* 415–434.

Derlega, V. J., Metts, S., Petronio, S., & Margulis, S. T. (1993). *Self-disclosure.* Newbury Park, CA: Sage.

DeSteno, D., Bartlett, M. Y., Braverman, J., & Salovey, P. (2002). Sex differences in jealousy: Evolutionary mechanism or artifact of measurement? *Journal of Personality and Social Psychology, 83,* 1103–1116.

de Waal, F. B. M. (2002). Evolutionary psychology: The wheat and the chaff. *Current Directions in Psychological Science, 11,* 187–191.

Diamond, L. M. (2001). Contributions of psychophysiology to research on adult attachment: Review and recommendations. *Personality and Social Psychology Review, 5,* 276–295.

Dickens, W. J., & Perlman, D. (1981). Friendship over the life-cycle. In S. Duck & R. Gilmour (Eds.), *Personal relationships 2: Developing personal relationships* (pp. 91–122). London: Academic Press.

Diener, E. (2000). Subjective well-being: The science of happiness and a proposal for a national index. *American Psychologist, 55,* 34–43.

Dijkstra, P., Groothof, H. A. K., Poel, G. A., Laverman, T. T. G., Schrier, M., & Buunk, B. P. (2001). Sex differences in the events that elicit jealousy among homosexuals. *Personal Relationships, 8,* 41–54.

Dindia, K. (1997). Self-disclosure, self-identity, and relationship development: A transactional/dialectical perspective. In S. Duck (Ed.), *Handbook of personal relationships: Theory, research and interventions* (2nd ed.) (pp. 411–426). New York: Wiley.

Dindia, K. (2000). Relational maintenance. In C. Hendrick & S. S. Hendrick (Eds.), *Close relationships: A sourcebook* (pp. 287–299). Thousand Oaks, CA: Sage.

Dindia, K., & Allen, M. (1992). Sex-differences in self-disclosure: A meta-analysis. *Psychological Bulletin, 112,* 106–124.

Dion, K. (1977). The incentive value of physical attractiveness for young children. *Personality and Social Psychology Bulletin, 3,* 67–70.

Dion, K., Berscheid, E., & Walster, E. (1972). What is beautiful is good. *Journal of Personality and Social Psychology, 24,* 285–290.

Drigotas, S. M., & Rusbult, C. E. (1992). Should I stay or should I go? A dependence model of breakups. *Journal of Personality and Social Psychology, 62,* 62–87.

Drigotas, S. M., Rusbult, C. E., & Verette, J. (1999). Level of commitment, mutuality of commitment, and couple well-being. *Personal Relationships, 6,* 389–409.

Duck, S. (1982). A topography of relationship disengagement and dissolution. In S. Duck (Ed.), *Personal relationships 4: Dissolving personal relationships* (pp. 1–30). New York: Academic Press.

Duck, S. (1984). A perspective on the repair of personal relationships. Repair of what, when? In S. Duck (Ed.), *Personal relationships 5: Repairing personal relationships* (pp. 163–184). New York: Academic Press.

Duck, S. (1994). Steady as (s)he goes: Relational maintenance as a shared meaning system. In D. J. Canary & L. Stafford (Eds.), *Communication and relational maintenance* (pp. 45–60). San Diego: Academic Press.

Duck, S. (Ed.). (1997). *Handbook of personal relationships: Theory, research and interventions* (2nd ed.). New York: Wiley.

Duck, S., & Montgomery, B. M. (1991). The interdependence among interaction substance, theory, and methods. In B. M. Montgomery & S. Duck (Eds.), *Studying interpersonal interaction* (pp. 3–15). New York: Guilford.

Duck, S., & Sants, H. (1983). On the origins of the specious: Are personal relationships really interpersonal states? *Journal of Social and Clinical Psychology, 1,* 27–41

Duck, S., & Wood, J. T. (1995). For better, for worse, for richer, for poorer: The rough and the smooth of relationships. In S. Duck & J. T. Wood (Eds.), *Confronting relationship challenges.* Thousand Oaks, CA: Sage.

Dugan, E., & Kivett, V. R. (1998). Implementing the Adams and Blieszner conceptual model: Predicting interactive friendship processes of older adults. *Journal of Social and Personal Relationships, 15,* 607–622.

Dutton, D. G., & Aron, A. P. (1974). Some evidence for heightened sexual attraction under conditions of high anxiety. *Journal of Personality and Social Psychology, 30,* 510–517.

Eagly, A. H., & Wood, W. (1999). The origins of sex differences in human behavior. *American Psychologist, 54,* 408–423.

Ebbesen, E. B., Kjos, G. L., & Konecni, V. J. (1976). Spatial ecology: Its effects on the choice of friends and enemies. *Journal of Experimental Social Psychology, 12,* 505–518.

Ekman, P., Friesen, W. V., & Ancoli, S. (1980). Facial signs of emotional experience. *Journal of Personality and Social Psychology, 39,* 1125–1134.

Ekman, P., Friesen, W. V., & Tomkins, S. S. (1971). Facial affect scoring technique: A first validity study. *Semiotica, 3,* 37–58.

Eldridge, N. S., & Gilbert, L. A. (1990). Correlates of relationship satisfaction in lesbian couples. *Psychology of Women Quarterly, 14,* 43–62.

Emery R. E., Laumann-Billings, L., Waldron, M. C., Sbarra, D. A., & Dillon, P. (2001). Child custody mediation and litigation: Custody, contact, and coparenting 12 years after initial dispute resolution. *Journal of Consulting and Clinical Psychology, 69,* 323–332.

Erber, R., & Erber, M. W. (2001). *Intimate relationships: Issues, theories, and research.* Boston: Allyn & Bacon.

Erbert, L. A. (2000). Conflict and dialectics: Perceptions of dialectical contradictions in marital conflict. *Journal of Social and Personal Relationships, 17,* 638–659.

Falbo, T., & Peplau, L. A. (1980). Power strategies in intimate relationships. *Journal of Personality and Social Psychology, 38,* 618–628.

Fast, J. (1970). *Body language.* New York: M. Evans.

Feeney, J. A. (1999). Issues of closeness and distance in dating relationships: Effects of sex and attachment style. *Journal of Social and Personal Relationships, 16,* 571–590.

Feeney, J. A., & Noller, P. (1996). *Adult attachment.* Thousand Oaks, CA: Sage.

Feeney, J. A., Noller, P., & Roberts, N. (2000). Attachment and close relationships. In C. Hendrick & S. S. Hendrick (Eds.), *Close relationships: A sourcebook* (pp. 185–201). Thousand Oaks, CA: Sage.

Fehr, B. (1988). Prototype analysis of the concepts of love and commitment. *Journal of Personality and Social Psychology, 5,* 557–579.

Fehr, B. (1993). How do I love thee? Let me consult my prototype. In S. Duck (Ed.), *Individuals in relationships* (pp. 87–120). Newbury Park, CA: Sage.

Fehr, B. (1996). *Friendship processes*. Thousand Oaks, CA: Sage.

Fehr, B. (2000). The life cycle of friendship. In C. Hendrick & S. S. Hendrick (Eds.), *Close relationships: A sourcebook* (pp. 71–82). Thousand Oaks, CA: Sage.

Fehr, B., & Broughton, R. (2001). Gender and personality differences in conceptions of love: An interpersonal theory analysis. *Personal Relationships, 8,* 115–136.

Fehr, B., & Russell, J. A. (1991). The concept of love viewed from a prototype perspective. *Journal of Personality and Social Psychology, 60,* 425–438.

Feingold, A. (1988). Matching for attractiveness in romantic partners and same-sex friends: A meta-analysis and theoretical critique. *Psychological Bulletin, 104,* 226–235.

Feingold, A. (1992). Gender differences in mate selection preferences: A test of the parental investment model. *Psychological Bulletin, 112,* 125–139.

Felmlee, D. H. (1995). Fatal attractions: Affection and disaffection in intimate relationships. *Journal of Social and Personal Relationships, 12,* 295–311.

Felmlee, D. H. (1998). "Be careful what you wish for . . .": A quantitative and qualitative investigation of "fatal attractions." *Personal Relationships, 5,* 235–253.

Field, N. P., Hart, D., & Horowitz, M. J. (1999). Representations of self and other in conjugal bereavement. *Journal of Social and Personal Relationships, 16,* 407–414.

Field, N. P., & Sundin, E. C. (2001). Attachment style in adjustment to conjugal bereavement. *Journal of Social and Personal Relationships, 18,* 347–361.

Fincham, F. D., Beach, S. R. H., & Kemp-Fincham, S. I. (1997). Marital quality: A new theoretical perspective. In R. J. Sternberg & M. Hojjat (Eds.), *Satisfaction in close relationships* (pp. 275–304). New York: Guilford.

Fincham, F. D., Beach, S., & Nelson, G. (1987). Attribution processes in distressed and nondistressed couples: 3. Causal and responsibility attributions for spouse behavior. *Cognitive Therapy and Research, 11,* 71–86.

Fincham, F. D., & Bradbury, T. N. (1993). Marital satisfaction, depression, and attributions: A longitudinal analysis. *Journal of Personality and Social Psychology, 64,* 442–452.

Fincham, F. D., Paleari, F. G., & Regalia, C. (2002). Forgiveness in marriage: The role of relationship quality, attributions, and empathy. *Personal Relationships, 9,* 27–37.

Fine, M. A. (2000). Divorce and single parenting. In C. Hendrick & S. S. Hendrick (Eds.), *Close relationships: A sourcebook* (pp. 139–152). Thousand Oaks, CA: Sage.

Fine, M. A., Coleman, M., & Ganong, L. H. (1999). A social constructionist multi-method approach to understanding the stepparent role. In E. M. Hetherington (Ed.), *Coping with divorce, single parenting, and remarriage* (pp. 273–294). Mahwah, NJ: Erlbaum.

Finkel, E. J., Rusbult, C. E., Kumashiro, M., & Hannon, P. A. (2002). Dealing with betrayal in close relationships: Does commitment promote forgiveness? *Journal of Personality and Social Psychology, 82,* 956–974.

Finkenauer, C., & Hazam, H. (2000). Disclosure and secrecy in marriage: Do both contribute to marital satisfaction? *Journal of Social and Personal Relationships, 17,* 245–263.

Fitzgerald, N. M., & Surra, C. A. (1981). Studying the development of dyadic relationships: Explorations into a retrospective interview technique. Paper presented at the National Council on Family Relations Pre-Conference Workshop on Theory and Methodology, Milwaukee, WI.

Fitzpatrick, M. A. (1987). Marriage and verbal intimacy. In V. J. Derlega & J. H. Berg (Eds.), *Self-disclosure: Theory, research and therapy* (pp. 131–154). New York: Plenum.

Fitzpatrick, J., & Sollie, D. L. (1999). Unrealistic gendered and relationship-specific beliefs: Contributions to investments and commitment in dating relationships. *Journal of Social and Personal Relationships, 16,* 852–867.

Fletcher, G. J. O., Simpson, J. A., & Thomas, G. (2000). The measurement of perceived relationship quality components: A confirmatory factor analytic approach. *Personality and Social Psychology Bulletin, 26,* 340–354

Flora, J., & Segrin, C. (2000). Relationship development in dating couples: Implications for relational satisfaction and loneliness. *Journal of Social and Personal Relationships, 17,* 811–825.

Foa, U.G., Converse, Jr., J., Törnblom, K.Y., & Foa, E.B. (Eds.). (1993). *Resource theory: Explorations and applications*. San Diego: Academic Press.

Folkes, V. S., & Sears, D. O. (1977). Does everybody like a liker? *Journal of Experimental Social Psychology, 13,* 505–519.

Foot, H. C., Smith, J. R., & Chapman, A. J. (1979). Non-verbal expressions of intimacy in children. In M. Cook & G. Wilson (Eds.), *Love and attraction*. Oxford, England: Pergamon.

Ford, C. S., & Beach, F. A. (1951). *Patterns of sexual behavior*. New York: Harper & Row.

Fox, G. L., & Murry, V. M. (2000). Gender and families: Feminist perspectives and family research. *Journal of Marriage and the Family, 62,* 1160–1172.

Frank, E., & Brandstätter, V. (2002). Approach versus avoidance: Different types of commitment in intimate relationships. *Journal of Personality and Social Psychology, 82,* 208–221.

Frazier, P., Arikian, N., Benson, S., Losoff, A., & Maurer, S. (1996). Desire for marriage and life satisfaction among unmarried heterosexual adults. *Journal of Social and Personal Relationships, 13,* 225–239.

Frazier, P. A., & Cook, S. W. (1993). Correlates of distress following heterosexual relationship dissolution. *Journal of Social and Personal Relationships, 10,* 55–67

French, J. R. P., & Raven, B. (1960). The bases of social power. In D. Cartwright & A. Zander (Eds.), *Group dynamics: Research and theory* (2nd ed.) (pp. 607–623). New York: Harper & Row.

Friedman, H. S., Riggio, R. E., & Casella, D. F. (1988). Nonverbal skill, personal charisma, and initial attraction. *Personality and Social Psychology Bulletin, 14,* 203–211.

Furstenberg, F. F., & Kiernan, K. E. (2001). Delayed parental divorce: How much do children benefit? *Journal of Marriage and the Family, 63,* 446–457.

Gaertner, L., & Foshee, V. (1999). Commitment and the perpetration of relationship violence. *Personal Relationships, 6,* 227–239.

Gaines, S. O., Jr. (1995). Relationships between members of cultural minorities. In J. T. Wood & S. Duck (Eds.), *Under-studied relationships: Off the beaten path* (pp. 51–88). Thousand Oaks, CA: Sage.

Gaines, S. O., Jr., Granrose, C. S., Rios, D. I., Garcia, B. F., Page, M. S., Farris, K. R., & Bledsoe, K. L. (1999). Patterns of attachment and responses to accommodative dilemmas among interethnic/interracial couples. *Journal of Social and Personal Relationships, 16,* 277–287.

Gaines, S. O., Jr., & Liu, J H. (2000). Multicultural/multiracial relationships. In C. Hendrick & S. S. Hendrick (Eds.), *Close relationships: A sourcebook* (pp. 97–108). Thousand Oaks, CA: Sage.

Gaines, S. O., Jr., Rios, D. I., Granrose, C. S., Bledsoe, K. L., Farris, K. R., Page Youn, M. S., & Garcia, B. F. (1999). Romanticism and interpersonal resource exchange among African American-Anglo and other interracial couples. *Journal of Black Psychology, 25,* 461–489.

Ganong, L. H., & Coleman, M. (1994). *Remarried family relationships*. Thousand Oaks, CA: Sage.

Ganong, L. H., & Coleman, M. (2000). Remarried families. In C. Hendrick & S. S. Hendrick (Eds.), *Close relationships: A sourcebook* (pp. 155–168). Thousand Oaks, CA: Sage.

Garcia, S. D., & Rivera, S. M. (1999). Perceptions of Hispanic and African-American couples at the friendship or engagement stage of a relationship. *Journal of Social and Personal Relationships, 16,* 65–86.

Garrido, E. F., & Acitelli, L. K. (1999). Relational identity and the division of household labor. *Journal of Social and Personal Relationships, 16,* 619–637.

Glass, S. P., & Wright, T. L. (1992). Justifications for extramarital relationships: The association between attitudes, behavior, and gender. *Journal of Sex Research, 29,* 361–387.

Glick, P., & Fiske, S. T. (2001). An ambivalent alliance: Hostile and benevolent sexism as complementary justifications for gender inequality. *American Psychologist, 56,* 109–118.

Goldsmith, D. J., & Dun, S. A. (1997). Sex differences and similarities in the communication of social support. *Journal of Social and Personal Relationships, 14,* 317–337.

Gonzales, M. H., Davis, J.M., Loney, G. L., Lukens, C. K., & Junghans, C. M. (1983). Interactional approach to interpersonal attraction. *Journal of Personality and Social Psychology, 44,* 1192–1197.

Gottman, J. M. (1993a). A theory of marital dissolution and stability. *Journal of Family Psychology, 7,* 57–75.

Gottman, J. M. (1993b). The roles of conflict engagement, escalation, and avoidance in marital interaction: A longitudinal view of five types of couples. *Journal of Consulting and Clinical Psychology, 61,* 6–15.

Gottman, J. M. (1994). Why marriages succeed or fail. New York: Simon & Schuster.

Gottman, J. M., Coan, J., Carrere, S., & Swanson, C. (1998). Predicting marital happiness and stability from newlywed interactions. *Journal of Marriage and the Family, 60,* 5–22.

Gottman, J. M., & Levenson, R. W. (1988). The social psychophysiology of marriage. In P. Noller & M. A. Fitzpatrick (Eds.), *Perspectives on marital interaction* (pp. 182–199). Philadelphia: Multilingual Matters.

Gottman, J. M., & Levenson, R. W. (2000). The timing of divorce: Predicting when a couple will divorce over a 14-year period. *Journal of Marriage and the Family, 62,* 737–745.

Gottman, J. M., & Notarius, C. I. (2000). Decade review: Observing marital interaction. *Journal of Marriage and the Family, 62,* 927–947.

Gouldner, A. W. (1960). The norm of reciprocity: A preliminary statement. *American Sociological Review, 25,* 161–178.

Greenblat, C. S. (1983). The salience of sexuality in the early years of marriage. *Journal of Marriage and the Family, 45,* 289–299.

Grote, N. K., & Clark, M. S. (2001). Perceiving unfairness in the family: Cause or consequence of marital distress? *Journal of Personality and Social Psychology, 80,* 281–293.

Grote, N. K., & Frieze, I. H. (1994). The measurement of friendship-based love in intimate relationships. *Personal Relationships, 1,* 275–300.

Grote, N. K., & Frieze, I. H. (1998). "Remembrance of things past": Perceptions of marital love from its beginnings to the present. *Journal of Social and Personal Relationships, 15,* 91–109.

Guerrero, L. K. (1997). Nonverbal involvement across interactions with same-sex friends, opposite-sex friends and romantic partners: Consistency or change? *Journal of Social and Personal Relationships, 14,* 31–58.

Gurung, R. A. R., & Duong, T. (1999). Mixing and matching: Assessing the concomitants of mixed-ethnic relationships. *Journal of Social and Personal Relationships, 16,* 639–657.

Gurung, R. A. R., Sarason, B. R., & Sarason, I. G. (1997). Personal characteristics, relationship quality, and social support perceptions and behavior in young adult romantic relationships. *Personal Relationships, 4,* 319–339.

Haas, S. M., & Stafford, L. (1998). An initial examination of maintenance behaviors in gay and lesbian relationships. *Journal of Social and Personal Relationships, 15,* 846–855.

Hahn, J., & Blass, T. (1997). Dating partner preferences: A function of similarity of love styles. *Journal of Social Behavior and Personality, 12,* 595–610.

Halford, W. K., Hahlweg, K., & Dunne, M. (1990). The cross-cultural consistency of marital communication associated with marital distress. *Journal of Marriage and the Family, 52,* 487–500.

Hall, E. T. (1966). *The hidden dimension.* New York: Doubleday.

Hammer, L. B., Allen, E., & Grigsby, T. D. (1997). Work-family conflict in dual-earner couples: Within-individual and crossover effects of work and family. *Journal of Vocational Behavior, 50,* 185–203.

Hansson, R. O., & Hayslip, B. (2000). Widowhood in later life. In J. H. Harvey & E. D. Miller (Eds.), *Loss and trauma: General and close relationship perspectives* (pp. 345–357). Philadelphia: Brunner-Routledge.

Harlow, H. F. (1974). *Learning to love.* New York: Jason Aronson.

Harlow, H. F., & Harlow, M. K. (1966). Learning to love. *Scientific American, 54,* 244–272.

Harlow, H. F., & Harlow, M. K. (1970). The young monkeys. In P. Cramer (Ed.), *Readings in developmental psychology today.* Del Mar, CA: CRM Books.

Hart, S. (2001). *Preventing sibling rivalry.* New York: Free Press.

Harter, S., Waters, P. L., Pettitt, L. M., Whitesell, N., & Kofkin, J. (1997). Autonomy and connectedness as dimensions of relationship styles in men and women. *Journal of Social and Personal Relationships, 14,* 147–164.

Harvey, J. H., & Hansen, A. M. (2000). Loss and bereavement in close romantic relationships. In C. Hendrick & S. S. Hendrick (Eds.), *Close relationships: A sourcebook* (pp. 359–370). Thousand Oaks, CA: Sage.

Harvey, J. H., Hendrick, S. S., & Tucker, K. L. (1988). Self-report methods in studying close relationships. In S. Duck (Ed.), *Handbook of personal relationships: Theory, research and interventions* (pp. 99–113). New York: Wiley.

Harvey, J. H., & Omarzu, J. (1997). Minding the close relationship. *Personality and Social Psychology Review, 1,* 224–240.

Harvey, J. H., Weber, A. L., & Orbuch, T. L. (1990). *Interpersonal accounts: A social psychological perspective.* Cambridge, MA: Basil Blackwell.

Hatfield, E., & Rapson, R. L. (1994). Love and intimacy. In H. Friedman (Ed.), *Encyclopedia of mental health* (pp. 583–592). San Diego: Academic Press.

Hatfield, E., & Rapson, R. L. (1996). *Love and sex: Cross-cultural perspectives.* Boston: Allyn & Bacon.

Hatfield, E., & Sprecher, S. (1986a). Measuring passionate love in intimate relations. *Journal of Adolescence, 9,* 383–410.

Hatfield, E., & Sprecher, S. (1986b). *Mirror, mirror . . . The importance of looks in everyday life.* Albany, NY: SUNY Press.

Hatkoff, T. S., & Lasswell, T. E. (1979). Male-female similarities and differences in conceptualizing love. In M. Cook & G. Wilson (Eds.), *Love and attraction: An international conference* (pp. 221–227). Oxford, England: Pergamon.

Hayashi, G. M., & Strickland, B. R. (1998). Long-term effects of parental divorce on love relationships: Divorce as attachment disruption. *Journal of Social and Personal Relationships, 15,* 23–38.

Hays, R. B. (1984). The development and maintenance of friendship. *Journal of Social and Personal Relationships, 1,* 75–98.

Hazan, C., & Shaver, P. (1987). Romantic love conceptualized as an attachment process. *Journal of Personality and Social Psychology, 52,* 511–524.

Heavey, C. L., Christensen, A., & Malamuth, N. M. (1995). The longitudinal impact of demand and withdrawal during marital conflict. *Journal of Consulting and Clinical Psychology, 63,* 797–801.

Heider, F. (1958). *The psychology of interpersonal relations.* New York: Wiley.

Hendrick, C., & Brown, S. R. (1971). Introversion, extraversion, and interpersonal attraction. *Journal of Personality and Social Psychology, 20,* 31–36.

Hendrick, C., & Hendrick, S. S. (1986). A theory and method of love. *Journal of Personality and Social Psychology, 50,* 392–402.

Hendrick, C., & Hendrick, S. S. (1990). A relationship specific version of the Love Attitudes Scale. *Journal of Social Behavior and Personality, 5,* 230–254.

Hendrick, C., & Hendrick, S. S. (Eds.). (2000). *Close relationships: A sourcebook.* Thousand Oaks, CA: Sage.

Hendrick, C., Hendrick, S. S., & Dicke, A. (1998). The Love Attitudes Scale: Short Form. *Journal of Social and Personal Relationships, 15,* 147–159.

Hendrick, S. S. (1981). Self-disclosure and marital satisfaction. *Journal of Personality and Social Psychology, 40,* 1150–1159.

Hendrick, S. S. (1988). A generic measure of relationship satisfaction. *Journal of Marriage and the Family, 50,* 93–98.

Hendrick, S. S. (1995). *Close relationships: What couple therapists can learn.* Pacific Grove, CA: Brooks/Cole.

Hendrick, S. S. (2001). Intimacy and love. In J. Worell (Ed.), *Encyclopedia of women and gender* (Vol. 1, pp. 633–643). San Diego: Academic Press.

Hendrick, S. S., Dicke, A., & Hendrick, C. (1998). The Relationship Assessment Scale. *Journal of Social and Personal Relationships, 15,* 137–142.

Hendrick, S. S., & Hendrick, C. (1987). Multidimensionality of sexual attitudes. *Journal of Sex Research, 23,* 502–526.

Hendrick, S. S., & Hendrick, C. (1992). *Liking, loving, and relating* (2nd ed.). Pacific Grove, CA: Brooks/Cole.

Hendrick, S. S., & Hendrick, C. (1993). Lovers as friends. *Journal of Social and Personal Relationships, 10,* 459–466.

Hendrick, S. S., & Hendrick, C. (1995). Gender differences and similarities in sex and love. *Personal Relationships, 2,* 55–65.

Hendrick, S. S., & Hendrick, C. (2000). Romantic love. In C. Hendrick & S. S. Hendrick (Eds.), *Close relationships: A sourcebook* (pp. 203–215). Thousand Oaks, CA: Sage.

Hendrick, S. S., & Hendrick, C. (2002). Linking romantic love and sex: Development of the Perceptions of Love and Sex Scale. *Journal of Social and Personal Relationships 19,* 361–378.

Hendrick, S. S., Hendrick, C., & Adler, N. L. (1988). Romantic relationships: Love, satisfaction, and staying together. *Journal of Personality and Social Psychology, 54,* 980–988.

Hendrick, S. S., Hendrick, C., Shoemaker, S., & Inman-Amos, J. (1995, June). Relationship attitudes after family divorce. Poster presented at the Annual Conference of the International Network on Personal Relationships, Williamsburg, VA.

Hetherington, E. M. (Ed.). (1999). *Coping with divorce, single parenting, and remarriage.* Mahwah, NJ: Erlbaum.

Holmes, J. G., & Rempel, J. K. (1989). Trust in close relationships. In C. Hendrick (Ed.), *Review of personality and social psychology: Close relationships* (Vol. 10, pp. 187–219). Newbury Park, CA: Sage.

Holtzworth-Munroe, A. (2000). A typology of men who are violent toward their female partners: Making sense of the heterogeneity in husband violence. *Current Directions in Psychological Science, 9,* 140–143.

Holtzworth-Munroe, A., Stuart, G. L., Sandin, E., Smutzler, N., & McLaughlin, W. (1997). Comparing the social support behaviors of violent and nonviolent husbands during discussions of wife personal problems. *Personal Relationships, 4,* 395–412.

Homans, G. C. (1961). *Social behavior: Its elementary forms.* New York: Harcourt, Brace & World.

Horowitz, M. J., Bonanno, G. A., & Holen, A. (1993). Pathological grief: Diagnosis and explanation. *Psychosomatic Medicine, 55,* 260–273.

Howard, J. A., Blumstein, P., & Schwartz, P. (1986). Sex, power, and influence tactics in intimate relationships. *Journal of Personality and Social Psychology, 51,* 102–109.

Howard, J. W., & Dawes, R. M. (1976). Linear prediction of marital happiness. *Personality and Social Psychology Bulletin, 2,* 478–480.

Hrdy, S. B. (1999). *Mother nature: Maternal instincts and how they shape the human species.* New York: Ballantine Books.

Huston, M., & Schwartz, P. (1995). The relationships of lesbians and of gay men. In J. T. Wood & S. Duck (Eds.), *Under-studied relationships: Off the beaten path* (pp. 89–121). Thousand Oaks, CA: Sage.

Huston, T. L., Caughlin, J. P., Houts, R. M., Smith, S. E., & George, L. J. (2001). The connubial crucible: Newlywed years as predictors of marital delight, distress, and divorce. *Journal of Personality and Social Psychology, 80,* 237–252.

Hyde, J. S., & Durik, A. M. (2000). Gender differences in erotic plasticity—evolutionary or sociocultural forces? Comment on Baumeister (2000). *Psychological Bulletin, 126,* 375–379.

Ickes, W., & Barnes, R. D. (1978). Boys and girls together—and alienated: On enacting stereotyped sex roles in mixed-sex dyads. *Journal of Personality and Social Psychology, 36,* 669–683.

Ickes, W., Bissonnette, V., Garcia, S., & Stinson, L. (1990). Implementing and using the dyadic interaction paradigm. In C. Hendrick & M. S. Clark (Eds.), *Review of personality and social psychology: Research methods in personality and social psychology* (Vol. 11, pp. 16–44). Newbury Park, CA: Sage.

Inman, C. (1996). Friendships among men: Closeness in the doing. In J. T. Wood (Ed.), *Gendered relationships* (pp. 95–110). Mountain View, CA: Mayfield.

Jacobson, N. S., & Christensen, A. (1996). *Integrative couple therapy: Promoting acceptance and change.* New York: W. W. Norton.

Jacobson, N. S., & Gottman, J. M. (1995). *When men batter women: New insights into ending abusive relationships.* New York: Simon & Schuster.

Jankowiak, W. R., & Fischer, E. F. (1992). A cross-cultural perspective on romantic love. *Ethnology, 31,* 149–155.

Jacquet, S. E., & Surra, C. A. (2001). Parental divorce and premarital couples: Commitment and other relationship characteristics. *Journal of Marriage and the Family, 63,* 627–638.

Johnson, F. L. (1996). Friendships among women: Closeness in dialogue. In J. T. Wood (Ed.), *Gendered relationships* (pp. 79–94). Mountain View, CA: Mayfield.

Johnson, M. P. (1995). Patriarchal terrorism and common couple violence: Two forms of violence against women. *Journal of Marriage and the Family, 57,* 283–294.

Johnson, M. P., Caughlin, J. P., & Huston, T. L. (1999). The tripartite nature of marital commitment: Personal, moral, and structural reasons to stay married. *Journal of Marriage and the Family, 61,* 160–177.

Johnson, M. P., & Ferraro, K. J. (2000). Research on domestic violence in the 1990s: Making distinctions. *Journal of Marriage and the Family, 62,* 948–963.

Jones, W. H., Hansson, R. O., & Cutrona, C. (1984). Helping the lonely: Issues of intervention with young and older adults. In S. Duck (Ed.), *Personal relationships 5: Repairing personal relationships* (pp. 143–161). New York: Academic Press.

Jones, W. H., Sansone, C., & Helm, B. (1983). Loneliness and interpersonal judgments. *Personality and Social Psychology Bulletin, 9,* 437–441.

Jourard, S. M. (1964). *The transparent self.* Princeton, NJ: Van Nostrand Reinhold.

Karney, B. R., & Bradbury, T. N. (1995). The longitudinal course of marital quality and stability: A review of theory, method, and research. *Psychological Bulletin, 118,* 3–34.

Karney, B. R., & Frye, N. E. (2002). "But we've been getting better lately": Comparing prospective and retrospective views of relationship development. *Journal of Personality and Social Psychology, 82,* 222–238.

Kashy, D. A., & Levesque, M. J. (2000). Quantitative methods in close relationships research. In C. Hendrick & S. S. Hendrick (Eds.), *Close relationships: A sourcebook* (pp. 3–17). Thousand Oaks, CA: Sage.

Kaslow, F. (1993). Attraction and affairs: Fabulous and fatal. *Journal of Family Psychotherapy, 4,* 1–34.

Kaufman, J., & Zigler, E. (1993). The intergenerational transmission of abuse is overstated. In R. J. Gelles & D. R. Loseke (Eds.), *Current controversies on family violence* (pp. 209–221). Newbury Park, CA: Sage.

Keeley, M. P., & Hart, A. J. (1994). Nonverbal behavior in dyadic interactions. In S. Duck (Ed.), *Dynamics of relationships* (pp. 135–162). Thousand Oaks, CA: Sage.

Kelley, H. H. (1979). *Personal relationships: Their structures and processes.* Hillsdale, NJ: Erlbaum.

Kenrick, D. T. (1995). Evolutionary theory versus the confederacy of dunces. *Psychological Inquiry, 6,* 56–62.

Kenrick, D. T., & Trost, M. R. (1989). A reproductive exchange model of heterosexual relationships: Putting proximate economics in ultimate perspective. In C. Hendrick (Ed.), *Close relationships* (pp. 92–118). Newbury Park, CA: Sage.

Kenrick, D. T., & Trost, M. R. (1993). The evolutionary perspective. In A. E. Beall & R. J. Sternberg (Eds.), *The psychology of gender* (pp. 148–172). New York: Guilford.

Kerckhoff, A. C., & Davis K. E. (1962). Value consensus and need complementarity in mate selection. *American Sociological Review, 27,* 295–303.

Kiecolt-Glaser, J. K., & Newton, T. L. (2001). Marriage and health: His and hers. *Psychological Bulletin, 127,* 472–503.

Kiecolt-Glaser, J. K., Newton, T., Cacioppo, J. T., MacCallum, R. C., Glaser, R., & Malarkey, W. B. (1996). Marital conflict and endocrine function: Are men really more physiologically affected than women? *Journal of Consulting and Clinical Psychology, 64,* 324–332.

Kinsey, A.C., Pomeroy, W. B., & Martin, C. E. (1948). *Sexual behavior in the human male.* Philadelphia: Saunders.

Kinsey, A. C., Pomeroy, W. B., Martin, C. E., & Gebhard, P. H. (1953). *Sexual behavior in the human female.* Philadelphia: Saunders.

Kirkpatrick, L. E., & Hazan, C. (1994). Attachment styles and close relationships: A four-year prospective study. *Personal Relationships, 1,* 123–142.

Kirkwood, C. (1993). *Leaving abusive partners: From the scars of survival to the wisdom for change.* Newbury Park, CA: Sage.

Kitson, G. C., & Morgan, L. A. (1990). The multiple consequences of divorce: A decade review. *Journal of Marriage and the Family, 52,* 913–924.

Klein, R. C. A., & Lamm, H. (1996). Legitimate interest in couple conflict. *Journal of Social and Personal Relationships, 13,* 619–626.

Kleinke, C. L. (1986). Gaze and eye contact: A research review. *Psychological Bulletin, 100,* 78–100.

Klinetob, N. A., & Smith, D. A. (1996). Demand-withdraw communication in marital interaction: Tests of interspousal contingency and gender role hypotheses. *Journal of Marriage and the Family, 58,* 945–957.

Knee, C. R. (1998). Implicit theories of relationships: Assessment and prediction of romantic relationship initiation, coping, and longevity. *Journal of Personality and Social Psychology, 74,* 360–370.

Knee, C. R., Nanayakkara, A., Victor, N. A., Neighbors, C., & Patrick, H. (2001). Implicit theories of relationships: Who cares if romantic partners are less than ideal? *Personality and Social Psychology Bulletin, 27,* 808–819.

Knobloch, L. K., Solomon, D. H., & Cruz, M. G. (2001). The role of relationship development and attachment in the experience of romantic jealousy. *Personal Relationships, 8,* 205–224.

Knox, D., Daniels, V., Sturdivant, L., & Zusman, M. E. (2001). College student use of the internet for mate selection. *College Student Journal, 35,* 158–160.

Knudson-Martin, C., & Mahoney, A. R. (1998). Language and processes in the construction of equality in new marriages. *Family Relations, 47,* 81–91.

Koeppel, L. B., Montagne-Miller, Y., O'Hair, D., & Cody, M. J. (1993). Friendly? Flirting? Wrong? In P. J. Kalbfleisch (Ed.), *Interpersonal communication: Evolving interpersonal relationships* (pp. 13–32). Mahwah, NJ: Erlbaum.

Koss, M. P., & Cook, S. L. (1993). Facing the facts: Date and acquaintance rape are significant problems for women. In R. J. Gelles & D. R. Loseke (Eds.), *Current controversies on family violence* (pp. 104–119). Newbury Park, CA: Sage.

Kurdek, L. A. (1991). The dissolution of gay and lesbian couples. *Journal of Social and Personal Relationships, 8,* 265–278.

Kurdek, L. A. (1994). Areas of conflict for gay, lesbian, and heterosexual couples: What couples argue about influences relationship satisfaction. *Journal of Marriage and the Family, 56,* 923–934.

Kurdek, L. A. (1998). Relationship outcomes and their predictors: Longitudinal evidence from heterosexual married, gay cohabiting, and lesbian cohabiting couples. *Journal of Marriage and the Family, 60,* 553–568.

Kurdek, L. (2001, June). Research on gay and lesbian couples. Invited presentation at the International Network on Personal Relationships/International Society for the Study of Personal Relationships Conference, Prescott, AZ.

Kurdek, L. A., & Schmitt, J. P. (1986). Relationship quality of partners in heterosexual married, heterosexual cohabiting, and gay and lesbian relationships. *Journal of Personality and Social Psychology, 51,* 711–720.

La France, M. (2001). Review of *A natural history of rape: Biological bases of sexual coercion,* by R. Thornhill & C. T. Palmer. *Contemporary Psychology APA Review of Books, 46,* 377–379.

Langley, R., & Levy, R. C. (1977). *Wife beating: The silent crisis.* New York: Dutton.

Lasswell, T. E., & Lasswell, M. E. (1976). I love you but I'm not in love with you. *Journal of Marriage and Family Counseling, 38,* 211–224.

Laumann, E. O., Gagnon, J. H., Michael, R. T., & Michaels, S. (1994). *The social organization of sexuality: Sexual practices in the United States.* Chicago: University of Chicago Press.

Lawrance, K., & Byers, E. S. (1995). Sexual satisfaction in long-term heterosexual relationships: The interpersonal exchange model of sexual satisfaction. *Personal Relationships, 2,* 267–285.

Lear, D. (1997). Sex and sexuality: *Risk and relationships in the age of AIDS.* Thousand Oaks, CA: Sage.

Lee, J. A. (1973). *The colors of love: An exploration of the ways of loving.* Don Mills, Ontario, Canada: New Press.

Levine, D. (2000). Virtual attraction: What rocks your boat. *CyberPsychology and Behavior, 3,* 565–573.

Levine, S. (2001, June 11). No safety in the numbers: AIDS rises among the young. *U.S. News & World Report,* p. 31.

Levinger, G. (1979a). Marital cohesiveness at the brink: The fate of applications for divorce. In G. Levinger & O. C. Moles (Eds.), *Divorce and separation.* New York: Basic Books.

Levinger, G. (1979b). A social exchange view on the dissolution of pair relationships. In R. L. Burgess & T. L. Huston (Eds.), *Social exchange in developing relationships* (pp. 169– 193). New York: Academic Press.

Levinger, G. (1980). Toward the analysis of close relationships. *Journal of Experimental Social Psychology, 16,* 510–544.

Levinger, G. (1983). Development and change. In H. H. Kelley, E. Berscheid, A. Christensen, J. H. Harvey, T. L. Huston, G. Levinger, E. McClintock, L. A. Peplau, & D. R. Peterson (Eds.), *Close relationships* (pp. 315–359). New York: Freeman.

Levinger, G. (1997). Prologue. In R. J. Sternberg & M. Hojjat (Eds.), *Satisfaction in close relationships* (pp. 1–4). New York: Guilford.

Levinger, G., & Snoek, J. D. (1972). *Attraction in relationship: A new look at interpersonal attraction.* Morristown, NJ: General Learning Press.

Levinson, D. S. (1997). Young widowhood: A life change journey. *Journal of Personal and Interpersonal Loss, 2,* 277–291.

Levy, J. A. (1994). Sex and sexuality in later life stages. In A. S. Rossi (Ed.), *Sexuality across the life course* (pp. 287–309). Chicago: University of Chicago Press.

Lippert, T., & Prager, K. J. (2001). Daily experiences of intimacy: A study of couples. *Personal Relationships, 8,* 283–298.

Liu, C. (2000). A theory of marital sexual life. *Journal of Marriage and the Family, 62,* 363–374.

Lloyd, S. A., & Cate, R. M. (1985). The developmental course of conflict in dissolution of premarital relationships. *Journal of Social and Personal Relationships, 2,* 179–194.

Lloyd, S. A., & Emery, B. C. (2000a). The context and dynamics of intimate aggression against women. *Journal of Social and Personal Relationships, 17,* 503–521.

Lloyd, S. A., & Emery, B. C. (2000b). *The dark side of courtship: Physical and sexual aggression.* Thousand Oaks, CA: Sage.

Long, E. C. J. (1990). Measuring dyadic perspective-taking: Two scales for assessing perspective-taking in marriage and similar dyads. *Educational and Psychological Measurement, 50,* 91–103.

Lund, M. (1985). The development of investment and commitment scales for predicting continuity of personal relationships. *Journal of Social and Personal Relationships, 2,* 3–23.

Lyons, R. F., Sullivan, M. J. L., Ritvo, P. G., & Coyne, J. C. (1995). *Relationships in chronic illness and disability.* Thousand Oaks, CA: Sage.

Maccoby, E. (1990). Gender and relationships: A developmental account. *American Psychologist, 45,* 513–520.

Marshall, L. L., Weston, R., & Honeycutt, T. C. (2000). Does men's positivity moderate or mediate the effects of their abuse on women's relationship quality? *Journal of Social and Personal Relationships, 17,* 660–675.

Marston, P. J., Hecht, M. L., Manke, M. L., McDaniel, S., & Reeder, H. (1998). The subjective experience of intimacy, passion, and commitment in heterosexual love relationships. *Personal Relationships, 5,* 15–30.

Marston, P. J., Hecht, M. L., & Robers, T. (1987). 'True love ways': The subjective experience and communication of romantic love. *Journal of Social and Personal Relationships, 4,* 387–407.

Martin, L. L., & Seta, J. J. (1983). Perceptions of unity and distinctiveness as determinants of attraction. *Journal of Personality and Social Psychology, 44,* 755–764.

Mathias-Riegel, B. (1999, September–October). Intimacy 101: A refresher course in the language of love. *Modern Maturity, 42W,* 46–49, 84.

McAdams, D. P. (1988). Personal needs and personal relationships. In S. Duck (Ed.), *Handbook of personal relationships: Theory, research and interventions* (pp. 7–22). New York: Wiley.

McLanahan, S. S. (1999). Father absence and the welfare of children. In E. M. Hetherington (Ed.), *Coping with divorce, single parenting, and remarriage* (pp. 117–145). Mahwah, NJ: Erlbaum.

McLoyd, V. C., Cauce, A. M., Takeuchi, D., & Wilson, L. (2000). Marital processes and parental socialization in families of color: A decade review of research. *Journal of Marriage and the Family, 62,* 1070–1093.

Meeks, B. S., Hendrick, S. S., & Hendrick, C. (1998). Communication, love, and relationship satisfaction. *Journal of Social and Personal Relationships, 15,* 755–773.

Mellen, S. L. W. (1981). *The evolution of love.* San Francisco: Freeman.

Messman, S. J., Canary, D. J., & Hause, K. S. (2000). Motives to remain platonic, equity, and the use of maintenance strategies in opposite-sex friendships. *Journal of Social and Personal Relationships, 17,* 67–94.

Metts, S., Sprecher, S., & Regan, P. C. (1998). Communication and sexual desire. In P. A. Andersen & L. K. Guerrero (Eds.), *Handbook of communication and emotion: Research, theory, applications, and contexts* (pp. 353–377). San Diego: Academic Press.

Meyers, S. A., & Berscheid, E. (1997). The language of love: The difference a preposition makes. *Personality and Social Psychology Bulletin, 23,* 347–362.

Michael, R. T., Gagnon, J. H., Laumann, E. O., & Kolata, G. (2001). Sex and society. In A. J. Cherlin (Ed.), *Public and private families: A reader.* Boston: McGraw Hill.

Mikulincer, M., & Segal, J. (1990). A multidimensional analysis of the experience of loneliness. *Journal of Social and Personal Relationships, 7,* 209–230.

Milardo, R. M., & Helms-Erikson, H. (2000). Network overlap and third-party influence in close relationships. In C. Hendrick & S. S. Hendrick (Eds.), *Close relationships: A sourcebook* (pp. 33–45). Thousand Oaks, CA: Sage.

Milkie, M. A., & Peltola, P. (1999). Playing all the roles: Gender and the work-family balancing act. *Journal of Marriage and the Family, 61,* 476–490.

Miller, L. C., Berg, J. H., & Archer, R. L. (1983). Openers: Individuals who elicit intimate self-disclosure. *Journal of Personality and Social Psychology, 44,* 1234–1244.

Monsour, M. (1992). Meanings of intimacy in cross- and same-sex friendships. *Journal of Social and Personal Relationships, 9,* 277–295.

Monsour, M. (1994). Similarities and dissimilarities in personal relationships: Constructing meaning and building intimacy through communication. In S. Duck (Ed.), *Dynamics of relationships* (pp. 112–134). Thousand Oaks, CA: Sage.

Monsour, M. (2002). *Women and men as friends: Relationships across the life span in the twenty-first century.* Mahwah, NJ: Erlbaum.

Montgomery, B. M. (1988). Quality communication in personal relationships. In S. Duck (Ed.), *Handbook of personal relationships: Theory, research and interventions* (pp. 343–359). New York: Wiley.

Montgomery, M. J., & Sorell, G. T. (1997). Differences in love attitudes across family life stages. *Family Relations, 46,* 55–61.

Morrow, G. D., Clark, E. M., & Brock, K. F. (1995). Individual and partner love styles: Implications for the quality of romantic involvements. *Journal of Social and Personal Relationships, 12,* 363–387.

Morton, T. L. (1978). Intimacy and reciprocity of exchange: A comparison of spouses and strangers. *Journal of Personality and Social Psychology, 36,* 72–81.

Muehlenhard, C. L. (1988). Misinterpreted dating behaviors and the risk of date rape. *Journal of Social and Clinical Psychology, 6,* 20–37.

Muehlenhard, C. L., Friedman, D. E., & Thomas, C. M. (1985). Is date rape justifiable? The effects of dating activity, who initiated, who paid, and men's attitudes toward women. *Psychology of Women Quarterly, 9,* 297–310.

Mulrine, A. (2002, May 27). Risky business. *U.S. News & World Report,* pp. 42–49

Murray, S. L., & Holmes, J. G. (1997). A leap of faith? Positive illusions in romantic relationships. *Personality and Social Psychology Bulletin, 23,* 586–604.

Murray, S. L., Holmes, J. G., Bellavia, G., Griffin, D. W., & Dolderman, D. (2002). Kindred spirits? The benefits of egocentrism in close relationships. *Journal of Personality and Social Psychology, 82,* 563–581.

Murray, S. L., Holmes, J. G., & Griffin, D. W. (1996a). The benefits of positive illusions: Idealization and the construction of satisfaction in close relationships. *Journal of Personality and Social Psychology, 70,* 79–98.

Murray, S. L., Holmes, J. G., & Griffin, D. W. (1996b). The self-fulfilling nature of positive illusions in romantic relationships: Love is not blind, but prescient. *Journal of Personality and Social Psychology, 71,* 1155–1180.

Murstein, B. I. (1976). *Who will marry whom?* New York: Springer.

Murstein, B. I., & Adler, E. R. (1995). Gender differences in power and self-disclosure in dating and married couples. *Personal Relationships, 2,* 199–209.

Murstein, B. I., & Christy, P. (1976). Physical attractiveness and marriage adjustment in middle-aged couples. *Journal of Personality and Social Psychology, 34,* 537–542.

Myers, D. G. (2000). The funds, friends, and faith of happy people. *American Psychologist, 55,* 56–67.

Myers, D. G. (2002). *Social psychology* (7th ed.). New York: McGraw Hill.

Neimeyer, R. A., & Mitchell, K. A. (1988). Similarity and attraction: A longitudinal study. *Journal of Social and Personal Relationships, 5,* 131–148.

Neria, Y., Guttmann-Steinmetz, S., Koenen, K., Levinovsky, L., Zakin, G., & Dekel, R. (2001). Do attachment and hardiness relate to each other and to mental health in real-life stress? *Journal of Social and Personal Relationships, 18,* 844–858.

Newcomb, T. M. (1961). *The acquaintance process.* New York: Holt, Rinehart & Winston.

Nezlek, J., Wheeler, L., & Reis, H. T. (1983). Studies of social participation. In H. T. Reis (Ed.), *Naturalistic approaches to studying social interaction* (pp. 57–73). San Francisco: Jossey-Bass.

Nolen-Hoeksema, S., McBride, A., & Larson, J. (1997). Rumination and psychological distress among bereaved partners. *Journal of Personality and Social Psychology, 72,* 855–862.

Noller, P., & Venardos, C. (1986). Communication awareness in married couples. *Journal of Social and Personal Relationships, 3,* 31–42.

Ognibene, T. C., & Collins, N. L. (1998). Adult attachment styles, perceived social support and coping strategies. *Journal of Social and Personal Relationships, 15,* 323–345.

O'Grady, K. E. (1989). Physical attractiveness, need for approval, social self-esteem, and maladjustment. *Journal of Social and Clinical Psychology, 8,* 62–69.

Orbuch, T. L., Veroff, J., Hassan, H., & Horrocks, J. (2002). Who will divorce: A 14-year longitudinal study of black couples and white couples. *Journal of Social and Personal Relationships, 19,* 179–202.

Paikoff, R. L., & Brooks-Gunn, J. (1991). Do parent-child relationships change during puberty? *Psychological Bulletin, 110,* 47–66.

Parks, M. R., & Floyd, K. (1996). Meanings for closeness and intimacy in friendship. *Journal of Social and Personal Relationships, 13,* 85–107.

Pasch, L. A., Bradbury, T. N., & Davila, J. (1997). Gender, negative affectivity, and observed social support behavior in marital interaction. *Personal Relationships, 4,* 361–378.

Pasley, K., Kerpelman, J., & Guilbert, D. E. (2001). Gendered conflict, identity disruption, and marital instability: Expanding Gottman's model. *Journal of Social and Personal Relationships, 18,* 5–27.

Patterson, C. J. (2000). Family relationships of lesbians and gay men. *Journal of Marriage and the Family, 62,* 1052–1069.

Pennebaker, J. W. (1990). *Opening up: The healing power of confiding in others.* New York: William Morrow.

Peplau, L. A. (2001). Rethinking women's sexual orientatation: An interdisciplinary, relationship-focused approach. *Personal Relationships, 8,* 1–19.

Peplau, L. A., & Spaulding, L. R. (2000). The close relationships of lesbians, gay men, and bisexuals. In C. Hendrick & S. S. Hendrick (Eds.), *Close relationships: A sourcebook* (pp. 111–123). Thousand Oaks, CA: Sage.

Perry-Jenkins, M., Repetti, R. L., & Crouter, A. C. (2000). Work and family in the 1990s. *Journal of Marriage and the Family, 62,* 981–998.

Pestrak, V. A., Martin, D., & Martin, M. (1985). Extramarital sex: An examination of the literature. *International Journal of Family Therapy, 7,* 107–115.

Peterson, D. R. (1983). Conflict. In H. H. Kelley, E. Berscheid, A. Christensen, J. H. Harvey, T. L. Huston, G. Levinger, E. McClintock, L. A. Peplau, & D. R. Peterson (Eds.), *Close relationships* (pp. 360–396). New York: Freeman.

Pfeiffer, S. M., & Wong, P. T. P. (1989). Multidimensional jealousy. *Journal of Social and Personal Relationships, 6,* 181–196.

Prager, K. J. (1995). *The psychology of intimacy.* New York: Guilford.

Prager, K. J. (2000). Intimacy in personal relationships. In C. Hendrick & S. S. Hendrick (Eds.), *Close relationships: A sourcebook* (pp. 229–242). Thousand Oaks, CA: Sage.

Prager, K. J., & Burhmester, D. (1998). Intimacy and need fulfillment in couple relationships. *Journal of Social and Personal Relationships, 15,* 435–469.

Prins, K. S., Buunk, B. P., & Van Yperen, N. W. (1993). Equity, normative disapproval and extramarital relationships. *Journal of Social and Personal Relationships, 10,* 39–53.

Raphael, B., & Dobson, M. (2000). Bereavement. In J. H. Harvey & E. D. Miller (Eds.), *Loss and trauma: General and close relationship perspectives* (pp. 45–61). Philadelphia: Brunner-Routledge.

Rawlins, W. K. (1992). *Friendship matters: Communication, dialectics, and the life course.* New York: Aldine de Gruyter.

Reeder, H. M. (2000). 'I like you . . . as a friend': The role of attraction in cross-sex friendship. *Journal of Social and Personal Relationships, 17,* 329–348.

Regan, P. C., & Berscheid, E. (1995). Gender differences in beliefs about the causes of male and female sexual desire. *Personal Relationships, 2,* 345–358.

Regan, P. C., & Berscheid, E. (1999). *Lust: What we know about human sexual desire.* Thousand Oaks, CA: Sage.

Regan, P. C., Kocan, E. R., & Whitlock, T. (1998). Ain't love grand! A prototype analysis of the concept of romantic love. *Journal of Social and Personal Relationships, 15,* 411–420.

Reis, H. T., & Shaver, P. (1988). Intimacy as an interpersonal process. In S. Duck (Ed.), *Handbook of personal relationships: Theory, research and interventions* (pp. 367–389). New York: Wiley.

Ridley, C. A., Wilhelm, M. S., & Surra, C. A. (2001). Married couples' conflict responses and marital quality. *Journal of Social and Personal Relationships, 18,* 517–534.

Risman, B. J., & Johnson-Sumerford, D. (1998). Doing it fairly: A study of postgender *marriages. Journal of Marriage and the Family, 60,* 23–40.

Robak, R. W., & Weitzman, S. P. (1998). The nature of grief: Loss of love relationships in young adulthood. *Journal of Personal and Interpersonal Loss, 3,* 205–216.

Roberts, L. J. (2000). Fire and ice in marital communication: Hostile and distancing behaviors as predictors of marital distress. *Journal of Marriage and the Family, 62,* 693–707.

Rogers, S. J., & DeBoer, D. D. (2001). Changes in wives' income: Effects on marital happiness, psychological well-being, and the risk of divorce. *Journal of Marriage and Family, 63,* 458–472.

Rohner, R. P., & Veneziano, R. A. (2001). The importance of father love: History and contemporary evidence. *Review of General Psychology, 5,* 382–405.

Rollins, B., & Cannon, K. (1974). Marital satisfaction over the family life cycle: A reevaluation. *Journal of Marriage and the Family, 36,* 271–282.

Roloff, M. E., Soule, K. P., & Carey, C. M. (2001). Reasons for remaining in a relationship and responses to relational transgressions. *Journal of Social and Personal Relationships, 18,* 362–385.

Rose, A. J., & Asher, S. R. (2000). Children's friendships. In C. Hendrick & S. S. Hendrick (Eds.), *Close relationships: A sourcebook* (pp. 47–57). Thousand Oaks, CA: Sage.

Rosenblatt, P. C. (1977). Needed research on commitment in marriage. In G. Levinger & H. L. Raush (Eds.), *Close relationships: Perspectives on the meaning of intimacy* (pp. 73–86). Amherst: University of Massachusetts Press.

Rossi, A. S. (Ed.). (1994). *Sexuality across the life course.* Chicago: University of Chicago Press.

Rowatt, W. C., Cunningham, M. R., & Druen, P. B. (1999). Lying to get a date: The effect of facial physical attractiveness on the willingness to deceive prospective dating partners. *Journal of Social and Personal Relationships, 16,* 209–223.

Rubenstein, C. M., & Shaver, P. (1982). In search of intimacy. New York: Delacorte Press.

Rubin, Z., & Mitchell, C. (1976). Couples research as couples counseling. *American Psychologist, 31,* 17–25.

Rusbult, C. E. (1983). A longitudinal test of the investment model: The development (and deterioration) of satisfaction and commitment in heterosexual involvements. *Journal of Personality and Social Psychology, 45,* 101–117.

Rusbult, C. E., & Buunk, B. P. (1993). Commitment processes in close relationships: An interdependence analysis. *Journal of Social and Personal Relationships, 10,* 175–204.

Rusbult, C. E., Johnson, D. J., & Morrow, G. D. (1986). Impact of couple patterns of problem solving on distress and nondistress in dating relationships. *Journal of Personality and Social Psychology, 50,* 744–753.

Rusbult, C. E., Wieselquist, J., Foster, C. A., & Witcher, B. S. (1999). Commitment and trust in close relationships: An interdependence analysis. In J. M. Adams & W. H. Jones (Eds.), *Handbook of interpersonal commitment and relationship stability* (pp. 427–449). New York: Kluwer Academic/Plenum.

Rusbult, C. E., & Zembrodt, L. M. (1983). Responses to dissatisfaction in romantic involvements: A multidimensional scaling analysis. *Journal of Experimental Social Psychology, 19,* 274–293.

Ruvolo, A. P. (1998). Marital well-being and general happiness of newlywed couples: Relationships across time. *Journal of Social and Personal Relationships, 15,* 470–489.

Ruvolo, A. P., & Veroff, J. (1997). For better or for worse: Real-ideal discrepancies and the marital well-being of newlyweds. *Journal of Social and Personal Relationships, 14,* 223–242.

Sagrestano, L. M. (1992). Power strategies in interpersonal relationships: The effects of expertise and gender. *Psychology of Women Quarterly, 16,* 481–495.

Sagrestano, L. M., Christensen, A., & Heavey, C. L. (1998). Social influence techniques during marital conflict. *Personal Relationships, 5,* 75–89.

Saitzyk, A. R., Floyd, F. J., & Kroll, A. B. (1997). Sequential analysis of autonomy-interdependence and affiliation-disaffiliation in couples' social support interactions. *Personal Relationships, 4,* 341–360.

Samter, W., Whaley, B. B., Mortenson, S. T., & Burleson, B. R. (1997). Ethnicity and emotional support in same-sex friendship: A comparison of Asian-Americans, African-Americans, and Euro-Americans. *Personal Relationships, 4,* 413–430.

Sanderson, B., & Kurkek, L. A. (1993). Race and gender as moderator variables in predicting relationship satisfaction and relationship commitment in a sample of dating heterosexual couples. *Family Relations, 42,* 263–267.

Sanderson, C. A., & Cantor, N. (2001). The association of intimacy goals and marital satisfaction: A test of four mediational hypotheses. *Personality and Social Psychology Bulletin, 27,* 1567–1577.

Santrock, J. W., & Sitterle, K. A. (1987). Parent-child relationships in stepmother families. In K. Pasley & M. Ihinger-Tallman (Eds.), *Remarriage and stepparenting: Current research and theory* (pp. 273–299). New York: Guilford.

Sarason, I. G., Sarason, B. R., Shearin, E. N., & Pierce, G. R. (1987). A brief measure of social support: Practical and theoretical implications. *Journal of Social and Personal Relationships, 4,* 497–510.

Satterfield, A. T., & Muehlenhard, C. L. (1997). Shaken confidence: The effects of an authority figure's flirtatiousness on women's and men's self-rated creativity. *Psychology of Women Quarterly, 21,* 395–416.

Scanzoni, J., Polonko, K., Teachman, J., & Thompson, L. (1989). *The sexual bond: Rethinking families and close relationships.* Newbury Park, CA: Sage.

Schachter, S. (1964). The interaction of cognitive and physiological determinants of emotional state. In L. Berkowitz (Ed.), *Advances in experimental social psychology* (Vol. 1, pp. 49–80). New York: Academic Press.

Schachter, S., & Singer, J. E. (1962). Cognitive, social and physiological determinants of emotional state. *Psychological Review, 69,* 379–399.

Schaffer, H. R. (1971). *The growth of sociability.* Baltimore: Penguin.

Schiavi, R. C. (1994). Effect of chronic disease and medication on sexual functioning. In A. S. Rossi (Ed.), *Sexuality across the life course* (pp. 313–339). Chicago: University of Chicago Press.

Schmitt, D. P., & Buss, D. M. (2001). Human mate poaching: Tactics and temptations for infiltrating existing mateships. *Journal of Personality and Social Psychology, 80,* 894–917.

Schmitt, D. P., Shackelford, T. K., Duntley, J., Tooke, W., & Buss, D. M. (2001). The desire for sexual variety as a key to understanding basic human mating strategies. *Personal Relationships, 8,* 425–455.

Schneider, C. S., & Kenny, D. A. (2000). Cross-sex friends who were once romantic partners: Are they platonic friends now? *Journal of Social and Personal Relationships, 17,* 451–466.

Schofield, M. J., & Kafer, N. F. (1985). Children's understanding of friendship issues: Development by stage or sequence? *Journal of Social and Personal Relationships, 2,* 151–165.

Schütz, A. (1999). It was your fault! Self-serving biases in autobiographical accounts of conflicts in married couples. *Journal of Social and Personal Relationships, 16,* 193–208.

Seccombe, K. (2000). Families in poverty in the 1990s: Trends, causes, consequences, and lessons learned. *Journal of Marriage and the Family, 62,* 1094–1113.

Selman, R. L. (1981). The child as a friendship philosopher. In S. R. Asher & J. M. Gottman (Eds.), *The development of children's friendships* (pp. 242–272). New York: Cambridge University Press.

Seltzer, J. A. (2000). Families formed outside of marriage. *Journal of Marriage and the Family, 62,* 1247–1268.

Shackelford, T. K. (1998). Divorce as a consequence of spousal infidelity. In V. C. de Munck (Ed.), *Romantic love and sexual behavior: Perspectives from the social sciences* (pp. 135–153). Westport, CT: Praeger.

Shanks, J. (2001, Spring). Ask the rabbi: What does Jewish tradition say about premarital sex and cohabitation? *Reform Judaism,* p. 96.

Sharpsteen, D. J., & Kirkpatrick, L. A. (1997). Romantic jealousy and adult romantic attachment. *Journal of Personality and Social Psychology, 72,* 627–640.

Shea, L., Thompson, L., & Blieszner, R. (1988). Resources in older adults' old and new friendships. *Journal of Social and Personal Relationships, 5,* 83–96.

Shibazaki, K., & Brennan, K. A. (1998). When birds of different feathers flock together: A preliminary comparison of intra-ethnic and inter-ethnic dating relationships. *Journal of Social and Personal Relationships, 15,* 248–256.

Shotland, R. L. (1989). A model of the causes of date rape in developing and close relationships. In C. Hendrick (Ed.), *Close relationships* (pp. 247–270). Newbury Park, CA: Sage.

Sillars, A., Roberts, L. J., Leonard, K. E., & Dun, T. (2000). Cognition during marital conflict: The relationship of thought and talk. *Journal of Social and Personal Relationships, 17,* 479–502.

Simons, R. L., Lin, K.-H., & Gordon, L. C. (1998). Socialization in the family of origin and male dating violence: A prospective study. *Journal of Marriage and the Family, 60,* 467–478.

Simons, R. L., Lin, K.-H., Gordon, L. C., Conger, R. D., & Lorenz, F. O. (1999). Explaining the higher incidence of adjustment problems among children of divorce compared with those in two-parent families. *Journal of Marriage and the Family, 61,* 1020–1033.

Simpson, J. A. (1990). Influence of attachment styles on romantic relationships. *Journal of Personality and Social Psychology, 59,* 971–980.

Simpson, J. A., & Gangestad, S. W. (2001). Evolution and relationships: A call for integration. *Personal Relationships, 8,* 341–355.

Singh, D. (1993). Adaptive significance of female physical attractiveness: Role of waist-to-hip ratio. *Journal of Personality and Social Psychology, 65,* 293–307.

Singh, D. (1995). Female judgment of male attractiveness and desirability for relationships: Role of waist-to-hip ratio and financial status. *Journal of Personality and Social Psychology, 69,* 1089–1101.

Smith, D. (2001, April). Researchers develop workshops tailored to gay and lesbian couples. *APA Monitor on Psychology, 32*(4), 20.

Smith, T. W. (1994). Attitudes toward sexual permissiveness: Trends, correlates, and behavioral connections. In A. S. Rossi (Ed.), *Sexuality across the life course* (pp. 63–97). Chicago: University of Chicago Press.

Snyder, M., Tanke, E. D., & Berscheid, E. (1977). Social perception and interpersonal behavior: On the self-fulfilling nature of social stereotypes. *Journal of Personality and Social Psychology, 35,* 656–666.

Sokolski, D. M., & Hendrick, S. S. (1999). Fostering marital satisfaction. *Family Therapy, 26,* 39–49.

Solomon, D. H., & Samp, J. A. (1998). Power and problem appraisal: Perceptual foundations of the chilling effect in dating relationships. *Journal of Social and Personal Relationships, 15,* 191–209.

Sprecher, S. (1987). The effects of self-disclosure given and received on affection for an intimate partner and stability of the relationship. *Journal of Social and Personal Relationships, 4,* 115–127.

Sprecher, S. (1994). Two sides to the breakup of dating relationships. *Personal Relationships, 1,* 199–222.

Sprecher, S. (2000, November). When the honeymoon occurs before marriage: A longitudinal investigation of sexual satisfaction, intimacy, and initiation in heterosexual relationships. Paper presented at the Annual Conference of the National Council on Family Relations, Minneapolis, MN.

Sprecher, S. (2001a). A comparison of emotional consequences of and changes in equity over time using global and domain-specific measures of equity. *Journal of Social and Personal Relationships, 18,* 477–501.

Sprecher, S. (2001b). Equity and social exchange in dating couples: Associations with satisfaction, commitment, and stability. *Journal of Marriage and Family, 63,* 599–613.

Sprecher, S., Aron, A., Hatfield, E., Cortese, A., Potapova, E., & Levitskaya, A. (1994). Love: American style, Russian style, and Japanese style. *Personal Relationships, 1,* 349–369.

Sprecher, S., & Felmlee, D. (1993). Conflict, love and other relationship dimensions for individuals in dissolving, stable, and growing premarital relationships. *Free Inquiry in Creative Sociology, 21,* 115–125.

Sprecher, S., Felmlee, D., Metts, S., Fehr, B., & Vanni, D. (1998). Factors associated with distress following the breakup of a close relationship. *Journal of Social and Personal Relationships, 15,* 791–809.

Sprecher, S., & McKinney, K. (1993). *Sexuality.* Newbury Park, CA: Sage.

Sprecher, S., & Metts, S. (1989). Development of the 'Romantic Beliefs Scale' and examination of the effects of gender and gender-role orientation. *Journal of Social and Personal Relationships, 6,* 387–411.

Sprecher, S., & Metts, S. (1999). Romantic beliefs: Their influence on relationships and patterns of change over time. *Journal of Social and Personal Relationships, 16,* 834–851.

Sprecher, S., & Regan, P. C. (1998). Passionate and companionate love in courting and young married couples. *Sociological Inquiry, 68,* 163–185.

Sprecher, S., & Regan, P. C. (2000). Sexuality in a relational context. In C. Hendrick & S. S. Hendrick (Eds.), *Close relationships: A sourcebook* (pp. 217–227). Thousand Oaks, CA: Sage.

Sprecher, S., Sullivan, Q., & Hatfield, E. (1994). Mate selection preferences: Gender differences examined in a national sample. *Journal of Personality and Social Psychology, 66,* 1074–1080.

Stack, S., & Eshleman, J. R. (1998). Marital status and happiness: A 17-nation study. *Journal of Marriage and the Family, 60,* 527–536.

Stafford, L., & Canary, D. J. (1991). Maintenance strategies and romantic relationship type: Gender and relational characteristics. *Journal of Social and Personal Relationships, 8,* 217–242.

Steil, J. M. (2000). Contemporary marriage: Still an unequal partnership. In C. Hendrick & S. S. Hendrick (Eds.), *Close relationships: A sourcebook* (pp. 125–136). Thousand Oaks, CA: Sage.

Steil, J. M., McGann, V. L., & Kahn, A. S. (2001). Entitlement. In J. Worell (Ed.), *Encyclopedia of women and gender* (Vol. 1, pp. 403–410). San Diego: Academic Press.

Steil, J. M., & Weltman, K. (1992). Influence strategies at home and at work: A study of sixty dual career couples. *Journal of Social and Personal Relationships, 9,* 65–88.

Sternberg, R. J. (1986). A triangular theory of love. *Psychological Review, 93,* 119–135.

Stewart, S., Stinnett, H., & Rosenfeld, L. B. (2000). Sex differences in desired characteristics of short-term and long-term relationship partners. *Journal of Social and Personal Relationships, 17,* 843–853.

Straus, M. A., & Gelles, R. J. (1990). *Physical violence in American families.* New Brunswick, NJ: Transaction.

Stroebe, M. S., Stroebe, W., Hansson, R. O., & Schut, H. (Eds.). (2001). *Handbook of bereavement research: Consequences, coping, and care.* Washington, DC: American Psychological Association.

Surra, C. A. (1990). Research and theory on mate selection and premarital relationships in the 1980s. *Journal of Marriage and the Family, 52,* 844–865.

Surra, C. A., & Gray, C. R. (2000). A typology of commitment to marriage: Why do partners commit to problematic relationships? In L. J. Waite, C. Backrach, M. Hindin, E. Thomson, & A. Thornton (Eds.), *The ties that bind: Perspectives on marriage and cohabitation* (pp. 253–280). New York: Aldine de Gruyter.

Surra, C. A., & Hughes, D. K. (1997). Commitment processes in accounts of the development of premarital relationships. *Journal of Marriage and the Family, 59,* 5–21.

Tannen, D. (1994). *Gender and discourse.* New York: Oxford University Press.

Teachman, J. D., Tedrow, L. M., & Crowder, K. D. (2000). The changing demography of America's families. *Journal of Marriage and the Family, 62,* 1234–1246.

Thibaut, J. W., & Kelley, H. H. (1959). *The social psychology of groups.* New York: Wiley.

Thompson, A., & Bolger, N. (1999). Emotional transmission in couples under stress. *Journal of Marriage and the Family, 61,* 38–48.

Thornhill, R., & Palmer, C. T. (2000). *A natural history of rape: Biological bases of sexual coercion.* Cambridge, MA: MIT Press.

Tidwell, M. O., Reis, H. T., & Shaver, P. R. (1996). Attachment, attractiveness, and social interaction: A diary study. *Journal of Personality and Social Psychology, 71,* 729–745.

Timmer, S. G., Veroff, J., & Hatchett, S. (1996). Family ties and marital happiness: The different marital experiences of black and white newlywed couples. *Journal of Social and Personal Relationships, 13,* 335–359.

Travis, C. B. (2001). Gender development: Evolutionary perspectives. In J. Worell (Ed.), *Encyclopedia of women and gender* (Vol. 1, pp. 493–505). San Diego: Academic Press.

Treas, J., & Giesen, D. (2000). Sexual infidelity among married and cohabiting Americans. *Journal of Marriage and the Family, 62,* 48–60.

Trivers, R. L. (1972). Parental investment and sexual selection. In B. Campbell (Ed.), *Sexual selection and the descent of man* (pp. 136–179). Chicago: Aldine de Gruyter.

Tucker, P., & Aron, A. (1993). Passionate love and marital satisfaction at key transition points in the family life cycle. *Journal of Social and Clinical Psychology, 12,* 135–147.

Utne, M. K., Hatfield, E., Traupmann, J., & Greenberger, D. (1984). Equity, marital satisfaction, and stability. *Journal of Social and Personal Relationships, 1,* 323–332.

Vangelisti, A. L., & Daly, J. A. (1997). Gender differences in standards for romantic relationships. *Personal Relationships, 4,* 203–219.

Vangelisti, A. L., & Young, S. L. (2000). When words hurt: The effects of perceived intentionality on interpersonal relationships. *Journal of Social and Personal Relationships, 17,* 393–424.

Vannoy, R. (1980). *Sex without love: A philosophical exploration.* Buffalo, NY: Prometheus Books.

Vittengl, J. R., & Holt, C. S. (2000). Getting acquainted: The relationship of self-disclosure and social attraction to positive affect. *Journal of Social and Personal Relationships, 17,* 53–66.

Vogel, D. L., Tucker, C. M., Wester, S. R., & Heesacker, M. (1999). The impact of sex and situational cues on the endorsement of traditional gender-role attitudes and behaviors in dating couples. *Journal of Social and Personal Relationships, 16,* 459–473.

Voss, K., Markiewicz, D., & Doyle, A. B (1999). Friendship, marriage and self-esteem. *Journal of Social and Personal Relationships, 16,* 103–122.

Waite, L. J., & Joyner, K. (2001). Emotional satisfaction and physical pleasure in sexual unions: Time horizon, sexual behavior, and sexual exclusivity. *Journal of Marriage and Family, 63,* 247–264.

Walen, H. R., & Lachman, M. E. (2000). Social support and strain from partner, family, and friends: Costs and benefits for men and women in adulthood. *Journal of Social and Personal Relationships, 17,* 5–30.

Walker, L. E. A. (1994). *Abused women and survivor therapy: A practical guide for the psychotherapist.* Washington, DC: American Psychological Association.

Walster, E., Aronson, V., Abrahams, D., & Rottmann, L. (1966). Importance of physical attractiveness in dating behavior. *Journal of Personality and Social Psychology, 4,* 508–516.

Walster, E., Berscheid, E., & Walster, G. W. (1973). New directions in equity research. *Journal of Personality and Social Psychology, 25,* 151–176.

Walster, E., & Walster, G. W. (1978). *A new look at love.* Reading, MA: Addison-Wesley.

Way, N., Cowal, K., Gingold, R., Pahl, K., & Bissessar, N. (2001). Friendship patterns among African American, Asian American, and Latino adolescents from low-income families. *Journal of Social and Personal Relationships, 18,* 29–53.

Weber, A. L., & Harvey, J. H. (1994). Accounts in coping with relationship loss. In A. Weber & J. H. Harvey (Eds.), *Perspectives on close relationships* (pp. 285–306). Boston: Allyn & Bacon.

Weigel, D. J., & Ballard-Reisch, D. S. (1999). All marriages are not maintained equally: Marital type, marital quality, and the use of maintenance behaviors. *Personal Relationships, 6,* 291–303.

Weishaus, S., & Field, D. (1988). A half century of marriage: Continuity or change? *Journal of Marriage and the Family, 50,* 763–774.

Weiss, R. S. (1998). A taxonomy of relationships. *Journal of Social and Personal Relationships, 15,* 671–683.

Werking, K. J. (1997). Cross-sex friendship research as ideological practice. In S. Duck (Ed.), *Handbook of personal relationships: Theory, research and interventions* (2nd ed., pp. 391–410). New York: Wiley.

West, C., & Zimmerman, D. H. (1987). Doing gender. *Gender and Society, 1*(2), 125–151.

West, L., Anderson, J., & Duck, S. (1996). Crossing the barriers to friendships between men and women. In J. T. Wood (Ed.), *Gendered relationships* (pp. 111–127). Mountain View, CA: Mayfield.

Wiederman, M. W., & Hurd, C. (1999). Extradyadic involvement during dating. *Journal of Social and Personal Relationships, 16,* 265–274.

Wiehe, V. R., & Richards, A. L. (1995). *Intimate betrayal: Understanding and responding to the trauma of acquaintance rape.* Thousand Oaks, CA: Sage.

Wilkie, J. R., Ferree, M. M., & Ratcliff, K. S. (1998). Gender and fairness: Marital satisfaction in two-earner couples. *Journal of Marriage and the Family, 60,* 577–594.

Winch, R. F. (1958). *Mate selection: A study of complementary needs.* New York: Harper & Brothers.

Winstead, B. A., Derlega, V. J., & Rose, S. (1997). *Gender and close relationships.* Thousand Oaks, CA: Sage.

Winter, D. G., Stewart, A. J., & McClelland, D. C. (1977). Husband's motives and wife's career level. *Journal of Personality and Social Psychology, 35,* 159–166.

Wood, J. T. (1995). Feminist scholarship and the study of relationships. *Journal of Social and Personal Relationships, 12,* 103–120.

Wood, J. T. (2000). *Relational communication: Continuity and change in personal relationships* (2nd ed.). Belmont, CA: Wadsworth.

Worell, J. (2001). *Encyclopedia of women and gender* (Vols. 1 and 2). San Diego: Academic Press.

Wortman, C. B., & Dunkel-Schetter, C. (1987). Conceptual and methodological issues in the study of social support. In A. Baum & J. E. Singer (Eds.), *Handbook of psychology and health, Vol. 5: Stress* (pp. 63–108). Hillsdale, NJ: Erlbaum.

Wright, R. A., & Contrada, R. J. (1986). Dating selectivity and interpersonal attraction: Toward a better understanding of the "elusive phenomenon." *Journal of Social and Personal Relationships, 3,* 131–148.

Young, K. S., Grifffin-Shelley, E., Cooper, A., O'Mara, J., & Buchanan, J. (2000). Online infidelity: A new dimension in couple relationships with implications for evaluation and treatment. *Sexual Addiction and Compulsivity, 7,* 59–74.

Zajonc, R. B. (1968). Attitudinal effects of mere exposure. *Journal of Personality and Social Psychology Monograph Supplement, 9*(2, part 2), 1–27.

Index

Note: *Bold numbers indicate pages on which key terms are cited.*

social support from, 63–64
stepfamilies. *See* remarriage/remarried families
stereotypes about, 190, 191
theories of, 190
traditional form of, 190, 191, 224–225
as types of relationships, 2
violence in, 66, 108, 154–159, 167, 214
work/employment and, 225–228
"fatal attractions," 26, 27
fathers
  bonding with infants by, 4–5
  divorce and, 178–180
feminist theory (on gender), 212, 213–214
First Years of Marriage study, 200
flirting, 35
friendships, 45–69
  of adolescents, 57–58, 63
  of adults, 58–59, 60
  age and, 52, 56–59
  attraction and, 26, 49, 54–55, 61
  best friends, 53
  body language in, 29
  of children, 56–57, 60, 146–147
  closeness in, 55
  communication in, 53, 54, 55–56, 59, 60, 123
  conflict in, 59, 146–147
  cross-sex types of, 45–47, 55, 59, 60–62
  cultural influences on, 52, 61
  definition of, **49**–50, 60
  deterioration of, 59
  development of, 54–56
  dialectics in, 50
  of elderly individuals, 58–59
  family relationships and, 57, 58–59
  lesbian relationships and, 195
  gender differences in, 52, 53, 58, 59–62, 222
  integration with other relationships, 58
  intimacy in, 55, 60
  jealousy in, 166
  marriage and, 58, 63
  parents/parenthood and, 58
  patterns of, 52–53
  personality and, 52, 53, 54–55
  physical attractiveness and, 31, 54
  relationship satisfaction in, 53, 54, 55, 60
  romantic relationships vs., 222
  same-sex types of, 55, 57–58, 60, 61, 195–197

scenarios about, 1, 45–49, 235
self-disclosure in, 50, 54, 60
sexual desire/behavior in, 50, 61
similarity in, 54–55
social networks of, 55–56
social support from, 63–64
theories of, 50–54
as type of relationship, 2
voluntary nature of, 49–50

gay (definition of), **194**. *See also* gay/lesbian relationships
gay/lesbian relationships, 194–198
  adoption in, 197, 198
  AIDS/HIV and, 195
  attitudes toward, 195, 197, 198
  attraction in, 195
  bereavement in, 180, 197
  breakup of, 170, 196–197
  children in, 197–198
  cohabitation in, 195, 203
  commitment in, 109, 196
  conflict in, 196–197
  couple types in, 196–197
  cultural influences on, 195, 197, 198
  dating/courtship and, 195–196
  death of partner in, 180, 197
  disclosure of partners in, 195, 197
  diversity and, 10
  friendships and, 195
  gender and, 195, 196, 214
  infidelity in, 195, 196
  physical attractiveness and, 195
  relational maintenance in, 195–196
  relationship satisfaction in, 109, 133, 195–196
  same-sex relationships vs., 195–197
  scenarios about, 14, 185–189, 240
  sexual desire/behavior in, 99, 108–109, 195
  social support for, 195, 196, 197
  violence in, 196
gender, 207–232
  accountability and, 212
  changing concept of, 229–230
  cultural influences on, 229–230
  definition of, **211**
  differences in behaviors related to. *See* gender differences